BECKETT AND MUSICALITY

Beckett and Musicality

Edited by
SARA JANE BAILES
AND
NICHOLAS TILL
University of Sussex, UK

Routledge
Taylor & Francis Group
LONDON AND NEW YORK

First published 2014 by Ashgate Publishing

2 Park Square, Milton Park, Abingdon, Oxfordshire OX14 4RN
52 Vanderbilt Avenue, New York, NY 10017

Routledge is an imprint of the Taylor & Francis Group, an informa business

First issued in paperback 2020

British Library Cataloguing in Publication Data
A catalogue record for this book is available from the British Library

The Library of Congress has cataloged the printed edition as follows:
Beckett and musicality / edited by Sara Jane Bailes and Nicholas Till.
pages cm
Includes bibliographical references and index.
ISBN 978-1-4724-0963-8 (hardcover)
1. Beckett, Samuel, 1906-1989 – Criticism and interpretation. 2. Music and literature. 3. Music in the theater. I. Bailes, Sara Jane. II. Till, Nicholas, 1955-

ML80.B42B43 2014
780.92–dc23

2014015547

ISBN 978-1-4724-0963-8 (hbk)
ISBN 978-0-367-66913-3 (pbk)

Contents

List of Figures

List of Music Examples

Notes on Contributors

Sara Jane Bailes is a theatre artist and Reader in Theatre and Performance Studies in the Drama Programme at the University of Sussex. Her scholarly and creative practice focuses on historical and contemporary experimental theatre making. She has directed and performed in many of Beckett's shorter works. She publishes and lectures internationally in a variety of live and web-based contexts and mentors young theatre practitioners. Her monograph, *Performance Theatre and the Poetics of Failure* (Routledge), was published in 2010.

Brynhildur Boyce has taught at Goldsmiths, University of London and at the University of Iceland. She guest-edited a special issue of *Nordic Irish Studies* on Samuel Beckett and has published a number of essays on Beckett, including one in *Irish Studies Review* that won the 2009 British Association for Irish Studies Postgraduate Prize. She completed her PhD at Goldsmiths in 2012 on communication in the radio plays of Samuel Beckett.

Kevin Branigan studied French and English Literatures at the National University of Ireland, Maynooth. He returned to the French Department to complete his PhD in 2006 as a Government of Ireland Scholar. His thesis was subsequently published as *Radio Beckett* in 2008 by Peter Lang. In January 2009 he discussed *Radio Beckett* on RTÉ radio's *The Arts Show*. He currently teaches French at NUI, Maynooth.

Mary Bryden is Professor of French Literature at the University of Reading. Her many books and articles on Beckett include the edited collection *Samuel Beckett and Music* (Oxford University Press, 1998) and a chapter 'Reflections on Beckett and Music, with a Case Study: Paul Rhys's *Not I*' in Lois Oppenheim (ed.), *Samuel Beckett and the Arts* (Garland, 1999). More recently, she has co-edited (with Margaret Topping) *Beckett's Proust/Deleuze's Proust* (Palgrave, 2009), which includes considerations of music.

David Foster is an artist and writer. He gained a PhD at the University of Reading in 2011 for a thesis combining theory and practice-based research in visual and musical aesthetics, centring on a study of the film adaptation of Beckett's *Comédie*. His articles have been published in *Screen*, the *Journal of Beckett Studies*, *Samuel Beckett Today/Aujourd'hui* and *Studies in European Cinema*. His essay 'The Artist-Photographer and the Problem of Commentary' appears in *The Reflexive Photographer* (MuseumsEtc, 2013), and he recently self-published the first volume in a projected series of photobooks documenting his ongoing project, *Detopia*.

Matthew Goulish is dramaturge for *Every house has a door*. His books include *39 Microlectures: In Proximity of Performance* (Routledge, 2000), *The Brightest Thing in the World: 3 Lectures from the Institute of Failure* (Green Lantern, 2012), and *Work from Memory: In Response to In Search of Lost Time by Marcel Proust*, a collaboration with the poet Dan Beachy-Quick (Ahsahta, 2012). He teaches writing at the School of the Art Institute of Chicago.

Catherine Laws is a pianist and musicologist. She is Senior Lecturer in Music at the University of York and a Senior Artistic Research Fellow at the Orpheus Institute, Ghent. As a performer, she specializes in contemporary music and performs with two contemporary ensembles, the music theatre group Black Hair, and experimental ensemble *[rout]*. She has published a range of articles focusing on the musicality of the work of Samuel Beckett and composers' responses to his texts and has recently completed a book, *Headaches Among the Overtones: Music in Beckett/Beckett in Music* for Rodopi Press (2013).

Franz Michael Maier is Privatdozent of Musicology at the Free University Berlin. He is interested in the work of Guido of Arezzo, Beethoven and Marcel Proust, and his main areas of research relate to theory of the elements of music, music in the nineteenth century, and the relation between music and literature. His book *Becketts Melodien* was published in 2006 (Koenigshausen and Neumann). Among his articles on Beckett and music are 'Two Versions of *Nacht und Träume*: What Franz Schubert Tells Us about a Favourite Song of Beckett' (*Samuel Beckett Today/Aujourd'hui* 18, 2007); 'The Idea of Melodic Connection in Samuel Beckett' (*Journal of the American Musicological Society*, 2008) and more recently 'Samuel Beckett, les douze sons de l'Empereur Hoâng-tí et le silence de l'Empereur Mou' which appears in the edited collection, *Beckett et la musique* (ed. David Lauffer and Geneviève Mathon, Presses Universitaires de Strasbourg).

Thomas Mansell was awarded a PhD by Birkbeck, University of London, for his thesis 'Beckett and Music: Incarnating the Idea' (2012). His work has been published in *Samuel Beckett Today/Aujourd'hui*, *Performance Research*, and in the anthology *Samuel Beckett's 'Endgame'* (ed. Mark S. Byron). In 2006 he was co-organizer of the centenary conference 'Beckett and Company', held at Goldsmiths and Tate Modern. He worked for several years as a ballet pianist, and now teaches piano and cello in London.

Christof Migone is an artist, curator and writer. His work and research delve into language, voice, bodies, performance, intimacy, complicity and endurance. He co-edited the book and CD *Writing Aloud: The Sonics of Language* (Errant Bodies Press, 2001) and his writings have been published in *Aural Cultures*,

S:ON, *Experimental Sound and Radio*, *Musicworks*, *Radio Rethink*, *Semiotext(e)*, *Angelaki*, *Esse*, *Inter*, *Performance Research* and others. A book compiling his writings on sound art, *Sonic Somatic: Performances of the Unsound Body* was published by Errant Bodies Press in 2012. He obtained a PhD from the Department of Performance Studies, Tisch School of the Arts, New York University in 2007. He currently lives in Toronto and is an Assistant Professor of New Media at Western University in London, Ontario.

Katarzyna Ojrzyńska is Assistant Lecturer in the Department of Studies in Drama and Pre-1800 Literature at the University of Łódź, Poland, where she completed her Master's dissertation 'The Human Body in the Plays of Samuel Beckett'. She is also a member of the Samuel Beckett Research Group affiliated with the University of Gdańsk, Poland. She was recently awarded her PhD and is now working on a monograph on dance in contemporary Irish drama. She has published articles on the works of Irish playwrights including William Butler Yeats, Samuel Beckett and Brian Friel.

Paul Rhys studied composition in the US and the UK and currently teaches at Anglia Ruskin University in Cambridge. Important works include *Chicago Fall* for acoustic/electronic ensemble performed at the Pompidou Centre in Paris, a Gloria for choir and orchestra and a piano concerto recently premiered in London by Ian Pace. He has completed two *Dialogues* for solo wind instruments and recorded birdsongs, one of which is recorded on the Lorelt CD label. Other works include *Three Songs* for orchestra setting poems by Primo Levi and *The Fruits of One Tree* taking its title from the writings of Baha'u'llah.

Maria Ristani holds a BA in English Language and Literature and an MA in English Literature and Culture from the Aristotle University of Thessaloniki where she teaches drama and performance art. She was awarded a PhD in 2013 from the same university for her thesis on the role of rhythm in the verbal and scenic idiom of Samuel Beckett's shorter plays. Her work has also been presented at a number of conferences and published in international journals and volumes.

Céline Surprenant is an Associate Researcher with the Chair of Modern and Contemporary French Literature held by Antoine Compagnon at the Collège de France, where she is part of a collaborative project investigating the history of scientific and literary disciplines in the nineteenth and twentieth century at the Collège de France. She was a Senior Lecturer in the School of English, University of Sussex (1996–2010) where she is now Visiting Senior Lecturer in French. She is the author of *Freud's Mass Psychology: Questions of Scale* (2003), *Freud: A Guide for the Perplexed* (2008) and has published articles on Beckett, Freud, Proust, Proust and Darwin, Ernest Renan and Jean-Luc Nancy.

Nicholas Till is Professor of Opera and Music Theatre in the Department of Music at the University of Sussex. He has written on a wide range of twentieth-century and contemporary art practices in opera, music, theatre, visual art, film and video and has worked for many years as an experimental theatre maker. He was one of the co-organizers, with Sara Jane Bailes, of the 'Beckett and Music' symposium at the University of Sussex in 2009, for which he directed a new Beckett-based music theatre work by Stefano Gervasoni. He is currently Leverhulme Research Fellow at the University of Sussex and is working on a book on early opera.

Acknowledgements

We would like to thank a number of people who have contributed to bringing this book into being: our colleague at the University of Sussex, Peter Boxall, who was the third co-organizer of the symposium which inspired and helped to develop this collection; the various contributors to the symposium, many of whom are represented here, but some of whom are not, and all of our students who helped make that event possible; in particular Heidi Bishop at Ashgate, who first approached us with an interest in publishing this book when she spotted the announcement for the symposium and was then admirably persistent in encouraging us to follow the project through, and hugely supportive in guiding the proposal and book through their various stages; Pam Bertram, our Senior Editor at Ashgate, who has expended great care on the final appearance of the book. Thanks to all of our contributors who have journeyed through with us to this end and for the stimulating and productive dialogues throughout. Finally, a special thanks to Christof Migone for allowing us to use his image for our cover.

Introduction
Beckett and Musicality

Sara Jane Bailes and Nicholas Till

The pervasiveness of music in Samuel Beckett's writing and discussions of the alliances between Beckett and musicality now constitute a familiar critical province within Beckett Studies, one that continues to be informed by the still emerging evidence of Beckett's own engagement with music throughout his personal and literary life, as well as by the ongoing interest of musicians and sound artists in Beckett's oeuvre. It is of little surprise that Beckett's lifelong relationship with the classical music repertoire is so evidently mapped throughout the two volumes of *The Letters of Samuel Beckett* (*1929–1940*; *1941–1956*), published in 2009 and 2011. In his correspondence, the writer's attendance at musical concerts and listening to old or new recordings is referred to as a matter of course in exchanges with friends, colleagues and acquaintances. Erudite in all matters that drew his interest, his knowledge and familiarity with the works of many composers (although, like John Cage, he had a deaf ear for Bach) is as apparent as his understanding of music's relation to his own writing and the often frustrating limitations of the fabric of language, which, for Beckett, often lacked the capacity to be either as porous or as polyphonic as musical composition. In music, Beckett was able to hear other potentialities for communication and expression, and his concern with the musicality of language – its rhythmic, sonorous and structural possibilities as composition – suggested a way in which the writer could expand a crucial dimension of writing as a practice made up of words that one 'hears', whether they are spoken or read. In Beckett's writing, words function not only as signifiers, they reach towards a place beyond meaning where a sense of the world is illuminated by the tonal and poetic qualities of language, shaped as much by a perfectly tuned ear for pattern and resonance as by an eye acutely trained on the intellectual value and weight of signification as words are meticulously arranged on the page.

In Beckett's works for theatre, as well as in his prose writings and poems, this engagement with music and musicality plays out in implicit and explicit ways. First, and perhaps most obvious, is the way in which his writing refers to and sometimes includes music by canonical composers such as Schubert and Beethoven: *All That Fall* includes passages from Schubert's string quartet 'Death and the Maiden'; *Nacht und Träume* incorporates the last seven bars of one of Schubert's songs; and the television play, *Ghost Trio*, includes passages from Beethoven's Piano Trio, Op. 70 No. 1, nicknamed the 'Ghost Trio'. Yet even when simply prescribing the inclusion of music in such a way in his plays, music is, as Mary Bryden points out, 'delicately woven into its dramatic fabric'.[1] It is never simply auxiliary, then, but rather part of the overall composition. Other works demand unspecified music as a compositional element, in dialogue or tension with text and image. In two of his radio plays, *Words and Music* and *Cascando*, Beckett engages directly with the tension between music and language, pitting them against each other as characters in the drama. There is also substantial evidence of his attempts to employ musical forms and devices in his prose and dramatic writings, from his first (unpublished) novel *Dream of Fair to Middling Women*, with its numerous references to musical forms (a digression is described as a 'cadenza'; repeated passages are 'da capo'; whispers are delivered 'pianissimo'; meanings are 'orchestrated'; particular scenes may be described as 'duos', 'trios'[2]) and its fanciful conceit of the characters as musical notes to be arranged like a melody, through *Murphy*, *Watt* (which contains two musical compositions by Beckett himself) and *Molloy* (in which the famous sucking-stones episode has been interpreted as a parody of serialism[3]), to a late work like *Quad*, described by Beckett as 'a static fugue'.[4]

Beckett was also interested in the philosophical aesthetics of music, in particular the writings of Schopenhauer, for whom the abstraction of music permitted more direct access to the underlying forces (or 'will') of the world than the representational arts such as painting or literature, which could only convey the idea of phenomenal reality. For Beckett, in music one is (arguably) released from the burden of literal and figurative meaning, as well as from the constraints of linear narrative form and mimesis in particular, as dominant organizing principles within realist drama which is so often dependent on the representation of events, persons and encounters. Music offered Beckett a model for a more suggestive and perhaps intuitive way of capturing the experience of human existence with an air of refined abstraction while it dispensed with irrelevant detail. 'Is there any reason', he enquired in his oft-cited letter to Axel Kaun (9 July 1937),

> why that terrifyingly arbitrary materiality of the word surface should not be dissolved, as for example the sound surface of Beethoven's Seventh Symphony is devoured by huge black pauses, so that for pages on end we cannot perceive it as other than a dizzying path of sounds connecting unfathomable chasms of silence?'[5]

---

1 Mary Bryden, 'Beckett and the Sound of Silence', in (ed.), *Samuel Beckett and Music* (Oxford, 1998), pp. 21–46 (p. 11).

2 See Eric Prieto, *Listening In: Music, Mind, and the Modernist Narrative* (Lincoln, NE, and London, 2002), p. 178.

3 Harry White, 'Something is Taking its Course: Dramatic Exactitude and the Paradigm of Serialism in Samuel Beckett', in Bryden (ed.), *Samuel Beckett and Music*, pp. 159–71 (p. 162).

4 Quoted in Bryden, 'Beckett and the Sound of Silence', p. 36.

5 *The Letters of Samuel Beckett*, vol. 1: *1929–1940*, ed. Martha Dow Fehsenfeld and Lois More Overbeck (Cambridge, 2009), pp. 518–9.

To be able to work with language as substance rather than surface, or to at least move between surface and depth, was a quest to which Beckett remained committed: to rethink the intrinsic way in which we understand the interpolation of surface and depth, where words are conceived as a surface one 'drills' into or 'a veil which one has to tear apart in order to get to those things (or the nothingness) lying behind it'.[6] In music, meaning emerges and spreads throughout a composition, rather than stabilizing a fixed set of ideas. In musical composition, motif, theme, repetition and silence can articulate a sense of progression, a moment of hiatus, an instance of return or an aporia with almost imperceptible precision whilst at the same time remaining diffuse. And for Beckett, as for John Cage, silence is considered to be 'part of a continuum of sound'.[7] Silence takes on concrete form, often becoming the means through which the desire for meaning to take place is articulated, even as one witnesses (as in 'hears' or 'sees') the thwarted efforts of such a necessity in that silence. There is always something to be heard; no ceasing of sound, in other words, merely those sounds that are more or less audible. If prose fiction and poetry were unable to deploy silence as an expressive component, then theatre finally delivered to Beckett what had been denied in these other forms.

Music meant many things to Beckett and informed the impulse, imagination and movement of his writing in such a profound way that he was able to investigate its correspondences across many forms. In the introduction to her edited collection *Samuel Beckett and Music* (1998), the first significant study of its kind to begin to articulate this rich area within Beckett Studies, Mary Bryden noted 'the protean function of music in Beckett's writing'.[8] In seeking to engage with Beckett the writer, it is not surprising, therefore, that critics and artists interpreting or drawing inspiration from his oeuvre often note, in addition to the element of musicality in Beckett's texts, the ways in which the reader/spectator's encounter with his work might similarly be considered 'musical', focused as much towards the realm of the acoustic and auditory as to the visual and the seen. In this respect musicians have learned from Beckett too: creating music for a production of *Comédie* (*Play*) in Paris in 1965, Philip Glass came to the realization that the play did not need his music, but rather, as he put it, that his own life in music had been fundamentally changed by his experience of the intrinsic musicality of Beckett's text. It is worth quoting Glass's insight in his own words for his subtle understanding of the phenomenology of his experience of the play, as reported by the music critic Joseph Roddy:

> Glass saw 15 to 20 performances of *Comédie* in Paris, and every time he would experience a catharsis, or epiphany, in a different spot in the play. 'That struck me as very odd,' he said. 'I thought that if the play were really a classical tragedy, that big emotion should hit me at the same place every night. But it was

6 Ibid., p. 518.

7 Bryden, 'Beckett and the Sound of Silence', p. 27.

8 Ibid., p. 2.

> always a different place. After a while I came to understand that the catharsis or epiphany happened very night when I reached a certain awareness of the play, and of myself.'[9]

Glass had recognized that *Comédie*'s gruelling method of repetitive variation conveyed affect through rhythm and pace, rather than meaning through dramatic narrative or structure. Such a process lies at the heart of Minimalism's own musical emphasis upon surface rather than depth, the tension between repetition and difference, and the play between movement and stasis. It may be that Beckett should be recognized, in addition to the more often cited musical forbears of Minimalism such as Satie or African drumming, as a progenitor of the most important musical development of the second half of the twentieth century.

But what, precisely, does it mean to say that a piece of prose or writing for theatre, radio or screen is 'musical' or that it is characterized by qualities that we usually associate with music? How might we better understand the ways in which the notion of musicality occupies the writing, reading and influence of Beckett's work beyond the more familiar tropes of literary criticism? This collection proposes a number of ways in which Beckett's works engage the notion of musicality and are engaged by and through musical composition, whether in the use of methods that relate to the processes of musical form (e.g. *Play* or *Ghost Trio*, a 'trio' that Beckett constructed according to the structural principles of Beethoven's music) or in aspects of writing that one attributes as 'musical', such as the lyricism, rhythm or dynamics of a text. Here, our knowledge of Beckett's working processes in the theatre is as important as what remains on the published page. Finally, the shift in attention from seeing to listening (from the visual to the aural plane, therefore) itself warrants critical attention, for in earlier as in later works (such as *All That Fall* written in 1956, *Not I* and *Ghost Trio*, written almost 20 years later, or the playlet, *Ohio Impromptu*, written in 1980), the act of listening – to music, to speech, to the reading out loud of a text or even just to silence – is itself foregrounded and dramatized. For Beckett, listening provided a way of approaching the predicament of one's existence and, in particular, encountering the self: a means of turning inwards – or rather, *tuning* inwards – towards a relationship of self *to itself*, as well as outwards to the encounter with the other and the material world. In his meditation on the act of listening, Jean-Luc Nancy states that 'to be listening will always, then, be to be straining toward or in an approach to the self (one should say, in a pathological manner, *a fit of self*: isn't [sonorous] sense first of all, every time, a *crisis of self*?)' Listening establishes a set of resonances: from self to itself, between self and subject or, as Nancy continues, 'one in the echo of the other and this echo is like the very sound of its sense'.[10] The sonorous (as opposed to the

[9] Joseph Roddy, 'Listening to Glass', in Richard Kostelanetz (ed.), *Writings of Glass: Essays, Interviews, Criticism* (Berkeley, Los Angeles and London, 1999), pp. 167–75 (p. 171).

[10] Jean-Luc Nancy, *Listening*, trans. Charlotte Mandel (New York, 2007), p. 9.

visual) operates through referral and resonance – it is not 'tendentially mimetic', therefore, as the visual is, but rather 'tendentially methexic (that is, having to do with participation, sharing or contagion)'.[11] The ability of the sonorous (and the act of listening as an operative mode particular to the sonorous) to invite, share and induce participation is, it would seem, key to the role and function of musicality as a non-mimetic yet reciprocal mode of exchange and relationality that extends throughout Beckett's work.

The chapters in this book address some of the above concerns and observations from a range of complementary perspectives. The book's origins were in a two-day symposium, 'Beckett and Music', held at the University of Sussex in February 2009.[12] One of the aims of that event was to begin to stage some of the conversations and equivalencies between written texts and musical compositions that Beckett was so attentive to throughout his writing career, and which scholars, composers, musicians and writers have engaged with in relation to that extensive body of work since. At the 'Beckett and Music' symposium, panels of papers were curated alongside performances of musical compositions, amongst those a staging of a hitherto unperformed music theatre piece, based on a poem by Beckett, by the Italian composer Stefano Gervasoni. Entitled *Pas si*, the piece was staged by one of the co-editors of this book (Nicholas Till)[13] and was presented along with performances of a number of Beckett-inspired musical works, including Paul Rhys's virtuoso solo piano piece *Not I* (discussed with insightful, personal detail by Rhys in this book) performed by Ian Pace, a staged presentation of *Cascando*, with music for solo cello written and performed by Peter Copley, and new works by Tom Hall and Fung Lam. Seven of the chapters in this book are based on papers given at that symposium (Boyce, Branigan, Mansell, Orzyńska, Rhys, Ristani and Surprenant) though all have since been developed considerably for this publication. Mary Bryden and Catherine Laws also contributed to the symposium, but their contributions here develop different materials. Franz Michael Maier's chapter was to have been presented at the symposium but instead appears here in print. In addition we invited a further three contributions: from David Foster, who attended the symposium, and from two artists who have responded to Beckett in highly distinctive ways that engage with translations and digressions in form – sound artist Christof Migone and theatre artist and writer Matthew Goulish. Finally, Sara Jane Bailes, co-organizer of the symposium (and co-editor of this book), contributed a new piece.

As noted earlier, Mary Bryden's *Samuel Beckett and Music* mapped out the field of study for Beckett's relationship with music decisively and included two definitive essays on some of the broader aspects of what music meant to Beckett, from Bryden herself and from Harry White. We are therefore particularly

---

11 Ibid., p. 10.

12 <http://www.sussex.ac.uk/cromt/archive/beckettandmusic>.

13 See Nicholas Till, 'Stefano Gervasoni's *Pas si*: Staging a Music Theatre Work Based on a Text by Samuel Beckett', *Contemporary Theatre Review* 23/2 (2013): 220–32.

delighted to be able to include a new essay by Mary Bryden in this collection. In addition, that collection contained a selection of essays on composers who have engaged with Beckett in different ways, such as Heinz Holliger, György Kurtág and Morton Feldman, and further interviews with Beckett-inspired composers, such as Luciano Berio and Philip Glass. A year later in 1999, Lois Oppenheim's collection *Samuel Beckett and the Arts* included further valuable reflections on Beckett's musical aesthetics by H. Porter Abbott, Daniel Albright and Charles Kranz. The present book adds to this body of understanding through closer focus on some specific works that incorporate music, such as Catherine Laws's chapter on Beckett's use of a Schubert song in the television play *Nacht und Träume* and Brynhildur Boyce's chapter on the incommensurability of words and music in the radio drama *Words and Music*. It also offers new reflections on some of the broader aspects of Beckett's relation to music, considering him as a writer for whom the concept of musicality must be understood as more than vague analogy (Ristani on the function of rhythm in Beckett's writing, Orzyńska on the idea of 'orchestration', Bryden on the relation of sound and silence in *Ghost Trio*). Sara Jane Bailes reflects on the musical correspondence implicit in the dialogic structural relations of reading and listening in both Beckett's and Maurice Blanchot's work, with particular reference to *Ohio Impromptu* in which Beckett establishes a musical counterpoint between Reader's words and Listener's pattern of insistent knocks. Kevin Branigan examines a composer's solution to supplying music for a lesser-known work in the Beckett canon, *Rough for Radio I*, whilst David Foster examines an even less familiar work, Marin Karmitz's 1966 film adaptation of *Comédie*, rediscovered only in 2000, to suggest analogies to 'atonality' for the film's visual composition. Through Beckett's engagement with Schopenhauer via Proust, Céline Surprenant tackles some of Beckett's earlier philosophical interests in music and in the formal possibilities of pastiche, whilst Franz Michael Maier examines a series of comments in a lecture by Beckett on Proust's contemporary, Gide, in order to begin to think about Beckett's search for a 'symphonic' mode of writing. Thomas Mansell considers Beckett's interest in dance as a physicalization of music, surveying Beckett's references to dance in his earlier prose works through to his obsessive concern for exactitude of gesture in his later work as director of his own plays. Finally, the book includes three chapters by artists who have responded in their own markedly different ways to Beckett's musicality: composer Paul Rhys discusses and reflects upon his approach to adapting *Not I* for solo piano, Christof Migone offers a recension of his radio work *Foursome* in which he invited four choreographers to make spoken and inscriptive transcriptions of *Quad*, and Matthew Goulish offers poetic reflections on the music of Morton Feldman while engaging with some of the resonances and particularities of Feldman's relationship to Beckett. The contributions in this collection span the entire arc of Beckett's production, from his early prose writings through the plays for theatre and radio to his late works for television. We have arranged them here approximately according to chronology to give the reader a sense of how Beckett's approach to music and musicality developed throughout his career, though the reader is also invited to discover alternative pathways through the chapters, each of which has its own distinctive engagement with the book's theme.

Together, the range of work included here exemplifies, we hope, the value of such an inventive and eclectic variety of approaches towards the expanding field of thinking about Beckett and musicality with regards to terms and modes of analysis, subject matter, writing styles, disciplinary and critical tools and so on. In addition, these chapters draw attention to some of the productive ways in which one might listen to and through the musical registers and nuances that help to define Beckett's work and which might parallel our more habitual tendency to 'see' what he wrote, particularly where his dramas are concerned. For in Beckett, it is not only that the function of music is protean; the modes of expression through which music manifests as a precisely structured exchange are transposed into the work and world of language and the stage. In his book on the musical turn in modernist writing Eric Prieto describes Beckett's 'musicalization of fiction' as being characteristic of the modernist search, from Mallarmé onwards, for modes of writing capable of conveying the complexity of consciousness, evident in writers as varied as Strindberg, Joyce, Eliot, Huxley, Pinget and Leiris.[14] Yet, the 'musicalization' of theatre, wherein Beckett is surely exemplary, is one of the definitive attributes that Hans-Thies Lehmann identifies in order to characterize the now ubiquitous concept of 'postdramatic theatre', itself indicative (despite Lehmann's disclaimers) of the postmodern turn in theatre.[15] Whether one understands this apparent paradox as evidence of the range of different functions that music served throughout Beckett's career, from his exuberant modernism to his ascetic yet wilfully promiscuous postmodernism, or as evidence of the continuing diversity of critical approaches to the understanding of Beckett's relation to music, we hope that this book will stimulate new modes of attention and listening for Beckett's musicality.

---

[14] Prieto, *Listening In*.

[15] Hans-Thies Lehmann, *Postdramatic Theatre*, trans Karen Jürs-Munby (London and New York, 2006).

Chapter 1

'Shades of Lessing': Beckett and the Aesthetics of the Modern Novel

Franz Michael Maier

In recent years, considerable effort has been made to understand Samuel Beckett's artistic beginnings. Increasingly, details of these beginnings have emerged, and their conditions and contexts have been reconstructed. Important steps in this research include Jean-Michel Rabaté's collection of articles on *Beckett avant Beckett* (1985), Eoin O'Brien and Édith Fournier's edition of Beckett's *Dream of Fair to Middling Women* (1992), John Pilling's *Beckett before Godot* (1997), his edition of Beckett's *Dream Notebook* (1999) and Brigitte Le Juez's account of Beckett as a lecturer at Trinity College, Dublin, *Beckett before Beckett* (2009). In 2009 Angela Moorjani indicated the importance of André Gide for the young Beckett who had been working on a monograph devoted to the author of *Les Faux-monnayeurs*. The publication of Beckett's *German Diaries* is announced for the near future.

There is an obvious reason for this interest in Beckett's artistic beginnings: the young Beckett was a critic as well as a writer. We read his letters, notes and reviews and find him elaborating upon art and art production. Studying the young Beckett, we hope to gain insight into the incubation of his artistic ideas which, in later years, become hidden behind a veil of enigmatic works and narratological silence. In this chapter, I wish to shed light on the young Beckett's ideas concerning narratology. In particular, I will discuss his distinction between 'melodic' and 'symphonic' narration. I draw particularly upon two quotations, one from Beckett's lectures at Trinity College in 1931 and another from his *German Diary* written in 1937.

In 1931 one of Beckett's students at Trinity College, Rachel Burrows, heard the writer speak about Gide's novel *Paludes* where he noted: 'Action instead of being treated melodically is treated symphonically – interest in potential, in milieu, unrealised actions etc.'[1] Beckett used a musical metaphor to explain Gide's poetics. His statement sounds important and can be easily memorized, because it is structured as a binary opposition. But what does Beckett mean to say? The statement is not at all clear. At first sight, it is not evident why a novelistic

1 The text given here was conveyed to me by John Pilling in a communication dated 3 Feb. 2011. See also John Pilling, *Beckett before Godot* (Cambridge, 2004), p. 240 n. 17. This chapter is an elaborated version of a paper first given at the International Conference 'Samuel Beckett: Out of the Archive', York, 2011.

description of 'potential' and 'milieu' should be called symphonic. In a later lecture, Beckett uses the same opposition again to illustrate Gide's *Bergsonisme*. As a characteristic trait of Gide he gives: 'Understanding Bergson (*symphonie* not *mélodie*; treatment of depth not of surface)'.[2] Evidently, Beckett adds a new layer of meaning to the well-known opposition of the two concurring musical principles of melody and symphony (or harmony) that, from Jean-Jacques Rousseau's *Essai sur l'origine des langues* (1781) onward, has been elaborated into oppositions such as sung versus orchestral, naive versus sophisticated, spontaneous versus planned and so on.

We learn that the treatment of action in traditional novels is different from its treatment in Gide's *Paludes*. Traditionally, action is based on and motivated by the character of the hero. The hero is attributed individual qualities and characteristics, and from them his deeds, accomplishments and failures spring. As the critic Albert Thibaudet put it in 1924 in a discussion of Balzac's novels, 'l'homme est donné avec son caractère fixé, et ses actes suivent son caractère [the hero is put in place with his character firmly defined, and his actions are the result of his character]'.[3] The hero in the novel *Jean-Christophe* for which, in 1916, Romain Rolland was awarded the Nobel Prize for Literature, may serve as an example. The story recounts the life of a musician and his search for his place in society. Jean-Christophe possesses individual traits and talents, and all his successes and failures evolve from these qualities. And while the story of his life turns out to be a long and winding *roman fleuve*, the identical self of the hero remains stable. The actions he takes and the conversions he undergoes only help him to discover this inner self. André Gide's *Paludes* offers a contrast to this.

Born in 1869 Gide was only three years younger than Rolland. *Paludes* appeared in 1895, long before the volumes of *Jean-Christophe* started to appear in 1904. The hero of *Paludes* is well characterized by the title for a planned monograph on Gide which Beckett, in September 1932, communicated to Thomas McGreevy: 'paralyzed in ubiquity'.[4] This title paraphrases the foreword of *Paludes*: 'Si nous savons ce que nous voulions dire, nous ne savons pas si nous ne disions que cela' [Even if we know what we wanted to say, we do not know whether we said more than that]'.[5] Besides writing his book, *Paludes*, Gide's hero does not do much in the traditional sense. He makes note of his plans and his actual accomplishments in his diary which consequently documents that he is not accomplishing anything.

---

2 Samuel Beckett, lectures on Gide and Racine, Trinity College Dublin, Michaelmas, 1931 (notes taken by Rachel Burrows, née Dobbin, TCD Mic 60), in Brigitte Le Juez, *Beckett before Beckett* (London, 2009), p. 44.

3 Albert Thibaudet, *Réflexions sur le roman* [1924], quoted in Michel Raimond, *La Crise du roman: Des lendemains du Naturalisme aux années vingt* (Paris, 1966), p. 447.

4 *The Letters of Samuel Beckett*, vol. 1: *1929–1940*, ed. Martha D. Fehsenfeld and Lois M. Overbeck (Cambridge, 2009), p. 123 n. 3.

5 André Gide, *Paludes*, Romans et récits: Œuvres lyriques et dramatiques 1, ed. Pierre Masson (Paris, 2009), p. 259.

While Rolland's Jean-Christophe, in his struggle for a decent position in a small world, is, as we may put it, 'acting from his heart', Gide's hero is paralysed by his sophisticated ways. He is not driven by an inner impulse that characterizes his centre; rather, what remains identical in him is the stasis that stems from his laziness. For the hero–narrator, this means a change from making plans and evaluating results toward the *imprévu négatif* – the 'unforeseen cancellation of plans'.[6] We can organize the two positions as follows:

Treatment of Action in Rolland's *Jean-Christophe*	Treatment of Action in Gide's *Paludes*
acting from the heart	paralysed in ubiquity
melodic treatment of action	symphonic treatment of action
interest in character of the hero	interest in potential and milieu
interest in accomplished actions	interest in unrealized actions (*imprévu négatif*)

Evidently, Beckett organized his lecture around polarities. He taught his students a scheme proposing new versus old novel, advanced versus traditional novel, and Gide versus Rolland.

The Role of Musical Metaphor

All this is evident. But why does Beckett express this clear contraposition by the less clear comparison with melody and symphony? Let us divide this question into two. First, is the musical metaphor elaborately and consistently integrated into Beckett's argumentation regarding Gide? Second, is the metaphor a constituent part of Beckett's intellectual universe at that time?

The answer to the first question would appear to be 'No, the metaphor does not fulfil an evident and clear function besides articulating an opposition between terms.' The metaphor does not give an immediately plausible explanation of the relation between the advanced and the traditional novel, and therefore Brigitte Le Juez could misread 'melodically' as 'methodically'.[7] We will see below that Beckett himself explains the opposition in question without any mention of music. The answer to the second question is 'Yes, the terms "melody" and "symphony" play an important role in Beckett's thoughts at that time'. With their help he integrates the discussion of old versus new novel into a context that he is constantly elaborating throughout the 1930s.

---

6 Ibid., p. 298; on keeping a diary and on rewriting diary entries, see pp. 266, 277, 296.

7 See Le Juez, *Beckett before Beckett*, p. 43.

Beyond Musical Metaphor

Beckett did not invent the scheme of new versus old ways of narration; rather, he adopted it from André Gide and Marcel Proust. Both participated in the 'culte de Dostoïevsky' that dominated literary criticism in early twentieth-century France.[8] In a 1923 collection of articles and lectures, Gide praised the Russian author for the new features of his novels. Four years earlier, we find the same praise of Dostoevsky in Marcel Proust. In *À l'ombre des jeunes filles en fleurs* (1919), we see the Proustian narrator travelling to the seaside with his grandmother. She gives him a volume of the letters of Madame de Sévigné to read and the narrator is fascinated by what he calls 'le côté Dostoïevski des *Lettres de Mme de Sévigné*' [the Dostoevskian side of Mme de Sévigné's letters]'.[9] Later in the novel, the narrator explains what the two have in common:

> Il est arrivé que Mme de Sévigné, comme Elstir, comme Dostoïevski, au lieu de présenter les choses dans l'ordre logique, c'est-à-dire en commençant par la cause, nous montre d'abord l'effet, l'illusion qui nous frappe. C'est ainsi que Dostoïevski présente ses personnages. Leurs actions nous apparaissent aussi trompeuses que ces effets d'Elstir où la mer a l'air d'être dans le ciel.
>
> [Mme de Sévigné sometimes, like Elstir or Dostoevsky, instead of presenting things in the logical order, that is to say starting with the cause, begins by showing us the effect, the illusion which strikes us. That is how Dostoevsky presents his characters. Their actions have as misleading an appearance as those Elstir paintings where the sea seems to be in the sky.][10]

Proust distinguishes the empirical order of events from the sequence of impressions a spectator experiences. Far from approving a misunderstanding of physical reality, he pleads for envisioning openly a complex situation without immediately reducing it to a plane of understanding whose metrics are predefined. Proust's narrator pleads in favour of the 'données immédiates' (immediately given data) of his consciousness (Bergson) and criticizes a logical and geometrical stratification of his experience. Several of these unclear and puzzling situations in which the perception of an event is divergent from its physical explication can be found in the Doncières episodes in the first part of *Le Côté de Guermantes*: the narrator hears the crackling of a chimney fire through a closed door and mistakes it for a crowd of people in conversation; he hears the ticking of a clock in a dark room and cannot locate it and so on.

---

8 Michel Raimond, *La Crise du roman*, p. 446.

9 Marcel Proust, *À la recherche du temps perdu*, ed. Jean-Yves Tadié (Paris, 1988), vol. 2, p. 14; Eng. trans.: *In Search of Lost Time*, ed. Christopher Prendergast (London, 2002) , vol. 2, p. 233.

10 Ibid., vol. 3, p. 880; Eng. trans., vol. 5, p. 350.

Beckett knew of this critical attitude toward the scheme of cause and effect. In his monograph *Proust*, he speaks of Proust's 'fine Dostoievskian contempt for the vulgarity of a plausible concatenation'. Some pages later he speaks of Proust's 'impressionism', which would free him from forcing the phenomena into 'a chain of cause and effect' and allow him to show the phenomena 'in the order and exactitude of their perception'.[11] In the same vein, he calls Gide's *Les Faux-monnayeurs* (which he considers the 'greatest book since Proust') an 'analytical novel refusing to commit itself to conclusions'.[12] For an alternative to logical conclusions, Beckett may have had in mind the Gidian narrator's remark on Madame Vedel: 'Il lui arrive assez souvent de ne pas achever ses phrases, ce qui donne à sa pensée une sorte de flou poétique. Elle fait de l'infini avec l'imprécis et l'inachevé. [She has a frequent habit of leaving her sentences unfinished, which gives her reflections a kind of poetic vagueness. She reaches the infinite by way of the indeterminate and the indefinite.]'[13] Beckett generalizes Proust's critique of 'cause and effect' into a critique of all the concepts with which we make the world the object of our rational understanding. In a long and detailed letter to Thomas McGreevy, he identified the same projection of predefined concepts into the phenomena in traditional landscape painting: 'all the anthropomorphized landscape ... all the landscape "promoted" to the emotions of the hiker, postulated as concerned with the hiker'. Beckett adds: 'What an impertinence, worse than Aesop & the animals.'[14] Beckett's criticism of general concepts of understanding (like cause and effect, like the reduction of the outer world to an echo of our needs) is based on Henri Bergson's critique of language: our logical approach to the world as represented by words gives us general concepts instead of the individual things and thus petrifies into an anthropocentric ontology what in truth is 'mobilité universelle' (universal mobility).[15] Beckett's statement in his Trinity College lecture on Gide, that 'language can't express confusion', sounds like a paraphrase of Bergson's' 'notre language est mal fait pour rendre les subtilités de l'analyse psychologique [our language is poorly designed to convey the subtleties of psychological analysis]'.[16]

---

[11] Samuel Beckett, *Proust*, in *Proust and Three Dialogues with Georges Duthuit* (London, 1965), pp. 81–2, 86.

[12] Beckett, lectures on Gide and Racine, in Le Juez, *Beckett before Beckett*, p. 43.

[13] André Gide, *Les Faux-monnayeurs*, Romans et récits: Œuvres lyriques et dramatiques 2, ed. Pierre Masson (Paris, 2009), p. 350; Eng. trans.: *The Counterfeiters*, trans. Dorothy Bussy, Kindle edn (New York, 1973).

[14] Samuel Beckett to Thomas McGreevy, 8 Sept. 1934, in *The Letters of Samuel Beckett*, vol. 1, p. 222.

[15] See Henri Bergson, *La perception du changement*, in *Œuvres*, ed. André Robinet (Paris, 1959), p. 1385; for 'nous ne voyons pas les choses mêmes [we do not see the things themselves]', see Henri Bergson, *Le Rire: Essai sur la signification du comique*, in *Œuvres*, p. 460.

[16] Beckett, lectures on Gide and Racine, in Le Juez *Beckett before Beckett*, p. 35; Henri Bergson, *Essai sur les données immédiates de la conscience*, in *Œuvres*, p. 13.

Besides Proust's epistemological openness for the unregulated and the unexpected (the *imprévu*), Beckett was attracted by a formal invention introduced by Gide. In an entry in his *Journal des Faux-monnayeurs* dated 21 November 1920, Gide distinguished narration in the traditional form of 'confessions' from narration in the new form of his evolving novel: confessions are made by an ego that is meant to stay with the contemplation of his very own deeds and responsibilities; a novel, on the other hand, can illuminate events by the perspectivism that results from a multiplicity of protagonists. The *primus confessor* is St Augustine, and it reminds us of his self-critical *Retractationes* when Gide remarks:

> Je fus amené, tout en l'écrivant, à penser que l'intimité, la pénétration, l'investigation psychologique peut, à certains égards, être poussée plus avant dans le 'roman' que même dans les 'confessions'. L'on est parfois gêné dans celles-ci par le 'je'.
>
> [Even while writing it [a chapter of his autobiography], I was led to think that intimacy, insight, psychological investigation can in certain respects be carried even further in the 'novel' than in 'confessions.' In the latter one is sometimes hampered by the 'I'.][17]

Gide finds the confessor's attitude self-centred and self-admiring and conceives of an alternative. But this does not imply a change in the object of his account. Before he sketches his new concept of dialogue, he emphasizes that he himself remains the one and only object of interest and the only source of experience: 'Tout ce que je vois, tout ce que j'apprends, tout ce qui m'advient depuis quelques mois, je voudrais le faire entrer dans ce roman, et m'en servir pour l'enrichissement de sa touffe. [Everything I have seen, everything I have learned, everything that has happened to me for several months, I should like to get into this novel, where it will serve to enrich the texture.]'[18] This remark makes clear that the following statement only regards the form of narration and does not question in any way the unity, integrity and consistency of the author's ego:

> Je voudrais que les événements ne fussent jamais racontés directement par l'auteur, mais plutôt exposés (et plusieurs fois, sous des angles divers) par ceux des acteurs sur qui ces événements auront eu quelque influence. Je voudrais que, dans le récit qu'ils en feront, ces événements apparaissent légèrement déformés ; une sorte d'intérêt vient, pour le lecteur, de ce seul fait qu'il ait à *rétablir*. L'histoire requiert sa collaboration pour se bien dessiner.

---

17 André Gide, *Journal des Faux-monnayeurs*, Romans et récits: Œuvres lyriques et dramatiques 2, ed. Pierre Masson (Paris, 2009), p. 529 (entry for 21 Nov. 1920); Eng. trans. *The Journal of the Counterfeiters*, trans. Justin O'Brien, Kindle edn (New York, 1973).

18 Ibid.

> [I should like events never to be related directly by the author, but instead exposed (and several times from different vantages) by those actors who will be influenced by those events. I should like the events to appear slightly warped; the reader will take a sort of interest from the mere fact of having to *reconstruct*. The story requires his collaboration in order to take shape properly.][19]

Gide demands from his reader a synthetic act in which he reconstitutes the initial unity and identity of the event that has been split into facets by the perspectivistic narration.

In his Trinity College lecture, Beckett revolts against Gide's motif of unity. He puzzles his students by describing Gide's poetics as oriented toward the 'integrity of incoherence'.[20] With this oxymoron, Beckett describes what he calls Gide's 'reconciliation between [the] authentic incoherence of post-Bergsonian thought and [the] coherence of Racinian statement'.[21] A critical yet reliable reporter, Beckett quotes from Gide's *Morceaux choisis* to underline that Gide's ego was strong, contracting and integrating and that Gide did not have any sympathy for disintegration: 'Les tendances les plus opposées n'ont jamais réussi à faire de moi un tourmenté. [The most antagonistic tendencies have never succeeded in making me a tormented soul.]'[22] In his own novel, *Dream of Fair to Middling Women* of 1932, however, Beckett would allow his hero to loudly reject the Gidian 'reconciliation':

> "There is no such thing" said Belacqua wildly "as a simultaneity of incoherence, there is no such thing as love in a thalamus."[23]

Beckett's Preferred Musical Metaphor

In all these reflections, Beckett does not make use of musical metaphor. Why, then, does he call action in the traditional novel 'melodic' and action in Gide's *Paludes* 'symphonic?' One could have expected otherwise, as Bergson explains 'mobilité universelle' – Beckett's 'confusion' – with the continuity of a melodic line.[24] But Burrows's notes document that in Beckett's scheme of melodic versus symphonic, Bergson was positioned on the side of symphony. Beckett identified one of Gide's main traits as: 'Understanding Bergson (*symphonie* not *mélodie*; treatment of depth not of surface)'.[25] In Burrows's notes, there is no trace of

---

19 Ibid.

20 Beckett, lectures on Gide and Racine, in Le Juez, *Beckett before Beckett*, p. 44.

21 Ibid., p. 35.

22 Ibid., p. 44. Gide's original text reads: 'un être tourmenté' (André Gide, *Morceaux choisis*, 20th edn (Paris, 1928), p. 434).

23 Beckett, *Dream of Fair to Middling Women*, ed. Eoin O'Brien and Edith Fournier (Dublin, 1992), p. 102.

24 See Bergson, *La Perception du changement*, pp. 1382–5.

25 Beckett, lectures on Gide and Racine, in Le Juez, *Beckett before Beckett*, p. 44.

Bergson's theory of melody.[26] Beckett's concept of 'melodic' must therefore be explained with reference to Arthur Schopenhauer, whose *World as Will and Representation* Beckett read in 1930. In §52 of this book, bass, tenor, alto and soprano are characterized as the four elements in music. Schopenhauer, a flutist, interprets the soprano as the leading voice and as the musical representation of the autonomous life of a human individual. He sees the melodic line of the soprano as a metaphor for the unbroken connection between a point of departure and a point of arrival in life that is made through a self-aware process of continuously progressing self-fulfilment:

> As [man] alone, because endowed with reason, constantly looks before and after on the path of his actual life and its innumerable possibilities, and so achieves a course of life which is intellectual, and therefore connected as a whole; corresponding to this, I say, the *melody* has significant intentional connection from beginning to end.[27]

Schopenhauer's metaphor of human life as a melody becomes evident if one thinks of a singer who follows the tune from note to note in a perfect legato with intellectual awareness and incessant intensity of performance. For a reader of Schopenhauer, Beckett's statement 'action is treated melodically' is perfectly clear: confronted with 'innumerable possibilities', man remains firmly himself, is not irritated in his planning and does not deviate from his path. This is the characteristic trait of Rolland's Jean-Christophe who is a person much to Schopenhauer's liking.

So is the Smeraldina-Rima, the prima donna of Beckett's first novel, *Dream of Fair to Middling Women*, the archetype of a melodic person. She conquers the hero of the novel, Belacqua, with a stringent 'master narrative': her life is focused on the music of Johann Sebastian Bach; she will move to Vienna and study the pianoforte. Her musical idol, Bach, was lauded during the 1920s for the contrapuntal 'linearity' of his music, a quality that causes Belacqua *Bachkrankheit*, that is, 'Bach disease'.[28] In her devotion to Bach, the Smeraldina makes Belacqua sick. This is a clear indication that she represents an old-fashioned position in *Dream of Fair to Middling Women*. The narrator ironizes 'melodic' narration as 'a lovely Pythagorean chain-chant solo of cause and effect, a one-figured teleophony

---

[26] For Bergson's concept of melody, see Franz Michael Maier, 'Melodisch, Melodie', in Karlheinz Barck et al. (eds), *Ästhetische Grundbegriffe: Historisches Wörterbuch in sieben Bänden* (Stuttgart, 2002), vol. 4, pp. 38–58 (p. 55).

[27] Arthur Schopenhauer, *The World as Will and Idea*, trans. R.B. Haldane and J. Kemp (London, 1883), vol. 1, p. 335. For Schopenhauer's terms 'intellectual' (*besonnen*) and 'connected' (*zusammenhängend*), see Franz Michael Maier, 'The Idea of Melodic Connection in Samuel Beckett', *Journal of the American Musicological Society* 61/2 (2008): 383–6.

[28] Beckett, *Dream of Fair to Middling Women*, p. 45. For 'linearity', see Ernst Kurth, *Grundlagen des linearen Kontrapunkts: Bachs melodische Polyphonie* (Bern, 1917).

that would be a pleasure to hear'.[29] The allusions are evident: 'chain-chant' instead of 'plain-chant' evokes a sequence of chapters that are diligently concatenated like the quotations in Thomas Aquinas's *Catena aurea*.[30] 'Cause and effect' refers to Proust: it identifies Proust's 'ordre logique' with 'ordre mélodique'.[31] 'Solo', 'one-figured' and 'teleophony' refer to Schopenhauer: his apotheosis of the soprano melody is interpreted as the praise of a single musical line that does not interact with other voices in symphony, but is oriented toward its own telos. Beckett's neologism 'teleophony' accentuates the opposition to symphony even more sharply than 'melody'.

The Concept of 'Symphony'

But what of 'symphony' and symphonic action? What sort of concept is this and why might Beckett have integrated it into his set of aesthetic terms? The philosophically stringent argumentation, the terminological accuracy and the elegant style of Schopenhauer's interpretation of human life as a melody did not conceal from Beckett that this interpretation rests on the assumption that every individual life finds its final fulfilment. This assumption requires a standpoint that sees life as a consummated whole and judges it from a point of view beyond time. From the standpoint of empirical existence, the future is open. There is a fundamental difference between singing the hymn *Deus, creator omnium* and living the life of one of his creatures: a melody one knows is completed, while even one's own life remains open. Beckett understood that the end of life is 'a termination but not a conclusion'[32] and in this light may have felt uneasy with Schopenhauer's speculative concept of melody. 'What is to become of me?' Beckett asked himself in December 1936.[33] With the instability Beckett felt about his own writing career, Schopenhauer's concept of life as an unbroken melodic line must have appeared to him as an untenable assumption. Even in *Endgame*, so many years later, the two antagonistic concepts are still present, exposed by the two protagonists:

> CLOV: Do you believe in the life to come?
> HAMM: Mine was always that.[34]

---

29 Beckett, *Dream of Fair to Middling Women*, p. 10.

30 For Beckett's concept of *catena* (chain), see his letter to Thomas McGreevy, 31 Jan. 1938: 'The rest of the essay … holds together perfectly. It is more "construit" perhaps, more Catena' (*The Letters of Samuel Beckett*, vol. 1, p. 598).

31 For 'ordre logique' see the quotation from Proust on p. 12 above.

32 Beckett, *Proust*, p. 68.

33 Samuel Beckett, *German Diary*, 13 Dec. 1936, in Mark Nixon, *Samuel Beckett's German Diaries 1936–1937* (London, 2011), p. 178.

34 Samuel Beckett, *Endgame*, in *The Complete Dramatic Works* (London, 1986), p. 116.

Clov talks about the coming eternal life, the *vita venturi saeculi* of the Christian *Credo*, in the sense in which the narrator of *Les Faux-monnayeurs* speaks of Madame Vedel: 'Elle attend de la vie future tout ce qui lui manque ici-bas [She expects from a future life all that is lacking to her in this one]',[35] while Hamm talks about the chronological sequence of years that come and pass.

Beckett's reserve against 'melodic fulfilment' is also a vivid young man's protest against the predetermined ways of bourgeois existence – the tradition of a university education, family life and a social and professional routine that he did not want to follow in the way his brother Frank continued their father's firm. Again, a negation was easier to give than a positive statement: 'I don't want to be a professor', Beckett wrote to Thomas MacGreevy on 11 March 1931.[36]

These reservations regarding linearity and continuity may have directed Beckett's thoughts toward the tradition of doubting a uniquely rationalist view of the world. In the notes on Stendhal in Beckett's *Dream Notebook* from the early 1930s the word *imprévu* is found three times.[37] In his letter dated 16 September 1934 to Thomas MacGreevy, Beckett also quotes from Stendhal: 'Maintenant la civilisation a chassé le hasard, plus d'imprévu. [Nowadays civilization has eliminated chance, and the unexpected never happens.]'[38] Beckett is interested in Stendhal's complaint about a world that is ruled by linear sequences of cause and effect. He sympathizes with attitudes which Michel Raimond later called the 'psychologie de la complexité et de l'illogisme [psychology of complexity and the illogical]'.[39] A fashionable expression of the Parisian 1920s for this complexity is *symphonique*. Literary critics praised Dostoevsky's novels for their 'ordre symphonique'.[40] In the same vein, Proust's hypotactical sentences are described as *symphonique* – they embrace a complex situation and surpass the monodic line of traditional narration.[41]

Compared to these vague *façons de parler*, Beckett uses 'symphonic' in a clear and distinct sense: it designates an alternative to linear discursivity, logic and 'melodic' coherence. Nemo, for example, one of the mysterious heroes of *Dream of Fair to Middling Women*, is called 'a symphonic, not a melodic, unit'.[42] Five pages later, the 'night firmament' with its stars is called a 'succinct constellations of genius', 'a network of loci that shall never be co-ordinate', 'the demented perforation of the night colander' and 'symphony without end'.[43] Regarding Nemo as well as the starry sky, Beckett refers to 'symphony' in the sense of the Greek

---

35 Gide, *Les Faux-monnayeurs*, p. 350.

36 *The Letters of Samuel Beckett*, vol. 1, p. 72.

37 Samuel Beckett, *Dream Notebook*, ed. John Pilling (Reading, 1999), pp. 127–8.

38 *The Letters of Samuel Beckett*, vol. 1, p. 228, 229 n. 6.

39 Raimond, *La Crise du roman*, p. 448; see also p. 449.

40 Ibid., p. 400.

41 Ibid., pp. 405, 282.

42 Beckett, *Dream of Fair to Middling Women*, p. 11.

43 Ibid., p. 16.

συμφωνία (*consonantia*): this term from ancient Greek musical theory signifies a conjunction of (two) elements that are different but fit well together: Nemo's character is, if not a complex harmony, then at least a constellation of multiple qualities; the stars allow the possibility of drawing an infinity of connecting lines between their positions. Later again, we see Belacqua and his Dublin girlfriend Alba 'pleasantly drunk' on the beach, and the narrator calls them 'less buttoned up in their cohesion, more Seventh Symphony and contrapanic-stuck, than usual'.[44] The first movement of Beethoven's Seventh Symphony resonates in Belacqua's head all the time – even the musical notes of one central motif pop up in the text twice – and the 'Beethoven pauses' in bars 53–62 of the symphony's first movement which did not make it into *Dream of Fair to Middling Women*, are present in *Ding-Dong*, the third story of *More Pricks than Kicks*. In these examples of symphonic action in Beckett's early novel and short stories, he refers to the eighteenth-century musical form *sinfonia*, an extended musical setting with contrasting themes and sections. Beckett identifies it with plurality, *imprévu*, dissonance and 'continuity bitched to hell'.[45]

The Concept of *Miteinander*

As we have seen, Beckett uses 'symphony' to describe the multifacetedness of the modern novel. An amalgam of συμφωνία and *sinfonia*, it comprises symphonic protagonists as well as symphonic action. The elaboration of these concepts was still on his agenda when, at the end of his visit to Germany in March 1937, he notes in his diary a conversation in Munich. In this note, which is the second quotation discussed in this article, Beckett differentiates the dichotomy of melody versus symphony into a more complex set of terms:

> Long discussion about theatre and film, which Eggers condemns, calls at the best intellectualism. Won't hear of possibility of word's inadequacy. The dissonance that has become principle and that the word cannot express, because literature can no more escape from *chronologies* to *simultaneities*, from *Nebeneinander* to *Miteinander*, [than] the human voice can sing chords. As I talk and listen realize suddenly how Work in Progress is the only [possible] development from Ulysses, the heroic attempt to make literature accomplish what belongs to music – the *Miteinander* and the *simultaneous*. Ulysses falsifies the unconscious, or the 'monologue intérieur', in so far as it is obliged to express it as a teleology.[46]

---

[44] Ibid., p. 188.

[45] Ibid., p. 138.

[46] Beckett, *German Diary*, 26 Mar. 1937, quoted in James Knowlson, *Damned to Fame: The Life of Samuel Beckett* (London, 1996), p. 258 (my italics); for a slightly different reading, see Nixon, *Samuel Beckett's German Diaries*, p. 167.

This proposes another version of Beckett's Bergsonist critique of language as seen in his Trinity College lecture. There, in 1931, he found words inadequate to deal with 'confusion', while now, in 1937, he finds them inadequate to deal with 'dissonance'. Also new in this note is the term *Nebeneinander*. Beckett found it so important for his deliberations on aesthetic multiplicity that he elaborated it into a set of four terms.

Nebeneinander stems from the monograph *Laokoon oder über die Grenzen der Mahlerey und Poesie* (1766) in which the poet and aesthetician Gotthold Ephraim Lessing discussed the story of Laocoon, his sons and the snakes. Lessing elaborated on the difference between a realization of this scene in literature and in sculpture. He distinguished these arts by their characteristic quality: literature is the art of the 'after-one-another', the *Aufeinander folgend* or *Nacheinander*, while the visual arts are the arts of the 'next-to-one-another', the *Nebeneinander*. James Joyce referred to this distinction at the beginning of the third chapter of *Ulysses*: 'Five, six: the *nacheinander*. Exactly: and that is the ineluctable modality of the audible. Open your eyes. No. Jesus! If I fell over a cliff that beetles o'er his base, fell through the *nebeneinander* ineluctably.'[47] Beckett was well aware of these concepts. 'Shades of Lessing', he noted in his diary on 11 February 1937 on the occasion of a discussion with Willi Grohmann on Klee and Picasso versus Joyce.[48] Six weeks later, in his diary entry of 26 March 1937, Beckett modified the Lessingian dichotomy by adding a third term. To the relations in time and space, *Nacheinander* and *Nebeneinander*, Beckett added the *Miteinander*, the 'with-one-another'. What sort of dimensionality is this? What is its relation to space and time?

The answer is given in the note itself: Beckett still had Joyce on his mind, whose *Ulysses* and *Work in Progress* he mentioned. In the third chapter of *Ulysses*, *Nacheinander* and *Nebeneinander* represent the Kantian forms of perception of the outer world: time and space. Stephen walks with his eyes closed and his mind dedicated to his inner world. In his note, Beckett qualified Joyce's way of conceiving this inner world (the unconscious, the *monologue intérieur*) as inadequate, because Joyce forced it into the inappropriate scheme of teleology. We already know this reproach: it is the argument against 'teleophony' and coherence from *Dream of Fair to Middling Women* that is repeated here. But the note hints at something more with the remark: 'Ulysses falsifies the unconscious.' The verb 'falsify' clearly hints at *Les Faux-monnayeurs*, the praised novel of incoherence in which, for Beckett, four kinds of falsification are demonstrated and overcome, among them 'falsification of art'.[49]

In order to explain the narratological problem that stands behind the 'teleological falsification' in *Ulysses*, Beckett made use of a musical example: a human voice cannot sing musical chords, that is, three or four musical tones

---

47 James Joyce, *Ulysses* (Oxford, 1998), p. 37.

48 Beckett, *German Diary*, 11 Feb. 1937, in Nixon, *Samuel Beckett's German Diaries*, p. 166.

49 Beckett, lectures on Gide and Racine, in Le Juez, *Beckett before Beckett*, p. 44.

that sound simultaneously. The *Miteinander* of tones in a chord is the unique musical kind of *Nebeneinander*: chords are multiplicities that neither blend their constituent parts nor segregate them in space, but organize them into a 'collocation' of its own.[50] This organization is what the Greeks called συμφωνία. Even if one considers overtone singing as a possible objection against Beckett's statement, elaborate chord progressions remain unattainable to the voice. It remains limited to melodic *Nacheinander*. With his introduction of *Miteinander* as the musical form of *Nebeneinander*, Beckett makes a substantial addition to the wealth of aesthetic concepts: even if man is an 'eye animal' and tends to organize (as Bergson complained) his concepts into the three dimensions of space, there are things that are neither extended in space nor apart from one another in space and yet still remain separate from one another. This was well known before Bergson: 'An object may exist and yet be no where. ... A moral reflection cannot be plac'd on the right or on the left hand of a passion, nor can a smell or sound be either of a circular or a square figure.'[51]

The musical tones are traditional inhabitants of this 'space without extension' – Marcel Proust laconically confirmed this tradition with his statement: 'Les sons n'ont pas de lieu [Sounds have no fixed point in space]'.[52] The interrelations between musical tones (whether sounding simultaneously in a chord or sequentially in a melodic line) are unique; they cannot without loss of information be embedded into a three-dimensional model. (All spatial representations of melodic relations are simplifications). These unique relations between the musical elements form the basis for metaphorical representations of complex relations in musical terms.

Why then did Beckett change from 'symphonic' to *Miteinander*? First, the epithet 'symphonic', as a consequence of its excessive use, had undergone a loss in significance – already in 1922, Friedrich Wilhelm Murnau advertised his silent film *Nosferatu* with the subtitle *Eine Symphonie des Grauens* (A Symphony of Horror). Secondly, 'symphonic' was never a well defined, autonomous term in Beckett's vocabulary – the antagonism to 'melodic' dominated its meaning. But the most important reason is Beckett's shift away from Joyce (and the teleological 'falsification' of the *monologue intérieur*) toward Gide (and the concept of a polyphony of protagonists' voices). Beckett's orientation toward Gide's idea of narrating events from different points of view is quite literally implicated in the word *Miteinander* (with-one-another), which indicates relations between human beings rather than logical or grammatical structures and which emphasizes the mutuality and liveliness of these relations. Unlike 'symphonic', *Miteinander* emphasizes the aspect of multiplicity in Gide's concept of perspectivism and

---

50 For the concept of 'collocation' in the theory of elementary perception, see Franz Brentano, 'Über Individuation sinnlicher Erscheinungen', in *Untersuchungen zur Sinnespsychologie* [1907] (Hamburg, 1979), p. 81.

51 David Hume, *A Treatise of Human Nature*, [1739/40], Bk 1, Pt 4, §5, ed. Lewis Amherst Selby-Bigge (Oxford, 1888), pp. 235–6.

52 Proust, *À la recherche du temps perdu*, vol. 2, p. 374; Eng. trans, vol. 3, p. 72.

eliminates the idea of unity so essential and dear to Gide.[53] *Miteinander* is a euphemism for 'authentic incoherence'.[54]

Beckett's notion of *Miteinander* is connected to the Lessingian *Nebeneinander* by an intermediate term. In 1879 the philosopher Hermann Lotze – a specialist in the field of space and spaces – described the visually and geometrically non-representable relations of consonant tones as *ortlos auseinander*, as 'apart without being in different places'.[55] Seen in these contexts, Beckett's concept of *Miteinander* is a marvellous addition to Lessing. Alas, the note in the *German Diary* develops it no further.

Analysis of the *Miteinander*

Still, the note makes it clear that *Miteinander* is the ideal that the modern novel should accomplish. The *Miteinander* of 1937 is the elaboration of the 'symphonic' of 1931. The continuation of the note shows that the aesthetic questions of the early 1930s were still on Beckett's mind: 'I provoke loud amusement by description of a man at such a degree of culture that he cannot have a simple or even a predominating idea.'[56] This is another description of the mental state that Beckett described in 1932 as 'paralyzed in ubiquity', but in the meantime, Beckett refined the scheme he taught in Dublin in 1931. Instead of limiting himself to the binary opposition of 'melodic' and 'symphonic', the Munich note juggles with the four terms 'chronologies', 'simultaneities', *Nebeneinander* and *Miteinander*. In the following attempts to organize these terms into a logical framework, three possible interpretations of their relation will be shown.

According to the first interpretation, the note in the *German Diary* is a mere repetition of the dualism of melodic and symphonic. It maintains a scheme of 'from A (melodic) to B (symphonic)', which it embellishes through two pairs of synonyms:

From melodic	to symphonic
From chronologies	to simultaneities
From *Nebeneinander*	to *Miteinander*

This interpretation raises the possible objection that only in one special instance is *Nebeneinander* a possible synonym for 'chronologies'. For example, Mark

53 See the quotations from Gide's *Journal des Faux-monnayeurs*, p. 14 above.

54 Beckett, lectures on Gide and Racine, in Le Juez, *Beckett before Beckett*, p. 35.

55 Hermann Lotze, *Metaphysik: Drei Bücher der Ontologie, Kosmologie und Psychologie*, ed. Georg Misch (Leipzig, 1912), p. 161.

56 Beckett, *German Diary*, 26 Mar. 1937, quoted in Knowlson, *Damned to Fame*, p. 258.

Nixon translates *Nebeneinander* as 'sequential'.[57] Nixon thinks of the words in a text: they stand side by side and are read one after the other. But in itself, *Nebeneinander* denotes a relation in space that has no connotation of time. This is the basis of Lessing's opposition of *Nebeneinander* and *Nacheinander*, in which it is *Nacheinander* that means 'sequential'.

The second interpretation reflects this objection. It reads *Miteinander* as an additional term that elaborates the 'from A to B' in 1931 into 'from A to B to C':

From melodic	to symphonic	
From **chronologies**	to **simultaneities** (*Nebeneinander*)	to *Miteinander*
From *Nacheinander*	to ***Nebeneinander***	to ***Miteinander***

The third interpretation is that of a full elaboration of the dualism of melodic and symphonic into a square of opposition, that is, into four positions with six relations among them:

Chronologies	**Simultaneities**
(***Nacheinander***)	
Literature	*Theatre and Film*
'action treated melodically'	
'one-figured teleophony'	
Nebeneinander	***Miteinander***
(next-to-one-another)	(with-one-another)
Calligrammes (Apollinaire)	*Music*
	'action treated symphonically'
	'dissonance'

In this scheme, the traditional 'melodic' novel is found under 'Chronologies' on the top left, whereas the novel with 'symphonically treated action' is located on the bottom right. Under *Nebeneinander*, a separate position in the logic square is given to the 'words' that, as Beckett puts it in *Dream of Fair to Middling Women*, 'relieved themselves under Apollinaire': in this poet's *Calligrammes* the letters are quite literally localized *Nebeneinander* – in horizontal, vertical and diagonal order: To the 'relief of the words', as Beckett says, their usual horizontal order is opened into a multiplicity of spatial orientations.[58] The lemma 'Simultaneities' finally denotes the genres the Munich discussion was concerned with: theatre and film.

---

57 Nixon, *Samuel Beckett's German Diaries*, p. 167.

58 See Beckett, *Dream of Fair to Middling Women*, p. 171.

Simultaneities in Film

'Simultaneities' is the catchword for the contemporary importance of Beckett's and Gide's aesthetic ideas: Stephen Gaghan's 2005 film *Syriana* is a recent example of the aesthetic ideal Beckett sketched in his 1937 *German Diary* entry. *Syriana* simultaneously tells four stories (a fifth was removed) which it scatters into a puzzle of scenes of about 90 seconds length each – there are 20 scenes in the first 30 minutes (the first act) of the film. As the scenes play in different locations, it is difficult to synthesize into a coherent line even those scenes that belong to the same sequence of one of the stories. The film quite literally demonstrates Beckett's statement that 'dissonance has become principle'. In the end, Gide's idea of a unity 'à rétablir' (to reconstruct) wins over Beckett's concept of totally abolishing any 'predominating idea': the reviewers of *Syriana* welcomed the authentic coherence of the underlying plot that gradually becomes visible as the film progresses.[59]

This chapter began with Beckett's characterization of Gide's *Paludes* as the 'symphonic' novel, posing the question: what might be the relation of Beckett the artist toward his aesthetic concepts of the 'symphonic' and the *Miteinander*? Beckett, who did not want to be a professor, did not restrict his activities to the Lessingian 'jeu charmant' (charming game) of general aesthetics but was oriented toward artistic production.[60] His *Dream of Fair to Middling Women* not only talks ironically about a 'purely melodic' novel,[61] but also confronts the reader with new ways of narration. There is a strange collocation of voices at the end of the chapter entitled 'Und':

> Thus dusk shall ere long gather about him–unless to be sure we take it into our head to scuttle at dead of night the brave ship where now he lies a-dreaming (creeks and springboards), the noble Hapak and all its freights, crew and cargo, and Belacqua along with his palpitations and adhesions and effusions and agenesia and wombtomb and aesthetic of inaudibilities.
>
> L'andar su che porta?.
>
> Oh but the bay, Mr Beckett, didn't you know, about your brow.[62]

We hear the narrator, we hear (without knowing who speaks) a famous quotation from Dante's Belacqua, and we hear a voice that talks to a mysterious 'Mr Beckett'. It is unclear who utters the words from Dante and who speaks to 'Mr Beckett'. From the point of view of pragmatics, all three voices share one and the same level of utterance – they speak as though they were voices in a musical setting. In

---

59 See Stephen Farber, 'A Half-Dozen Ways to Watch the Same Movie', *New York Times: Movies* (13 Nov. 2005), <http://www.nytimes.com/2005/11/13/movies/13farb.html?pagewanted=1>.

60 Samuel Beckett, *Le Monde et le pantalon* (Paris, 2010), p. 11.

61 Beckett, *Dream of Fair to Middling Women*, p. 10.

62 Ibid., p. 140–41.

Beckett's second novel, *Murphy*, we find an even more sophisticated constellation in the description of 'Murphy's mind' not 'as it really was' but as 'it felt and pictured itself to be'.[63] This indicates that in the conversation in Munich, Beckett was not lecturing on literary history but was rather confronting a contemporary narratological question of so complicated a nature that even Joyce's *Finnegans Wake* appeared to Beckett not as an accomplished answer but rather as another 'heroic attempt'. In that lively Munich conversation with its *Durcheinander* of voices, Beckett was arguing in favour of the artistic potential of theatre and film. The aesthetic concept that flashed through his mind along the associative lines of *Nacheinander*, *Nebeneinander* and *Miteinander* sheds light on the openness to a bounty of genres and media that would make Beckett's work, in the years to come, unique among the artistic creations of the twentieth century.

63 Samuel Beckett, *Murphy* (New York, 1957), pp. 10, 107.

Chapter 2

Beckett's *Proust*, Schopenhauer, and the Musical Art of Pastiche

Céline Surprenant

In 1931 Samuel Beckett published a study of Marcel Proust's partly posthumous seven-part novel *À la recherche du temps perdu* (1913–27), simply entitled *Proust*. *Du côté de chez Swann* – the first volume of the novel – had appeared in November 1913. Having written what he thought would form the first and the last volumes in 1913, Proust continued to expand and revise sections of the existing manuscript until his death in 1922. He did so especially during the First World War, working during this period on *Sodome et Gomorrhe* and the 'Albertine' sections. Interrupted during the conflict, the publication of the novel resumed in 1919 with *À l'ombre des jeunes filles en fleur*, and ended in 1927 with the posthumous publication of *Le Temps retrouvé*.[1] Proust (and editors after him) modified the outline of the novel and the number of volumes in which it was published throughout its editorial history. During the summer of 1930, Beckett read it twice in the 16-volume Gallimard edition published between 1927 and 1930.[2]

---

1 For a concise history of the genesis of the novel between 1908 and 1922, see Marion Schmid, 'The Birth and Development of *À la recherche du temps perdu*', in Richard Bales (ed.), *The Cambridge Companion to Proust* (Cambridge, 2006), pp. 58–73. In its final form the novel comprises the following parts that were published in varying numbers of volumes: *Du côté de chez Swann*, *À l'ombre des jeunes filles en fleur*, *Le Côté de Guermantes*, *Sodome et Gomorrhe*, *La Prisonnière*, *Albertine disparue (La Fugitive)*, and *Le Temps retrouvé*. References to the novel in this chapter are to the Pléiade edition in four volumes: Marcel Proust, *À la recherche du temps perdu*, ed. Jean-Yves Tadié (Paris, 1987–9). References to the English translation of the novel are from the six-volume translation by Charles Kenneth Scott Moncrieff and Terence Kilmartin, revised by Dennis Joseph Enright, *In Search of Lost Time* (New York, 2003). All translations of quotations (other than those from *À la recherche du temps perdu*) are by the author. The author is very grateful to Nick Till and Sara Jane Bailes for their helpful suggestions when revising the chapter.

2 See John Pilling, '*Proust* and Schopenhauer: Music and Shadows', in Mary Bryden (ed.), *Samuel Beckett and Music* (Oxford, 1998), pp. 173–8 (p. 176). In the Foreword to *Proust*, Beckett notoriously qualified the edition as 'abominable', referring to the typographical errors in it. For a description of Beckett's annotations on his copy of the novel, kept at the Beckett Archive in Reading, see John Pilling, 'Beckett's Proust', in Stanley E. Gontarski (ed.), *The Beckett Studies Reader* (Gainesville, FL, 1993), p. 26 n. 2.

Beckett, who had been a *lecteur d'anglais* at the École normale supérieure in Paris between 1928 and 1930 before writing *Proust*, did not at that time have today's critical editions documenting the genesis of the novel at his disposal. Even though he was commissioned to write a literary study of the writer, he adopted an irreverent attitude towards literary academic conventions and the psycho-biographical bias of the rare existing studies of Proust that had been published since Proust's death.[3] Throughout the seven sections of the book that deal with the themes of time, habit, memory, the 'Albertine tragedy'[4] and time regained in Proust's novel, and with the narrator's reflections on aesthetics and death, Beckett anticipated later critics. Among other points, he signalled the incessant 'mobility' of the characters and was one of the first reader–critics to be interested in the architecture of the novel, emphasizing the symmetrical structure whereby episodes come in pairs.[5] Beckett saw, for example, how listening to the sonata by the fictive composer Vinteuil in *Du côté de chez Swann* was mirrored by listening to Vinteuil's septuor described in the penultimate volume of the novel, denoting transformations in musical aesthetics from romantic to dissonant. Moreover, Beckett was one of the first critics to compare Proust to a number of philosophers, such as Descartes, Leibniz, Nietzsche and Schopenhauer, whom he happened to be reading in 1930.[6]

It is not only through his choice of themes and foci that Beckett anticipated later readers and critics of Proust. He also made a distinctive contribution through the style in which he chose to present *À la recherche du temps perdu*. Among other tactics, Beckett, the 'lecteur perspicace [perspicacious reader]', exaggerated apparently secondary aspects of the novel, such as the idea of the mathematical 'equation', with which *Proust* begins. The idea of the equation is found in *La Prisonnière*, which Beckett discussed in his section on the Albertine

---

3 Chatto & Windus commissioned the book in 1930, as a contribution to the Dolphin Series of Popular Literary Studies (see Luc Fraisse, 'Le "Proust" de Beckett: Fidélité médiatrice et infidélité créatrice', in Marius Buning, Matthijs Engelberts and Sjef Houppermans (eds), *Samuel Beckett: Crossroads and Borderlines*, *Samuel Beckett Today/ Aujourd'hui* 6 (Amsterdam and Atlanta, GA, 1997), pp. 365–86 (p. 369)).

4 The 'Albertine tragedy' refers to *La Prisonnière* and *Albertine disparue* (Fraisse, 'Le "Proust" de Beckett', p. 377).

5 Ibid., p. 374. See, for example, the passage on 'the perpetuum mobile of our disillusions' because 'the aspirations of yesterday were valid for yesterday's ego, not for to-day's'. The cause of the incessant mobility is the 'poisonous ingenuity of Time in the science of affliction' which results in the 'unceasing modification' of the subject's 'personality' (Samuel Beckett, *Proust*, in *Proust and Three Dialogues with Georges Duthuit* (London, 1999), pp. 14–15).

6 Ibid., p. 370. Beckett's philosophical approach to the novel was fed by his reading of Descartes, Kant and, according to Fraisse, Bergson's *L'Évolution créatrice* (see Fraisse, *L'Éclectisme philosophique de Marcel Proust* (Paris, 2013), p. 23). This does not mean that we can extract from either Proust or Beckett a coherent philosophical doctrine.

tragedy.[7] Beckett detached this term from its context and thus blurred its meaning, applying what Luc Fraisse has described as 'une technique de collage en mosaïque [a collage technique resembling mosaic]'.[8] The 'equation' however, like other mathematical metaphors that Beckett extracted and distributed throughout his study, is also a means of highlighting the tension between sensible experience and analytical reasoning upon which the narrator's aesthetic reflections on writing, visual art and music bear.[9]

Beckett 'took a deep and abiding interest' in music and mathematics for, as Mary Bryden suggests, 'they share a grounding in mensuration, and adherence to an abstract domain, a preoccupation with patterning and interconnection'.[10] As though he were anticipating the importance that 'counting ... rhythms, repetitions and variations' were to take in his later plays, the young writer seized on the musical theme of *À la recherche du temps perdu* and carefully annotated the pages of *Du côté de chez Swann* devoted to Swann's repeated listening to a phrase of the Vinteuil sonata, as I will discuss further below.[11] He concluded the book with an excursus on music in which music is described as 'the catalyctic element' of the novel. Beckett took this view from Jacques Benoist-Méchin, who in 1926 had underlined how music predominates in the novel because, among all other arts, it is the one that makes us most 'sensible à l'écoulement du temps [aware of the passing of time]'.[12] The 'Proustian demonstration' concerning music, Beckett claimed, thus echoing the 'Proustian equation' with which the book began, derived from Schopenhauer's metaphysics of music.[13] How does

---

7 Beckett, *Proust*, pp. 45–67.

8 Fraisse, 'Le "Proust" de Beckett', p. 378. For the passage where the narrator describes Albertine's lies in mathematical terms, see Proust, *À la recherche du temps perdu*, vol. 3, p. 850; Eng. trans., vol. 5, p. 397.

9 For an analysis of the logico-mathematical metaphors in the book, see Céline Surprenant, '"An Occult Arithmetic": The "Proustian Equation" according to Beckett's *Proust*', *Journal of Romance Studies* 7/3 (1997): 47–58. This chapter takes up and develops further the analyses carried out in that article.

10 Mary Bryden, 'Beckett and the Sound of Silence', in (ed.), *Samuel Beckett and Music*, pp. 21–46 (p. 40). The 'very process of counting, in its rhythms, repetitions and variations, becomes a defining feature in some of Beckett's later short plays ... and intersects significantly with his interest in music, and the musical structure of many of his plays' (Gerald Macklin, 'Writing by Numbers: The Music of Mind in Samuel Beckett's *Pas*', *French Studies Bulletin*, 76 (2000): 10–13; see also Pascale Casanova's commentary on *Cap au pire* (*Worstward Ho* (1983)) as 'a developed (and resolved) equation' in *Beckett l'abstracteur: Anatomie d'une révolution littéraire* (Paris, 1997), pp. 31–2).

11 Bryden, 'Beckett and the Sound of Silence', pp. 31–2.

12 Léon Pierre-Quint quoted in Jacques Benoist-Méchin, *La Musique et l'immortalité dans l'œuvre de Marcel Proust* (Paris, 1926), p. 34 n. 1, quoted in Beckett, *Proust*, p. 92.

13 Fraisse, 'Le "Proust" de Beckett', p. 370; Arthur Schopenhauer, *The World as Will and Representation*, trans. R.B. Haldane and J. Kemp (London, 1909), vol. 1, pp. 330–47.

Beckett treat that philosophical source in which Proust was interested from his first writings onwards?[14]

Critics have both praised and dismissed Beckett's idiosyncratic reading of *À la recherche du temps perdu*, some seeing it as a feat of 'déformations créatrices [creative distortion]'[15] while others consider it a work which is 'obscurely worded and seriously under-argued'.[16] John Pilling has described the concluding passage on music in *Proust* as 'Beckett's only extended assessment of what music might mean', a somewhat striking affirmation given how the concluding lines are, indeed, under-argued and therefore hardly make for an extended assessment.[17] Nevertheless, if Beckett's reading of and commentary upon *À la recherche du temps perdu* was formative for the writer's subsequent work, this might have to do with his treatment of music in it, however abstract and suggestive that remained. The theme of music provided him with an opportunity not only to apply the 'Schopenhauer filter' to the novel, which other themes such as habit, love and death also allowed him to do, but also to emphasize and, so to speak, to turn into parody the conflicting alliance of intellect and sensation that music performs in the novel, as I aim to show in the rest of this chapter. It is thus worth re-examining *Proust* by focusing on Beckett's discussion of music, for it indexes his reading of the novel's other earliest critics and testifies to the popularity of Schopenhauer's views on music at the end of the nineteenth-century, views to which Proust's novel sends us back through its representation of the hearing of a fictive composer's music.

However, it is not only *À la recherche du temps perdu* that has been subjected to Beckett's 'creative distortions'. Schopenhauer, whose pronouncements on music Beckett cited only sparsely but from which he nevertheless drew substantially, is also the object of a transformative re-description. Schopenhauer's ideas on music, more particularly, allowed Beckett to highlight the opposition between the intellect and sensation, the importance of which in Proust's novel, he acutely

---

14 See Anne Henry, 'Proust du Côté de Schopenhauer', in (ed.), *Schopenhauer et la création littéraire en Europe* (Paris, 1989), pp. 149–64 (p. 151). According to Henry, Proust became interested in Schopenhauer's philosophy through music, thanks to his friendship with the composer Reynaldo Hahn. Henry was the first critic to systematically argue, that Proust had transposed into a novel nineteenth-century philosophy, most particularly that of Schelling and Schopenhauer that had been assimilated by French philosophers who were taught to the young Proust at the *lycée* and during his philosophy studies at the Sorbonne between 1889 and 1895 (*Marcel Proust: Théories pour une esthétique* (Paris, 1981); see Fraisse, *L'Éclectisme*, p. 307). Proust also took an interest in Schopenhauer via Maupassant and Wagner, the latter being a constant reference in Proust's correspondence and novel. On Wagner and Proust, see Françoise Leriche, 'Wagner', in Annick Bouillaguet and Brian G. Rogers (eds), *Dictionnaire Marcel Proust* (Paris, 2004), pp. 1073–4.

15 Fraisse, 'Le *Proust* de Beckett', p. 378.

16 Ibid., p. 378; James Acheson, 'Beckett, Proust, and Schopenhauer', *Contemporary Literature*, 19/2 (1978): 165–79 (p. 165).

17 Pilling, '*Proust* and Schopenhauer', p. 173.

perceived.[18] Beckett may have carried out a 'very original endeavour'[19] in *Proust*, yet, through the theme of music, we discover that his study of *À la recherche du temps perdu* owes a great deal to the early reception of Proust and that Beckett had been a perspicacious reader, too, of Proust's early critics.

Music in Proust

In Proustian studies, the theme of music has recurred 'avec la régularité du pendule [with the regularity of a pendulum]'.[20] When Beckett stated in *Proust* that 'one could write an entire book on music in Proust, in particular of the music of Vinteuil: the Sonata and the Septuor', he was in fact referring to existing critical works written during the 1920s.[21] Since the earliest criticism, it had been deemed that music plays a revelatory role in *À la recherche du temps perdu*. Benoist-Méchin believed that 'de tous les arts, c'est peut-être la musique que Proust a traité le plus magistralement [music is, of all the arts, the one that Proust has most consummately represented]' and that music occupies 'la place plus élevée [the highest place]' in the novel.[22] Charles du Bos stated that 'toutes les fois où dans son œuvre [la musique] intervient, Proust est par elle aussitôt porté au sommet de sa puissance [every time that music plays a part in his work, Proust is, through it, immediately brought to the height of his power]'.[23] Arnaud Dandieu judged that, together with Ruskin's influence, music had been for Proust, 'l'initiatrice indispensable [the essential initiator]',[24] while a later critic, Georges Piroué, presented *À la recherche du temps perdu* 'comme l'équivalent d'une composition musicale [as being the equivalent of a musical composition]', a description that no doubt comes from the importance of Wagner and the leitmotiv in the novel.[25]

---

[18] That opposition in Proust sends us back to nineteenth-century sources, such as Hippolyte Taine's *De l'intelligence* (Paris, 1870) and, more generally, late nineteenth-century works in psychological sciences, from which Proust also drew and which can be explored, among others, through Donald Wright's study, *Du discours médical dans* À la recherche du temps perdu: *Science et souffrance* (Paris, 2007). Henry believes that Proust's recourse to human sciences, such as psychological ones, had mitigated his importation into the novel of Schopenhauer's pessimism. See Henry, 'Proust du côté de Schopenhauer', p. 158. The editor of *Du côté de chez Swann* underlined the opposition between the metaphors of liquid substance associated with sensation, as opposed to that of architecture with the intellect (Proust, *À la recherche du temps perdu*, vol. 1, p. 1239).

[19] Fraisse, *L'Éclectisme*, p. 23.

[20] Jean Nattiez, *Proust musicien* (Paris, 1984), p. 13.

[21] Beckett, *Proust*, p. 91.

[22] Benoist-Méchin, *La Musique*, pp. 31–2.

[23] Charles du Bos, *Approximations* (Paris, 1922), p. 94.

[24] Arnaud Dandieu, *Marcel Proust: Sa révélation psychologique* (Paris, 1930), p. 112.

[25] Georges Piroué, *Proust et la musique du devenir* (Paris, 1960), p. 170.

Benoist-Méchin argued that it is difficult to say 'où la musique commence et où elle cesse [where music begins and where it stops]' in the novel because 'elle déborde de beaucoup sur les passages qui lui sont plus particulièrement assignés [it extends beyond passages that are specifically devoted to it]'.[26] Music, together with painting and writing, is an element of the 'story of a vocation' that the novel tells, through the scenes of listening to fictive compositions by Vinteuil, the character whom Proust described as 'une des clés de voûte de sa construction Romanesque [one of the cornerstones of his novelistic composition]'.[27] Passages devoted to the hearing of Vinteuil's music condense many of the narrator's concerns, notably on aesthetics, posterity and the role of the intellect in the enjoyment of art and music. The recitals of Vinteuil's music that are described more than once take place at different stages of the narrator's life, and constitute steps in his aesthetic education and thinking. It is possible to relate the fictional musical pieces in the novel to precise musical compositions and ideas from the *fin-de-siècle* French school of music (most notably those of Camille Saint-Saëns, César Franck and Gabriel Fauré) of which the narrator was fond during his adolescence, and to Wagner and Beethoven, who replaced his early preferences during his years of maturity.[28] There is an emphasis on change both in musical compositions themselves and in musical taste.

It thus matters that the experience of listening to Vinteuil's music is repeated, because it is not only that we see the composer's œuvre evolve with the passing of time, but listening more than once to a piece of music modifies it in the ears of the listener. It is these modifications, within a single hearing of a piece and from one hearing to the next, that we follow through Swann's repeated hearings of Vinteuil's music as relayed by the narrator, for whom the sonata at first remained 'invisible', until, much later in life, Vinteuil's septuor serves as the support for the narrator's understanding of what art and music should be.[29]

Vinteuil's Music

Although Vinteuil's music pervades the entire work, only a small number of the pages devoted to it include technical terms of musical analysis. Instead, they consist

---

26 Benoist-Méchin, *La Musique*, p. 35. For a compilation of all the guises of music in the novel, see Leriche, 'Wagner'.

27 Quoted in Proust, 'Notice', in *À la recherche du temps perdu*, vol. 3, p. 1685.

28 Antoine Compagnon, *La Troisième République des lettres* (Paris, 1989); Cécile Leblanc, 'Proust et la "bande à Franck": Présence et influence de la musique française de la fin du dix-neuvième siècle', in Nathalie Mauriac Dyer, Kazuyoshi Yoshikawa and Pierre-Edmond Robert (eds), *Proust face à l'héritage du* XIX*e siècle*: *Tradition et métamorphose* (Paris, 2012), pp. 203–17.

29 Proust, *À la recherche du temps perdu*, vol. 3, pp. 753–68; Eng. trans., vol. 5, pp. 283–95.

of the narrator's describing, qualifying and comparing the movement of the sound of the notes of Vinteuil's 'petite phrase' in terms other than musical.[30] Vinteuil's music allows the reader to witness the attempted conversion of sensory perception into intellectual equivalents. However, the conversion is never quite realized. The narrator insists on the negative role that the 'formes du raisonnements [rational discourse]'[31] play in this matter, because they make the musical object disappear. The rational approach to music thus never completely holds. Hearing music is represented in terms of an alternation between the exercise of reason and sensory experience.

The first time Swann hears a particular phrase of the sonata that detaches itself from the rest, he perceives the 'qualité matérielle des sons sécrétés par les instruments [the material quality of the sounds which those instruments secreted]'.[32] In the midst of his listening, however, something detaches itself from the line of the violin, in a 'clapotement liquid [sort of liquid rippling of sound]',[33] which creates an 'impression … confuse', that is, 'une de ces impressions qui sont peut-être pourtant les seules purement musicales, inétendues, entièrement originales, irréductibles à tout autre ordre d'impressions. Une impression de ce genre, pendant un instant, est pour ainsi dire *sine materia* [so confused an impression, one of those that are, notwithstanding, our only purely musical impressions, limited in their extent, entirely original, and irreducible to any other kind. An impression of this order, vanishing in an instant, is, so to speak, an impression *sine materia*]'.[34] From the description of that first perception follows another related to the way in which memory transcribes it, 'comme un ouvrier qui travaille à établir des fondations durables au milieu des flots [like a labourer who toils at the laying down of firm foundations beneath the tumult of the waves]'.[35] Memory makes the line no longer 'insaisissable [ineffable]',[36] for Swann now 's'en représentait l'étendue, les groupements symétriques, la graphie, la valeur expressive; il avait devant lui cette chose qui n'est plus de la musique pure, qui est du dessin, de l'architecture, de la pensée, et qui permet de se rappeler la musique [was able to picture to himself its extent, its symmetrical arrangement, its notations, the strength of its expression; he had before him that definite object which was no longer pure music but rather design, architecture, thought, and which allowed the actual music to be recalled]'.[37] Music expands the soul, but soon 'les notes que nous entendons alors, tendent déjà, selon leur hauteur et leur quantité, à couvrir devant nos yeux des surfaces de dimensions variées … à nous donner des sensations de largeur, de

30 Nattiez, *Proust musicien*, p. 25.

31 Proust, *À la recherché du temps perdu*, vol. 1, p. 343; Eng. trans., vol. 1, p. 420.

32 Ibid., vol. 1, p. 205; Eng. trans., vol. 1, p. 250.

33 Ibid.

34 Ibid., vol. 1, pp. 205–6; Eng. trans., vol. 1, p. 250.

35 Ibid., vol. 1, p. 206; Eng. trans., vol. 1, p. 251.

36 Ibid.

37 Ibid.

ténuité, de stabilité, de caprice [the notes which we hear at such moments tend to spread out before our eyes, over surfaces greater or smaller according to their pitch and volume … to give us the sensation of breath or tenuity, stability or caprice]'.[38]

The 'petite phrase', which for Swann condenses Vinteuil's music, is tied to the progress of Swann and Odette's love. Changes in the perception of it are subjective changes that mark the changes in Swann's relation to his love object. When he later hears the sonata again, notes can then be grasped through analytical categories, for once Odette had ceased to love him, the motif that he had perceived as a 'mystérieuse entité [mysterious entity]'[39] and which gave a confused impression could become again the object of a reasoned apprehension. The subjective experience of love had until then subtracted it from an analytical grasp, from rational discourse. The narrator underlines the two ways in which to account for the aesthetic effect of the romantic sonata. It can be described in terms of the 'faible écart entre les cinq notes qui la composaient et au rappel constant de deux d'entre elles [the closeness of the intervals between the five notes of which it is composed and the constant repetition of two of these]'.[40] Yet, this explanation is invalid because, in creating its effect, the pianist did not dispose of a 'clavier mesquin de sept notes [a miserable stave of seven notes]', but rather, 'un clavier incommensurable [an immeasurable keyboard]',[41] composed of 'un millions de touches de tendresse, de passion, de courage, de sérénité [millions of keys of tenderness, of passion, of courage, of serenity]'[42] to be discovered by composers. That first listening – which is relayed through the memory of the narrator's hearing of the dissonant Vinteuil septuor – demonstrates that music can trigger a reasoned, intellectual listening as well as a poetical, sensible one.[43]

Just as water would appear to be consubstantial with music in the passages describing the recitals, the enjoyment of a musical object goes together with the rejection of reasoning. The musicologists' methods that are based on reasoning are the negative side of the 'direct impression' of music, even though something in music, as in other subjective experiences, invites precisely such reasoning. Within *À la recherche du temps perdu*, listening to music is thus not only the experience of sensible and qualitative essences. It also provides a concrete form to tensions within and beyond the apprehension of music itself.

Critical analyses of music in Proust from the early 1920s relate this tension within the experience of music to Schopenhauer's ideas about music, which, according to Fraisse, allows us to represent the uncapturable, because it gives us

---

38 Ibid., vol. 1, p. 206; Eng. trans., vol. 1, p. 250.

39 Ibid., vol. 1, p. 343; Eng. trans., vol. 1, p. 420.

40 Ibid.

41 Ibid.

42 Ibid., vol. 1, p. 344; Eng. trans., vol. 1, p. 421.

43 To illustrate the rational side of Vinteuil's art, the narrator compares it to the naturalist Lavoisier's work (ibid., vol. 1, pp. 343–5; Eng. trans., vol. 1, p. 423).

access to the will yet without any of its objectification in words or images.[44] In an oft-quoted interview published in *Le Temps* (12 November 1913), following the publication of *Du côté de chez Swann*, Proust stated:

> S['il se] permet de raisonner sur [son] livre, c'est qu'il n'est à aucun degré une œuvre de raisonnement; c'est que ses moindres éléments [lui ont été] fournis par [sa] sensibilité, qu [il les a] d'abord aperçus au fond de [lui]-même, sans les comprendre, ayant autant de peine à les convertir en quelque chose d'intelligible que s'ils avaient été aussi étrangers au monde de l'intelligence que, comment dire? un motif musical.
>
> [If he allows himself to reason about his book, it is because the latter is in no way borne out of reasoning; it is because it is his sensibility that had provided it with its slightest elements, which he had first perceived in himself, without understanding them, having as much trouble converting them into something intelligible as if they had been as foreign to the work of the intellect as, how should I say, a musical motif?][45]

Proust was defending himself against the charge that he was presenting mere intricacies. What was at stake, he objected, were realities that required a particular clarification and that were distinct from logical ideas. The interview presented one of the underlying dualities of the novel in a chiasmus that recurs in Proust's writing whenever matters are concerned with the relationship between the intellect and sensibility. In order to emphasize the role of the senses in his work, Proust reminds us of the part reason plays.

The analogy between a direct apprehension of the book and that of a musical motif calls for a rapprochement with Schopenhauer, who affirms how the unmediated experience of art (with music as the singular case within the arts), excludes abstract understanding, even if this leaves us in obscurity. The case of music is complex, because given that music 'cannot free itself [from arithmetic] without entirely ceasing to be music', it would seem precisely to invite an abstract understanding.

Treating music as something that is foreign to the domain of the intellect, then, simplifies the problem of establishing the relation between music and the intellect, which Schopenhauer discussed in *The World as Will and Representation* when underlining the fact that music has a stronger effect on us than the other arts:

> [Music's] representative relation to the world must be very deep, absolutely true, and strikingly accurate, because it is instantly understood by every one, and has the appearance of a certain infallibility, because its form may be reduced to

44 Fraisse, *L'Éclectisme*, p. 821.

45 Proust, 'Swann expliqué par Proust', interview with Élie-Joseph Bois, in *Contre Sainte-Beuve*, ed. Pierre Clarac and Yves Sandre (Paris, 1971), p. 559.

> perfectly definite rules expressed in numbers, from which it cannot free itself without entirely ceasing to be music. Yet the point of comparison between music and the world, the respect in which it stands to the world in the relation of a copy or repetition, is very obscure. Men have practised music in all ages without being able to account for this; content to understand it directly, they renounce all claims to an abstract conception of this direct understanding itself.[46]

Compared with the other arts, which are the objectification of will through the representation of particular things that 'excite … the knowledge' of the Platonic Ideas, music is not 'the copy of the Ideas, but *the copy of the will itself*, whose objectivity the Ideas are'. It does not speak of shadows, but of 'the thing itself'.[47] In a book published the same year as *Du côté de chez Swann*, André Fauconnet situates music with respect to the duality between arithmetic and music, a duality that Beckett's take on music in Proust presupposes:

> Tandis que la première [arithmetic] fait appel à l'entremise des concepts abstraits et met en jeu notre entendement discursif, la seconde [music] agit sur nos sens, émeut notre coeur et stimule immédiatement nos facultés d'intuition. Toutes deux s'accordent dans la mesure où elles représentent deux copies d'un même texte. Le texte, c'est le vouloir vivre universel avec ses degrés d'objectivation et sa progression rythmée de la satisfaction au désir, du désir à la satisfaction. La copie directe, immediate, fidèle, au point de rester obscure à l'intelligence, comme son modèle même, c'est la musique. La traduction pensée commentée du texte nous la devons à l'arithmétique.
>
> [While the first one appeals to abstract concepts and calls into play our discursive understanding, the second one acts on our senses, moves our Heart and stimulates our intuitive faculty. They are in harmony with each other in so far as they represent two copies of the same text. The text is the universal will to live, with its degrees of objectification and its rhythmic progression from satisfaction to desire, and from desire to satisfaction. The direct, immediate, faithful copy, as faithful as to remain obscure to the intellect, as its very model, is music. Arithmetic takes care of the thoughtfully annotated translation of the text.][48]

Beckett does not enquire into Schopenhauer's theory of the gradation of the will in music, as reconstituted by Fauconnet. However, he emphasizes the way in which the affirmation of the uselessness of abstract reasoning and understanding can itself become a source of aesthetic creation, an idea upon which he drew throughout *Proust*. He does so in particular when discussing the reversals that occur

---

46 Schopenhauer, *The World as Will and Representation*, vol. 1, pp. 334–5.

47 Ibid., p. 336.

48 André Fauconnet, *L'Esthétique de Schopenhauer* (Paris, 1913), p. 351.

around what he called Proust's romantic and anti-intellectual stance, which Beckett associates with his 'substitutions of affectivity for intelligence ... his rejection of Concept in favour of the Idea, his scepticism before causality'.[49] In emphasizing the logico-mathematical register, Beckett reversed Proust's 'substitution of affectivity for intelligence' in order to re-affirm or to re-experience that substitution through his own writing.[50] The substitution that he praises in Proust inspires Beckett to re-describe the novel through an accumulation of reversals. In this way, involuntary memory restores 'more because less'; time is 'a condition of resurrection because an instrument of death', among other formulations.[51]

Music and Posterity

One function of music in *À la recherche du temps perdu* is to trigger a reflection on the progress and the obsolescence of aesthetic judgements, and that theme, to which Beckett does not directly refer, could be inspired by Schopenhauer, who also believed that works of art precede the public that appreciates them.[52] Proust concretized that idea through Vinteuil's music. Indeed not only does the narrator reflect on formal developments within Vinteuil's œuvre itself, but music also activates a reflection on how works of art create the public that will be able to appreciate them. These reflections on music and posterity occur in *À l'ombre des jeunes filles en fleur*, when the narrator remembers hearing Odette play Vinteuil's sonata, a memory that coincides with one of the stages in the narrator's aesthetic education. The complexity of certain works and our deficient faculty of memory mean that we are permanently listening to them for the first time. Time is needed 'pour pénétrer une œuvre un peu profonde [to penetrate a work of any depth]',[53] but the time needed for that to happen 'n'est que le raccourci et comme le symbole des années, des siècles parfois, qui s'écoulent avant que le public puisse aimer un chef-d'œuvre vraiment nouveau [is but the shortening and as if the symbol of years, sometimes of centuries, which pass by before the public should be able to appreciate a truly new work of art]'.[54] It takes time for an individual to appreciate a work, however; the work itself must create its posterity, which is both peculiar to and an extension of itself. The narrator stages that process in relation to the stages in his appreciation of Vinteuil's music, from incomprehension to understanding. When he did not understand it, he could at least enjoy hearing Mme Swann play it. As for Swann, he had rapidly overcome its novelty, by assimilating its memory with memories of his courtship with Odette, and with the human and geographical

49 Beckett, *Proust*, p. 81.

50 Ibid.

51 Ibid., pp. 33, 35.

52 Fraisse, *L'Éclectisme*, pp. 841–2.

53 Proust, *À la recherche du temps perdu*, vol. 1, p. 520; Eng. trans., vol. 2, p. 120.

54 Ibid., vol. 1, pp. 521–2; Eng. trans., vol. 2, pp. 120–21.

décor in which it took place, that is, images of the Verdurin salon and its actors, and the many places where Odette and he had dined together. The narrator reports Swann thus contradicting Schopenhauer's idea that music 'shows' 'la Volonté en soi [the will-in-itself]' or 'la Synthèse de l'infini' [the synthesis of the infinite]'.[55] Just as Swann had, so to speak, 'domesticated' the novelty of the sonata, future generations end up by assimilating even the most incomprehensible works of music or art. Thus it is for Beethoven, Impressionism, the search for dissonance, and the exclusive use of the Chinese scale, Cubism and Futurism: steps in the narrator's aesthetic education in which music figures prominently.

Beckett's *Proust* as Pastiche

Schopenhauer provided some of the themes of Beckett's study – notably those that related to Proust's so-called pessimism – even though Beckett did not seek to explicate Schopenhauer's philosophy any more than he wanted to explicate Proust.[56] Among the expressions of this pessimism, Beckett spoke of the way in which the 'observer *infects* the observed with its own mobility', of human intercourse in terms of 'two separate and immanent dynamisms related to no system of synchronization', and stated that 'all that is realized in Time (all Time produces), whether in Art or in Life', can never be possessed 'integrally at once', but only by 'a series of partial annexation'.[57] Other construals of Proust's pessimism relate to time – 'Memory and Habit are attributes of the Time cancer'[58] – to the law of memory or to habit. Granted Beckett might have drawn themes from many sources other than Schopenhauer, the philosopher appears as only one of the possible languages with which to render the novel's great themes. This is apparent in Beckett's presentation of habit, for example, in a procession of idioms. How to describe the 'general laws of habit' to which the laws of memory are subjected? There is more than one way in which to state this. We move from anthropomorphic metaphors – habit is represented as an 'agent of security', a 'minister of dullness' – to the language of moral discipline, the metaphor of a contract with renewable clauses, to habit described as the organizer of a 'team of syntheses' on 'labour-saving principles'.[59] Among these metaphors, the Proustian definition of habit is 'translated' in Schopenhauer's idiom, in brackets:

---

55 Ibid., vol. 1, p. 524; Eng. trans., vol. 2, p. 124.

56 For Rupert Wood, the Schopenhauer filter is a 'well-structured combination of pessimism and a tragic view of existence' ('An Endgame of Aesthetics: Beckett as Essayist', in John Pilling (ed.), *The Cambridge Companion to Beckett* (Cambridge, 1994), pp. 1–16 (p. 4)).

57 Beckett, *Proust*, pp. 18–19 (my emphasis).

58 Ibid., p. 19.

59 Ibid., pp. 21–3.

> Life is a succession of habits, since the individual is a succession of individuals; the world being a projection of the individual's consciousness (an objectivation of the individual's will, Schopenhauer would say), the pact must be continually renewed, the letter of safe-conduct brought up to date.[60]

Habit also 'hid[es] the essence – the Idea – of the object in the haze of conception – preconception', and towards habit we are in the position of the tourist who wishes to find his experience in the Baedeker and not the reverse.[61] Schopenhauer's ideas underlie the commentary and can be retrieved when necessary, as here concerning habit or in the conclusion of the book concerning music.

In 'An Occult Arithmetic: The "Proustian Equation" according to Beckett's *Proust*', I suggested that Beckett made a pastiche of Proust, as though he had been guided by Proust's description of the idea of the voluntary pastiche. 'Pastiche' here refers specifically to Proust's idiosyncratic definition of the word, which is worth recalling.[62] The coincidence between the writing and structure of Beckett's *Proust* and Proust's conception of pastiche is all the more striking in that Proust defined pastiche in musical terms. He formulated the conception in his article on Flaubert's style 'À propos du "style" de Flaubert', which he wrote in response to the French critic, Albert Thibaudet, after having himself written pastiches of Balzac, Flaubert, Sainte-Beuve, Henri de Régnier, the Goncourt brothers, Michelet, Émile Faguet, Ernest Renan and Saint-Simon.[63] For Proust, a writer is prompted to write a voluntary pastiche after having unconsciously recorded recurrent patterns, sounds, rhythms, words, turns of phrase and syntactical tics of a beloved author, then imitating and indeed reproducing them. In his article on Flaubert, he analysed what is original about Flaubert's writing with respect to conventional grammar against those critics who had deemed that Flaubert 'couldn't write'.[64] However, creating a pastiche is not an analytical activity; it is a means of consciously liberating oneself from the 'music' of particular writers by imitating them: the more successful the imitation of another writer's language, the

---

60 Ibid., p. 19.

61 Ibid., p. 23.

62 For a classic work on Proust's pastiche, see Jean Milly, *Les Pastiches de Proust* (Paris, 1970).

63 The pastiches were published in *Le Figaro* between 1900 and 1908 and then collected in a volume entitled *Pastiches et mélanges* in 1919, together with texts on Ruskin. 'À propos du "style" de Flaubert' was published in the *Nouvelle revue française* (1 Jan. 1920), in *Contre Sainte-Beuve*, pp. 586–600 and translated into English by John Sturrock as 'On Flaubert's "Style"' (in *Against Sainte-Beuve and Other Essays* (London, 1994), pp. 261–74).

64 Proust, 'On Flaubert's "Style"', p. 265. For the other texts of the dispute about correctness in grammar, see *Flaubert savait-il écrire: Une querelle grammaticale (1919–1921)*, ed. Gilles Philippe (Grenoble, 2004), and my review of it (Céline Surprenant, 'Couldn't Write', *Times Literary Supplement* (6 May 2005): 22).

more it will be possible to invent a new language.[65] Concerning Flaubert, Proust underlined the writer's incongruous use of the conjunction 'and', which 'does not have at all the aim assigned to it by grammar … it marks a pause in a rhythmical measure and divides up a description'.[66] Proust emphasized that style could be analysed with reference to music, even though in *À la recherche du temps perdu* music itself is not the object of musical analysis per se.

Another means of fabricating a pastiche is by merging many sentences together, so as to reveal the similarities between them in the manner of a composite photograph and create the typical sentence of an author. The process that Proust described appeals to memory. That creation occurs automatically, as it were, when our memory retains only certain features of a writer's sentences. Proust demonstrated that procedure with Théophile Gautier's writing in his preface to Ruskin – 'Journées de lecture I' – where he supposedly quoted one of Gautier's sentences only to reveal that he had in fact invented it by combining different parts of the writer's sentences: 'En réalité, cette phrase ne se trouve pas, au moins sous cette forme, dans *Le Capitaine Fracasse* [In point of fact, this sentence is not to be found in *Le Capitaine Fracasse*, at least in this form]'.[67] We encounter that procedure with Vinteuil's fictional musical 'phrase': it is a composite of many pieces of music by Saint-Saens, Schubert, Wagner, Franck and Fauré.[68]

In the section on the Albertine tragedy in *Proust*, Beckett discusses what is needed for deciphering Albertine's lies. He speaks of her lies as 'anagrams' that require 'translation', so 'I may go and see the Verdurins tomorrow', for example, means 'it is absolutely certain that I will go and see the Verdurins tomorrow'.[69] It is in this context that Beckett quotes more or less accurately the narrator's description of his mistrust of Albertine: 'My imagination provided equations for the unknown in this algebra of desires', which provides one of the plausible sources of the 'Proustian equation' of the first sentence of the book.[70] More generally, that 'the subject's permanent reality' should 'only be apprehended as a retrospective hypothesis', is another way of stating that the subject is constantly providing 'equations for the unknown in this algebra of desires'.[71] Albertine's lies are not the only utterances that require translation, at least for Beckett, as he submits the narrator's very utterances to similar kinds of translation, retaining certain terms of the original text while replacing others, creating resonances between the original

65 Proust, 'À propos du "style" de Flaubert', pp. 594–5.

66 For a close study of Proust's assimilation of Flaubert's writing into the novel, see Mireille Naturel, *Proust et Flaubert: Un secret d'écriture*, 2nd edn (Amsterdam and Atlanta, GA, 2007).

67 Marcel Proust, 'Journées de lecture', in *Contre Sainte-Beuve*, pp. 175; 'Days of Reading I', in *Against Sainte-Beuve*, p. 209.

68 See Proust, 'Notice', in *À la recherche du temps perdu*, vol. 1, pp. 1237–40.

69 Beckett, *Proust*, p. 55.

70 Ibid.

71 Ibid., p. 15.

and his re-description. Thus the 'quoted' sentence that presents the narrator as speaking of his 'imagination providing equations' is in fact the 'translation' of 'l'équation approximative à cette inconnue qu'était pour moi la pensée d'Albertine [the approximate equation of that unknown quantity which Albertine's thoughts were to me]'.[72] Beckett would seem to have adopted, in writing *Proust*, the process of translating lies into truth that the narrator ascribes to Albertine.

John Pilling's study of Beckett's annotations of certain words in the margins of *À la recherche du temps perdu* would seem to confirm the coincidence between pastiche and Beckett's creation and helps us read not only Beckett's later work but also *Proust* as a whole. It is the rapprochement between Proust's voluntary pastiche and Beckett's mode of composition that incites Fraisse to view Beckett's art of transformation as 'creative distortions'.[73] To view the book as a pastiche reinforces Pilling's idea that it is 'in no sense a limitation of Beckett's originality, that we find so many individual elements in Beckett that are derived, in one way or another from Proust', because, 'so much of the essay is "lifted" from Proust, and yet ... it is nonetheless an utterly original essay'.[74] In Beckett's paraphrasing of the novel, single words flag the provenance of particular passages, as Proust advocates the words in a pastiche should do. For example, although Beckett does not reference the passages he quotes from the novel, words such as 'copiable' in the 'copiable he does not see' are traceable to particular passages in the novel.[75] Pilling extends his remark beyond *Proust* and gives the example of the word 'cloison' that Beckett underlined in his copy of Proust's novel and that he finds in Beckett's later work.[76]

For Proust, not only is every pastiche concerned with the music of an author, but among the pastiches of Flaubert that he wrote, one consisted in adding a musical chapter entitled 'Mondanité et mélomanie' to Flaubert's *Bouvard et Pécuchet*, the posthumously published story of two enthusiastic companions who embark unsuccessfully upon acquiring an encyclopaedic knowledge of late nineteenth-century arts and sciences. Proust made the pastiche in echo of the efforts of the disciples of César Franck to introduce Wagner into the French musical scene.[77] In his discussion of pastiche as a means of understanding the style of a writer, music is not merely an analogy, especially with regard to Flaubert, since Proust discussed Flaubert's style not only in terms of the sound and music it creates, but also in terms of what he called the 'blanks', which refer to Flaubert's particular use of ellipses to portray the passage of time and to suggest successions of events. Without having established whether or not Beckett read Proust's article on Flaubert, we could relate Proust's interest in ellipses to Beckett's later cultivation of reduction and silences.

---

72 Proust, *À la recherche du temps perdu*, vol. 3, p. 850; Eng. trans., vol. 5, p. 397.

73 Fraisse, 'Le "Proust" de Beckett', p. 378.

74 Pilling, 'Beckett's *Proust*', pp. 23, 15.

75 Beckett, *Proust*, p. 83.

76 Pilling, 'Beckett's *Proust*', p. 23.

77 See Leblanc, 'Proust et la "bande à Franck"', p. 207.

Instead of saying that Beckett took 'the colour of the author about whom he is writing', it might be more precise to say that he developed Proust's 'music' (some of his metaphors, his imagery, his intellectual operations and anti-intellectual themes), but also his enrolment of music, into an art of commentary. To consider *Proust* as a pastiche draws our attention to the patterns, sounds and rhythms that Beckett imitated and made resound, notably through its comic tonality.[78]

In the vein of Pierre-Quint's study *Marcel Proust, sa vie, son œuvre* (1925), Beckett highlighted the comical aspects of the novel, and found music to be one the sources of the comic in it. Humour is not only Beckett's 'justified instrument of the critical surgery that lays bare a wound', as Pilling argues, it is also Proust's. Humour blurs the distinction between what belongs to one and to the other. Listening to music is a propitious ground for derision. The degree of a character's appreciation of music is proportional to the expressions that music makes him or her adopt, especially since the enjoyment is merely simulated. Hence, the habit of simulating a profound love of Wagner has forced Mme de Verdurin's forehead to take on 'enormous proportions'.[79]

A Pastiche of Schopenhauer on Music

Schopenhauer's ideas dominated the philosophical climate in which Proust began to write prose fiction and contribute to literary journals during the 1890s to the extent that *À la recherche du temps perdu* has been described as one of the most faithful, albeit fictional, transcriptions or translations of *The World as Will and Representation*.[80] Whether or not we agree with this idea, Beckett reproduces how Proust himself involved the philosopher's ideas in his fictional texts, at least when they are filtered through his characters. In Proust, the characters do not directly discuss philosophical ideas. For the most part, they are said to master such and such a philosopher's thinking, such as Mme de Cambremer with Schopenhauer's philosophy.[81] Granted that Beckett (knowingly or unknowingly) followed Proust's conception of pastiche, a question arises as to what exactly Beckett retained from Schopenhauer. In view of the sparseness of what he imports from the philosopher, is there in *Proust* any evidence of a philosophical engagement with music according to Schopenhauer? Or rather did Beckett simply select extracts on music from *The World as Will and Representation*, as he did with words and themes from Proust's novel and from its early critical reception?

---

78 Pilling, 'Beckett's *Proust*', pp. 12, 14; see Bryden, 'Beckett and the Sound of Silence', p. 51.

79 Proust, *À la recherche du temps perdu*, vol. 3, pp. 298, 755; Eng. trans., vol. 4, pp. 351–2, vol. 5, p. 283.

80 See Henry, 'Proust du Côté de Schopenhauer', p. 149.

81 Proust, *À la recherche du temps perdu*, vol. 4, pp. 318, 569; Eng. trans., vol. 6, pp. 60, 378 (on Schopenhauer and music).

Beckett does indeed identify certain words and ideas from the philosopher, but transforms, condenses, even distorts them, situating ideas alongside one another that Schopenhauer kept separate. For example, Beckett distorts Schopenhauer's treatment of opera – Schopenhauer is not as negative about opera as Beckett makes him out to be – and he links Schopenhauer's discussion of vaudeville to what the philosopher says of repetition in music, that is, to the 'da capo', which is entirely permissible in music, according to Schopenhauer, but which would be disagreeable in the arts of language. It is Beckett, rather than Schopenhauer, who links vaudeville and the da capo, by a comparison of vaudeville and opera. In view of the way in which 'opera is a hideous corruption of this most immaterial of all the arts: the words of a libretto are to the musical phrase that they particularize what the Vendôme column is to the ideal perpendicular', Beckett writes. Vaudeville 'at least inaugurates the comedy of an exhaustive enumeration'. Beckett then praises the convention of the da capo, as though it comes close to 'the comedy of exhaustive enumeration'.[82] According to Pilling, Beckett 'redistributed the elements he had retained from his reading of Schopenhauer', which could be an exact description of how he dealt with *À la recherche du temps perdu.*[83] Through the discussion of music, we discover the creative selectiveness that presides over Beckett's commentary more than we are able to spell out an extensive Beckettian, or even Proustian, metaphysics of music that could be demonstrated as inspired by Schopenhauer.

Given this selective treatment, it is significant that Beckett exaggerates Schopenhauer's rejection of Leibniz's view of music as 'an unconscious exercise in which the mind doesn't know it is counting'.[84] In view of the book's play with the mathematico-scientific register, why should Beckett insist on Schopenhauer's rejection of the Leibnizian view of music as 'occult arithmetic'?[85] Schopenhauer engaged in a discussion of the physics of harmonics and of the problem as to whether or not arithmetic was part of the pleasure one takes in music.[86] The passages on listening to Vinteuil's sonata in *À la recherche du temps perdu* echo that debate, albeit not in the philosophical idiom, when Swann passes from the appreciation of the fluid, yet un-extended entity of which music consists, to reasoning about its mathematical intervals. Beckett did not intervene or reconstitute Leibniz's or Schopenhauer's arguments, but rather isolated this as one of the motifs of his comic re-description of *À la recherche du temps perdu.*

For the young Beckett, music was one of the means through which Proust articulated what is 'entirely intelligible but nevertheless inexplicable', a paradox

---

82 Beckett, *Proust*, p. 92.

83 Pilling, '*Proust* and Schopenhauer', p. 177.

84 Leibniz, quoted in Schopenhauer, *The World as Will and Representation*, vol. 1, p. 257.

85 Beckett, *Proust*, p. 91.

86 Schopenhauer, *The World as Will and Representation*, vol. 1, p. 257.

of which Beckett was fond, according to Pilling.[87] Beckett says of Proust's demonstrations that he 'explains them in order that they may appear as they are – inexplicable'.[88] Pilling describes as a 'paradox' what was described above as the chiasmus in which Proust formulated the relation between sensation and the intellect and which comes close to the way Schopenhauer qualified music in terms of a 'clarification obscure' or as that which is 'capable de représenter l'irreprésentable [able to represent the unrepresentable]'.[89] That duality was a point of critical interest in the early reception of Proust's writing, from which Beckett drew, without always acknowledging his sources. Jacques Rivière, one of Proust's early critics and director of the *Nouvelle revue française*, asked whether the author of *À la recherche du temps perdu* did not in fact renew the tradition of the French analytical novel (in spite of what many readers perceived to be a disorderly accumulation of memories and sensations).[90] After the publication of *Du côté de chez Swann*, Proust had praised Rivière for perceiving that the novel was rigorously constructed.[91] The problem as to whether a literature of sensations could be analytical had spurred Proust's early critical interventions, notably concerning symbolist literature and its cultivation of obscurity. Proust contributed to these literary debates prior to writing, around 1908, the pages posthumously published and entitled *Contre Sainte-Beuve*, where he presented the formula of the contradiction between sensation and the intellect.[92]

In his discussion of music in Proust, Benoist-Méchin believed that, for the Proustian narrator, music is an 'instrument of knowledge'.[93] This would seem to apply to the role of music in Beckett's *Proust*, except that the latter is linked with the yearning for a contradictory state of affairs, for the experience of reasoned sensations. Beckett, then, did not only anticipate philosophical discussions of the novel and understand its structure. Well before the publication of *Contre Sainte-Beuve* in 1954, thanks to which readers could discover that *À la recherche du temps perdu* originated in a conversation between a narrator and his mother on the nineteenth-century literary French critic Sainte-Beuve's method, Beckett acutely pinpointed the opposition of intellect and sensation that Proust discussed in this 'conversation piece' that was expanded into the novel. He did so by paying attention to the fictional hearing of music in Proust as a 'situation' in which the

87 Pilling, '*Proust* and Schopenhauer', p. 177.

88 Beckett, *Proust*, p. 87.

89 Fraisse, *L'Éclectisme*, pp. 820–21.

90 Jacques Rivière, *Études (1909–1924): L'Œuvre critique de Jacques Rivière à la Nouvelle revue française*, ed. Alain Rivière (Paris, 1999), pp. 586–92.

91 'Enfin je trouve un lecteur qui devine que mon livre est un ouvrage dogmatique et une construction! [Finally I find a reader that has understood that my book is a dogmatic work and is a construction!]' (Marcel Proust to Jacques Rivière, 6 Feb. 1914, in *Marcel Proust: Lettres*, ed. Françoise Leriche et al. (Paris, 2004), pp. 667–8.

92 See 'Projets de préface', in *Contre Sainte-Beuve*, pp. 211–16.

93 Benoist-Méchin, *La Musique*, p. 89.

tension between sensation and the intellect is played out. Beckett's *Proust* thus brings us back to the inception of *À la recherche du temps perdu*, to the time when Proust was wondering whether he should write a novel or an essay.[94] According to Beckett's perspective, then, music distinguishes itself from the other arts not so much for the reasons that Schopenhauer adduced, but because it stands and makes one hover between both kinds of writing, as he was able to demonstrate in his novel of sorts on Proust.

[94] Between 1908 and 1911, Proust wrote notes and sketches in *Carnets 1*, including the following oft-quoted statement concerning the uncertainty as to the art form that his project should take: 'Faut-il en faire un roman, une étude philosophique, suis-je romancier? [Should I make of it a novel, a philosophical study, am I a novelist?]' (Marcel Proust, *Carnets*, ed. Florence Callu and Antoine Compagnon (Paris, 2002), pp. 50–51).

Chapter 3

Music and Metamusic in Beckett's Early Plays for Radio[1]

Katarzyna Ojrzyńska

Advocating an emotional rather than an intellectual approach to his theatre, Beckett once wrote the following famous words to Jessica Tandy about *Not I*: 'I hope the piece may work on the nerves of the audience, not its intellect'.[2] Thus, it seems logical that in his works the Irish dramatist endeavoured to achieve a certain effect of musicality, for, as Katharine Worth puts it simply, 'music must affect the emotional imagination of the listener in some way'.[3] Beckett frequently stressed the importance of the orchestration of various sounds and voices in his plays. One of the most representative examples of this idea can be found in a well-known statement made in a letter to Alan Schneider in which the playwright contends: 'My work is a matter of fundamental sounds (no joke intended) made as fully as possible, and I accept responsibility for nothing else'.[4] Although this comment was made specifically with reference to *Endgame*, it seems equally relevant to other dramatic works by Beckett whose musicality has interested numerous contemporary critics.

It should be stressed that although Beckett developed his own minimalist, but at the same time diverse, language of theatre, departing significantly from the domination of the word on stage, he strongly objected to the Wagnerian synthesis of the arts, advocating already in the early 1950s that 'a theatre [should be] reduced to its own means, speech and acting, without painting, without music, without embellishments'.[5] On another occasion, in a letter to his American

---

1 This chapter is a revised and expanded version of 'O muzyce i metamuzyce we wczesnych słuchowiskach Samuela Becketta', *Tekstualia* 20/1 (2010): 89–101. I am very grateful to Sara Jane Bailes and Nicholas Till for their helpful comments on the previous version of the chapter.

2 Quoted in Enoch Brater, 'The *I* in Beckett's *Not I*', *Twentieth Century Literature* 20/3 (1974): 189–200 (p. 200).

3 Katharine Worth, 'Words for Music Perhaps', in Mary Bryden (ed.), *Samuel Beckett and Music* (Oxford, 1998), pp. 9–20 (p. 11).

4 Samuel Beckett to Alan Schneider, 29 Dec. 1957, in *No Author Better Served: The Correspondence of Samuel Beckett and Alan Schneider*, ed. Maurice Harmon (Cambridge, MA, and London, 1998), p. 24.

5 Samuel Beckett to Georges Duthuit, 3 Jan. 1951, in George Craig et al. (eds), *The Letters of Samuel Beckett*, vol. 2: *1941–1956* (Cambridge, 2011), p. 218.

publisher, Barney Rosset, dated 27 August 1957, he firmly states: 'If we can't keep our genres more or less distinct, or extricate them from the confusion that has them where they are, we might as well go home and lie down.'[6] In the light of his views, Beckett turned to music as the most abstract of arts, since it displays a great degree of 'formal autonomy and unworldly self-sufficiency'.[7] Furthermore, it is conspicuous that the dramatist frequently used music in its purest theatrical form, in the fashion postulated by Jerzy Grotowski, who pursued his vision of the anti-eclectic and anti-synthetic poor theatre 'stripped of all that is not essential to it, reveal[ing] to us not only the backbone of the medium, but also the deep riches which lie in the very nature of the art-form'.[8] Beckett, of course, does not go as far as to eliminate 'music (live or recorded) not produced by the actors'[9] from his plays, yet he frequently employed the concept of the stage, screen or radio performance 'becom[ing] music through the orchestration of voices and clashing objects',[10] which is apparent in the musical quality of a number of his works written for various media.

What deserves particular attention is the way in which this area of Beckett's interests finds expression in his early radio plays, or, as Beckett called them, 'radio texts' – works created for the medium whose ephemeral, auditory nature shares properties with the experience of music.[11] Written in the 1950s, *All That Fall* and *Embers* retain certain elements of a stylized realistic convention and traditional plot and thus differ significantly from Beckett's later experiments with the arts of radio, theatre and film. What distinguishes these works in terms of musicality is their carefully organized rhythmical structure, the effective use of concrete musical scores intricately woven into their plots and, above all, their metamusical dimension, which renders the plays similar to polyphonic musical compositions orchestrated by the characters. Although the idea of orchestration can be found in a number of Beckett's works for the stage and film, it is his early radio plays that most comprehensively explore the notion of creativity and artistic control over the acoustic matter in musical terms, by drawing the listener's attention to the role of the protagonists as artists who give an aesthetic shape to their own and the audience's auditory experience.

---

6 Quoted in Clas Zilliacus, *Beckett and Broadcasting* (Åbo, 1976), p. 3.

7 Thomas Mansell, 'Different Music: Beckett's Theatrical Conduct', in Marius Buning et al. (eds), *Historicising Beckett: Issues of Performance*, *Samuel Beckett Today/Aujourd'hui* 15 (Amsterdam and New York, 2005), pp. 225–39 (p. 227).

8 Jerzy Grotowski, *Towards a Poor Theatre* (New York, 1968), p. 21.

9 Ibid.

10 Ibid.

11 James Jesson, '"White World. Not a Sound": Beckett's Radioactive Text in *Embers*', *Texas Studies in Literature and Language* 51/1 (2009): 47–65 (p. 47); Everett C. Frost, 'A "Fresh Go" for the Skull', in Lois Oppenheim (ed.), *Directing Beckett* (Michigan, 1997), p. 191.

According to James Knowlson, in his work as a director Beckett frequently used musical terms such as 'piano', 'fortissimo', 'andante', 'allegro', 'da capo', 'cadenza'.[12] Furthermore, actors who worked with Beckett and his texts often compare the plays to musical scores, rehearsals to being conducted or themselves to musical instruments.[13] Interestingly, the presence of the figure of an artist as a conductor, a peculiar alter ego of the author, can be easily traced in many of Beckett's radio plays, such as *Words and Music*, *Cascando* or *Rough for Radio I*, as well as in his works for the stage. The earliest texts in which the dramatist investigates this idea most fully are the two radio dramas discussed in this chapter.

All That Fall

Mrs Rooney, the protagonist of Beckett's first play for radio, *All That Fall* (1956), occupies a special position amongst the orchestrating figures in Beckett's work, since, contrary to the prevalent tendency among his characters to brood incessantly over the past and continuously to 'revolv[e] it all [in their] poor mind[s]',[14] most of the time she seems closely focused upon the 'here and now'. Relying on her direct everyday experience, she mediates this to the listeners in a musical form, demonstrating an apparently substantial degree of control over the presented acoustic material.

All That Fall is based on a fairly simple plot line. The protagonist, an old and decrepit Irish woman, walks to the nearby railway station to meet her husband and together they return home. Structurally sometimes compared to a sonata,[15] the drama can be divided into three 'movements', which Martin Esslin defines as: 'Maddy Rooney's anabasis, her wait at the station, her and Dan's katabasis',[16] understood both in kinetic terms as three phases of the physical journey and as parts of a musical composition. With regards to the metamusical dimension of the play, these movements may be seen as denoting the protagonist's diminishing orchestrating power. Gradually, Mrs Rooney's role in the radio drama changes, as, towards the end of her journey, she relinquishes the position of a conductor orchestrating the sounds of the play and accepts the role of an orchestrated subject. In this respect, the closing,

---

12 James Knowlson, *Damned to Fame: The Life of Samuel Beckett* (London, 1996), p. 665.

13 Cf. Irena Jun, interview by Antoni Libera, in Linda Ben-Zvi (ed.), *Women in Beckett* (Urbana and Chicago, 1990), pp. 47–50 (p. 48); Mary Bryden, 'Beckett and the Sound of Silence', in (ed.), *Samuel Beckett and Music*, pp. 21–46 (p. 44).

14 Samuel Beckett, *Footfalls*, in *The Complete Dramatic Works* (London, 1986), p. 400.

15 Kevin Branigan, *Radio Beckett: Musicality in the Radio Plays of Samuel Beckett* (Bern, 2008), p. 96.

16 Quoted in Frost, 'A "Fresh Go" for the Skull', p. 190.

katabatic movement can be compared to the final descent from the podium of the conductor – as Mrs Rooney yields to her husband's authority. It is conspicuous that, while such a reversal of power relations can be observed in a number of Beckett's plays, most notably in the case of Pozzo and Lucky in *Waiting for Godot*, in *All That Fall* this change is communicated in metamusical terms.

It should be stressed that Maddy plays the role of an orchestrator in a subjective sense. In the first production of the play for the BBC in 1957, having consulted with Beckett over the issue, the producer Donald McWhinnie used stylized sounds of nature in the play so as to suggest that it presents an image of reality filtered through Mrs Rooney's consciousness.[17] Consequently, the sounds evoked by Maddy Rooney can be interpreted both from a 'psychoacoustic perspective'[18] as a reflection of an individual aural landscape, and in artistic terms as an instance of creative self-fashioning through transforming one's acoustic experience into a musical score.

Although, as I hope to demonstrate, towards the end of the play it seems much diminished, Mrs Rooney's command over her acoustic environment, strongly present in the first movement of the drama, is most evident in the use of animal sounds. The play opens with '*Rural sounds. Sheep, bird, cow, cock, severally, then together. Silence.*'[19] What seems striking about these sounds is not only their intended artificial quality, but also the order of their occurrence. Filtered through Maddy Rooney's consciousness, the sounds are arranged in a fashion resembling an orchestra's tuning before playing the opening bars of a composition under the conductor's baton. This may be interpreted as either an illustration of the mechanisms of Mrs Rooney's attention, which she at first focuses on separate sounds, or as an indication of her using more conscious orchestrating measures. The latter idea is made even more explicit in the third movement of the play. Proposing a feminist reading and referring to the play's protagonist, Sarah Bryant-Bertail observes:

> Later on her way back home from the station with her husband, it is Maddy herself who names the animals, this time in an apparent effort to bring them back to life: 'All is still. No living soul in sight … The wind – (brief wind) – scarcely stirs the leaves and the birds – (brief chirp) – are tired of singing. The cows – (brief moo) – and sheep (brief baa) – ruminate in silence. The dogs (brief bark) are hushed and the hens (brief cackle) – sprawl torpid in the dusk …' (43–44). This passage is comical in effect, a parody of the voice of God/the Author on the day of creation. Here is an instance where the hierarchical values are reversed, because Maddy is reviving the living creatures even as she describes them dying out.[20]

---

17 Jeff Porter, 'Samuel Beckett and the Radiophonic Body: Beckett and the BBC', *Modern Drama* 53/4 (2010): 431–46 (pp. 440–41); Frost, 'A "Fresh Go" for the Skull', p. 196.

18 Frost, 'A "Fresh Go" for the Skull', p. 197.

19 Samuel Beckett, *All That Fall*, in *The Complete Dramatic Works*, p. 172.

20 Sarah Bryant-Bertail, 'The True-Real Woman: Maddy Rooney as *Picara* in *All That Fall*', available at <http://archive.today/Gnjvi>.

The passage discussed also reinforces a similarity between Maddy Rooney and the traditional depictions of Death in a *danse macabre* which underscores her role as the orchestrator. If we consider the nature of the medium for which the play was written, Maddy is the figure of authority who decides about life and death, since the existence of the characters and their world in a radio text depends on them being heard by the audience.

In fact, the play seems replete with allusions to the motif of the dance of death, which always recur in connection with the protagonist. One may, for instance, point to the use of Schubert's 'Death and the Maiden' string quartet both at the beginning and towards the end of Mrs Rooney's journey to and from the railway station, 'serving the play as both overture and coda'.[21] The main theme of the string quartet used in *All That Fall* perfectly conforms to the acoustic image of the suburban area deeply troubled with death and decay that is presented. The miserable condition of the Boghill community is most evident in the numerous complaints made by the neighbours the protagonist meets on her way to the railway station concerning their own poor health or the death and physical decay of their relatives. The idea of deterioration is further reinforced by the unreliability of the various means of transport they use, which all break down or fail, and the general atmosphere of the place stinking of rotten leaves like 'a dead dog'.[22] It is also conspicuous that, passing next to the building from which the music comes, Mrs Rooney murmurs Schubert's melody to the rhythm established by her shuffling feet. In this way, she reinforces the theme of decay, expresses her sympathy for the woman inside the house and becomes a chanting messenger or even an incarnation of Death, reminding Boghill denizens of their unavoidable fate, which can be inferred from their successive conversations: for instance, when Mr Slocum enquires, 'Are you going in my direction?', she answers: 'I am, Mr Slocum, we all are'.[23] The melody of Schubert's piece, which the protagonist murmurs in the opening of the play, may thus be seen as Mrs Rooney's attribute, an equivalent of the musical instruments with which the figure of Death was traditionally presented in images of the *danse macabre*.

Certain allusions to the dance of death and the similarity between Mrs Rooney and Death are also discernible in the scene in which the protagonist meets Miss Fitt, a self-centred and neurotic spinster, who spends most of the time 'alone with [her] Maker'.[24] Physically a direct opposite of the considerably overweight Mrs Rooney, Miss Fitt is a thin and bony creature concerned more with heavenly existence than with earthly bondage and the issues troubling other

---

21 Porter, 'Samuel Beckett and the Radiophonic Body', p. 435.

22 Beckett, *All That Fall*, p. 196; for a more detailed discussion of the notion of decay in the play, see Katarzyna Ojrzyńska, 'The Journey through the Dying World of Boghill in Samuel Beckett's Play *All That Fall*', in Magdalena Cieślak and Agnieszka Rasmus (eds), *Images of the City* (Cambridge, 2009), pp. 284–93.

23 Beckett, *All That Fall*, p. 177.

24 Ibid., p. 182.

people, in this way paradoxically contradicting the ideal of Christian charity. Miss Fitt's humming of the hymn 'Lead, Kindly Light' brings her into a mood of religious contemplation and distances her from everyday chores. Yet it is also an expression of fake piousness protecting the spinster from any interference from the outside that would distract her from the alternative reality she has created. The protagonist ingeniously mocks Miss Fitt also when she joins in her song. The flimsy humming is now overpowered by forceful singing (here Beckett uses the musical term 'forte'[25]). Mrs Rooney's disdain, however, consists not only in the tone of her voice but also in the uttered words, as she chooses to verbalize only those fragments of the hymn that concern the miserable condition of human existence and to introduce slight changes to the lyrics: '… the encircling gloo-oom … tum tum on me. [*Forte.*] The night is dark and I am far from ho-ome, tum tum –',[26] thus bringing the outraged spinster back down to earth. Furthermore, the protagonist reminds her companion that the hymn was chanted on the Titanic, which, owing to the scale of the catastrophe, serves as a direct reference to the wretched condition of Boghill's inhabitants, all of whom seem to be inevitably heading for extinction. This is also yet another allusion to the *danse macabre*, which has its roots in the legend of the Three Living and Three Dead, in which the latter inform the former about their unavoidable fate. Consequently, through the allusions to the dance of death motif, Beckett places emphasis on the position of Mrs Rooney as the orchestrator of life perceived as a journey towards death. It should be stressed at this point that human existence, as depicted in the Beckettian oeuvre, pertains to what Heidegger defines as 'being towards death' (*Sein-zum-Tode*). Presented sometimes literally (*Act Without Words I*) as thrown into the world (*Geworfenheit*),[27] the characters are offered very few stable points of reference or certainty, apart from the fact that eventually they will all die. Therefore, the figure of Mrs Rooney as an orchestrator in *All That Fall* additionally underscores the existentialist dimension of the play, in which living is tantamount to a long and painful process of dying.

At the same time, Beckett seems to mock the connection between his protagonist and Death in a crude, naturalistic way. Again alluding to the 'Death and the Maiden' theme in music and visual arts, the play explores the idea of the erotic lure of Death[28] in a grotesque fashion when the decrepit, gargantuan Mrs Rooney encourages the aged Mr Slocum to 'unlace [her] behind the hedge'.[29] Although Mr Slocum apparently resists the temptation, this does not undermine Mrs Rooney's

[25] Ibid., p. 184.

[26] Ibid. The original is 'Lead, Kindly Light, amid the encircling gloom,/Lead Thou me on!/The night is dark, and I am far from home,/Lead Thou me on!' (*Lyra Apostolica* (Derby and London, 1837), p. 28).

[27] Martin Heidegger, *Being and Time*, trans. John Macquarrie and Edward Robinson (Bodmin, 2001).

[28] See, for instance, Niklaus Manuel Deutsch's painting *Death and the Maiden* (1517).

[29] Beckett, *All That Fall*, p. 177.

position of power, which is most manifest in the way she orchestrates the acoustic dimension of the play.

In musical terms, what serves as the backbone of the composition of the first movement of the play is the sound of Mrs Rooney's tired footfalls, which creates a peculiar melody of deterioration and exhaustion. Beckett wrote to his friend, Nancy Cunard: 'in the dead of t'other night got a nice gruesome idea full of cartwheels and *dragging feet* and puffing and panting which may or may not lead to something'.[30] These sounds gave rise to *All That Fall* and constitute the core of its rhythmical structure, which, according to Donald McWhinnie, was amplified by the use of four animal sounds at the beginning of the play 'correspond[ing] exactly to the four-in-a-bar metre of Mrs. Rooney's walk to the station and back, which is the percussive accompaniment to the play'.[31] The idea of using this particular acoustic element as a skeleton to support the whole musical composition of the drama can be observed in a number of the playwright's later works such as *Footfalls* and *Quad*. One may suspect that it resulted from Beckett's being 'an attentive and courteous listener',[32] an observation that can be applied to both human relationships and his ability to absorb sounds from the environment. The shuffling quality of the steps marks Mrs Rooney's locomotive deterioration and her progress, or rather regress, towards the final stasis. As Mary Bryden maintains, 'the friction of feet is important, for it provides a constant reminder of the cost or effort of that movement, thus endowing an aerial play with a solidity of earth-bound resonance',[33] as if bringing the characters closer to the ground and, simultaneously, to the grave.

In the third movement of the play, the percussive thread becomes amplified by the blind Mr Rooney, who joins his wife on her homeward journey, and is further enhanced by the tapping and thudding noises he produces with his cane. These sounds alert the listener to the notion of visual impairment, which Beckett endows with a particular meaning, especially in his radio plays, due to the specificity of the medium which deprives the audience of the possibility to confront the sounds they hear with visual equivalents. For Worth, this also lends to the subjective and oneiric character of the dramatic piece: 'Beckett's handling of blindness takes us into a much more dream-like territory. The blind man's stick tapping the way in *All That Fall* contributes to a strange melody in which human voices, animal sounds, and the music of Schubert create the atmosphere of an inner landscape'.[34] Instead of gaining access to the objective world inhabited by the Beckettian characters,

---

30 Quoted in Knowlson, *Damned to Fame*, p. 428 (my italics).

31 Quoted in Frost, 'A "Fresh Go" for the Skull', p. 193. Frost, on the other hand, confesses: 'Try as I might, I could find no four-in-a-bar metre of Mrs. Rooney's walk to the station and back as a structural principle of the play' (ibid., p. 193).

32 Bryden, 'Beckett and the Sound of Silence', p. 24.

33 Ibid., p. 36.

34 Katharine Worth, 'Beckett and the Radio Medium', in John Drakakis (ed.), *British Radio Drama* (Cambridge, 1981), pp. 191–217 (p. 193).

the audience set out on a peculiar journey into the reality subjectively experienced by the protagonist.

Unlike the numerous others of Beckett's characters who are frequently presented as isolated and mostly focused on their past, Mrs Rooney does not seem alienated from her surrounding reality. She immerses herself in the sounds of the world and the melody of her own gait by means of which she orchestrates her own acoustic experience. She uses her body as a tool, an instrument that controls and complements the sounds she distils from her environment. The organization of the sonic texture of the play is therefore presented as a creative act and a symbol of control over life. This is why Mrs Rooney seems so desperate to manifest her presence at the railway station. After remaining silent for a moment, she announces: 'Do not imagine, because I am silent, that I am not present, and alive'[35] and later tries to outshout the noise of the train.[36] However, this form of reasserting her orchestrating power in fact anticipates her renunciation of her position of control in the third movement of the play.

In order to analyse the change in the power relations that takes place in *All That Fall*, let us return to the acoustic motif of the tapping of the stick. The sound reinforces the intrusive presence of Mr Rooney, accentuating his domineering position in the relationship with his wife. Although, as Jeff Porter observes, Maddy 'is the acoustic centre of the play, both a maker of sound and its hearer and, as such, enjoys an unusual degree of agency for a Beckett character',[37] she is not necessarily the one who holds power. As a matter of fact, acting as a vigorous and bawdy orchestrator in the first movement of the play, Mrs Rooney is degraded to a submissive position once she is accompanied by her husband, which is most evident in her desperate pleas: 'Put your arm round me ... Be nice to me!'[38] It is also conspicuous that Dan Rooney's short and frequently sharp comments provide a counterpoint to the lengthy sequences delivered by his wife. Consequently, these curt answers as well as the sound of the thudding stick in the third movement of the play can be associated with the notions of disciplining and curtailing the physical and verbal excess associated with the figure of Mrs Rooney, conspicuous in her talkativeness as well as the references to her overweight body and erotic desires. Dan Rooney, by contrast, serves as a proponent of emotional detachment and erotic moderation.

As a result, when seen from a metamusical perspective, the stick is no longer simply a symbol of impairment, for its sound gives an impression of a metronome that coordinates the moves of the couple. In this way, from a conductor orchestrating the rural sounds in the opening of the drama, Mrs Rooney later turns into an orchestrated subject or an instrument, while the object that should serve as a sign of Mr Rooney's physical incapacity and weakness eventually turns into a baton –

35 Beckett, *All That Fall*, p. 185.

36 Ibid., p. 187.

37 Porter, 'Samuel Beckett and the Radiophonic Body', p. 435.

38 Beckett, *All That Fall*, p. 197.

an attribute of a conductor's power. With this in mind, the earlier-mentioned scene where Mrs Rooney orders the elements of nature that she previously orchestrated to fall silent may be seen as an act in which she ultimately renounces the position of the conductor.

Embers

The instrumentation or orchestration of sounds in order to compose a coherent musical piece by the protagonist, who in this way imitates the creative process of the dramatist, contributes to a peculiar metamusical effect which may also be found in Beckett's later radio play *Embers* (1957). Although the drama can be successfully compared to a musical score, it seems that the plot resembles even more closely the act of composing or rehearsing a musical work for a ghostly radiophonic trio. As an artist, Henry is the only character in *Embers* whose 'being there' can be ascertained due to the background noises he produces, namely the sounds of his boots on the shingle. Apart from the truly spectral father, whose physical presence is questioned even by Ada, the existence of the remaining two characters cannot be verified in any other way than on the basis of their voices which, like most other sounds, seem to be evoked by the protagonist. The absence of noises resulting from, for instance, the movement and other 'symptoms' of physicality of the dramatis personae as well as the awkward quality of the voice of Henry's wife, which remains '*Low remote … throughout*',[39] have led most critics to interpret the 'acousmatic'[40] play as Henry's 'soulscape' or 'skullscape'[41] of sounds orchestrated by the protagonist himself.

The sonic element that most often manifests itself as independent of Henry's will is the constant rhythmical background accompaniment of the sea. At the same time, more than being an element of the objective reality experienced by the audience, the sea is part of Henry's soulscape. For the protagonist, it belongs to the domain of dreams and retrospections, for 'the sound is so strange, so unlike the sound of the sea, that if you didn't see what it was you wouldn't know what it was'.[42] The soothing quality of the sound of waves beating against the shore introduces a dreamy atmosphere to the play, bringing it closer to the oneiric and

39 Samuel Beckett, *Embers*, in *Complete Dramatic Works*, p. 257.

40 Porter, 'Samuel Beckett and the Radiophonic Body', p. 437. Porter borrows the term from Michel Chion, who in *Audio-Vision: Sound on Screen* defines the acousmatic voice as one that 'creates a mystery of the nature of its source, its properties and its powers, given that causal listening cannot supply complete information about the sound's nature and the events taking place' (quoted ibid., pp. 437–8).

41 Marjorie Perloff, 'The Silence that is not Silence: Acoustic Art in Samuel Beckett's *Embers*', in Lois Oppenheim (ed.), *Samuel Beckett and the Visual Arts: Music, Visual Arts, and Non-Print Media* (New York, 1998), pp. 247–68.

42 Beckett, *Embers*, p. 253.

retrospective *That Time* (1974–6). The steady musical background of the sea can be compared to a lullaby that offers Henry access to his memories, which he uses as raw material that needs to be harnessed and aestheticized to be transformed into a musical composition. This is most conspicuous in the passage in which Henry temporarily gains control over the acoustic elements that constitute his vision. In the scene where the protagonist recalls a series of Ada's reprimands, the volume of the sea is increased and serves as an accompaniment to the dialogue of the characters, which underscores Henry's orchestrating agency:

> ADA: … Don't stand there thinking about it. [*Pause.*] Don't stand there staring. [*Pause*...] Don't wet your good boots. [*Pause.*]
> HENRY: Don't, don't … .
> …
> ADA: [*Twenty years earlier, imploring.*] Don't! Don't!
> HENRY: [*Ditto, urgent.*] Darling!
> ADA: [*Ditto, more feebly.*] Don't!
> HENRY: [*Ditto, exultantly.*] Darling![43]

The waves become increasingly rough and loud towards the end of their duet when the listener hears the amplified cry of Ada and the waves, which James Jesson reads in purely sexual terms as Henry's 'sexual triumph' over his partner[44] rather than an amusing marital farce. More importantly, though, the fragment proposes a rare moment when the protagonist is able to control the incessant roll of the sea, which here seems subjected to his artistic vision. In terms of metamusicality, the excerpt illustrates Henry's attempt to orchestrate the sounds in his head into a musical form similar to a comic operetta, which accentuates his desire for artistic control over the acousmatic environment.

Another measure taken by Henry to give proper acoustic shape to the hum of the sea is presented towards the end of the play. He announces: 'Thuds, I want thuds! … Not this … [*Pause.*] … sucking!'[45] and demonstrates the quality of the sound that he wishes to obtain to serve as the percussive background for his musical piece by dashing two big stones together. This primitive gesture suggests not so much imitating nature but harnessing it and using it for artistic aims. It may be seen as a creative act that goes beyond representation towards human creativity. This supports the interpretation of the protagonist as the author's alter ego. As a director Beckett was often meticulous about the acoustic quality of his plays, as for instance in the cases of *Not I* and *Footfalls*, and sometimes resorted to demonstration. Lawrence Shainberg recalls that during the 1980 production of *Endgame* at the Riverside Studios, Beckett had a clear idea of how Nagg should knock on the lid of Nell's dustbin at the beginning of the play: 'Beckett demonstrated the sound he

---

43 Ibid., pp. 259–60.

44 Jesson, '"White World. Not a Sound"', p. 53.

45 Beckett, *Embers*, pp. 260–61.

wanted using his bony knuckle on the lid, and after Mandell had tried it six or seven times – not "Tap, tap, tap, tap," or "Tap ... tap ... tap ... tap," but "tap, tap ... tap, tap" – appeared to be satisfied'.[46] Such satisfaction is not, however, granted to the main character of *Embers*.

Since his struggle with the sound of the ebb and flow of the sea most of the time results in failure, Henry evokes alternative sonic elements that could serve as a rhythmical backbone of his piece: the drip, which proves unsuccessful due to its association with water, as well as the beat of horse hooves and of a ruler. Interestingly, Henry perceives an intrinsic bond between the hooves and the temporal aspect of human existence when he ponders the possibility of training a horse to 'mark time with its four legs'.[47] The sound seems to be related to the passage of time as opposed to the character's absorption in the past. Yet even the hooves are not totally disconnected from the evoked memories of the years gone by. Like in Yeats's play *Purgatory*, the sound is closely associated with the troubling images of the past, namely with the haunting scene in which Henry recalls his daughter, Addie, riding a horse, concluding with a climactic and truly ghastly '*wail amplified to paroxysm*'[48] uttered to the rising tempo marked by a galloping horse. A similar musical and emotional escalation takes place when a moment earlier the girl participates in piano lessons.

Comparable to the relationship between the conductor and the orchestra, the connection between artist and artistic material which does not easily lend itself to creative control or appropriation corresponds to the relationship between Henry and his daughter. In the two subsequent retrospections, rhythmical and hard sounds, similar to those produced by Henry with the stones, are connected with Addie and the leisure-time activities she is involved in but apparently does not enjoy. At first, we hear the girl performing one of Chopin's waltzes to the accompaniment of her music master beating time with a cylindrical ruler. Despite her effort, Addie repeatedly makes the same error by playing the lower note E instead of F. In the subsequent retrospection, the girl is riding a horse and the sound of the ruler is replaced with the beat of hooves, which again imposes a certain disciplining rhythm upon her. Reflecting the status of the family, the activities aim at her gradual introduction into society where demonstrating impeccable manners plays a crucial role. Thus, the acoustic elements communicate the idea of civilizing the child, appropriating her body and mind to certain norms. In the artistic sense, Addie is shapeless matter which needs to be given proper contour: Beckett conveys this in a musical fashion. The scenes under discussion can also be read as a metamusical, self-ironic commentary on the artist's, in this case Henry's, struggle for control, coherence and perfection. Much like his artistic creation – the story of Bolton that incessantly meanders away from its conclusion – Addie resists any framework one

---

46 Lawrence Shainberg, 'Exorcizing Beckett', available at <http://www.samuel-beckett.net/ShainExor1.html>, p. 3.

47 Beckett, *Embers*, p. 257.

48 Ibid., p. 259.

tries to impose on her; she escapes the attempts of orchestrating her behaviour, tending towards chaos, acoustically discernible in her loud paroxysmal wail. In metamusical terms, she is an insubordinate musician who rebels against the conductor whose directions she is unwilling or unable to follow.

In a way, Henry alludes to the stereotypical figure of a conductor as a despot, while his connection with the women whose voices he attempts to orchestrate can be compared to the patriarchal nineteenth-century concept of a musical 'marriage ... with the orchestra in the role of wife, and the conductor as husband'.[49] Due to Addie's rebellious nature, so defined a relationship is bound to fail in the play, which seems to be typical of more contemporary conductor–orchestra relations. As Barbara Pollack explains, 'as the 20th century progressed, it became more common for conductors to project their own personalities and fantasies onto the orchestra, and the musicians, in turn, projected theirs back onto the conductor'.[50] This observation seems equally relevant to Henry's relationship with his wife, especially at the end of the play, when he implores her to continue her story: 'Drive on, drive on! ... Keep on, keep on!'[51] Yet, when after a while Ada announces that she has nothing more to say, Henry seems powerless and unable to prevent her departure.

With regard to the metamusical dimension of the play, it is crucial to notice that in the play Henry also acts as a self-orchestrator. This is most conspicuous in the opening of the drama, when he urges himself to move and thus produce specific sounds with exclamations: 'On. [*Sea. Voice louder.*] On! [*He moves on. Boots on shingle. As he goes.*] Stop. [*Boots on shingle. As he goes, louder.*] Stop! [*He halts. Sea a little louder.*] Down. [*Sea. Voice louder.*] Down! [*Slither of shingle as he sits...*]'.[52] Not unlike Mrs Rooney, Henry uses his body as a tool that may help him to realize his artistic vision. His inner compulsion to create forces him to expose himself physically to the sound of the waves – an element stimulating him to pursue his creative endeavour.

In some respects, one may notice certain parallels between the protagonist of *Embers* and the Irish Cuchulain as presented in Yeats's dramatic oeuvre. Margaret Harper observes that

> In general, the Cuchulain plays feature female characters ... who are associated with water, shorelines and the borders of territories, including the borders between the living and the dead. This hero is noticeably surrounded by the water ... So Cuchulain is, I think, islanded. ... In other words, the myth of Cuchulain,

---

49 Barbara Pollack, 'The Effective Conductor: A Matter of Communication and Personality', in Glenn Daniel Wilson (ed.), *Psychology and Performing Arts* (Amsterdam, 1991), pp. 155–64 (p. 157).

50 Ibid., p. 156.

51 Beckett, *Embers*, p. 262.

52 Ibid., p. 253.

as interpreted by Yeats, is about being caught in a failed definition, floating in indefiniteness, with the problem of completion perpetually deferred.[53]

Although Henry hardly resembles the heroic figure of the legendary Irish warrior from Yeats's plays, the metaphor used by Harper seems highly relevant to the spiritual condition of Beckett's protagonist seen as a liminal figure suspended between reality and the world of his memories, between dreams and phantasmagorias and between the world of the living and the realm of the dead. Not unlike Cuchulain, Beckett's protagonist attempts to combat the waves, which in the play are clearly associated with the female element.[54] To achieve this aim he resorts to artistic activity.

In fact, Henry's creative striving for control over the acoustic environment of the play is most visible in the tension between him and the sea. Lawley argues that 'Beckett is well aware of the traditional connections of the sea with creativity. [Therefore, it can be] regarded, though in a harshly ironic light, as a major element in the creative process. For without his sea Henry would presumably have no need to create.'[55] The protagonist seeks inspiration from the sounds of nature, which, however, need to be artistically refashioned to be a part of his composition. Similar to Cuchulain in Yeats's *At the Hawk's Well*, the main character of *Embers* may either surrender to the lure of passivity or actively participate in shaping his fate as an artist and a conductor, somewhat similar to the Irish warrior in his struggle with his ghostly orchestra. Finally, like a conductor, isolated on a podium, he seems equally 'islanded' as Yeats's hero. Surrounded by the unruly sounds, he seems engaged in never-ending artistic strife.

This notion of loneliness is strongly underscored in the final part of the play, when, apart from the beat of the waves, all the voices evoked by Henry fall silent and the protagonist loses his creative control over them. At the beginning of his final story, the main character in vain tries to evoke the ghostly Ada and the sound of the hooves. Nor does the sea obey his last order: 'Not a sound',[56] which could bring the orchestrated musical piece to a close. What Henry is left with is the unfinished story of Bolton, which serves as the opening and coda of his musical piece and as a memoir of his failure as an orchestrator to bring it to a proper conclusion. Having returned to dull, everyday reality, he can only wait for

53 Margaret Harper, 'Yeats's Wild West: Cuchulain and the Cowboy' (plenary lecture presented at the DUCIS conference 'A New Ireland? Representations of History Past and Present in Literature and Culture', Falun, 3–4 Nov. 2011).

54 When Henry exclaims: 'Listen to it! ... Lips and claws! ... Get away from it! Where it couldn't get at me!' (Beckett, *Embers*, p. 258), the personified sea acquires a specifically female bodily shape.

55 Paul Lawley, '*Embers*: An Interpretation', available at <http://www.english.fsu.edu/jobs/num06/jobs06.htm>.

56 Beckett, *Embers*, p. 254.

another spark of creative inspiration, which will allow him to 'Fail again. Fail better', to use Beckett's famous words from *Worstward Ho*.[57]

Metamusic in Other Plays by Beckett

The metamusical motif of orchestration also recurs in Beckett's later plays for radio. In a similar vein as in *Embers*, in *Cascando* (1961) Beckett focuses on the idea of an unfinished musical narrative which troubles the protagonist. In his attempt to bring the story of Woburn, possibly his alter ego, to an end, the Opener orchestrates the sounds of the Voice and the Music into a coherent acoustic piece. Although the protagonist seems largely successful in his endeavours and towards the end the two sonic elements are harmoniously combined 'as though they had linked their arms',[58] the play is left open ended as if in anticipation of a finale that never takes place.

It needs to be emphasized that the Opener holds a substantial degree of control over his acoustic environment, which can be seen as a projection of his own psyche. The acoustic matter seems to be subjected to his conductorial will, which he several times comments on with satisfaction: 'Good'.[59] This is unusual for Beckettian characters, whose orchestrating attempts are notoriously bound to failure. Such is, for instance, the case of *Words and Music* (1961), which illustrates in acoustic terms the decline of the orchestrating power of the character named Croak. At first presented as a royal figure of authority, who conducts his orchestra (Music) and soloist (Words) in an authoritarian way and is addressed by them in a humble fashion, at the end of the drama he seems unable to perform his function any longer and lets his orchestrating attribute – a club – fall to the ground. Although Words and Music eventually achieve a certain harmony, Croak renounces his power and leaves to the sound of shuffling slippers, either too overwhelmed by the achieved effect, which instead of comfort brings him pain, or perhaps unwilling to finish his work, for fear that completion would amount to silence and creative emptiness. After his departure, Words tries to take over the role of the orchestrator and implores Music to continue its performance. The achieved effect is far from satisfactory, and Words concludes with a deep sigh.

What sheds further light on the play are Beckett's own words to Katharine Worth regarding *Words and Music*: 'Music always wins',[60] alluding to the complex power relations between Words and Music in this radio drama. From the very beginning the relationship between these two 'characters' seems tense. This is most conspicuous in the way they interrupt each other's performances either with the orchestra's chaotic tuning or the soloist's groans and verbal protestations. In

57 Samuel Beckett, *Worstward Ho* (London, 1987), p. 7.

58 Samuel Beckett, *Cascando*, in *Complete Dramatic Works*, p. 303.

59 Ibid., pp. 301, 303.

60 Katharine Worth, 'Words for Music Perhaps', p. 210.

the end Music prevails, as it sets the tune of the final performance and thus prompts Words's singing. In fact, it appears it is Music that holds the real orchestrating power over both Croak's emotions and the soloist's performance and in this way manifests its supremacy over the verbal order.

Finally, I want to turn to the metamusical tension between the conductor and the insubordinate acoustic matter which is particularly noticeable in some of Beckett's works for the stage, such as *Not I* (1972) and *Footfalls* (1975). In both plays the concept of self-orchestration is explored. In the case of *Footfalls*, Beckett again alludes to the notion of conducting/composing by means of adjusting the acoustic material to the percussive line of the protagonist's gait. The protagonist orchestrates the sound of her own movement and speech and complements the musical piece with a contrapuntal melody line in the form of words delivered by her mother, whose voice May possibly hears only in her head.

In *Not I*, in which it is possible to see Mouth and Auditor as representative of two aspects of one personality, Beckett again recycles the idea of tension between the conductor and the orchestrated subject. While Mouth occupies the upstage position, the mysterious figure of Auditor, clothed in loose black djellaba, remains in the background. Most critical interpretations of the play seem to be based on the assumption that Auditor serves as 'a physical representation of an internal force that is developing clearly in dialogue',[61] in which (s)he silently participates. Yet it needs to be stressed that the attempts to exert pressure on Mouth by the mysterious figure are also conveyed in a metamusical fashion and, as in the case of *Embers*, result in the ultimate failure. The effects of the possible communication between the characters are conspicuous in the violent refusal of Mouth to perform her monologue in the first person. The aggressive exclamation '... what?.. who?.. no!.. she!..'[62] is followed by Auditor's gesture that 'consists in simple sideways raising of arms from sides and their falling back'.[63] Although Beckett specified in his stage directions that the raising of arms aims to communicate 'helpless compassion',[64] it is also reminiscent of a conductor's gesture indicating a crescendo. In the context of the play, it may be seen as an expression of a wish to increase the intensity of the internal struggle within the orchestrated character, which will eventually lead to relinquishing the third person. After each failed attempt to sustain the moment of doubt and thus control Mouth's performance, Auditor's gesture 'lessens … till scarcely perceptible at [the] third [repetition]'.[65] As in the case of the sea in *Embers*, after the conductor's failure, the 'unorchestrable' sounds do not cease but continue their unruly existence. In fact, by carrying on with her monologue, Mouth paradoxically reaffirms her creative identity, since the chaotic form of her speech, which seems almost literally

---

61 Stanley E. Gontarski, *The Intent of Undoing in Samuel Beckett's Dramatic Texts* (Bloomington, IN, 1985).

62 Samuel Beckett, *Not I*, in *Complete Dramatic Works*, pp. 377, 379, 381–2.

63 Ibid., p. 375.

64 Ibid.

65 Ibid.

dismembered by the character's teeth, creates a new, musical rather than narrative quality with its hypnotic flow and numerous echoes.

Conclusion

To recapitulate, analysis of the metamusical dimension of Beckett's early plays for radio sheds light both on the power relations between the characters and on the nature of the creative process of composing and conducting. Not unlike many of Beckett's plays for the stage, the radio texts discussed can be read both as musical scores and works about orchestrating, combining sound and voice together into well-arranged pieces of music. Still, this metamusical dimension seems most evident in the dramas written for a medium that operates exclusively with sound. Relying solely on the sonic experience, Beckett's early radio plays provide a self-ironic commentary on the playwright's own process of writing, understood as parallel to composing. In a broader sense, they address the notions of individuality and subjectivity in experiencing the world as well as the idea of human creative propensity. In the end, this seems to inspire Beckett's characters to give musical shape to their experience, transforming it into a work of art.

Chapter 4

Tuning In/Tuning Up: The Communicative Efforts of Words and Music in Samuel Beckett's *Words and Music*

Brynhildur Boyce

I

The radiogenic notion of 'tuning in' is, this chapter will argue, central to Samuel Beckett's third play for radio, *Words and Music*, written in 1961. While the experience of listening to analogue radio – of tuning in, that is, to a particular frequency – supplies the notion, the figure of speech is commonly used to articulate the activity of comprehension within the process of communication. In both cases, the listener must situate the transmission, contextualize the form and 'tune in' to the sender's meaning. This, however, is no mean feat, as communication is the result not of perfect attunement but of two communicators' efforts to draw near and understand each other, despite having no assurance that they can or do. The philosopher of language Donald Davidson – whose investigation of communication will be central to the argument presented here – states, to this end, that 'making sense of the utterances and behaviour of others ... requires us to find a great deal of reason and truth in them'.[1] Furthermore, he suggests that just as such charitable pragmatism at most 'maximises agreement', so the method of making sense, or of interpreting, can only ever be 'one of getting a best fit'.[2] This notion of achieving a 'best fit' between different communicative ontologies resonates, I would argue, with the radiogenic activity of 'tuning in'. The former, Davidson tells us, is always temporary, since we continually 'adjust our theory [of interpretation] to fit the inflow of new information';[3] while the latter, as Steven Connor reminds us, is a similarly volatile process, by which the radio listener 'repeatedly constitutes his or her relation to the device and [its] transmissions'.[4] There is, in other words, a slippage at the heart of this activity, and, by highlighting

---

1 Donald Davidson, *Inquiries into Truth and Interpretation* (Oxford, 1984), p. 153.

2 Ibid., p. 136.

3 Ibid., p. 279.

4 Steven Connor, 'I Switch Off: Beckett and the Ordeals of Radio', in Debra Rae Cohen, Michael Coyle and Jane Lewty (eds), *Broadcasting Modernism* (Gainesville, FL, 2009), p. 289.

the inherent misalignment between communicants, the notion of 'tuning in' can serve as a reminder that every act of communication involves the effort to overcome this essential incompatibility.

Words and Music presents a decidedly disjunctive communicational situation, which is made immediately obvious through its structure. In a letter to his American publishers Grove Press, Beckett called the play a 'text–music tandem',[5] and the text does, indeed, appear to be at the fore in this tandem. The eponymous characters of Words and Music are ordered by a figure called Croak to express, first separately and then together, certain subjects of his choosing: 'love', 'age' and finally 'the face'. To this end, they gradually develop songs together: thus, Music proposes melodies while Words supplies the lines, and both fine-tune their contributions in a bid to make them fit. Through this interaction, Music and Words attempt to overcome their essential incommensurability and tune in to each other's form of expression. However, while ostensibly delineating an escalating process of creative cooperation between these characters, the play in fact omits half of that exchange, supplying only the lines spoken by Words (whom Croak calls Joe) while leaving Music (or Bob) a blank. And words, what is more, take the place of a score, providing textual notation in the form of '*love and soul music*', '*spreading and subsiding music*' or '*warmly sentimental*'. Beckett, in other words, neither composed the music to be played nor indicated that an existing piece should be used, and thus extended a permanent invitation to a composer – any composer – to give the character of Music expression.[6] None of the compositions specifically written for the part should, in extension, be regarded as providing a definitive interpretation of it, since Music remains, in the play, undefined and open-ended.

Much has nevertheless been made of the supposedly authorized status of John Beckett's composition for the part of Music, which he wrote for the BBC production of *Words and Music* originally broadcast on 13 November 1962. This status rests, it appears, on the fact that he was the first composer to work on the play and that he happened to be Beckett's cousin. Katharine Worth thus wonders whether 'Beckett would be willing to have a character so well established as *his* Music unstitched and remade [my italics]', since he and his cousin 'had no doubt worked closely on *Words and Music*'.[7] Worth's second assumption,

---

5 Clas Zilliacus, *Beckett and Broadcasting: A Study of the Works of Samuel Beckett for and in Radio and Television* (Åbo, 1976), p. 99.

6 This is in contrast to most of his other works in which music is incorporated. His first radio play, *All That Fall*, thus names the Schubert piece that is heard, while the plays *Embers*, *Ghost Trio* and *Nacht und Träume* specify not only the pieces (by Chopin, Beethoven and Schubert respectively) but even the bars that are to be played. For the 'threne' heard in the novel *Watt*, on the other hand, Beckett himself composed both a rhythmic score and the melody sung by the soprano.

7 Katharine Worth, 'Words for Music Perhaps', in Mary Bryden (ed.), *Samuel Beckett and Music* (Oxford, 1998), pp. 9–20 (p. 12). Worth produced the second English language recording of *Words and Music* in 1973. Wishing to use one for teaching purposes and unable

regarding the Becketts' collaboration, is simply wrong: in 1962, Beckett wrote to the director Alan Schneider that 'John Beckett has done his music for *Words & Music* (BBC). No idea yet what he has done, but have full confidence.'[8] I would argue that Worth's first assumption, concerning the authorship of Music, is equally unfounded. It is not *Samuel* Beckett's but rather *John* Beckett's Music that is well established, existing as it does as both a score and a recording. Some decades later, when Everett Frost was preparing his production of the play, Beckett stated that 'it would be 'impossible' for [Frost] to use the John Beckett score'.[9] I would suggest that this was not merely due to the fact that his cousin had, by that point, withdrawn permission to use it. More significantly, the very nature of the play dictates that Music must, in Worth's words, be 'remade' for each production.

I propose three ways in which one might approach *Words and Music*. One might, firstly, focus entirely on the text, as the only tangible aspect of the work-as-conceived-by-Beckett and the only source of ascertainable information about Music. This may, however, appear to reveal 'a major weakness in the text: the simplicity of [musical] direction' and lead to dissatisfaction with Beckett's apparent 'naivety … that composers will have an intuitive comprehension of such directions as "*soft music worthy of foregoing, great expression*"'.[10] Received as pure text, however, the play – as linguistic and not musical notation – must naturally deliver a 'simplistic' account of Music: indeed, it is this thematically important incommensurability of words and music that necessitates the play's structurally significant call for a composer's contribution. An exclusive focus on the text may, on the other hand, lead to the conclusion that Beckett 'had a clear, if general, idea of the kind of music he wanted', but this attributes to the words a musical knowledge and compositional ability that they cannot possess.[11] It is more common for strictly textual interpretations to view Music not as the sum of its brief directions but as the representative of a metaphysical, Schopenhauerian

---

to borrow the BBC's recording, she made a production with the Audio-Visual Centre at the University of London, for which she commissioned new music from the British composer Humphrey Searle. Beckett himself suggested that she approach Searle.

8 In Maurice Harmon (ed.), *No Author Better Served: The Correspondence of Samuel Beckett and Alan Schneider* (Cambridge, MA, 1998), p. 122.

9 Everett C. Frost, 'The Note Man on the Word Man: Morton Feldman on Composing the Music for Samuel Beckett's *Words and Music* in *The Beckett Festival of Radio Plays*', in Bryden (ed.), *Samuel Beckett and Music*, pp. 47–55 (p. 47). Frost produced and directed a recording of *Words and Music* in 1987, for Voices International. This production, which was part of Frost's 'Beckett Festival of Radio Plays' and broadcast in the States on National Public Radio, used new music by the American composer Morton Feldman. Beckett suggested Feldman for the job, having been pleased with *Neither*, the opera written by the composer to the short text 'Neither', provided by Beckett specifically for that purpose.

10 Kevin Branigan, *Radio Beckett: Musicality in the Radio Plays of Samuel Beckett* (Bern, 2008), p. 229.

11 Eric Prieto, *Listening In: Music, Mind, and the Modernist Narrative* (Lincoln, NE, 2002), p. 199.

conception of music, which recognizes the above-mentioned incommensurability. This perspective will be discussed towards the end of this chapter, since it would distract from the structural point being made here. At this stage, suffice it to say that by (necessarily) drawing on a conceptual notion of music, textual analyses ignore the fact that the play was designed to be broadcast on the radio. As a purely textual object it is therefore incomplete, since Music has yet to be not only composed but also performed.

The second possibility is to regard the work as being a co-production between Beckett's text and a particular composer's music. Katharine Worth gives an account of the way in which Humphrey Searle's 'temperamentally in tune' music 'released the meanings' sought by the text;[12] while Everett Frost notes that as 'the composition of a great artist in his own right, [Morton] Feldman's score struggles under the collaboration with Beckett's text ... much as, in the play itself, Bob [Music] struggles with Joe [Words]'.[13] Such approbation implies that the text may be so perfectly matched by a complementary music as to be completely fulfilled, but this perspective was rejected by Beckett who, as he explained to the BBC producer Donald McWhinnie, approved of John Beckett's score for its 'spirit not of reinforcement but of otherness'.[14] The notion of a perfect musical match fails, moreover, to acknowledge the inherent incompletion of the work. As a gap that is permanently structured into the play, the character of Music can be neither definitively interpreted nor decisively performed into being, and each production can therefore only make a suggestion about the work but never fully realize it.

This brings us to the third possibility, and the one followed in this chapter, which is to regard *Words and Music* as consisting of Beckett's text and a series of Music-shaped, musically undefined gaps. This has the advantage of maintaining, on two levels, the contrary open-endedness of the play. Firstly, by acknowledging both the text's authority – in the sense that it invites and structurally controls the musical filling of those gaps – and its simultaneous yielding, to a composer, of authorial control within each gap. Secondly, by recognizing that, since those gaps are an integral part of the play, they can never be conclusively filled but must continually be filled anew, from production to production. This is not, however, an unproblematic position, requiring as it does the juggling of mutually exclusive perspectives. The text is both insufficient to, and the only permanent part of, the work. *Words and Music* exists, if not primarily then certainly most steadfastly, as words on a page, and as such it effectively invites the reader to fill the gaps and complete the dialogue by conceptualizing the absent Music through the utterances of Words. The impulse to focus exclusively on the text is thus unavoidable and

12 Worth, 'Words for Music Perhaps', pp. 12, 16.

13 Everett C. Frost, 'Fundamental Sounds: Recording Samuel Beckett's Radio Plays', *Theatre Journal* 43/3 (1991): 361–76 (p. 374).

14 Lois More Overbeck, 'Audience of Self/Audience of Reader', *Modernism/modernity* 18/4 (2011): 721–37 (p. 729).

possibly even requisite, but it is at the same time inadequate to a full understanding of the play, which requires its performance, that is, the addition to it of music. All discussion of Words and Music's interaction is, in this context, deeply problematic and can only be conducted from the perspective of the former character. On the one hand, as I will argue, the gaps in the play are crucial to our understanding of it; but on the other, no understanding is possible unless the gaps are – temporarily – filled in a particular production. This contradiction informs the following analysis, the scope of which is deliberately demarcated by the dealings of Words and Music. My interest, in this chapter, is in their disjunctive relation, and while the third character of the play, Croak, may instigate their attempt to tune in to each other, their continued interaction is, as we shall see below, the result of their own efforts. Croak is therefore not a prominent presence in this analysis.

II

Words and Music are, as Words puts it, 'cooped up' together, a description loaded with a sense of resented unity or united division, and their problematic co-habitation is confirmed by the 'loathing' with which Words speaks to Music, as it is by Croak's entreaty that they are friends.[15] Yet the start of the play is marked not by a lack of interaction, but by interaction of a curiously disconnected kind. Words and Music 'speak' at, rather than with, each other: it is as though they are merely going through the conversational motions, separated not so much from each other as from communication itself. Having prepared themselves for Croak's arrival by 'tuning up' – Music in the orchestral sense, Words by rattling off a speech on 'sloth' – they have no difficulty in tuning in to what Croak announces as the first 'theme tonight ... love'.[16] Words has merely to substitute the word 'love' for 'sloth' in order to re-use his speech:

> WORDS: [*Orotund.*] Love is of all the passions the most powerful passion and indeed no passion is more powerful than the passion of love. [*Clears throat.*] This is the mode in which the mind is most strongly affected and indeed in no mode is the mind more strongly affected than in this. [*Pause.*]
> CROAK: *Rending sigh. Thump of club.*
> WORDS: [*As before.*] By passion we are to understand a movement of the mind pursuing or fleeing real or imagined pleasure or pain. [*Clears throat.*] Of all –
> CROAK: [*Anguished.*] Oh!

The stale non-specificity of the phrases is betrayed when Words stumbles over the subject matter, returning briefly to 'sloth':

[15] Samuel Beckett, *Words and Music*, in *The Complete Dramatic Works* (London, 1986), p. 287.

[16] Ibid., p. 288.

> WORDS: Of all these movements then and who can number them and they are legion sloth is the ... LOVE is the most urgent and indeed by no manner of movement is the soul more urged than by this, to and – [*Violent thump of club.*]
> CROAK: Bob.
> WORDS: From.
> [*Violent thump of club.*]
> CROAK: Bob! [...] Love!
> MUSIC: *Rap of baton on stand. Soft music worthy of foregoing, great expression* [...].[17]

Repetition takes the place of contextually specific expression in the opening section of the play, which is characterized by the kind of disconnection crystallized in the passage above. By transferring his speech wholesale from rehearsal to performance, Words shows himself to engage in no meaningful way with his ostensible 'theme tonight', and this detachment is all the more pointed considering that engagement is the very essence of love. Emerging as a fully formed, standardized template, his self-absorbedly circular composition seeks no contact with its audience either. The polished rings of his rhetoric resemble arid exercises in sentence structure rather than attempts to articulate and convey thought, an effect presumably mirrored by Music's 'worthy' rejoinder. This disengagement is mirrored structurally as Words and Music, in accordance with Croak's strictly alternating focus, deliver their material in separate doses, the one falling silent before the other begins. Croak's regular shifts in focus, moreover, undermine the force of his reactions, which – as when he utters an '[*Anguished.*] Oh!' on hearing of 'real or imagined pleasure or pain' – come to resemble not the purposeful absorption of meaning so much as knee-jerk mimesis, one empty gesture mirroring another.

After interrupting Words's rehearsed declamation with a 'violent thump of [his] club', Croak calls on Music to express 'Love'. Greeting the '*Soft music worthy of foregoing*' with the same thump and '[*Anguished.*] Oh!' as he did the speech, he then demands that the music be played again, 'Louder!'[18] His reasons for doing so are difficult to gauge. The bombastic music that results – '*fortissimo, all expression gone*' – may, however, be said to actualize the hollow, inflated quality of the sentiments being proclaimed and to reflect the empty sounds – whether verbal or musical – that here deliver the mere shapes of those sentiments. The characters perpetuate through mechanical repetition the framework of communication, while demonstrating neither the desire to convey meaning nor the desire to grasp it. It is not that they have trouble comprehending one another, but rather that comprehension is irrelevant. What is absent is the impulse towards, and the effort to achieve, understanding, an impulse that must underpin the very process of communication; and since nothing is communicated, it stands to reason that 'all expression [is] gone'.

---

[17] Ibid.

[18] Ibid.

Words and Music are given a new theme, that of 'age', for which Words's set speech is of no use and about which he struggles to speak coherently: '[*Faltering.*] Age is ... age is when ... old age I mean ... if that is what my Lord means ...'.[19] Music, on the other hand, launches directly into '*Age music*' as he did before with '*Love music*'. Croak's response is again to 'violent[ly]' interrupt their individual efforts, and in a change of tactic he commands them to work together. While this could arguably be for the benefit of Words, that he might be stimulated by Music's expressiveness, there is another, more methodological explanation for Croak's decision. If the composer Morton Feldman is to be believed, any direct musical engagement with what he terms a universal concept – such as age – is bound to result in a 'cliché type of response': 'music ... has terrific power', he explained to Everett Frost, but 'when [it] is universal, it never gets beyond the level of, say, a Shostakovich. It's freshman universal.'[20] Regarded in this light, Music's response to the theme of age is likely to be formulaic, and it therefore stands to reason that Croak should seek to complicate the concept and thereby enrich its expression, by forcing its interpreters towards a more complex, jointly developed understanding of it. Feldman's solution, in his composition for the play, was to focus not on the concept of age itself but rather on the 'technical way of arriving at it', generating through music – through, for instance, the use of pizzicato – the experiential nature of age that he felt was conveyed, in an equally technical manner, by the 'halting' language of Words. It is in precisely this way, as we shall see, that both Music and Words come to express what Feldman calls the 'quintessence of the material'.

Feldman used the same word to describe the effect of Beckett's text 'Neither', which he felt provided 'the quintessence, something that just hovered'.[21] He further explained that every line of the text – which traces an oscillating movement 'to and fro', 'back and forth', from 'self' to 'unself' – is 'really the same thought said in another way ... getting deeper and deeper saturated into the thought'.[22] Feldman sought, in his opera *Neither*, to likewise 'hold the moment', using as his compositional methodology what he termed a floating focus, in order to express the thought 'in another way ... through the language of another register, the language of another colour'.[23] Returning to *Words and Music*, the eponymous

---

19 Ibid., p. 289.

20 Morton Feldman, *Morton Feldman Says: Selected Interviews and Lectures 1964–1987*, ed. Chris Villars (London, 2006), p. 235. Feldman's suggestion that the 'universal' emotions conveyed by Shostakovich's music are simplistic and formulaic was perhaps confirmed by Shostakovich's declaration, at the premiere of his Fifth Symphony in 1937: 'The theme of my symphony is the making of a man. ... In the finale, the tragically tense impulses of the earlier movements are resolved in optimism and the joy of living' (quoted in Michael Steinberg, *The Symphony: A Listener's Guide* (Oxford, 1995), pp. 547–8).

21 Feldman, *Morton Feldman Says*, p. 75.

22 Ibid., p. 194.

23 Ibid., pp. 76, 194.

characters might be said to join forces in the pursuit of the quintessence of age, which lies, it follows, in a focused, technically executed 'saturation' in the subject matter. What follows is the painstaking, technical process of articulation, through the medium of song.

Words utters a line to which Music responds – either modifying what Words has just said or anticipating the next line – in accordance with which Words then tries to sing; and gradually, as words are combined with music, a narrative on age emerges.

> CROAK: Together. [*Pause. Thump.*] Together! [*Pause. Violent thump.*] Together, dogs!
> MUSIC: *Long la.* [...]
> WORDS: [*Trying to sing.*] Age is when ... to a man ...
> MUSIC: *Improvement of above.*
> WORDS: [*Trying to sing this.*] Age is when to a man ...
> MUSIC: *Suggestion for following.*
> WORDS: [*Trying to sing this.*] Huddled o'er ... the ingle ... [*Pause. Violent thump. Trying to sing.*] Waiting for the hag to put the ... pan in the bed ...
> MUSIC: *Improvement of above.*
> WORDS: [*Trying to sing this.*] Waiting for the hag to put the pan in the bed.
> MUSIC: *Suggestion for following.*
> WORDS: [*Trying to sing this.*] And bring the ... arrowroot ... [*Pause. Violent thump. As before.*] And bring the toddy.[24]

The orotund, rhetorical, monotonous style of before has been replaced by a faltering, open-ended and dialogic manner. Far from being a vehicle for pre-formed, uncontextualized bombast, the act of utterance has become a means of searching for and shaping the phrases that ring true. As evidence that this is indeed the case, one might point to the complex manner in which old age is here evoked. At a semantic level, it emerges with such precision that 'arrowroot', associated in the Victorian period with childhood, becomes in the hands of the nurse-like 'hag' a signifier of second infancy.[25] The replacement of this porridge by the more age-appropriate toddy only serves to confirm the evocation. The sentence stretches out, what is more, postponing its delivery of meaning, delaying its explanation of the 'when' that will describe what 'age is', and as such it enacts the endlessness of old age, demonstrating syntactically the way in which time is protracted by the anticipation of an ever-deferred conclusion. The contrast between this comprehensive eloquence and the earlier estranging and estranged rhetoric could not be starker.

It makes no sense, when dealing only with the text, to make any comparable assertion about the substance of Music's contribution. Many critics have nevertheless attempted just that. Clas Zilliacus thus states that 'Music ... introduces

---

24 Beckett, *Words and Music*, pp. 289–90.

25 Boiled with water or milk to produce a thin porridge, arrowroot was given, as an easily digestible food, to children and invalids in the nineteenth century.

the face theme into the Age song';[26] Shimon Levy maintains that 'Music … elicits memories through the power of association';[27] and Elissa Guralnick explains that 'when Joe/Words speaks in sympathy with Croak, he mainly expresses regret and incurable longing – sentiments with which Music accords'.[28] These descriptions have no basis in the unspecified 'improvements' and 'suggestions' – which, to be sure, run the gamut from 'warm' to 'discreet' – that make up the Music of the text. As Guralnick's comment makes clear, all the sentiments and actions critically ascribed to Music are in fact transferred from Words: all, that is, apart from one specific action. The text contains numerous directions concerning the different *ways* in which the music is played – '*humble*', '*soft*', '*fortissimo*' – but only once does it prescribe *what* is played. Music's first utterance, after being commanded to interact with Words, is thus specified as being a '*long la*', a tone with certain highly significant connotations.[29] In the solmization system – which in fact takes two quite distinct forms – commonly used to teach music, each note of a seven-tone scale is associated with a particular syllable of the sequence do, re, mi, fa, so, la, ti. In some countries, such as Britain, Ireland and Germany, the 'movable-do' system is used, in which the syllables are relative designators: 'do' corresponds to the tonic, or keynote, on which the scale is based, and thus is C in C major, but D in D major. The note designated by 'la' varies accordingly, being A in C major, but B in D major. Conversely, France, Italy and other Latin countries use the 'fixed-do' system, in which the syllables are absolute designators: irrespective of the key, 'do' is fixed to C and the syllables name the notes, such that 'la' is always A. If, as here, the key is unspecified, it is natural to assume that we are in C major, the most neutral of scales and the default example used in music theory, and in this case 'la' denotes the note A. In its '*long la*', Music might therefore be said to be playing 'A' for 'age'.

When ordered to collaborate on this universal concept, Music no longer reacts (solely) to it as a concept, but rather focuses on the 'technical' means – both letters and notes – by which it may be reached. By playing 'la' Music reverts, in an appropriately musico-linguistic conceit, to the fundamentals to produce a precisely pitched tonal expression of the theme and thus articulates, in a very literal manner, a particular quintessence of age. The non-linguistic speech sound 'la' forms, in this way, a meeting place between the verbal and the musical, pointing in one direction to a particular letter, and in the other to a particular note. As though this were a singing lesson, Words is invited to respond in kind, and to conflate words and music by '*trying to sing*' his first phrase to the same note. It is to just such a 'long la', the A note played on an oboe, that an orchestra tunes just before a

---

[26] Zilliacus, *Beckett and Broadcasting*, p. 113.

[27] Shimon Levy, *Samuel Beckett's Self-Referential Drama: The Sensitive Chaos* (Brighton, 2002), p. 91.

[28] Elissa S. Guralnick, *Sight Unseen: Beckett, Pinter, Stoppard, and Other Contemporary Dramatists on Radio* (Athens, OH, 1996), p. 89.

[29] Beckett, *Words and Music*, p. 289.

concert, and the suggestion of convergence thus contained in the note suggests that Words and Music may likewise be able to 'tune in' to each other. This is precisely the effect achieved in both the Voices International and the RTÉ productions, in which Morton Feldman's and Paul Clark's Music, respectively, play a multi-instrumented A note,[30] and in both cases Words responds by singing 'Age is when …' on that note.

In a discussion of tuning, which he characterizes as the manual effort to situate a listener and transmitter in 'the same zone of reception', Steven Connor observes that 'at the beginning of *Words and Music* … the controlling or summoning voice [of Croak] attempts to synchronize the two agencies … who represent words and music'.[31] However, while Croak's command that they perform 'Together!' certainly provides the impetus, I would argue that any form of synchronization between Words and Music is due to their own, technical endeavours to enter the 'same zone', which is to say, to merge their modes of expression. The most significant aspect of these endeavours, however, is not the result so much as simply the effort made by the two figures to draw near in this way.

Following the line of argument I have been advancing, Words and Music must enter a structure conducive to the transmission of expression – a structure of communication, that is – before they are able to express anything. Only by articulating to each other, it seems, can they locate in themselves a conception of age, and only by interpreting the other's ideas and engaging with the other's mode of expression can they stimulate further expression both in each other and in themselves. In this way, they work to dovetail each stage of their contributions before proceeding to the next. Starting, in the passage quoted above, with the 'la', Music makes a series of '*Suggestion*[*s*] *for following*' to which Words attempts to sing a phrase, after which Music in turn plays an '*Improvement of above*', to which Words again tries to sing the same phrase. The object of the improvements is unclear: are they meant to bring Words's response into line with the original, musical suggestion, or do they perhaps retrospectively adjust that suggestion so that it better corresponds with Words's interpretation of it?

Further possibilities are suggested by the various compositions written for the play. John Beckett's 'improvements' tend to supply a short, new musical phrase that does not correspond to what Words has just sung, but which he is easily able to follow, and in this way the BBC's Music makes sure that Words keeps abreast of the musical direction. Each of Paul Clark's improvements also presents a new melody, which likewise bears no resemblance to what Words has just sung, but unlike John Beckett's these melodies become increasingly long and complex, and

30 Raidió Teilifís Éireann (RTÉ), the Irish national broadcaster, recorded and broadcast all of Beckett's radio plays in 2006 to celebrate the centenary of his birth. Made in association with the theatre company Gare St Lazare Players Ireland, which has specialized in Beckett's works, these recordings were directed by Judy Hegarty Lovett, with original music by the British composer Paul Clark.

31 Connor, 'I Switch Off', p. 289.

Words is increasingly unable to sing them. Music seems, therefore, deliberately to cleave from and outpace Words in the RTÉ recording. In contrast, Morton Feldman's improvements repeat the previous suggestion – which Words has sung – but on a different instrument, moving, for instance, from marimba to flute. These instrumental variations serve to demonstrate the infinite expressive possibilities of the same basic refrain, and the effect is to simultaneously confirm and ever so slightly unfix the communion between Music and Words. In the Voices International production, Words and Music are thus essentially on the same wavelength yet not entirely in synch. The effect generated by the textual directions thus varies from production to production, primarily because each compositional decision reverberates through, and shapes anew, the nature of Words and Music's relation. What may appear straightforward on the page is, in short, anything but that in performance.

Whatever the result of the suggestions and improvements, the (textual) impression given is that Music seeks both to coordinate his and Words's efforts and to demonstrate that co-ordination. Similarly, after each of Music's responses Words repeats with more confidence the line he at first sang hesitantly, as though finding in the reply sufficient evidence of Music's engagement with his phrase: sufficient evidence, that is, that his phrase fulfils the objective of all utterances, namely to have an effect on the listener and provoke interpretation. This apparent reassurance has an immediate, reciprocal effect on Words himself: in sending his line back he extends it slightly, possibly beyond the parameters of the previous musical suggestion, as though wishing to provoke a reaction before continuing. The possible outcomes of this interaction are, however, manifold, as a comparison of the three recordings addressed in this chapter makes clear. In the BBC recording, Words speaks the extended line, for which Music provides a melody, to which, in turn, Words sings the line and then speaks a new extension. The sense of their close and careful cooperation is thus tempered by the fact that they do not merge: Words sets the textual direction, but waits for Music to lead the musical way. In the RTÉ recording, on the other hand, Words tries to sing the extended line to the previous melody, and then tries (without much success) to sing it again to Music's new suggestion. This version of the situation reflects Eric Prieto's assumption that 'Music has now adopted a leading role [... and] Words can only do his best to keep up' by mistakenly trying to second-guess Music's decisions.[32] Conversely, in the Voices International recording, Words and Music can best be described as co-elaborating the song, by gradually building on each other's contributions. Thus, Words re-uses and extends the previous melody, and Music endorses that by repeating the phrase, albeit with the kind of instrumental variation described above. In this way, both Words and Music keep the conversational ball incrementally rolling.

MUSIC: *Suggestion for following.*
WORDS: [*Trying to sing this.*] She comes in the ashes ... [*Imploring.*] No!

---

[32] Prieto, *Listening In*, p. 225.

> MUSIC: *Repeats suggestion.*
> WORDS: [*Trying to sing this.*] She comes in the ashes who loved could not be ... won or ... [*Pause.*]
> MUSIC: *Repeats end of previous suggestion.*
> WORDS: [*Trying to sing this.*] Or won not loved ... [*Wearily.*] ... or some other trouble ... [*Pause. Trying to sing.*] Comes in the ashes like in that old –
> MUSIC: *Interrupts with improvement of this and brief suggestion.*
> WORDS: [*Trying to sing this.*] Comes in the ashes like in that old light ... her face ... in the ashes … .[33]

Through this kind of constant, mutual stimulation, they reach out to each other and seek convergence. Mere interaction – as at the start of the play – is not enough: there must be palpable attentiveness and reaction. It might be argued that it is only now, when communicating with an other, that these characters' utterances have meaning, since it is only now they have meaning to express.

III

Donald Davidson argues that language is a social affair, stating that 'speaking a language requires that there be an interpreter',[34] since 'one must always intend to … hav[e] one's words interpreted'.[35] However, and importantly for our present purposes, 'communication does not demand that any two people speak the same language'.[36] Indeed, 'it is probably the case that no two people actually do speak the same language', since 'they don't … have to mean the same thing by the same words',[37] but 'if communication succeeds, speaker and hearer must assign the same meaning to the speaker's words',[38] which is to say, the hearer must assign the speaker's meaning to the words as uttered by the speaker. 'The aim of interpretation', Davidson declares, 'is not agreement but understanding';[39] meaning emerges from a process of 'triangulation':

> To understand the speech of another … we must entertain the same propositions, with the same subject matter, and the same concept of truth. Communication depends on each communicator having, and correctly thinking that the other has, the concept of a shared world, an intersubjective world. But the concept of an

---

33 Beckett, *Words and Music*, p. 290.

34 Donald Davidson, *Subjective, Intersubjective, Objective* (Oxford, 2001), p. 114.

35 Davidson, *Inquiries into Truth and Interpretation*, p. 272.

36 Donald Davidson, *Truth, Language and History* (Oxford, 2005), p. 96.

37 Davidson, *Subjective, Intersubjective, Objective*, pp. 115, 121.

38 Davidson, *Inquiries into Truth and Interpretation*, p. 277.

39 Ibid., p. xvii.

> intersubjective world is the concept of an objective world, a world about which each communicator can have beliefs.[40]

Our common concept of truth depends not on sameness of belief – since that would be impossible to verify – but on a readiness and ability to understand the other's belief; and such understanding can only arise when both parties interact with a common object.

> Our sense of objectivity is the consequence of [a] sort of triangulation, one that requires two creatures. Each interacts with an object, but what gives each the concept of the way things are objectively is the base line formed between the creatures by language.[41]

Meaning emerges at the intersection of the speaker's intention and the hearer's interpretation and is established anew by the particulars of each communicative situation. Irrespective of whether the communicators are unknown or familiar to one another, each new dialogue triggers a fresh process of triangulation, since 'truth for a language [is] relative to [both] a time and a speaker'.[42] Furthermore, not only is comprehension site-specific, it also continues to evolve during that specific situation as both communicators move along the 'base line' towards each other and towards a sense of mutual objectivity. Continually evolving understanding entails a similarly evolving method of interpretation, which Davidson terms a 'passing theory', since it consists of equal parts anticipation and modification and is constantly being renewed. We necessarily start with what he calls a 'prior' theory of interpretation – an assumption, that is, of how we may understand the speaker – but as the dialogue progresses we alter that theory, 'revising past interpretations ... in the light of new evidence' and adjusting our current interpretations to try to 'yield the speaker's intended interpretation':[43] we adjust, in effect, our interpretation of that intended interpretation. It therefore follows that 'the longer talk continues the better our theory becomes', which is to say, the more tailor-made it becomes.[44]

This might explain why the discourse on love – which, as we have seen, is not at all site-specific – provokes no interpretation and produces no meaning. In contrast, when developing their song on age, Words and Music are effectively building the kind of triangular structure outlined above, in that they interact, on the one hand, with the 'object' of age and, on the other, with each other's understanding of that object. For this mutually beneficial arrangement to continue, each must assume – without for obvious reasons being able to

40 Davidson, *Subjective, Intersubjective, Objective*, p. 105.

41 Ibid.

42 Davidson, *Inquiries into Truth and Interpretation*, p. 131.

43 Davidson, *Truth, Language and History*, pp. 100, 99.

44 Davidson, *Inquiries into Truth and Interpretation*, p. 279.

ascertain it – that the other responds in a more or less understandable and more or less complementary way to the shared stimulus. Words and Music's active engagement with each other's utterances has thus far been referred to as a process of tuning in. Alternatively, they might be said to be constructing triangulated, passing theories about one another, as evidenced by their suggestions, improvements and attempts to sing, which pattern forth a shifting network of expectation, adjustment and interpretation. Comprehension, in this respect, is a performance between speaker and interpreter, and we might recall that Words and Music are indeed performing – in an immediate sense for Croak – and that the subject of their performance is their communication 'together'. What is more, as we saw above, each actual performance – which is to say, each production of the play – establishes a new conversational situation and, as the dynamics of the dialogue alter, so the methods, or theories, of interpretation must change. Finally, following Davidson, it does indeed appear to be the case that the longer Words and Music's 'talk' continues, the better their theories of interpretation become. If the 'Age Song' demonstrates their struggles to tune in to each other, the 'Wellhead Song' with which the play ends arguably displays the fruits of those efforts. It emerges fully formed, and Words and Music seem, in it, to be in a state of attunement.

A bridge is formed between the two songs by Words's detailed meditation on a woman's face – the 'face in the ashes' with which the 'Age Song' concludes – and the 'Wellhead Song' issues naturally from this description:

> WORDS: ... a little colour comes back into the cheeks and the eyes ... [*Reverently.*] ... open. [*Pause.*] Then down a little way ... [*Pause. Change to poetic tone. Low.*]
> Then down a little way
> Through the trash
> To where ... towards where ...
> [*Pause.*]
> MUSIC: *Discreet suggestion for above.*
> WORDS: [*Trying to sing this.*]
> Then down a little way
> Through the trash
> Towards where ...
> [*Pause.*]
> MUSIC: *Discreet suggestion for following.*
> WORDS: [*Trying to sing this.*]
> All dark no begging
> No giving no words
> No sense no need ...
> [*Pause.*]
> MUSIC: *More confident suggestion for following.*
> WORDS: [*Trying to sing this.*]
> Through the scum

Down a little way
To where one glimpse
Of that wellhead.[45]

Words and Music appear to have reached a state of equilibrium: they are, as it were, tuned in to the same wavelength. When Words pauses it is not, as before, to obtain stimulation and reassurance but rather, simply, to allow Music to contribute. The ease with which Words attempts to sing, moreover – delivering without hesitation each subsequent section of the poem – indicates that he knows both what to say and, importantly, how to fit it to Music's proposals. His '*trying to sing*' seems now to have qualitative rather than ontological implications: there seems no longer to be a question of whether he can sing at all, merely of how well he does it. Likewise, Music has neither to repeat nor to improve his suggestions, his greater confidence suggesting that he too is accurately anticipating Words's next utterances. This tallies with Davidson's assertion that, for successful communication to take place, both parties' passing theories of interpretation must converge, since 'the speaker must "go on" more or less as the other expects'.[46]

The close structural correspondence between *Words and Music* and Davidson's theories of meaning and understanding may, as argued above, usefully illuminate the play. This illumination culminates in what is, for our purposes, perhaps the most significant element of Davidson's thinking, namely his lucid articulation of an arrestingly optimistic view of communication, a view that he readily acknowledges is both a choice and, quite simply, necessary. Underlying and facilitating successful communication is something he calls a 'principle of charity', which he defines as a means of optimizing understanding by maximizing intelligibility. 'Charity is forced on us', he declares; 'whether we like it or not, if we want to understand others, we must count them right in most matters'.[47] Just as the interpreter, to this end, 'read[s his] own logic into the thoughts of a speaker',[48] so the speaker's intention – concerning the way he wishes his words to be understood – is to some extent dictated by his belief about the interpreter's logic in understanding those words.[49] In short, Davidson's principle of charity highlights the way in which we instinctively converge as communicants and emphasizes the good will that leads to and serves to maintain comprehension. In a pragmatic bid to maximize our chances of understanding and being understood, we keep the conversation going by modifying our passing theories in favour of our communicant and in this way work to diminish the gap between us. Everything, it appears, is commensurable, because we wish it so.

---

45 Beckett, *Words and Music*, p. 293.

46 Davidson, *Subjective, Intersubjective, Objective*, p. 115.

47 Davidson, *Inquiries into Truth and Interpretation*, p. 197.

48 Davidson, *Subjective, Intersubjective, Objective*, p. 149.

49 Davidson, *Truth, Language and History*, p. 122.

IV

Words and Music, however, presents the inherent dichotomy of such a perspective. The dialogic momentum indicated by the sequence 'WORDS: ... MUSIC: ... WORDS: ...', for instance, encourages the kind of (text-based) supposition we find in Elissa Guralnick's analysis of the play: 'Since conversation implies at least a modicum of mutual understanding, the mere fact that Joe and Bob can talk to one another [suggests that] words have attained the condition of music' and that the two have converged.[50] Such a conclusion, however, is based on a Davidsonian, charitable assumption: only half of the exchange is available to us, and so it is the 'fact' of the conversation that is, in fact, implied. A Guralnick-like reader of the play, in other words, interprets generously, compensating for her lack of knowledge about Music by conjecturing a correspondence between the eponymous characters' 'talk' and charitably reading Words's logic into the utterances – which is to say, the indeterminate improvements and suggestions – of Music. In this, the reader mirrors what Words himself must do. However, if the process of interpretation entails communicators' pragmatic acceptance of what Davidson calls 'a best fit', it follows that they will never fit hand-in-glove, and the more effort they put into tailoring their agreement, the more pronounced will be its slippage. When, at the start of the play, Words and Music are detached and disconnected from the communicative impulse, and thus from each other, their inherent misalignment is of little importance, but this changes as soon as they begin drawing near to one another.

Significantly, it is at the very moment when Words and Music seem to be converging that the material of their union, the 'Age Poem', starts to crack open:

> Age is when to a man
> Huddled o'er the ingle
> Shivering for the hag
> To put the pan in the bed
> And bring the toddy
> She comes in the ashes
> Who loved could not be won
> Or won not loved
> Or some other trouble
> Comes in the ashes
> Like in that old light
> The face in the ashes
> The old starlight
> On the earth again.[51]

---

50 Guralnick, *Sight Unseen*, p. 89.

51 Beckett, *Words and Music*, p. 291.

The poem establishes a tangible sense of presence, partly through the vividness of the verbs – 'huddled' and 'shivering' – and partly through the concrete particularity of 'the pan', 'the bed' and 'the face'. At the same time, however, it is riddled with absence. The man derives no warmth from the fire over which he shivers, its burnt-out ashes serving only to make palpable the lack of heat. He is likewise out of synch with the woman with whom, loving and winning in turn, he never quite merges. Her face is doubly removed, on the one hand there in the ashes, like the memory of some long-extinguished passion, and on the other looking down on him with a chilly, distant starlight gaze. This disjunction is reflected in the syntactic void around which the poem revolves, the undefined 'when' that, as we saw above, continually delays the delivery of meaning concerning what 'age is'. Eventually, this elongated metaphor on age recedes even from itself. In his discussion of metaphor, the philosopher Paul Ricoeur stated that any 'shift from literal to figurative sense [is] a metaphor' and that to 'speak by means of metaphor is to say something different 'through' some literal meaning'.[52] Davidson adds that 'the literal meaning [of a metaphor is] latent … while the figurative meaning carries the direct load'.[53] Here, however, the literal meaning becomes dominant as the poem, increasingly fixated on the face, becomes absorbed in the ashes. Age is hardly expressed 'through' these images, for they chiefly express themselves, and when a shift is again made to a metaphoric meaning, what is shown in the starlight is not age but 'the face'. In attempting to grasp it, in other words, the poem slips past its ostensible subject matter, as though they were irreconcilably misaligned. This fissuring of the word surface serves, finally, to emphasize the glaring gap at the heart of the play, which in turn becomes a stark reminder of the disjunctive relations between all communicants. Such inherent out-of-tuneness, along with the attempts to overcome this essential misalignment, is, finally, writ large in the play's juxtaposition of its two very different forms of expression, music and words.

V

A discussion of the ontological distinction between words and music, let alone an attempt to define each, is beyond the scope of this chapter. If verbal and musical meaning, however, are agreed to be encoded in essentially different ways, it follows that the characters Music and Words fundamentally lack each other's codes. A brief example, concerning the 'long la' played by Music, should serve to demonstrate this. In the correlation between the letter 'A', the speech sound 'la' and a tone measured at the frequency of 440Hz, a particular note, as we have seen, can not only be identified but also positioned within a scale pattern, and in this way the verbal and the musical are merged. Yet this equation also demonstrates their separateness, since that which unites them is the very thing that sunders them.

[52] Paul Ricoeur, *The Rule of Metaphor*, trans. Robert Czerny (London, 1986), p. 188.

[53] Davidson, *Inquiries into Truth and Interpretation*, p. 250.

'A' is the first letter of the alphabet, but when transposed to the neutral, default key of C it is the sixth note. What is more, it can denote anything from the first to the seventh note of a scale, depending on the particular keynote. Its identity slips, in this way, as it moves from one context to another, and what is revealed, in this rather literal manner, is the incommensurability of music and words. The attempt, as here, to translate the signs of the one by the signs of the other results in slippage: the letters of the alphabet cannot quite tune in, as it were, to the notes of the musical scale. This is not to deny that the two may interact – *Words and Music* does, after all, trace their efforts to do just this – but merely to suggest that each system may recognize, and yet not fully decipher, the meaning of the other. As such, the pairing of words and music enacts an extreme example of the radical interpretation necessary to, but unable completely to effect, communication.

Words and Music effectively pulls the rug out from under itself in this way, by demonstrating the leap of faith that is made in every act of communication. If Davidson chooses to highlight the ability of communicative good will to maximize communicants' sense of convergence – which in turn suggests that everything they encounter may ultimately be subsumed within their conceptual schemes – Beckett is more circumspect, pointing towards the gaping obstacles that are ignored in the effort to achieve this convergence. While this may, in relation to Davidson's optimism, seem a pessimistic position, I would argue that it is merely pragmatic. *Words and Music* recognizes the gap between different modes of communication; what is more, it acknowledges and delineates the impulse to bridge that gap. For Morton Feldman – whose composition for the part of Music demonstrates just this gapful quality – communication stems not from 'mutual understanding' but rather from a situation in which 'people don't understand each other … because then … an effort is being made'.[54]

An awareness of this incommensurability lies behind the most common kind of analysis of the musical aspect of the play, which views Music not as an indeterminate, unknown communicant – nor, indeed, as bodied forth by any of the actual compositions written and performed for the play – but as the representative of a philosophical notion of music: specifically, the notion developed by Arthur Schopenhauer, for whom music is 'the most direct, intuitive form of access to an underlying reality which is essentially resistant to discursive articulation'.[55] This critical approach is typified, on the one hand, by Martin Esslin's contrast between a 'verbal [i.e. rational] … [and] a musical (i.e. emotional) stream of consciousness'[56] and, on the other, by the opposition Eric Prieto draws between words, 'which, having a *post rem* relationship to phenomena, can never fully express them', and music, which has an '*ante rem* access to unmediated reality' but 'cannot …

54 Feldman, *Morton Feldman Says*, p. 59.

55 Andrew Bowie, *Music, Philosophy and Modernity* (Cambridge, 2007), p. 121.

56 Martin Esslin, *Mediations: Essays on Brecht, Beckett and the Media* (London, 1980), p. 136.

name that which it expresses'.[57] Such interpretations build on Schopenhauer's observation that 'concepts are the *universalia post rem*, while music gives the *universalia ante rem*'.[58]

As a justification for this line of interpretation, critics of *Words and Music* tend to point to the influence of Schopenhauer on Beckett's early prose works, in particular the novel *Dream of Fair to Middling Women* (1932) – which may be read as an attempt to realize, in literary form, Schopenhauer's aesthetics of music – and the monograph *Proust* (1931), in which music is described in Schopenhauerian terms as 'the Idea itself, unaware of the world of phenomena ... ideal and invisible'.[59] While such theoretical, textualized analysis certainly recognizes a vital difference between words and music, it nevertheless confers on the latter a singular, ontologically consistent value that is at odds with Beckett's own understanding of music, an understanding that ranged from the theoretical to a lifelong and deep engagement with the practice of music.[60] He played the piano throughout his life and sometimes sang, he tried his hand at composing, and he devoted a great deal of time to listening to musical performances, often comparing different recordings of the same piece. It should therefore be clear, as Catherine Laws points out, that for Beckett, 'music is not simply "Music" ... but rather a huge muddle of musics'.[61] The singular value extracted from Schopenhauer's thinking is also at odds with the way in which Beckett's use of music developed in his work. A conceptual analysis may suit his early prose, in which music does, indeed, feature as an abstract, idealized entity; but it will not suffice for works calling, as very many of his later plays do, for the incorporation of real, performed music. It must, in short, be unadvisable to extract from *Dream of Fair to Middling*

---

57 Prieto, *Listening In*, pp. 216, 227.

58 Arthur Schopenhauer, *The World as Will and Representation*, trans. Judith Norman and Alistair Welchman, ed. Christopher Janaway, Judith Norman and Alistair Welchman (Cambridge, 2010), vol. 1, p. 291. Schopenhauer draws on the medieval problem of universals. The concepts of the human mind, which were held to be posterior to the things they represent, were known as *universalia post rem*, or universals after the thing; while divine ideas – answering to the ideal essences of Plato's Forms or Ideas – were *universalia ante rem*, or universals before the thing. Arguing that music possesses a 'universal language', Schopenhauer writes that it 'gives the *universalia ante rem*' by 'provid[ing] the innermost kernel, prior to all form – the heart of things' (ibid.).

59 Ibid., vol. 1, p. 92; for a critical examination of the 'muffled' nature of this supposed influence, see John Pilling, '*Proust* and Schopenhauer: Music and Shadows', in Mary Bryden (ed.), *Samuel Beckett and Music* (Oxford, 1998), pp. 173–8.

60 It also ignores Schopenhauer's sensible warning that, for 'a man [to] assent with genuine conviction to the explanation of the significance of music here to be given, ... he should often listen to music' (*World as Will and Representation*, vol. 1, 257).

61 Catherine Laws, 'Music in *Words and Music*: Feldman's Response to Beckett's Play', in Angela Moorjani and Carola Viet (eds), *Samuel Becket: Endlessness in the Year 2000, Samuel Beckett Today/Aujourd'hui* 11 (Amsterdam and New York, 2001), pp. 279–90 (p. 280).

Women and *Proust* a textual articulation of music and apply it to a work, written 30 years later, that requires music to be sounded. Certainly, any notion – rejected by Laws – that *Words and Music* treats Music 'as a pure idea', 'the same in any realization',[62] is directly contradicted both by the open-ended, collaborative nature of the play and by its staging of Words and Music's perpetual struggle to understand each other.

VI

This discussion of *Words and Music* opened by arguing against a purely textual interpretation of the play, on the grounds that such a reading will either explain the character of Music away in metaphysical terms or conclude that any compositional realization of it has already been decided by the text. It is with good reason that Stephen Benson asks why 'critics are content to interpret a play explicitly concerned with [the] relation [of music and the spoken word] without hearing a note of music and to interpret not only its conceptual framework, but also its content', but the answer is surely not, as Benson concludes, simply that 'Beckett makes relatively clear the conceptual underpinning of Music, and so allows the part to be read without being heard'.[63] That underpinning, as we have seen, is commonly understood in Schopenhauerian terms, terms that lead Benson to view music as 'an objectifying art, called upon to enact abstract categories of human feeling'.[64] However, while Schopenhauer writes that 'melodies are … like universal concepts',[65] Feldman states that universal music is a cliché, and since it is a Feldman, rather than a Schopenhauer, who is invited to fill the play's Music-shaped, musically undefined gaps, it seems abundantly clear that an abstract, prescribed notion of music is not what is required. *Words and Music* exists, of course, as a published text and may legitimately be received as such. Subtitled 'A Piece for Radio', however, it is at the same time designed to be performed and so is incomplete until acoustically joined by composed music. I would argue that whatever meaning the play has resides, on the one hand, in the unknowability of Music when the play is silently read and, on the other, in the actual coming together of text and composition. In place of a purely textual interpretation I propose, in brief, this two-fold, continually inconclusive perspective.

It would, for this reason, be to radically misunderstand the play if one were to argue, as Guy Debrock does, that 'Beckett provides for the music to be in the form of words' and that his 'word-gestures [are] by themselves sufficient clues'

62 Ibid., p. 279.

63 Stephen Benson, 'Beckett, Feldman, Joe and Bob: Speaking of Music in *Words and Music*', in Suzanne M. Lodato and David Francis Urrow (eds), *Essays on Music and the Spoken Word and on Surveying the Field* (Amsterdam, 2005), p. 166.

64 Ibid., p. 169.

65 Schopenhauer, *World as Will and Representation*, p. 291.

to a composer, who '"merely" [has] to actualize Beckett's virtual music'.[66] By accepting at face value what Prieto terms the 'semantic muteness of Music'[67] and by giving the last word on the subject to the musical indications of the text, such an interpretation would reduce the play to a stable, fully authorized and thus fully interpretable script. This, however, brushes aside the problematic fact that Music, on the page, is an unknown quantity – whose 'muteness' may invite, but ultimately resists, charitable actualization – and, in performance, is an actual, individual participant in an evolving communicative event. More precisely, the character of Music is, at any one moment, the sum total of a particular composition and its particular realization – the specific communicative efforts, in other words, of a composer and a group of musicians – as it encounters and engages with the Words of Beckett's text. Since this sum total is necessarily different in each such performed encounter, it makes no sense to talk of a static, virtual music. Any discussion of the incommensurability of music and words must instead consider the practical problems of their actual interaction. Everett Frost points out that 'whenever the score varies, the play varies'.[68] I would go further and argue that the play varies even when the score or particular performer remains the same.[69] Structurally, *Words and Music* requires a real act of communication not only to take place, but to continue taking place from production to production, which in turn necessitates new, evolving and passing theories of interpretation from its participants. Words tries to sing in accordance with Music, but, however well he refines his passing theory for one particular dialogic partner, the next will demand of him a new theory. What, in short, is presented by *Words and Music* is the never stable, never conclusive nature of communication, the slightly-out-of-tune relation between communicants, and their continual, arguably bootless yet always optimistic, struggle to bridge the gap between them.

---

66 Guy Debrock, 'The Word Man and the Note Man: Morton Feldman and Beckett's Virtual Music', in Lois Oppenheim (ed.), *Samuel Beckett and the Arts: Music, Visual Arts and Non-Print Media* (New York, 1999), pp. 67–82 (pp. 79–80).

67 Prieto, *Listening In*, p. 218.

68 Everett C. Frost, Preface to Samuel Beckett, *'All That Fall' and Other Plays for Radio and Screen* (London, 2009), pp. vii–xxiii (p. xi).

69 Morton Feldman's Music thus appears in two recordings of the play – by Voices International and Westdeutscher Rundfunk (1996) – while Patrick Magee portrayed Words in both the BBC's and Katherine Worth's productions. Two very different performances are the result in each case, due to the two very different interactions between the characters.

Chapter 5
Atonality and Eternity: The Musical Language of *Comédie*

David Foster

In January 1966, in a studio on the Rue Mouffetard in Paris, a small cast and crew came together to produce a highly unusual piece of cinema. Filmmaker Marin Karmitz, theatre director Jean-Marie Serreau, film editor Jean Ravel, sound engineer Luc Perini, and actors Eléonore Hirt, Michael Lonsdale and Delphine Seyrig, collaborated with the writer and dramatist Samuel Beckett to create a screen adaptation of the latter's stageplay, *Comédie*. Directing the project was the Romanian-born, French-raised Karmitz, a graduate of the prestigious Paris film school, IDHEC, an acolyte of the *nouvelle vague*, whose aesthetics were also being shaped by the work of other eminent exponents of late modernism in mid-1960s Paris: the music of Pierre Boulez, the paintings of Jean Dubuffet and the novels of Marguerite Duras.[1] The latter had written the script for his first major directorial project, the short film *Nuit Noire Calcutta* (1964). Filming on *Comédie* lasted around a fortnight, and Beckett, who was present throughout, seems to have had a significant hand in the work's creation, not least because he had already spent a great deal of time rehearsing the same cast for *Comédie*'s stage production.[2] After a lengthy editing process with which Beckett was also closely involved, the completed film received a largely unfavourable reception at its Venice Film Festival premiere, following which it appears to have been more or less forgotten and not seen publicly again until June 2000 when it was shown at the Musée d'Art Moderne de la Ville de Paris as part of a group show called 'Voilà, le monde dans la tête'. An exhibition at the Anthony Reynolds Gallery in London followed in December 2000, and the film has subsequently been shown widely in several exhibitions in Europe and beyond.[3]

---

1 Karmitz discusses these influences and others in Marin Karmitz and Elisabeth Lebovici, 'Entretien', in Caroline Bourgeois (ed.), *Comédie* (Paris, 2001), pp. 14–25.

2 Jean-Marie Serreau was the putative director of the Paris production of *Comédie*, but, as James Knowlson recounts in his biography of Beckett, Serreau was often preoccupied with other aspects of the heterogeneous bill that *Comédie* was part of, and Beckett was left to rehearse the cast 'practically single-handed'. Given Beckett's exacting nature and the rigours of the play, it is perhaps not surprising that it took 'nearly four months of rehearsals' for *Comédie* to meet Beckett's demanding standards. See James Knowlson, *Damned to Fame: The Life of Samuel Beckett* (London, 1996), p. 515.

3 The film is not commercially available. My thanks to Galerie Carlier Gebauer for allowing me to view a copy of the film.

Since its re-emergence, scholars have provided insightful overviews of the film,[4] examining issues around its adaptation and its relation to the theatrical original,[5] as well as exploring its formal and spatial structure.[6] This chapter also engages with issues of form and structure but does so specifically in order to address one of *Comédie*'s most striking expressive aspects, an aspect that can be broadly described as its musicality. The study is predominantly concerned with drawing an analogy between the film's images, structures and sounds, and recognized musical forms and language – specifically, the language of atonality. This gives rise to an exploration of the semantics of atonality in relation to the film. Finally, I suggest that this atonal language is incorporated into a style and patterning that is characteristic of aspects of musical Minimalism.

The original stage version of *Comédie* is, of course, the French translation of Beckett's *Play*, the mise-en-scène of which consists solely of three funerary urns lined up side by side, from whose mouths three heads protrude: a man (M) in the centre, and a woman on each side (W1 and W2), all facing front. Situated at floor level between the urns and the audience is a spotlight that moves between the faces of the three protagonists, which sometimes splits in three to illuminate them simultaneously. The figures speak when, only when and always when their faces are illuminated by the spotlight, and their lines are delivered at a 'rapid tempo throughout'.[7] *Play* is divided into three distinct sections which Beckett described as the Chorus, the Narration and the Meditation.[8] In the Chorus, all three protagonists are illuminated and so speak their 'largely unintelligible'[9] lines together. In the next section, the Narration, each takes it in turn to relate her/his own perspective on a series of events in which they were involved. The story related is a typical narrative of adultery: the man is married to one of the women, conducts an affair with the other, confesses his dalliance to his wife but fails to leave his mistress, then disappears completely. Both wife and mistress believe that he has ended up with the other. In the final section, the Meditation, the protagonists reflect on the

---

4 See Michael Glasmeier and Gaby Hartel, '"Three Grey Disks": Samuel Beckett's Forgotten Film, *Comédie*', in Bourgeois (ed.), *Comédie*, pp. 77–85; Graley Herren, 'Different Music: Karmitz and Beckett's Film Adaptation of *Comédie*', *Journal of Beckett Studies* NS 18/1–2 (2009): 10–31.

5 See Graley Herren, *Samuel Beckett's Plays on Film and Television* (Basingstoke, 2007), ch. 8.

6 See David Foster, 'Spatial Aesthetics in the Film Adaptation of Samuel Beckett's *Comédie*', *Screen* 53/2 (2012): 105–17; id., 'Becoming Present, Becoming Absent: Movement and Visual Form in the Film Adaptation of *Comédie*', *Journal of Beckett Studies* NS 21/2 (2012): 157–80.

7 Samuel Beckett, *Play*, in *The Complete Dramatic Works* (London, 1986), p. 307.

8 It was in conversation with Martin Esslin in 1966 that Beckett labelled the three sections in this way (see Martin Esslin, *Mediations: Essays on Brecht, Beckett, and the Media* (London, 1980), p. 139).

9 Beckett, *Play*, p. 307.

circumstances in which we see them – compelled to speak by the spotlight – and on the aftermath of the affair. All three sections are then repeated, and Beckett gives the option to repeat the three sections exactly or to introduce an element of variation relating to the strength of the light and the characters' voices, and/or the order in which the lines are delivered.

Critics have long approached readings of Beckett's *Play* in musical terms. As Maurice Blackman notes, 'nearly all commentators rely sooner or later on musical terminology or musical analogy in discussing *Play*. [It is] a piece of chamber music, as it were, cast in a rondo form and deploying language in a distinctly musical way.'[10] The film adaptation of *Comédie*, whilst radically different in many respects, does retain all of the stage version's musical elements, whilst adding a crucial medium-specific aspect, that of montage.[11] Indeed, whilst the musical elements of the stage version derive almost entirely from the vocal content and vocal structure of the play, one of the driving principles of this chapter is the proposition that in the film version one of the primary ways in which we experience not only those vocal elements, but also the visual content and structure and the interplay between the two, is closely comparable or even tantamount to the manner in which we experience music.

The objection immediately arises that 'the manner in which we experience music' is not only extremely complex but also highly contested, so let us clarify the kind of response being referred to. To refer to *Comédie*'s musicality is to refer, initially, to a response that is primarily physiological, as opposed to intellectual, analytical or theoretical. As Michael Glasmeier and Gaby Hartel suggest, the 'purely phonetic sound poetry' of *Comédie*'s mostly indecipherable speech works in tandem with the dynamic and 'rhythmic montage of the images' to stimulate a response that 'gets a grip on the viewer's "nervous system"'.[12] Of course, a physiological stimulus is not necessarily musical, but the specific content of *Comédie*'s tableaux, and the montage of those tableaux, imbues the piece with a manifest sense of musicality. Specifically, the sparse tableaux that make up all of the film's images – three monochrome figures, each comprising a funerary urn from which a talking head protrudes, depicted at varying depths in relation to both the frame and each other – embody an interplay of distinct and clearly delineated elements of repetition and variation, both in terms of the composition of each individual arrangement and in contraposition to every other arrangement in the film. That is to say, all of the film's tableaux are different versions of the same pattern, variations on a theme: figures suspended in an apparently infinite space, each of whom has clearly discernible but fluctuating spatial relations to two other figures with near-identical attributes and similarly discernible but fluctuating

---

10 Maurice Blackman, 'The Shaping of a Beckett Text: *Play*', *Journal of Beckett Studies* os 10 (1985): 87–107 (p. 88).

11 There is not the space here to describe the many differences between film and play. Useful sources include the essays by Herren cited above.

12 Glasmeier and Hartel, '"Three Grey Disks"', p. 7.

spatial relations to the frame inside which it is depicted. It is this aesthetic impression – that the mise-en-scène of the film is composed only and entirely out of these sparse, shifting differential relations – that gives rise to a primary experience of the montage that is commensurable or even homologous with the way in which we experience music.

The idea that it is not just aural but visual material that can produce a musical effect is not new: film theorists from Eisenstein to Deleuze have written of the visual music of montage. As one scholar paraphrases the latter in an article on the former's resonance with Beckett: 'Film montage, as a system, creates a mechanism that "invades" the nervous system by creating what may be called shock waves, to which the body responds by mapping its rhythms, as in the bodily response to the feelings evoked by music.'[13] But how might this immediate, somatic way of experiencing the work be explored in a scholarly context? Short of examining a viewer's actual physiological response to the work, we must, conversely, return to a mode of analytical, theoretical discourse and, specifically, a mode of analogical discourse. In fact, it is axiomatic that an analogical mode of one kind or another is unavoidable when using a different medium – in this case verbal language – to describe music: the attempt to represent it in another form, regardless of whether analogy or metaphor is conspicuously employed, can only ever point towards a *likeness* of the music itself.

The analogical mode of the present study works to equate *Comédie*'s visual, vocal and structural material with musical parallels, with the result that an extensive translation of the piece into an entirely musical framework is described. A large part of this translation is founded on a suggestion that the language and structure that the film employs to stimulate an initially physiological response may be considered analogous to the defining characteristic of atonal music, namely, the absence of a tonal centre. The analogy is followed through to suggest that the semantics of such atonality – most notably the expression of a refusal of conclusivity and arrival – might be understood to reflect the semantics that permeate *Comédie*. Having constructed a detailed impression of the film as music, the study concludes by suggesting that the piece's atonality is incorporated into a style and patterning redolent of certain strains of musical Minimalism, on account of its highly repetitive patterning and reductive tonal palette. Further, I suggest that the overall music of the piece might even be understood to embody a kind of transition between these two major tendencies within twentieth-century music: atonality and Minimalism.

The chapter's methodology, then, encompasses a twin approach. It attempts to point towards the film's tangible musical affectivity: that is, it tries to account for a partly synaesthetic response in which one might 'hear' both its visual

[13] Jean Antoine-Dunne, 'Beckett and Eisenstein on Light and Contrapuntal Montage', in Angela Moorjani and Carola Viet (eds), *Samuel Becket: Endlessness in the Year 2000, Samuel Beckett Today/Aujourd'hui* 11 (Amsterdam and New York, 2001): 315–23 (pp. 320–21).

and its aural material as music. In order to do this, it also comprises a partially imaginative exercise (on the part of both writer and reader) whereby the film's material is theoretically translated into musical parallels, such that one might recreate, either mentally or in actuality, the music thus described. Like any interpretation, the study does not claim to offer objective understanding; rather its modus operandi is one of suggestion. The musical parallels are no more than propositions that work to intimate (indeed cannot do more than intimate) a musical experience of the film. Since the methodological status of the analogy is suggestive in this way, its semantic implications – which chiefly result from the conceit of comparing the film's visual and aural aesthetic to that of musical atonality – take on a similar status. That is, the interpretive possibilities that are outlined do not purport to rest on any kind of stable foundation. Instead, the analogy and its interpretive implications are suspended, rather like the figures themselves, reflecting the film's own open-endedness. In fact, I want to suggest that the critical value of the chapter might be found not merely in the discussion of eternality that it alights on – a subject which has been discussed at length in countless studies of Beckett's work – but particularly in the method this study proposes: the journey rather than the arrival remains the main locus of significance, again reflecting the work under discussion. The method illuminates a range of both productive and problematic aspects inherent to a discourse that translates aesthetic forms between a triumvirate of media – image, sound and the written word – in several combinations. It comprises a heuristic and somewhat experimental mode of analysis in which music, analogy and theory are combined to think systematically about the composition and structure of a cinematic work, both as a whole and in its various constituent parts.

An Analogy between Image and Music

We can begin to formulate the analogy by making the straightforward suggestion that the appearance of a figure on screen is analogous to the sounding of a single note, the duration of the note equating to the duration of the figure's appearance in one position. So when all three are depicted on screen at the same time, this is analogous to the simultaneous sounding of three notes, in other words, a three-note chord. The figures are near-identical in their basic appearance, in that they all comprise the same basic shape, visual texture and chromaticity, and so, despite some facial differences, it seems reasonable to suggest that the basic tone-colour or texture of all three notes is also close to being identical (the implications of the figures not always being depicted with their urns is addressed in due course). Where the figures obviously differ from each other is in their positioning: their spacing in relation to one another and in relation to the frame of the screen. Let us posit these differential spatial relations as analogous to differential musical relations of *pitch*.

The configuration in which the three figures are first depicted – at equal size, in a line with a narrow interval of empty space between each urn – is replicated

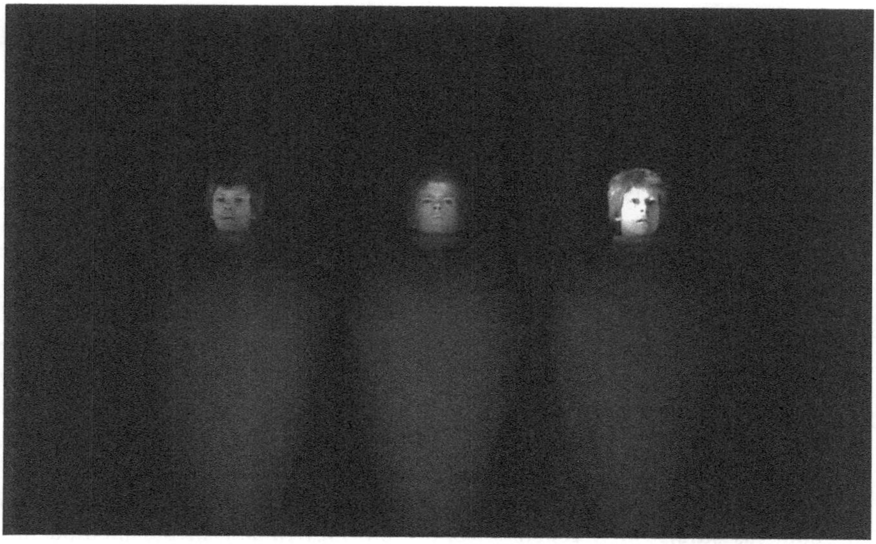

Figure 5.1 Still from Samuel Beckett and Marin Karmitz, *Comédie*, 1966. 35mm film transferred to DVD; 18.43 mins. Courtesy of Marin Karmitz

as the figures' depicted magnitude increases, at six different scales in total. The proportions of the tableau are maintained in its replication: that is, the spacing between the figures stays the same whenever they are shown depicted in this visually balanced way (which they always are until, in the second section of the film, we see them depicted at different depths in relation to each other). Let us call this configuration the 'basic tableau' or, rather, the 'basic chord' of the piece (see Figure 5.1).

In considering what kind of chord we might compare this 'basic tableau' to, for obvious reasons, a triad of some kind immediately suggests itself: the term 'triad' occasionally referring to any chord of three notes, but almost always used in music to designate 'a chord of three notes, consisting of a given note with the third and fifth above it. The third may be major or minor, the fifth perfect, augmented or diminished.'[14] Evidently, there is a clear interval between the three figures in every instance of the basic chord and, importantly, both intervals are of equal width and remain proportionally the same throughout, suggesting that the triad we might compare this image to would be one with equal intervals between its first and third notes and its third and fifth notes. So what kind of triad has intervals of equal width between notes? There are two main possibilities: an augmented triad, which has an interval of four semitones between notes and is thus composed of a major third and an augmented fifth; and a diminished triad, which has an interval

[14] *Oxford English Dictionary*, online edn, June 2013, <http://www.oed.com/>, s.v. 'Triad'.

of three semitones between notes and is thus composed of a minor third and a diminished fifth. Additionally of course, we could choose instead to analogize the tableau to a three-note chord that is not triadic in the usual sense, and posit an interval between notes of one, two, five or more semitones instead. However, it is to the characteristics of a diminished triad which, in forging a productive analogy, the tableau can be most meaningfully compared.

A diminished triad comprises a tonic, a minor third and a diminished fifth. This last note, the diminished fifth, gives the defining interval of the chord, which is also known as a tritone, because the interval is three whole tones from the tonic. Deryck Cooke writes:

> The interval between the tonic and the sharp fourth [i.e. the diminished fifth] should normally act as a modulation to the dominant [i.e. the perfect fifth]; but when it is exposed without any resolution of any kind, and becomes an 'essential' note, a tension in its own right … it acts as a 'flaw' which destroys the integrity of the tonic key – thus removing the music outside the categories of human joy and sorrow inherent in the major and minor systems.[15]

This is the defining characteristic of the diminished triad that makes for a fitting and apposite comparison with the 'basic tableau' of the film's three figures. It allows us to denote the three tones of a triad to the figures, without any of those notes being a tonal centre. So, from left to right across the triad, we can denote F2[16] as the tonic, H as the minor third, and F1 as the diminished fifth, and yet each of the three notes is of equal status, is a 'tension in its own right'. This engenders an 'atonal equilibrium'[17] between all three tones, and, as in the notes of the dodecaphonic scale of Arnold Schoenberg's atonal system, the three figures 'become equal in their structural standing'.[18] Indeed, one scholar writes of this idea as nothing less than 'a definite conclusion: Any tendency for a tonality to emerge may be avoided by introducing a note three whole tones distant from the key note of that tonality.'[19] It follows that we could denote the triad from right to left instead, and the analogy would remain unchanged: the interval between F1 and F2 will be that of a tritone regardless of which is denoted as the tonic and which as the diminished fifth, and without any tonal centre to the piece, and without other tones outside those of the diminished triad, the designations of the tones are emptied of exterior reference.

Crucially though, the three tones of a diminished triad remain meaningful in relation to each other. For although the analogy bestows equal status upon all three

---

15 Deryck Cooke, *The Language of Music* (Oxford, 1959), p. 84.

16 The figures' designations – which stand for 'Homme', 'Femme 1' and 'Femme 2' – are taken from the playscript (Samuel Beckett, *Comédie et actes divers* (Paris, 1972), p. 9).

17 Reginald Smith Brindle, *Serial Composition* (Oxford, 1966), p. 66.

18 Bryan Simms, *The Atonal Music of Arnold Schoenberg, 1908–1923* (Oxford, 2000), p. 28.

19 Ibid.

figures, the basic facts of a triad's spacing mean that, clearly, the three notes do not quite all share the same tensions. Each figure/note shares a tension, a relationship, with the other two, but whilst H shares an identical tension – a minor third – with both F1 and F2, they share a different tension with each other, namely a tritone. If we consider what we know about the actual text of *Play*, or perhaps the simple fact that in the film we can identify what the figures' genders are, the structure of these dynamics makes sense: the relationship between H and F1 and the parallel relationship between H and F2 are characterized by the same tension, whilst the relationship between F1 and F2 is characterized by a quite different tension. It seems particularly apposite that the minor third is an interval of consonance, whilst the tritone – an interval equal to two minor thirds – is one of dissonance. Such relations reflect those of the figures' fraught 'eternal triangle'. That is, in terms of our whole chord, it is as though the intervals between H and each of the Fs are both set up in perpetuity as relations of *potential* consonance, but that because of the equally perpetual presence of the other F completing the triad, this potential consonance of the minor third is always disrupted by the dissonant tritone interval; thus we never 'hear' the consonant minor third, and only dissonance is expressed through the tensions between the figures themselves. The overall piece however, as it comprises only the three notes of the diminished triad, expresses no consonance or dissonance, but is entirely atonal.

How, then, does the analogy account for the changes in the depicted position of the figures? If we consider that the figures are essentially static upon a single diegetic plane, whilst the camera's images engender the variations in the depicted magnitude of the figures,[20] then the six manifestations of this 'basic chord' are in one aspect unchanging – namely, in the static relation between the figures/notes themselves – and in one aspect subject to variation, that is, in their changing relation to the framing camera. So, in what does the variation consist? Considering that we have analogized differences of tonal pitch with the spacing of the figures along the screen's horizontal axis, it would perhaps seem to follow that the differentiation in the figures' relation to the camera – the differentiation in their magnitude in relation to the frame along the axis of depth – should be analogized to a separate quality of the note. The quality of volume (as in amplitude) immediately suggests itself, especially as the figures do, in the way in which we perceive them, increase and decrease in magnitudinal volume along the axis of depth. But whilst such a comparison would perhaps be possible, it is also conceivable to analogize the figures' variation in their spatial relation to the frame in terms of pitch too. The reason that it makes sense to do this is because 'what has been termed the "basic

[20] The variation in the depicted magnitude of the figures is achieved through post-production editing of the filmed material. Sometimes, parts of one frame are interpolated within another, arguably creating the cubist-like impression of a single plane seen perspectivally. The result can still be understood to constitute 'the camera's images', even though such photographic vision is radically different to that seen in more conventional cinema. See Foster, 'Spatial Aesthetics'.

miracle of music", namely, the octave',[21] means that pitch can be understood to possess two different expressive attributes, to operate, in a sense, in two different dimensions: that of 'pitch height', which is 'used to refer to perceived musical pitch that occurs independent of the octave',[22] and that of 'pitch chroma', which 'refers to the perceived musical pitch of corresponding notes across octaves'.[23]

We can therefore posit that each one of the figures is denoted by one particular chromatic value, and this denotation does not change; however, the *octaval* pitch of the note – the pitch height – does change, and this is dictated by the figures' depicted placement upon the continuum of depth. In terms of our musical analogy then, the camera operates both as a kind of conductor (a mode of musical direction that has often been brought to bear on the interpretation of *Play*, among other Beckett works[24]) and as a kind of composer/transposer, as a modulator of frequency and also a controller of the pace and rhythm at which these different frequencies are sounded. The figures in one sense remain the same, each remaining forever characterized by the same essential chromatic value, but are transposed octavally by the frequency modulation of the framing camera. Ernst Levy describes this kind of transposition effectively: 'Here are two tones, different, yet so alike that we call them by the same name, taking them to form an identity – a peculiar, unique sort of identity: two and yet one':[25] different and yet the same. So, whilst every one of the film's tableaux that depicts all three figures is analogous to the sounding of a diminished triad, with the intervallic tensions remaining unchanged, the tonal tensions are subject to variation. We can turn to Levy again to illustrate the point, who describes the triad as 'the second "miracle of music"',[26] continuing:

> Every interval name has a twofold meaning: it points both to a character and a distance. The term *third*, for instance, designates, on one hand, a distance: it is the third (diatonic) tone from a starting point. It also designates, on the other hand, a relationship between two tones. If one of the tones is transposed by an octave, away from the other tones [then] the melodic relation has changed. Not so the harmonic relation. A third remains a third at whatever octave distance the tones might be placed.[27]

In this way it might be suggested that the camera's ability to give an impression or illusion of depth to two-dimensional space is analogous here to the manner in

---

21 Ernst Levy, *A Theory of Harmony* (Albany, NY, 1985), p. 53.

22 E. Bruce Goldstein, *Encyclopedia of Perception* (London, 2010), vol. 1, p. 152.

23 Ibid.

24 See Thomas Mansell, 'Different Music: Beckett's Theatrical Conduct', in Marius Buning et al. (eds), *Historicising Beckett/Issues of Performance*, *Samuel Beckett Today/Aujourd'hui* 15 (Amsterdam and New York, 2005), pp. 225–39.

25 Levy, *A Theory of Harmony*, 54.

26 Ibid.

27 Ibid.

which octave transpositions of tone give an impression of depth to music. Thus the montage of the film embodies, or 'enfigures', a form of relational motion: a musical motion in which no thing moves. This is what we see, or 'hear', in *Comédie*: dynamic movement without the displacement of objects, a 'pure motion' or, rather, a purely relational motion. Of course, montage can often express this kind of musical motion, although arguably seldom with the 'purity' that is achieved in *Comédie* through the spareness of its mise-en-scène.

Such an approach might be further consolidated by considering more closely the range of planes upon which the figures are depicted, and noting that the figures' depiction is restricted to only a handful of specific planes along the axis of depth. Moreover, there is always a considerable differential between each of the planes upon which they are seen. In all, there are nine different planes. As well as the six planes on which the 'basic tableau' appears, there are an additional three planes, depicting figures in three different magnitudes of close-up (and without their urns: a point discussed in due course). All of the planes that are occupied in the frames showing figures upon two different planes simultaneously can also be matched to these nine planes. So, analogously this dictates that the piece is played out across a nine-octave range, a frequency range which, appositely in terms of our analogy, spans almost the whole auditory range of human hearing (which is, of course, also the range within which all music is composed and experienced). To be exact, 'frequencies audible to the average human ear are in the range between 20 and 20,000Hz'.[28] Given that an octave transposition consists in a doubling or halving of frequency, the range of average human hearing can be calculated as being a little short of ten octaves (a ten octave range would span from 20 to 20,480Hz).

Another way to approach this idea is through the identification of a structural motif of doubling in the spacing of the triad in terms of both its intervallic tensions along the horizontal axis and its tonal tensions along the axis of depth. That is, the intervallic value of a minor third is doubled to give a tritone, which gives the unchanging intervallic tensions of our diminished triad. A tritone symmetrically divides the octave, so a doubling of its interval produces an octave interval. An octave interval is defined by its ratio of 2:1: that is, a frequency is doubled or halved to transpose it up or down by an octave, and this doubling and halving is made manifest along the continuum of depth to give the different octaval frequencies, the variable tonal tensions, of the piece. The tensions between the notes remain defined by the same ratio, but upon the screen's horizontal axis, this ratio applies to the intervallic tensions, whereas, upon the screen's axis of depth, the ratio applies to the tonal tensions.

It should be noted that an analogy based on this series of octaval transpositions is not logically perfect in terms of the change in the figures' depicted size. Were it an ideal comparison, the figures would of course halve and double in their depicted size along the nine planes picked out of the continuum. Clearly this is not quite the case, so the analogy represents an interpretive strategy that partially imposes a

[28] Dipak Basu (ed.), *Dictionary of Pure and Applied Physics* (London, 2001), p. 151.

Figure 5.2 Still from Samuel Beckett and Marin Karmitz, *Comédie*, 1966. 35mm film transferred to DVD; 18.43 mins. Courtesy Marin Karmitz

meaningful musical structure onto that of the film, as opposed to one that precisely mirrors the film's images. Arguably, this slight mismatch is justifiable in terms of the interpretive ideas that the analogy proposes.

The next question that presents itself concerns the direction of the frequency continuum. We can address this by considering what frequency actually is: namely the number of wave cycles completed over a given time, the difference between high and low frequencies being that the former completes more wave cycles over a given time than the latter. So, if we treat the camera as the modulator of frequency, then the length of time it takes to complete a cycle between modulator and modulated will shorten as the proximity between the frame of the camera and the figures increases, and thus the images of greatest apparent magnitude, the extreme close-ups, are 'heard' as the highest pitched notes in the piece. If we are considering the pitch continuum as the nine octaves that span the range of human hearing, then that is a very shrill pitch indeed, whilst those of the smallest apparent magnitude can be analogized as the notes of lowest pitch.

A coherent idea of how *Comédie*'s images might 'sound' is taking shape, but there are two further analogous qualities to consider: the dynamics (as in loudness) of the notes, and the texture/timbre of the notes. Regarding the former, it is worth turning to Lawrence Marks, an expert in the study of synaesthesia, on the findings of 'sensory psychophysical experiments':

> When the reader or listener encounters a synesthetic metaphor, a metaphor of light and sound, the loudness tends to imply a perceptually equivalent level

> of brightness, or the brightness a perceptually equivalent level of loudness, in accordance with an implicit or explicit sensory correspondence between these two instantiations of intensity.[29]

Let us then go along with this straightforward conclusion that 'there is a synesthetic association between brightness and loudness' and consider the relative intensity of light to equate with the relative intensity of amplitude: the brighter the image, the louder the note.[30] In order to confirm such an equation, we only have to consider that if a figure were not illuminated at all, it would not be visible on screen, and thus, in our analogy, a note would not sound.

This equation of brightness and loudness proves important in addressing our final analogous quality, that of the notes' timbre, a consideration of which proves rather more complicated. The analogy began by equating the appearance of each figure with the sounding of a note, so it follows that the timbre or texture of this note might be compared to the pictorial content of the figure as it appears on screen. However, whilst the analogous qualities between music and images that we have dealt with so far operate along a continuum, both timbre and pictorial imagery clearly do not. As Roger Scruton notes, 'timbre, and tone-colour generally, presents no parallel system of musical organization, on a par with rhythm, melody and harmony'.[31] This fact helps to demonstrate why the equation of timbre with picture is entirely appropriate, but leaves us with some fairly insurmountable difficulties in terms of describing the specific type of sound with which we might compare the image. However, the way in which the images appear can tell us something quite important about the characteristics of the kind of note to which we might compare them: specifically, when we see a figure or figures appear on, or disappear from, the screen and 'move' between one cut and the next, they do not fade in or fade out (except at the very beginning of the film) but appear or disappear instantaneously. Furthermore, the level of illumination given to the figures frequently varies during a single composition (as the spotlight moves among them): that is, in terms of our analogy, during a single sounding of a chord. We can surmise from both observations that the kind of note to which we might compare the figures would have to be one whose amplitude does not decay (not the kind of sound made by, for example, a piano or other instrument which hammers or plucks a string, instruments which produce a sound which almost instantly decays), in other words, a drone and, furthermore, one that can increase and decrease in amplitude during a single sounding of a note. If we were to consider the physical cause of such a note, many instruments would satisfy these conditions, but such requirements certainly narrow the field and, more importantly, give us a much greater appreciation of the texture of *Comédie*'s 'music'.

[29] Lawrence Marks, 'Synesthesia and the Arts', in W.R. Crozier and A.J. Chapman (eds), *Cogntive Processes in the Perception of Art* (Amsterdam, 1984), pp. 427–59 (p. 436).

[30] Ibid., p. 438.

[31] Roger Scruton, *The Aesthetics of Music* (Oxford, 1997), p. 77.

A further aspect of the figures' appearance tells us something more about the timbre of their analogous sound, that is, the fact that the basic pictorial content of the figures changes and so, therefore, must the timbre of the note. This change consists, of course, in whether a figure is depicted as the juxtaposition of a head and an urn or just as a head, and analogizing this difference in timbre can tell us something about the timbre itself. That is, the head–urn combination can be understood as producing a tone with a more complex texture than the tone produced by the head on its own, and one way in which we might approach the notion of a tone's complexity is by considering the phenomenon of its overtones (and Beckett would no doubt consider the present discussion as exemplifying the 'headaches' among them of which he spoke).[32] It is worth citing two explanations of this phenomenon:

> A tone produced by any musical instrument is not just a single tone, but is a simultaneous spectrum of other less obviously heard tones. These tones are called overtones, also known as harmonics, partial tones, or partials. The first harmonic with the lowest frequency is called the fundamental tone. The fundamental tone is acoustically louder than all the other overtones and determines the pitch of the composite tone.[33]

> Musical sound sources produce a complex amalgam of partial tones that perceptually coalesce as a single tone having a fundamental pitch and a specific timbre, or tone color. The timbre of a complex tone is affected by the number, the frequencies, and the amplitudes of these partial tones.[34]

The incorporation of this factor into the analogy tells us something about the notes' timbre in the following way. Firstly, if we consider that throughout the piece, the urn is always given a markedly lower level of illumination than the heads, then it makes sense to analogize the urn as comprising the note's overtones; the urn being the partials of the tone that sound much more 'quietly' than the head, which we can analogize as the fundamental tone. Secondly, if we consider the urn's relative size compared to the head of the figures, our analogy would dictate that the urn 'sounds' at a relative frequency that is considerably higher than that of the heads, so again this coheres with our equation of the urns with overtones, and the heads with fundamental tones. Thirdly, if this is the case, then it also seems to make sense that the planes closest to the camera are only ever occupied by heads alone, (see Figure 5.2) for we can consider that the overtones sounded by these high-

---

[32] See Maurice Harmon (ed.), *No Author Better Served: The Correspondence of Samuel Beckett and Alan Schneider* (Cambridge, MA, 1998), p. 24.

[33] Evangelos Sembos, *Principles of Music Theory* (Morrisville, NC, 2006), p. 93.

[34] Burdette Green and David Butler, 'From Acoustics to *Tonpsychologie*', in Thomas Christensen (ed.), *The Cambridge History of Western Music Theory* (Cambridge, 2002), pp. 246–71 (p. 250).

frequency notes would be beyond the range of human hearing. Furthermore, given *Comédie*'s confusion of parts and wholes, it seems particularly apt that the very phenomenon of a tone comprising a fundamental tone and its overtones embodies a kind of tautological paradox, in that the fundamental tone is both a part and a whole: the fundamental tone is the composite tone and one of its constituents. In this way, Beckett's 'fundamental sound'[35] can be seen in the present context to describe the head on its own and also the whole figure. As the *OED* definition of a fundamental makes clear: it is 'the tone produced by the vibration of the *whole* of a sonorous body, as distinguished from the higher tones or harmonics produced by that of its parts'.[36]

The Musicality of the Voice

Having proposed a musical analogy of *Comédie*'s visual content, we can now turn to a discussion of the film's aural content, before considering more thoroughly the overall effect and meaning of the whole of the film's 'music'. Clearly, the film's aural content is entirely comprised, apart from the crackle of the optical soundtrack, of oral content: torrents of words that spill forth from the mouths of the three figures, the rapidity of which produces a kind of hyper-vocalization, with only short fragments of it comprehensible in the way we usually receive language (already rapid speech was further accelerated with a machine called a phonogène:[37] a device which enabled early manifestations of what later became known as 'timestretching', that is, changing the temporal rate of an audio signal without altering the pitch). As Glasmeier and Hartel write of *Comédie*'s speech, 'language no longer serves narrative or commentatory purposes. It has been turned by Beckett into structured noises ... manipulated into a virtual rhythm-machine.'[38]

In his essay 'The Grain of the Voice', Roland Barthes makes a distinction between two modes of vocalization which he calls the 'pheno-song' and the 'geno-song'. The former refers to 'everything in the performance which is in the service of communication, representation, expression',[39] whereas

> the geno-song is the volume of the singing and speaking voice, the space where significations germinate 'from within language and in its very materiality'; it forms a signifying play having nothing to do with communication, representation (of feelings), expression; it is that apex (or that depth) of production where the melody really works at the language – not at what it says, but the voluptuousness

35 See Harmon (ed.), *No Author Better Served*, p. 24.

36 *Oxford English Dictionary*, s.v. 'Fundamental' (my italics).

37 See Karmitz and Lebovici, 'Entretien', p. 21.

38 Glasmeier and Hartel, '"Three Grey Disks"', p. 79.

39 Roland Barthes, *Image Music Text*, trans. Stephen Heath (London, 1977), p. 182.

> of its sounds-signifiers, of its letters – where melody explores how the language works and identifies with that work.[40]

We might conceptualize *Comédie*'s voices in just this way: as tending towards a geno-song of abstract sound as opposed to a pheno-song of representative language; as spoken words striving to return to their origin in abstract noise, becoming absolute sound, tending towards the condition of melody. *Comédie*'s voices form the sound of a melody searching for itself, seeking to become purer, to become an abstraction. Their speech worms ceaselessly into the material of language, working at the negation of words, to become anti-words, to become music.

Each voice is almost continually monotone: the torrent of speech that each of the three figures deliver remains pitched almost constantly at the same three different levels (and each figure does pitch their speech at a noticeably different frequency to each other, the two Fs unsurprisingly being relatively close in tone and of a much higher frequency than H), though there are occasionally some brief flourishes of tonal variety. This monotony is no impediment to an ascription of melody to these voices: quite the reverse in fact, as such a sustained delivery at one particular pitch arguably works to highlight the voice's inherent tonal quality. And, of course, tone is only one of the components of melody, the others being rhythm and, to a lesser extent, tempo.

Voice as Melody; Image as Harmony

Having approached the aural/oral elements of *Comédie* as the film's melodic content, we might posit the film's visual elements in our analogy as the piece's harmonic content. Of course, these two elements of music form an opposition that cannot be decisively uncoupled. Almost all music contains melodic aspects within its harmony and harmonic aspects within its melody, and indeed this is the case with *Comédie* too. In the Chorus sections, for example, when all three figures speak together, the melodies of their speech become harmonic or, rather, they become disharmonic. In terms of the film's harmonic content, like all variable harmony, this takes on melodic characteristics simply on account of its movements. Even discounting these particular ways in which harmony can be heard melodically and melody heard harmonically, these two musical phenomena are always inextricably related. As Victor Zuckerkandl writes:

> when we hear a piece of music of the 'melody-plus-harmony' type, we do not experience two movements going on side by side, one of single tones, melody, the other of chords, harmony; we experience one integrated tonal motion.[41]

---

40 Ibid.

41 Victor Zuckerkandl, *The Sense of Music* (Princeton, NJ, 1971), p. 218.

This integration characterizes the experience of *Comédie*'s music too, in that the way in which the melody of the speech affects us varies quite considerably depending on the 'sounds' made by the harmony of the film's images. For example, the speech we hear and see emanating from a figure when it is depicted in isolated close-up (when the harmony consists of a single, very high-pitched note) has a markedly different affective power from the speech we hear when all three figures are seen (when the harmony is one of the many variations of the triadic chord). As Karmitz himself has remarked, on the subject of the film's extreme close-ups: 'Mais sur quel mot isole-t-on un personnage? C'est un question qui m'obséde encore. [But on which word should the figure be isolated? It is a question that obsesses me still.]'[42] That this question appears to be so enduringly enigmatic is unsurprising, as the shape, pattern, movement and rhythm of the whole montage seems to be governed both by the content of the speech, and by certain formal and kinetic concerns connected with the piece's overall intensive trajectory.[43] To some extent then, a balance has been struck, in that, whilst the montage is being shaped in a particular way, cuts are executed upon particular words and around particular segments of speech, and the choice of these particulars is not solely dependent on the overall shaping, but equally seems to be based on a kind of musical or intuitive sensibility regarding the sound of the speech. The resulting effect is one in which harmony and melody – and perhaps most importantly, their rhythms – are engaged in a contrapuntal way: complementing one another and interrelating with each other, as opposed to one being in the service of the other. Put simply, the manner in which we receive the vocal/melodic content of the film is influenced and affected by the manner in which we receive the montagic/harmonic content and vice versa. What we see changes what we hear, and what we hear changes what we see. Even if we leave the analogy with music to one side, there is something here of the synaesthetic.

The analogy with atonality seems fitting with regards to the vocal/melodic content of the piece too. Each of the three voices sustains the same pitch throughout the piece and so there is no tonal movement in the melody (bar the occasional lapse, something we might connect to the impossibility of absolute atonality, as noted below), and the three voice-tones together create a chord with no aural sense of a tonal centre and one that actually sounds remarkably similar to the triadic atonality to which we have compared the film's images. When we hear the three voices speak together in the Chorus sections or hear them abutting each other in the other sections, the combination of the three tones sounds harmonically dissonant in a way not dissimilar to a diminished triad, simply in terms of the perpetual unresolvedness that the three monotone voices evoke. It seems clear that, just as the film's images lack any kind of ground, centre, origin or destination (discussed further below), its voices – both their

---

42 Karmitz and Lebovici, 'Entretien', p. 23.

43 See Foster, 'Becoming Present, Becoming Absent', pp. 166–9.

many individual fragments of melody and their melodies taken as a whole – are characterized in the same way.

The Semantics of Atonality

Approaching *Comédie* as a work of atonality seems appropriate not only in terms of the equal tonal status it bestows upon each of the figures, but in terms of the shape and structure of its montagic movement: movement which is analogous, as we have already determined, to the harmonic movement of music: a motion in which no thing moves. That is, just as atonality is defined by the absence of a tonal centre, and thus 'harmony ceases to communicate the place of departure, and also the destination',[44] in *Comédie* there is no single shot which we might locate as the central image of the film, against which the montagic movement of the film moves away from and returns. Whilst the 'basic tableau' can be seen as a kind of provisionally foundational image, there is no one magnitude of the tableau which we can definitively identify as being located in the centre of the frequency range, for two examples of its depiction can be seen to occupy the mid-range of the continuum and neither can be said to be located more centrally than the other. Just as the only true point of departure and arrival in atonal music is the silence that precedes and follows the piece, only the image of the blank, black screen can be seen in this way in *Comédie*.

In his analysis of the tritone, the musicologist Heiner Ruland crystallizes this idea of open-endedness, exploring the notion that the atonal expresses the eternal:

> What makes the tritone a *diabolus* [is] that it dissolves the threshold between inner world and outer world and permits the untransformed inner world to work into the outer world. [We can] draw the boundary between inner world and outer exactly there, between fourth and fifth. We can also begin to sense dimly in the tritone how two worlds that are diametrically opposed as regards time, the inner world and the outer world, resolve themselves into a unity when they are experienced from the aspect of eternity – and this is the truly atonal experience of the tritone.[45]

The tritone, exposed without resolution, by engendering the atonal, simultaneously engenders a sense of the eternal, of infinite time. Schoenberg considered atonality in the same way:

---

44 Ernst Bloch, *Essays on the Philosophy of Music*, trans. Peter Palmer (Cambridge, 1985), p. 229.

45 Heiner Ruland, *Expanding Tonal Awareness: A Musical Exploration of the Evolution of Consciousness Guided by the Monochord*, trans. John Logan (London, 1992), p. 96.

> The analogy with infinity could hardly be made more vivid than through a fluctuating, so to speak, unending harmony, through a harmony that does not always carry with it certificate of domicile and passport carefully indicating country of origin and destination.[46]

To be more precise then, what an atonal piece expresses is the endlessness of itself, of its musical space. Perhaps it would therefore be accurate to suggest that the ending of a truly atonal piece of music is a contradiction in terms and thus a kind of impossibility: that, by ending, a piece of music negates any claim to absolute atonality. Perhaps a piece that is truly atonal never ends or at least points towards its never-ending, as *Play* and *Comédie* do through use of the da capo repeat and by 'concluding' with an indication that, were it not for the constraints of performance/exhibition, they would cycle on endlessly. (Of course, in the age of the looping video installation, such constraints no longer exist.)

The dissolution of a distinction between internal and external time raises some fundamental questions with regards to the conscious status of *Comédie*'s figures, questions that Beckett confronts and presents us with in much of his work: namely, what would it mean to be eternally conscious? Is consciousness not predicated on its own finitude? If not, how would a conscious mind manifest a consciousness of its own eternity? In this connection, it is worth recalling Ruland's claim that the dissolution of the boundary between inner and outer worlds is 'what makes the tritone a *diabolus*': that is, there is something inherently malevolent, or at least *inhuman*, within this conception of infinity. Theodor Adorno considered atonal music in a similar way:

> [The twelve-tone] technique further approaches the ideal of mastery as domination, the infinity of which resides in the fact that nothing heteronomous remains which is not absorbed into the continuum of this technique. Infinity is its pure identity. It is, however, the suppressing moment in the domination of nature, which suddenly turns against the subjective autonomy and freedom itself, in the name of which this domination found its fulfilment. ... It is a closed system – one which is opaque even unto itself – in which the configuration of means is directly hypostatized as goal and as law.[47]

Adorno's comment can be seen to describe the 'closed system' of *Comédie* quite accurately, which, being 'opaque even unto itself', is also simply a state unto itself. The system has no 'goal' or end beyond its always already constituted 'configuration of means'. There is nothing outside the continuum. Despite some apparent level of consciousness, the inhabitants of this system have no autonomy

---

46 Arnold Schoenberg, *Theory of Harmony*, trans. Roy Carter (Berkeley, 1992), p. 129.

47 Theodor Adorno, *Philosophy of Modern Music*, trans. Anne Mitchell and Wesley Blomster (London, 2003), p. 66.

in terms of their own involvement within it. And yet the elements that organize the 'technique' of the 'sounds' the figures articulate – the modulation of frequency and rhythm and the varying levels of illumination – cannot be said to be exterior to them. That which is modulated remains a property of the note itself. The system, the whole state that the film represents, is beyond conceptions of interiority and exteriority: it suggests a state of absolute betweenness. This is the paradox of eternal consciousness: to be eternally conscious is to dissolve the boundary between interior and exterior time and to be divested, therefore, of the consciousness of temporality; and, since temporality is that which, in making consciousness present to itself, engenders consciousness in itself, the dissolution of temporality is simultaneously the dissolution of consciousness. This suggests the possible impossibility of eternal consciousness represented by the experience of *Comédie*'s figures, articulated through their atonal 'music'. And of course, atonality itself, as I have hinted already, is a kind of possible impossibility. According to Schoenberg:

> Everything implied by a series of tones constitutes tonality, whether it be brought together by means of direct reference to a single fundamental or by more complicated connections. … A piece of music will always have to be tonal in so far as a relation has to exist from tone to tone by virtue of which the tones, placed next to or above one another, yield a perceptible continuity. The tonality may then be neither perceptible nor provable; these relations may be obscure and difficult to comprehend, even incomprehensible.[48]

Were it possible for a piece of music to be truly atonal, there would perhaps be nothing more one could say about it beyond the significance of this atonality. Yet there is always a great deal more to a putatively atonal piece of music beyond the articulation of its atonality, just as there is always immeasurably more to tonal music than simply an articulation of the key in which it is composed, and likewise there is far more to *Comédie* than an articulation of the infinite. A piece's tonality or lack of it is only one of a combination of elements that cohere to form a musical work, and, indeed, this study has proposed an extensive impression of the totality of the film's content *as* music, enabling us to conclude by summarizing the work's overall music that we have outlined and to then consider some of its affinities with aspects of musical Minimalism.

The Film as Music and Its Relation to Minimalism

One of the most striking aspects of *Comédie*'s overall soundscape lies in its intense, even maddening, repetitiveness and a sustained, almost obsessive focus on just three chromatic tones, in both its harmonic and melodic aspects. In the harmony, these three tones are sounded at nine different octaval pitches, employing the whole

48 Schoenberg, *Theory of Harmony*, p. 432.

spectrum of the auditory range. In the melody, the three tones clearly sound at the same three pitches throughout (these may or may not be the same tones as those of the harmony; to resolve this question would perhaps be to push the analogy too far). Semantically, it is as though the music is perpetually and obsessively – though by no means systematically – probing at the same thing, or rather the same three things, as if continually interrogating, repeatedly questioning, perhaps repeatedly posing a question, perhaps repeatedly posing the same question: the same unanswerable question, the same unaskable question. When we come to consider the rhythms of the piece, the harmony is rhythmically very variable and unpredictable, sometimes moving between chord variations rapidly, sometimes sounding the same chord for an extended period of time. On the other hand, the rhythm of the melody is always rapid and fairly uniform in its machine-gun-like delivery. The sound of the counterpoint certainly creates some quite exhilarating moments of interplay at several different points in the piece. Taken altogether, the music amounts to a highly intense, hyper-iterative study of just a handful of specific tones.

The style of composition most often associated with atonality is, of course, Serialism, and works in this style, by definition, do not restrict themselves to just a few specific tones; on the contrary, they use 'all 12 notes of the chromatic scale in any order selected by the composer'.[49] On the other hand, some of the most notable early manifestations of what came to be known as Minimalism – a movement often considered to be a reaction to the austerity of Serialism and a return to tonality – are often characterized by the reductive tonal palette we have identified in *Comédie*. This is certainly the case with respect to seminal pieces by two of the central figures in the movement's early development: Terry Riley and Philip Glass.

A well-established relationship already exists between Glass's early work and the stage version of *Play/Comédie*: Glass has described how 'as theater music, *Play* had [a] crucial effect on my thinking'[50] and on the development of his ideas concerning the importance of an audience's role in 'completing' a work of art. More pertinent to the present discussion is the fact that 'the first piece of music Glass still includes in his corpus'[51] was a piece he composed for a 1966 production of *Play*,[52] and the clear significance that *Play* had in the development of Glass's ideas concerning musical form and thus in the development of Minimalist idioms. Indeed, Glass notes that his prolonged engagement with *Play* was a 'formative

[49] Michael Kennedy, *The Concise Oxford Dictionary of Music*, 4th edn (Oxford, 1996), p. 666.

[50] Philip Glass, *Opera on the Beach* (London, 1988), p. 35.

[51] Edward Strickland, *Minimalism: Origins* (Bloomington, IN, 2000), p. 205.

[52] Somewhat remarkably, this Paris production – by the theatre collective that would later become Mabou Mines – took place in the same city and in the same year as the film adaptation of *Comédie*. Despite its location however, this was a production of the English-language *Play*.

experience' that 'set the direction which eventually led to the ensemble music'[53] and that he viewed the work and listened to a recording of his piece 'many, many times'.[54] No score or recording of Glass's music for *Play* appears to exist now, but he has described it as a work characterized by 'a highly reductive, repetitive style'[55] that used 'rhythmic structure to generate an overall form'.[56] In more detail:

> A piece of music based on two lines, each played by soprano saxophone, having only two notes so that each line represented an alternating, pulsing interval. When combined, these two intervals (they were written in two different repeating rhythms) formed a shifting pattern of sounds that stayed within the four pitches of the two intervals. The result was a very static piece that was full of rhythmic variety.[57]

One scholar has noted how the structure of the piece 'imitates the spareness and stark formality of *Play*, without the attempt to trace any "dramatic" trajectory of recognition and revelation'.[58] This interpretation could equally be applied to the 'music' of *Comédie* that we have outlined, but there are also further aspects of Glass's composition that highlight the proto-Minimalism reflected in the film's musical style. Glass's description of a 'static piece full of rhythmic variety' sounds almost paradoxical, but it is strikingly reminiscent of the way in which *Comédie*'s figures are simultaneously represented as static and dynamic through the film's montage, a phenomenon that manifests in the foregoing musical analogy as harmonic stasis in intervallic tension alongside harmonic movement in both rhythm and tonal tension. Two further interrelated characteristics of the piece point towards some core characteristics of early Minimalism that are clearly manifest in *Comédie*'s 'music': its stripped-down tonal palette and its use of highly repetitive tonal structures, these two features being co-dependent.

Ultimately then, *Comédie*'s arrangement of its atonal language into the kind of sparse, insistently repetitive structures we associate with Minimalism might alert us to the way in which the film reflects some of the predominant aesthetic concerns of its day. To read the film's 'music' in the way proposed is to assimilate something of the changing face of the mid-century musical avant-garde, when the strictures and severity of largely European modes of atonality and Serialism were being challenged by the radically different systems of a predominantly American Minimalism. Perhaps we can see, or rather 'hear', this shift being played out through the music created by the language, formal patterning of, and interrelation between, *Comédie*'s sounds and images.

---

53 Glass, *Opera on the Beach*, p. 35.

54 Ibid.

55 Ibid., pp. 18–19.

56 Ibid., p. 38.

57 Ibid., p. 19.

58 Daniel Albright, *Beckett and Aesthetics* (Cambridge, 2003), p. 147.

Chapter 6

Richard Rijnvos and *Rough for Radio I*: Towards the Enrichment of an Impoverished Text

Kevin Branigan

> Come on, Gogo, return the ball, can't you, once in a way?
>
> Samuel Beckett, *Waiting for Godot*

With each of his successive radio plays, Samuel Beckett offered an ever-more intense study of the isolation of the individual from society. *Rough for Radio I* is one of his most extreme expressions of such alienation. Here the listener is presented with a character, simply named He, who occupies a nondescript interior, and a scenario that abandons any sustained development of plot or character. This absence of remarkable detail or dramatic action might result in the work's total oblivion were it not for its most striking quality: despite being a portrait of isolation, *Rough for Radio I* is an open-ended text.

This chapter examines *Rough for Radio I*, which I describe as a 'hemi-text'. The term seeks to describe a work that is unfinished by its very nature, as it requires artistic input from another complementary field in order to complete it. That is to say, an artist or composer must provide the other side of the creative dialogue before the two hemi-texts sound as one artistic whole. As Vladimir berates Estragon in *Waiting for Godot* for his reticence in replying to him, *Rough for Radio I* is a study of an individual who, despite an apparent need for company, is reluctant to respond to the concerns and questions of his visitor. *Rough for Radio I* invites the composer to complete a creative dialogue, thereby transcending the communicative dead-ends which abound in the text. First, I will briefly trace the musical development of Beckett's radio works before I examine the themes and structure of *Rough for Radio I*, as well as the specific qualities which the Dutch composer, Richard Rijnvos, brings to his English language production, titled *Radio I*.

Beckett's radio plays offer an ideal introduction to the development of his aesthetic, from the Joycean-influenced hiberno-modernism of *All That Fall* (1956) to an austere and less allusive style in *Embers* (1959), *Words and Music* (1962), *Cascando* (1963), and *Rough for Radio I* (1961) and *Rough for Radio II* (1976). *All That Fall* is brimful of energy, movement and music, despite being a sardonic presentation of degeneration, sterility and death. The music of Schubert is heard as Maddy Rooney trudges to Boghill station to collect her blind husband, Dan. The theme of premature death suggested by Schubert's lied 'Death and the Maiden' pervades the play and yet Beckett's heroine exhibits an admirable ability to laugh heartily at such suffering. *Embers* strikes a more sombre tone, and, while it also occurs in an external location, movement is reduced to a few footfalls on a pebble strand in contrast to the earlier pastoral walk to and from Boghill train station. A gloomy organ-like sound representing the sea and a few misplayed bars of Chopin are now the musical fare, and the characters Henry interacts with are ghostly figures, perhaps mere figments of his imagination. Radio is the perfect medium for such an ambiguous interplay between presence and absence. For this reason Beckett resisted non-radio productions of *All That Fall* and *Embers*. In radio broadcast it is possible to convey the haziness of Maddy Rooney's perception of reality: she is our medium or guide, however unreliable. Likewise in *Embers*, the audience relies upon Henry's insistence that the strange background sound is that of the sea, that his wife Ada joins him briefly and that his mute, blind father is beside him on the strand. Beckett's own reflections on *All That Fall* are indicative of the intrinsic radio qualities of all his work for this medium:

> It is no more theatre than *Endgame* is radio and to 'act' it is to kill it. Even the reduced visual dimension it will receive from the simplest and most static of readings ... will be destructive of whatever quality it may have and which depends on the whole thing's coming out of the dark.[1]

Following his first two radio plays, Beckett made a radical shift from dramas that provided more conventional characterization and plot and which were located in an exterior natural setting. In these earlier works music was used to underpin movement and pacing, and the audience was eased into the broadcast by familiar classical pieces. Subsequently Beckett abandoned the use of past musical masters in favour of music that had to be written specifically for each new radio play. In *Words and Music* creative conflict is conveyed, where Words and Music represent respectively thoughts and emotions locked in a strained performance for Croak, the listener. Music has personality; he can be cheeky and uncooperative as he reacts to the banal poetic impromptus of Words. Beckett's sense of both radio-specific drama and music alters between *Words and Music* and *Rough for Radio I*. Croak is a demanding listener whose emotional reactions and wishes influence the performance by Words and Music. As such, this is an instance of the potential for creative interplay between audience and performers, as well as between fellow performers. By contrast, the central character in *Rough for Radio I* listens to a transmission of music and a voice that he cannot interact with, neither of which can interact with each other either.

Rough for Radio I is a bewilderingly simple radio play. 'He' is preoccupied by musical sounds and a voice that emanate separately from a radio-like transmitter.

[1] Samuel Beckett to Barney Rosset, 27 Aug. 1957, in Clas Zilliacus *Beckett and Broadcasting: A Study of the Works of Samuel Beckett for and in Radio and Television* (Åbo, 1976), p. 6.

He is visited by 'She' who listens intently and then leaves him, none the wiser. She is unable to comprehend his obsession with these sounds. Their conversation is strained; He only answers her questions, if at all, after some prodding:

> SHE: Are these two knobs?
> HE: Yes.
> SHE: Just push? [*Pause.*] Is it live? [*Pause.*] I ask you is it live.
> HE: No, you must twist. [*Pause.*] To the right.[2]

She's efforts at small-talk and the apparent compliment about his Turkoman rug fall flat. He feels no obligation to reply. Her questions and those of the radio audience are either left unanswered or else answered insufficiently. Is she allowed to sit on the hassock? Can she have light or heat? Can he explain the nature of music and voice? Is he concerned if she walks into the house garbage on her way out? In this vatic text, Beckett withholds valuable detail which might enlighten the listener. We may contrast He's reticence with Maddy's efforts in *All That Fall* to paint her surroundings for the listener, describing the racecourse, the laburnum tree and other significant details along the roadway. As unreliable as her perception of reality might be, she addresses the radio listener directly and aids her/his visualization.

Following She's departure, He becomes highly anxious as he detects fundamental changes in the music and voice. He telephones his doctor and begs him to visit. He explains that the music and voice are no longer sounding separately but are playing together and are coming to an end:

> HE: [*With music and voice.*] Yes … wait … [*Music and voice silent. Very agitated.*] Yes … yes … no matter … what the trouble is? … they're ending … ENDING … .[3]

The responses of the doctor's secretary, and of the doctor himself, appear dismissive. He hangs up and is left alone, the sole entity able to comprehend the gravity of what he hears. The only indication given by Beckett concerning a change to the music and the voice is that, following He's second phone call, they begin to emanate together and become ever fainter. As voice and music converge and falter, He is faced with the prospect of death or creative oblivion which is placed in counterpoint with the exuberance of new life, about which he hears over the phone: two confinements and a breech birth gain priority over his existential handwringing.

While *Rough for Radio I* was first published in English in 1976, it was originally written in French in 1961 and published in 1973 by Éditions de Minuit as *Esquisse radiophonique*. There is conflicting information concerning

2 Samuel Beckett, *Rough for Radio I*, in *Collected Shorter Plays of Samuel Beckett* (London, 1984), p. 108.

3 Ibid., p. 110.

a French language version. In a letter to Richard Rijnvos, Edward Beckett refers to a France Culture (ORTF) production in 1962.[4] However, in correspondence with Clas Zilliacus in 1975, Samuel Beckett was unaware of any such French broadcast.[5] Zilliacus points out that *Esquisse radiophonique* was completed just before Beckett commenced work on *Cascando* and argues that it may be treated as a 'proto-*Cascando*'.[6] While the two plays are superficially similar, *Cascando* is more ostensibly about an unresolved creative process. In contrast with He, Opener, the narrator, is generally more at ease and in control of the voice and music he listens to. Beckett also provides a full text for Voice in the play. Had *Esquisse radiophonique* remained unpublished, the suggestion that it was an unfinished draft of *Cascando* would be more plausible. Beckett's decision to publish it suggests that he considered it as a separate work.

Martin Esslin, who in 1976 sought permission from Beckett to produce *Rough for Radio I* for the BBC, notes the significance of the radio-like apparatus as well as the technical radio term 'live', used by She.[7] It is perhaps understandable that he should identify radiophonic qualities in the description of this machine, with the implication that the play is a commentary on the nature of radio. Unlike a normal radio set, however, the two knobs mentioned do not permit tuning in to a station and regulation of volume. One knob on the machine accesses music; the second accesses a voice. He indicates to She that these knobs are to be turned to the right. Strangely, while a click is heard which indicates that She or He is turning them on, there is no such sound to indicate that they have been turned off. The pauses that occur in the transmission of the voice and music allow her to reflect and ask questions about what she hears. She realizes that even when she hears the music and voice together they are not *actually* together; they are separate transmissions heard simultaneously:

> SHE: What is it like together?
> [*Pause.*]
> HE: To the right, madam.
> [*Click.*]
> MUSIC: [*Faint, brief.*] ....
> MUSIC, VOICE: [*Together.*] ....
> [*Silence.*]
> SHE: They are not together?

4 Richard Rijnvos, 'What is it Like Together? Genesis of the First Production of Beckett's Radio I', in Marius Buning and Lois Oppenheim (eds), *Beckett in the 1990s, Samuel Beckett Today/Aujourd'hui* 2 (Amsterdam and Atlanta, GA, 1993), pp. 103–10 (p. 109).

5 Zilliacus, *Beckett and Broadcasting*, p. 122.

6 Ibid, p. 119.

7 Martin Esslin, *Mediations: Essays on Brecht, Beckett and the Media* (London, 1983), p. 142.

HE: No.
SHE: They cannot see each other?
HE: No.
SHE: Hear each other?
HE: No.
SHE: It's inconceivable![8]

Her demand that what she hears be played louder is futile.[9] There is no volume control on the apparatus and, in the absence of explanation, she remains mystified. She is typical of the listener faced with a sparse text. She makes an earnest attempt to comprehend what she hears, and while she might grapple with radiophonic terminology, the above questions and her subsequent query as to the 'conditions' to which voice and the music are subject merit a more considered response than He provides.[10] But in contrast with a similarly elliptical but closed prose text, *Company* (1980), *Rough for Radio I* is open to completion by a possibly more expansive composer.

In 1989 Richard Rijnvos was commissioned by the Dutch Broadcasting Corporation to represent the Netherlands at the Prix Italia in 1991. The corporation stated: 'It would be appreciated if typical radio aspects, such as our electronic studio equipment, would be involved'.[11] Rijnvos produced music and vocal text for Beckett's *Rough for Radio I* and presented it under the title *Radio I.* This title differentiates it from Beckett's skeletal text. In so doing, Rijnvos is calling attention to the fact that his production is not intended as an unproblematic completion of the text for broadcast. Indeed, this would be impossible, as Beckett's text gives no significant detail concerning the nature of the crucial components of voice and music. Instead *Radio I* treats the text as an *objet trouvé*, in relation to which Rijnvos constructs a sound structure using his own musical score and a vocal sample. Although Rijnvos's musical influences are eclectic, a major one was that of the New York School composers, notably John Cage and Morton Feldman. Rijnvos met John Cage for the first time in The Hague in 1988. From this moment on there is a marked shift in Rijnvos's conception of composition, including a radical move towards incorporating music and sounds that are not of his own making into his work. This perhaps explains his attraction to *Rough for Radio I*, as Beckett also requires the inclusion of sounds which are not determined by him.

Rijnvos's interest in *Rough for Radio I* is as much due to its musical and structural challenges as to any desire to further clarify any message embedded in the text:

8 Beckett, *Rough for Radio I*, p. 108.
9 Ibid.
10 Ibid.
11 Rijnvos, 'What is it Like Together?', p. 103.

> In my opinion the only form of radio-making which shows an explicitly medium-bound character is the radio play, so this is what I decided to make. If it is the composer's intention to base his work on an already existing text, rather than conceiving his own, it may be self-evident that he will look for a text in which the music is not, as usual, merely functional … but in which the music is allotted an intrinsic role such as we find in the texts for radio by Samuel Beckett where the music is made part of the 'dramatis personae'.[12]

The composer's attention to the formal aspects of the play is crucial to its success, as Beckett, since his critique of Joyce in *Work in Progress*, professed an admiration for material in which form and content are complementary:

> The form, structure, and mood of an artistic statement cannot be separated from its meaning, its conceptual content; simply because the work of art as a whole *is* its meaning, what is said in it is indissolubly linked with the *manner* in which it is said, and cannot be said in any other way.[13]

In a play that is divested of the normal requirements of narrative or characterization, this attention to structure is indispensable if the producer wishes to put across a work which, while obscure in meaning, is nonetheless not abstract in form. What links the open form and structure of the play to its subject is the recurrence of incomplete and strained conversations. For even the apparent conversation between He and She is undermined by the pockets of silence that separate each exchange. Rijnvos highlights the problematic nature of their dialogue by allowing pauses of up to 10 seconds between their lines. If they are isolated, then they share this property with the multitude of other incomplete dialogues that occur in the play.

Rough for Radio I may be regarded in different ways as a result of this incomplete series of conversations. It may be interpreted as a pessimistic expression of humankind's isolation from reality and humanity. However, it is significant that the completion of the play requires a musical component. Beckett seems to suggest that something additional to his own voice is required in order to achieve a less problematic communication or expression. His relative lack of technical musical expertise obliged him to seek a dialogue with a composer. The composer is fluent in a language which Beckett apprehends intuitively but cannot speak; a form of communication which he believes has not been 'condemned to explicitness'.[14]

In *Rough for Radio I*, Rijnvos found a form for the presentation of music that is uniquely radiophonic since it is a text in which music's role is specific but its nature is undefined. The principal clue identified by Rijnvos relating to the function of the music is found in the brief discussion between He and She quoted above, in

12 Ibid., p. 103.

13 Martin Esslin, *The Theatre of the Absurd* (London, 1987), p. 44.

14 Lawrence Shainberg, 'Exorcising Beckett', *Paris Review* 29/104 (1987): 100–136 (p. 116).

which She observes: 'They are not together? … They cannot see each other? … Hear each other?'[15] Upon turning the first knob, she hears music faintly. When it ceases she exclaims 'but there are more than one!'[16] She may be referring to the number of radio channels, but her astonishment may also be due to her sense that the different musical elements emanate from different transmissions. Rijnvos also assumes a separation of musical sources. Since it is difficult to convey this to the listener without the benefit of visual cueing, Rijnvos presents an aid to the listener by recording each instrument in his ensemble separately and in contrastive sound ambiences. This permits a degree of differentiation in the broadcast:

> I ultimately chose for writing music in seven instrumental layers. These layers are: 1. bass flute, 2. oboe, 3. clarinet, 4. trombone, 5. piano (doubling celesta) and tubular bells, 6. violin (solo) and 7. string trio. Other than instrumental identity, these independently composed layers differ in each acoustical quality with which they are recorded, again independently of each other. The clarinet, for example, is recorded very close by in the dry acoustics of a direction room, and the trombone from afar in a resounding staircase (by way of which it approaches the sound of an eerily close mist horn at sea).[17]

The British composer Christopher Fox also observed that 'the clarinet is close and dry, the trombone distant and surrounded by resonance. Each layer of Rijnvos's music is more or less long-breathed, registrally conjunct; together the layers exude a remote calm quite at odds with the mixture of exasperation and confusion of *He* and *She*.'[18]

Rijnvos's compositional and production choices for *Radio I* may be seen as reflecting the influence of the New York School, in particular that of Cage, whose emphasis on indeterminacy is crucial. One of the American composer's greatest achievements was to question our conceptual relationship with sounds. Cage gained notoriety for *4'33"* (1952), a piece for piano where the pianist sits at the keyboard but does not play. Instead the audience's attention focuses upon the ambient sounds that surround her/him, sounds which s/he might customarily try to ignore while concentrating upon a performance. This typifies Cage's challenge to audiences to consider all sounds as inherently musical. One of Cage's own early influences was the French artist Marcel Duchamp whose use of *objets trouvés* suggested that all items, even a urinal (*Fountain*, 1917), can be considered art works when presented within the framework of a gallery. Cage advocated bringing elements that he had not composed into his work, as well as developing methods to allow indeterminacy as part of his compositional process. The instructions

15 Beckett, *Rough for Radio I*, p. 108.

16 Ibid.

17 Rijnvos, 'What is it Like Together?', p. 106.

18 Christopher Fox, 'Square Dances: The Music of Richard Rijnvos', *Musical Times* 140/1869 (1999): 22–30 (p. 25).

derived from non-musical elements such as the Chinese book of chance, *I Ching*, might be used to generate the sequences of notes, along with structure, rhythmic characteristics and other musical parameters. Cage's collection of lectures and essays, *Silence*, has become a seminal manifesto for a musicality that celebrates the sounds that surround us: 'One may give up the desire to control sound, clear his mind of music, and set about discovering means to let sounds be themselves rather than vehicles for man-made theories or expressions of human sentiments.'[19]

Rijnvos's music for *Radio I* gives a similar impression of chance juxtapositions. In the texture of the composition different motifs may be identified at first hearing and others revealed with repeated listening and familiarity. The piano tones outline groups of the intervals that reoccur throughout; punctuating high and low-pitched notes are played at various stages by all instruments. The dreamlike quality of the piece is reinforced by a recurring oboe motif, by long notes played on trombone and by chiming tones on tubular bells. The oboe motif has a strong melodic pattern, formed of slurred leaping intervals of ninths, sevenths and closer intervals of sixths, fourths and seconds. At times this motif becomes insistent and disjointed, while at others it is quieter and almost plaintive. Intervals which make up this motif occur widely among the other instruments in different registers and in elongated or shortened note duration. While the recording of each musical instrument is separate, the listener is the fixed point and determines any sense of order or progression that may occur in the overall soundscape. Is it possible as a listener not to detect consonance between the separate elements heard? For He, such convergence or resolution of the sounds would seem to defy their essential nature. His distress is in marked contrast to that of Opener in *Cascando*, who likewise listens to Voice and Music. While aware that these two are not linked, Opener delights in perceiving such temporal concordance despite the spatial separation of what he hears. He feels like an astronomer who admires the shape of a constellation whose stars are light years away from one another: 'From one world to another, it's as though they drew together.'[20]

The other half of the radio transmission that preoccupies He is the voice. The vaguest of directions are given concerning the nature of this voice, and no indication is made as to what it says. For his proposed 1976 BBC production, Martin Esslin had suggested to Beckett that the voice be 'no more than a faint mumbled murmur'. However, Beckett did not approve of this idea and, despite Esslin's enthusiasm for the piece, decided not to proceed with the project.[21] *Rough for Radio I* contrasts, then, with *Words and Music* and *Cascando* which, though similar in theme and structure, contain specific text for Words and Voice. There are also more specific directions as to the nature of the music in both works, and Beckett took great care to discuss the composition for the initial productions with,

19 John Cage, *Silence* (London, 1978), p. 10.

20 Beckett, *Cascando*, in *Collected Shorter Plays*, p. 141.

21 Esslin, *Mediations* , p. 144.

respectively, John Beckett and Marcel Mihalovici. Rijnvos feels that Beckett's omission of any indication concerning the voice, 'really lets us down', but he believes that we can still gather 'that the voice originates from a man and that he is alone'.[22] We cannot tell whether this should be an incoherent mumble or a clearly heard vocal text. Rijnvos seeks a solution to the hole left in the text by Beckett by using a recording of the voice of John Cage. This calls to mind Cage's *Empty Words* (1974) in which he read Henry David Thoreau's *Journal* against a recording of dawn at his New York home. Here words are savoured for their musicality rather than their semantic significance.

Cage was consulted by Rijnvos concerning his inclusion in *Radio I* and considered it a 'very elegant' idea.[23] Rijnvos has been described by Christopher Fox as a 'tidy' composer and this insertion could not be any tidier.[24] It complements the metaphysical distress of He, who is haunted by phenomena that are beyond his control. Cage's voice proposes a series of workaday considerations, questions and declarations that receive no response. He was recorded by Rijnvos at the Royal Conservatory in The Hague in 1988 as he arranged a workshop with the workshop's participants, and the younger composer then isolated the parts of the recording that featured only Cage's rambling voice. The series of statements and unanswered questions is uncannily suited to Beckett's text, which contains many such one-sided conversations. Below is a sample of what Cage says:

> Is there any one else?
> What?
> She's not here?
> She's not coming?
> I won't be any place.
> Now we have only the one left.
> And they don't seem to be speaking.
> That means that you both you'll have to both do both of these things before tomorrow noon.[25]

Rijnvos uses Cage's isolated words in order to fill the void in the Beckett text. As such, it is an appropriate choice, bearing similarities with He's one-sided phone conversations. The composer had previously experimented with what he called 'time brackets', the inclusion of non-composed sounds in a score, which he learned from Cage, in *Study in Five Parts for Piano* (1986–7). This is an intricate piece for piano, recorded by John Snijders with a duration of just over 14 minutes. Despite the demanding nature of the piece for the musician, it is concluded by the insertion of a recorded plucked violin string. Rijnvos juxtaposes the simplicity of the time

22 Rijnvos, 'What is it Like Together?' p. 107.

23 Ibid., p. 108.

24 Fox, 'Square Dances', p. 22.

25 Rijnvos, 'What is it Like Together?', p. 108.

bracket with the demanding nature of the composition for piano. As Christopher Fox suggests, 'the effect is like a window thrown open, a brief glimpse out of a crowded room into a quiet other landscape in which time is measured differently'.[26]

Beckett's short story *Dante and the Lobster* (1934) contains an instance of a similar appearance of a voice previously unheard at its conclusion. The story ends as its protagonist Belacqua guiltily boils a lobster alive. He consoles himself with the sentiment that at least the lobster will have a quick death. A three-word retort completes the story: 'It is not'.[27] Is this meant to be the voice of the lobster, a divine interjection, an authorial voice or a combination of all three? Similarly, the linear progression of *Embers* is punctured by involuntary flashbacks to intense moments, voices and sounds in Henry's life.

Rijnvos's production of *Radio I* is 27 minutes in duration and features Joan Plowright as She and Michael Gough as He. The music is performed by the Ives Ensemble. There are long pauses, averaging 7 seconds, between the actors' dialogue. A click is heard as She or He turn the knobs to the right. We hear the music first for 37 seconds. Contrary to the direction for faint music in the text, the music throughout the production is perfectly audible and the instruments are played mezzo-piano. The effect is impassive, as though the musicians were disinterested performers. The voice is then heard for 30 seconds: like the instruments, his voice is dreamy throughout the entire play, except for once when we hear excitement as he chirps 'I can't wait!' The listener can savour each musical and vocal element without searching for progression or dramatic climax. When She wonders what voice and music will sound like together, we hear these elements side by side, voice for 40 seconds, music for 30. Following She's departure, He turns the knobs and this time we hear music played for 2 minutes' duration. Voice then joins after 35 seconds. The only discernible difference now is that Rijnvos's music is heard played forte. He, however, is convinced that they are now playing together and are fading. As She shouted 'Louder' earlier, He now calls 'Come on! Come on!'[28] He tries to influence their progression despite agreeing with the doctor that 'there is nothing to be done'.[29] He is mysteriously able to turn them off when speaking to the doctor or his secretary. We hear music and voice for 2 minutes and 30 seconds following the secretary's first call, for 1 minute and 45 seconds following the doctor's call and for 1 minute and 10 seconds at the end, marking a clear diminution throughout. At this final point Rijnvos still chooses to play Cage's voice and the music at the same level as before. Instead, he differentiates this passage by a gradual withdrawal of all instruments except for celesta and bells.

---

[26] Fox, 'Square Dances', p. 22.

[27] Samuel Beckett, *Dante and the Lobster*, in *More Pricks Than Kicks* (London, 1979), p. 19.

[28] Beckett, *Rough for Radio I*, p. 110.

[29] Ibid.

As Cage's questions are left unanswered in the Rijnvos production, the composer seems to be making us aware of the unresolved nature of Beckett's hemi-text. The result of this completion of the artistic conversation between Beckett and Rijnvos is risky. Rijnvos completes the work without the personal collaboration accorded by Beckett to Marcel Mihalovici in his composition for *Cascando* or to John Beckett in his composition for *Words and Music*. A scrupulous deference to Beckett's wishes is recorded in *The Art of Radio* by Donald McWhinnie, the author's principal BBC producer, and in *Mediations* by Martin Esslin, who also produced and directed a number of his radio and stage plays. It would appear that both of these highly accomplished producers felt a sense of failure if Beckett was dissatisfied with what he heard. An example of this is when Beckett listened back to Esslin's radio adaption of *Play*: 'I remember that playback in my office very vividly. Beckett sat through the whole play with an enigmatic and inscrutable expression on his face. When it was all over, he said: "I don't like it at all. You got it wrong."'[30]

Of course Beckett was entitled to offer an opinion on such productions. However, many of the productions of the radio plays display an emphasis on achieving a definitive interpretation as desired by the author. Hence, we see Everett C. Frost noting that the animal sounds of McWhinnie's BBC production of *All That Fall* had 'failed to please Beckett and he urged us to get the actual sounds of the animals if we possibly could'.[31] Beckett's death in 1989 meant that Rijnvos was liberated from a need to seek the author's interpretation when approaching this text. He is not concerned with seeking a definitive understanding of *Rough for Radio I*; he is aware that his is but one interpretation amongst many.

Communication becomes particularly difficult when we consider a Beckett text. *Rough for Radio I* is a distillation of the author's abandonment of content, of affecting the pose of 'a non-knower, a non-can-er', as Beckett described himself in an interview with Israel Shenker in 1956.[32] The result of the Rijnvos production is the creation of various ill-matched couples. They are together more through fate than choice, and their communication is endangered by misinterpretation. Beckett and Rijnvos achieve a crucial artistic coupling in *Radio I*: in Rijnvos's presentation of Beckett's text, Cage's voice couples briefly and incommensurably with music, just as He and She meet briefly for their uncomfortable exchanges.

---

30 Esslin, *Mediations* , p. 139.

31 Samuel Beckett to Barney Rosset (his publisher at Grove Press), 27 Aug. 1957, quoted in Everett C. Frost, 'A "Fresh Go" for the Skull: Directing *All That Fall*, Samuel Beckett's Play for Radio', in Lois Oppenheim (ed.), *Directing Beckett* (Ann Arbor, MI, 1994), pp. 186–219 (p. 194).

32 Israel Shenker, 'An Interview with Beckett', *New York Times* (5 May 1956), in Lawrence Graver and Raymond Federman (eds), *Samuel Beckett: The Critical Heritage* (London, 1979), p. 148.

As a result of such an impoverished text, any addition can potentially create a richer work. Beckett was wary of the changes that music might bring to his austere texts. He was somewhat surprised that John Beckett's music for the radio production of *Molloy*, featuring Patrick Magee, did not overwhelm the prose: 'I was also extremely pleased with the music. I had wondered a bit if the text would take it'.[33] In *Radio I* Rijnvos assumes an equal status with the author in order to bring the text to life and to make these two hemi-texts sound together.

---

33 Samuel Beckett (Molien, Ussy-sur-Marne) to Donald McWhinnie, 11 Dec. 1957 (previously on deposit at Beckett Archive, Reading, now privately owned).

Chapter 7
Articulated Arrhythmia: Samuel Beckett's Shorter Plays

Maria Ristani

The Rhythmic Register of Beckett's Shorter Plays

When asked about her rehearsal work on Samuel Beckett's *Rockaby* (1980), actress Billie Whitelaw stated: 'I am beating time the whole time. Also, even if at first the script is not fully understood I know that if I get the rhythm and music of it right it works'.[1] Whitelaw's reference to Beckett's writing in terms of a particular rhythm and as a music score should come as no surprise in view of the playwright's striking awareness of and sensitivity to timing, repetition, durational patterns, pulse, tempi and those elements in drama which border on music and which Beckett meticulously specified in his dramatic work, more strikingly so in the minimalist plays written after the early 1960s. Beckett seems to have been intrigued by the 'ghastly grinning on' of time,[2] which he attempted to organize musically and carve out in rhythm, holding time back in repetitive patterns or dragging it on in hurried, animated staccatos. An emancipated rhythmic text thus resounds in his writings, 'on-beat, off-beat, between-beat, delaying, dragging, precipitating, syncopating'.[3]

To speak of Beckett's dramatic writing as 'rhythmic' immediately summons questions of order, structuring and control. This is how the rhythmic quality of his work has been read, and quite rightly so, as there is no doubt that shaping and containing in rhythmic pattern stand at the core of Beckett's oeuvre. Think of the visual ballet in *Come and Go* (1965), the strictly choreographed movement of May in *Footfalls* (1975) or the patterned resonance of movement and language in *Rockaby*. Rhythm is here the faithful guardian of form. Usurping the role traditionally provided by syntactic and punctuation devices or narrative links and chronological chains, it functions as structural agent and cohesive pattern: it binds verbal flow in repeated refrains, arrests bodily motion in choreographed schemas and adds to the aesthetic integrity of Beckett's mise-en-scène by arranging sonic

[1] Janet Goodridge, *Rhythm and Timing of Movement in Performance: Drama, Dance and Ceremony* (London, 1999), p. 56.

[2] Samuel Beckett, *A Piece of Monologue*, in *Collected Shorter Plays of Samuel Beckett* (London, 2006), p. 265.

[3] Goodridge, *Rhythm and Timing of Movement in Performance*, p. 57.

and visual stimuli in patterned echoes and cross-feedback loops. Critics have emphasized Beckett's typically modernist emphasis on structure and form, reading this rhythmic register as part of the playwright's move away from the referential quality of gestural or verbal language (most strikingly felt in his shorter plays) and towards a more formally oriented abstraction.

But is rhythm in Beckett entirely a formal preoccupation? My study takes its cue from this question, examining the way the rhythmic in Beckett seems to propose something more complex and profound than the mere provision of pattern and order. Without refuting the structured and structuring nature of rhythmicity, I aim, however, to unsettle this assumption, proposing a re-definition of rhythm as both structure-producing interruption and inventive motility – rhythm as an interplay of both constraint and release. My main contention is that Beckett found in rhythm an alternative to conventional syntax – an edifice, in other words, on which to negotiate the drying up or dissolution of language – but also a way to transform the representational strategies of his playtexts. Significantly more than an abstract formal shape, rhythmic patterning in Beckett's writing becomes a dramaturgical operation which activates, as we shall see, alternate modes of expression, embodiment and representation. Examples might be drawn from Beckett's entire oeuvre. The present analysis will, however, be limited to his shorter plays, where he strips language of ornamental inflections and becomes still more meticulous with the timing of the words and the accompanying gestures, thus allowing the rhythmic quality of his work to surface and dominate.[4]

The Concept of Rhythm

When addressing the concept of rhythm, one is presented with a series of apparent contradictions and problematic dichotomies that cannot be ignored. The word comes into English through Latin from the ancient Greek ῥυθμός, the etymological root of which can be traced to the ancient Greek verb ῥέω (to flow) that brings in the idea of flux, of continuous movement across boundaries (as in a stream), of unrestrained motility. This affinity that the word etymologically holds to flux and flowing is, however, not semantically verified by the actual usage of the term in modern languages or in the vocabulary of ancient Greek thought where it originally appeared. The French structural linguist, Émile Benveniste, thanks to whom the polyvalent topic of rhythm attracted renewed attention in theoretical linguistics in the second half of the twentieth century, undertakes in his article 'The Notion of "Rhythm" in its Linguistic Expression' to trace the different inflections and uses of the term in multiple ancient Greek texts (at least up to the Attic period). In his attempted overview Benveniste concludes that,

[4] This is often referred to as Beckett's 'later drama'; this period begins with *Play* (1962–3) and includes the dramatic works written thereafter.

regardless of its etymological inflection, the word 'rhythm' almost invariably bore the meaning of '"distinctive form, proportioned figure, arrangement, disposition" in conditions of use which are otherwise extremely varied'.[5] Benveniste traces the first appearance of the word in Archilochus, a Greek poet of the seventh century BCE whose work has survived only in fragments. Archilochus' use of the term 'rhythm' bears almost no relation to our modern understanding of the word. It is still relevant, though, to the idea of pattern and form, denoting in the poet's lines a distinctive form of temper or character: γίγνωσκε δ' οἷος ῥυσμὸς ἀνθρώπους ἔχει (learn to know the *dispositions* which men have).[6] The same understanding of rhythm as concerned with schema and form is echoed, as Benveniste observes, in the greatest part of ancient theoretical literature. The insistent association of rhythm with *metron* (measure) and *peras* (limit) by Greek authors proves in itself the emphasis placed on rhythmicity 'for its function of "limiting" the possibilities' and generating what is proportional, finite and precisely measurable.[7] This framing of rhythm qua order and proportion was, for instance, evident in Plato's philosophical treatises. Plato consistently emphasized the capacity for rhythmic/harmonic configurations as the basis for a proper education and, above all, as a distinguishing privilege of humanity over disorderly beasts. In his discussion of choric art in *Laws*, he theorized rhythm as the orderly schemata projected by the body in tune with, and in adherence to, the metrical form of the text. In fact, Plato's definition of rhythm as an 'ordering of movement (*kiniseos taxis*) distinct from the "non-rhythm" of kinetic chaos or kinetic continuum'[8] is what basically underlies our traditional understanding of the term as metrical constraint and ordering pattern.

Interestingly enough, within the modern conceptual frame of the word 'rhythm' (at least with regard to Western thought), there is also very little reference to the notion of flow, stream or gush which the morphological link of the word with ῥέω implies. For the most part, the abundant existing definitions of the term allude to order, structure and metricity, invariably relating rhythm to

5 Emile Benveniste, *Problems in General Linguistics*, trans. Mary Elizabeth Meek (Coral Gables, FL, 1971), p. 285.

6 Ibid., p. 284. Benveniste is here using Bergk's translation of Archilochus. The same passage has been translated differently by Werner Jaeger, who interprets rhythm as holding pattern or containing force, and reads the same lines as: 'understand the rhythm which holds mankind in its bonds' (see Werner Jaeger, *Paideia: The Ideals of Greek Culture*, vol. 1: *Archaic Greece: The Mind of Athens*, trans. Gilbert Highet [New York, 1986], p. 125). Despite the differing interpretations of the lines, it is clear that rhythm is used by Archilochus in the sense of arranging pattern and form. In its original appearance the word had no musical connotations; the first use of the word 'rhythm' with musical reference can be traced later to Xenocrates in the fourth century BCE.

7 Lewis Rowell, 'The Subconscious Language of Musical Time', *Music Theory Spectrum* 1 (1979): 96–106 (p. 104).

8 Goodridge, *Rhythm and Timing of Movement in Performance*, p. 43.

issues of 'recurrence, regularity, pattern, periodicity, or … meter, measure and cadence in poetry and music'.[9] Both music theory and general discourse have long suppressed the propulsive nature of the rhythmic, referring it, as already shown, to a stable matrix of calculable coordinates. This is at least what a quick overview of standard dictionary entries reveals: rhythm has been identified as 'an ordered recurrent alternation of strong and weak elements in the flow of sound and silence in speech',[10] an 'agreeable succession of rising and falling sounds' in poetry and prose,[11] a pattern of recurrence in environmental and cosmic cycles, a 'grouping of … sounds, principally by means of duration and stress' in music[12] or 'a regularly recurrent quantitative change in a variable biological process'.[13] The prevalent etymological account of the word has even been revised with new perspectives that dispute rhythm as a nominal derivative of ῥέω (to flow), and propose the root *ry* (*ery*) or *w'ry* instead (to pull, draw, hold, restrain) as a possible origin. Two prominent classicists, Werner Jaeger and Trasyboulos Georgiades, both favour this alternate derivation of the word which indicates a static nature for rhythmicity and is thus more in tune with its spatial and metric conception as featured in ancient Greek writings or even later. In his *Paideia: The Ideals of Greek Culture*, Jaeger asserts that 'if rhythm "holds"' – as translated in passages from Archilochus and Aeschylus – 'it cannot be a flux … but *pause*, the steady limitation of movement'.[14]

Rhythm: A 'Fluid Form'

In his treatment of this disputed etymology and its apparent contradiction with semantics, Émile Benveniste, however, does not seek to exorcise this discrepancy. On the contrary, he welcomes the tension between flowing (etymology) and shaping (semantic usage) as constitutive of the actual meaning of the word. According to the French linguist, a closer look at the pre-Platonic use of the term reveals that the word 'rhythm' did refer to schema and form, yet a form 'which does not have organic consistency' but is 'assumed by what is moving, mobile and fluid … [and thus is] improvised, momentary, changeable'.[15] Benveniste cites many examples of the (pre-Platonic) use of 'rhythm' which suggest the notion of dynamic shape rather than the idea of fixed and immutably structured form that

9 Haili You, 'Defining Rhythm: Aspects of an Anthropology of Rhythm', *Culture, Medicine and Psychiatry* 18/3 (1994): 361–38 (p. 362).

10 *Merriam Webster's Encyclopaedia of Literature* (Springfield, MA, 1995), *s.v.* 'rhythm'.

11 Philip B. Gove (ed.), *Webster's New Dictionary of Synonyms* (Springfield, MA, 1973), *s.v.* 'rhythm'.

12 *The New Grove* (London, 1980), *s.v.* 'rhythm'.

13 *Merriam-Webster's Medical Dictionary* (Springfield, MA, 1995), *s.v.* 'rhythm'.

14 Jaeger, *Paideia*, vol. 1, p. 126.

15 Benveniste, *Problems in General Linguistics*, pp. 285–6.

Plato later attached to the semantics of rhythm. It was only really with Plato (for whom, as we have seen, rhythm referred to movement determined by measure and numerical regulations) that this dialectic of containment and flow was suppressed in favour of a more mechanical understanding of the term, one that is still alive both in musical theory and in general discourse.

Speaking of rhythm as fitting a 'specific modality of the "form" of things',[16] a fluid form, Benveniste highlights an ambivalence that is by no means restricted to the use of the term in ancient Greek literature. It is actually inherent in the very concept of rhythmicity. Immutably structured yet infinitely renewable, rhythm involves a dialectic between schematic form and flowing movement. In what seems a contradiction, it is both the flow of action in its wave dynamics and energy register and that which holds, confines and shapes this flow. Rhythm is, as it were, a form–force compound: in its Janus-faced quality, it features as a calculated constraint running through potentially incalculable movement. To quote W.B. Yeats from *The Symbolism of Poetry*, rhythm sounds 'an alluring monotony' hushing and comforting us in its reassuring periodicity, 'while it holds us waking by variety … keep[ing] us in that state of perhaps real trance'.[17] The challenge resides, as we shall see, in finding the vocabulary to address this expressive intensity ('trance') which the patterned language of rhythmicity ('alluring monotony') activates and which displaces received structures of representation and meaning.

This new understanding of rhythm as dynamic form, fuelled more-or-less by Benveniste's contribution (Amittai F. Aviram speaks of 'post-Benveniste theorists' in his overview of the existing rhythm literature)[18] was particularly resonant during the 1960s and 1970s when Beckett composed his shorter plays. During this same period Julia Kristeva, to whom I shall refer later, drew attention to pre-linguistic rhythms and 'pulsions' through her *Revolution in Poetic Language* of 1974, while a few years later the poet and translator Henri Meschonnic problematized the typical alignment of rhythm and measure in his *Critique du rythme* (1982). In the 1980s the social theorist Henri Lefebvre wrote his innovative *Éléments de rythmanalyse* (*Elements of Rhythmanalysis*),[19] a true 'manifesto for the centrality of rhythm in analyses of the urban and the

---

[16] Ibid., p. 286.

[17] William Butler Yeats, *Essays and Introductions* (London, 1961), p. 159.

[18] Amittai F. Aviram, 'The Meaning of Rhythm', in Massimo Verdicchio and Robert Burch (eds), *Between Philosophy and Poetry: Writing, Rhythm, History* (London, 2002), pp. 161–70 (pp. 161–2).

[19] Lefebvre turned to the concept of rhythm in his late writings. *Éléments de rythmanalyse*, part of his series Critique of Everyday Life, was published posthumously in 1992. Rhythmanalysis was also the topic of two shorter pieces, co-written with Catherine Régulier: 'The Rhythmanalytical Project' and 'Attempt at the Rhythmanalysis of Mediterranean Cities'. These were all published in *Rhythmanalysis: Space, Time and Everyday Life*, trans. Stuart Elden (New York, 2004).

everyday'.[20] His rhythmanalytical project was intended as an '*analytic* operation that consists in opening and unwrapping' the polyrhythmic bundle that our living body forms, traversed as it is by physiological, environmental or socio-cultural rhythms.[21] Though in the process of Lefebvre's analysis his attention is taken up more by the cultural appropriation and production of 'natural rhythms' – a process he calls 'dressage' – his starting point is still, the irreducibility of the rhythmic. Rhythm, he argues, 'appears as regulated time, governed by rational laws, but in contact with what is least rational in human being: the lived, the carnal, the body'.[22] It lends itself to objective, mathematical approximations and triggers the reasoning mind in its articulation of measurable, patterned clock-time (what Platonic definition and all concomitant metrical approaches have emphasized) as much as it is intertwined with the flowing temporality of the lived, which is in excess of any regular patterning. This is what Lefebvre reads as the blending of the structured and the lived lying at the heart of rhythmicity, with the law of numbers and the quantifiable *metron* (metre) meddling with the vital, visceral body or the unpredictably polyrhythmic everyday life.

Beckett's work shares, as it were, this same understanding of rhythm as an intensive form–force. Testing its possibilities at both edges, Beckett works on the essential ambivalence of rhythm as both regulated form and as that which releases affect and motility. He weaves, as we shall see, sharply angled rhythmic shapes which ultimately transform and mobilize the representational values of his texts, directing us to what Patrice Pavis described in his analysis of rhythm in performance as 'a rhythmic schema that is very different from that of conventional semantics'.[23] This activates a different language of expression which, as the playwright himself desired, would 'work on the nerves of the audience, not its intellect'.[24] This rhythmic form was best described by Beckett himself in a letter to his younger contemporary Harold Pinter (1961): 'If you insist on finding form [for my plays] I'll describe it for you. I was in hospital once. There was a man in another ward, dying of throat cancer. In the silences I could hear his screams continually. That's the only kind of form my work has.'[25] Affective energy and force, contained within a palpable schema; this is the form–force that Beckett's works assume. In the following sections I will examine how this dynamic compound of hold and release is woven through Beckett's writing and, more particularly, in his later work for the theatre.

---

20 Elizabeth Lindley and Laura McMahon (eds), *Rhythms: Essays in French Literature, Thought and Culture* (Oxford, 2008), p. 17.

21 Lefebvre, *Rhythmanalysis*, p. 9.

22 Ibid.

23 Patrice Pavis, *Analyzing Performance: Theater, Dance, and Film*, trans. David Williams (Ann Arbor, MI, 2003), p. 146.

24 Stanley E. Gontarski (ed.), *The Theatrical Notebooks of Samuel Beckett: The Shorter Plays* (New York, 1999), p. xvii.

25 Quoted in Deirdre Bair, *Samuel Beckett: A Biography* (London, 1980), p. 560.

Rhythmic Structuring: The Later Plays

Writing and also directing work for the stage after the late 1950s, Beckett was all the more concerned with the tension and dynamics of live performance where the material body and its lived experience become the focus of attention.[26] Issues of pouring out, revolving, modulating, relenting, buzzing or freezing and throttling – to note some of the phrases recurrently featuring in his stage directions or actual dramatic text – are now of paramount importance. In his effort to anchor and register in his scripts the energy flow of the performative, Beckett seems to adopt a composer's tactics and turns to music's handling of continued energy. Rather than channelling performance flow into an interconnected system of causal logic or a linear arrangement of beginnings and ends, Beckett instead opts for carefully construed, alternating blocks of breaks and spasms (as in *Play*), of motion and rest (as in *Rockaby*), of breaks and repeat (as in the knock–repeat–knock sequence of *Ohio Impromptu*), or of theme and variation (as in the mutually resonant phrases and gestures of the three women in *Come and Go*). By clearly notating the rests, the repeats and the accents, he works his way through sequences, links, counterpoints, interruptions and pauses, anchoring energy flow in rhythm. Let us look, for example, at the rhythmically patterned text of *Play* which features Beckett's first systematic use of rhythm as an integral element of both dramatic structure and meaning. After a '*largely unintelligible*' opening chorus,[27] the first section of the text flows as follows:

> w1: I said to him, Give her up. I swore by all I held most sacred –
> [*Spot from w1 to w2.*]
> w2: One morning as I was sitting stitching by the open window she burst in and flew at me. Give him up, she screamed, he's mine. Her photographs were kind to her. Seeing her now for the first time full length in the flesh I understood why he preferred me.
> [*Spot from w2 to M.*]
> M: We were not long together when she smelled the rat. Give up that whore, she said, or I'll cut my throat – [*Hiccup.*] Pardon – so help me God. I knew she could have no proof. So I told her I did not know what she was talking about.
> [*Spot from M to w2.*]

[26] These are the years when Beckett was directly engaged with practical stage work, turning to directing his own plays, starting with *Endspiel* (*Endgame*) at the Schiller-Theater in Berlin in 1967. His acquaintance with and active involvement in the mechanics of performance, with the insights that it necessarily brought to light, had an undeniable effect on his writing. Stanley Gontarski reads the minimalist, pattern-oriented aesthetic of the late plays as directly linked with Beckett's gradual transformation 'from playwright to theatre artist' (see 'Revising Himself: Performance as Text in Samuel Beckett's Theatre', *Journal of Modern Literature* 22/1 [1998]: 131–45).

[27] Beckett, *Play*, in *Collected Shorter Plays*, p. 147.

> W2: What are you talking about? I said, stitching away. Someone yours? Give up whom? I smell you off him, she screamed, he stinks of bitch.[28]

As the usual sequential patterns of dramatic writing are abandoned (such as chronological schemata, interaction patterns, dramatic cohesion or storytelling continuity), the synapses in an otherwise fragmented text are now repetitions, doublings back and variations ('Give her up'/'Give him up'/'Give up that whore'/'Give up whom?'), insistent interruptions ('or I'll cut my throat – [*Hiccup.*] Pardon –'/'I swore by all I held most sacred –'), symmetries ('[*Spot from W2 to M.*]'/'[*Spot from M to W2.*]'), or counterpoint patterns ('So I told her I did not know what she was talking about'/'What are you talking about? I said, stitching away'), with the narrative thus progressing along in in-built rhythmic lines. The rhythmic schema that these constraints give rise to is very precise: a flowing movement incessantly interrupted in a violent staccato, all the more so as the tempo to which it beats is frenetic ('*Rapid tempo throughout*'[29]). The lighting spot, which James Knowlson aptly compares to a 'conductor's baton',[30] seems to set the repetitively syncopated rhythm of the piece: it flashes on and off each speaker's face, lets them gasp one sentence and often cuts them off before completion, thus imposing a recurring caesura on both scenic and verbal language. The play comprises short, apparently disjointed energy particles, which Beckett likened to the movement of a lawn mower in rehearsals: 'a burst of energy followed by a pause, a renewed burst followed by yet another pause'.[31] In fact, the image of the 'old hand mower',[32] the sound heard outside W2's apartment while M is trying to part from her, is central in the play itself: 'a little rush, then another'.[33] Writing in *Play* becomes writing in rhythm, as prosodic concerns (utterance tempo, energy and rhythm of the oral delivery) as well as rhythmic constraints (interchange of pauses and sounds) override plot, character or dialogue considerations.

This primary concern with rhythmic structuring is evident in all aspects of Beckett's work at the time, whether translating his works and revising earlier ones or rehearsing his plays and directing his actors. Before the 1964 production of *Play* (directed by George Divine), Beckett was now-famously described by Billie Whitelaw as cutting out words, dots and letters for the lines to fit in a tighter rhythmic shape: 'page 2, speech 4, fifth word. Will you make these three dots, two dots?', Whitelaw remembers him asking.[34] When directing, Beckett

---

28 Ibid., p. 148.

29 Ibid., p. 147.

30 James Knowlson, *Damned to Fame: The Life of Samuel Beckett* (London, 1997), p. 444.

31 Chris Ackerley and Stanley E. Gontarski, *The Grove Companion to Samuel Beckett: A Reader's Guide to His Works, Life, and Thought* (New York, 2004), p. 445.

32 Beckett, *Play*, p. 150.

33 Ibid., p. 151.

34 Billie Whitelaw, *Billie Whitelaw ... Who He?* (New York, 1996), p. 78.

would regularly hold rehearsals for tone, pitch and rhythm where the actors 'worked like machines, beating time with [their] fingers'[35] as he spoke aloud the lines for them to hear their pulse or acted out the movements in all their rhythmic specificity – a true conducting ritual, as it has often been described by actors who worked alongside him. Dramaturgical elements such as character or story were clearly less important to him than rhythmic and sonic explorations. As McCarthy remarks, 'fundamentally, Beckett allow[ed] the actor to organize an energy flow, rather than a flow of emotions' by tuning into the rhythm required.[36] While rehearsing *Happy Days* with Brenda Bruce in 1962, as James Knowlson relates in his biography of Beckett, he 'even brought a metronome into the theatre and set it down on the floor, saying, "This is the rhythm I want." To the actress's astonishment, he then left it ticking relentlessly away'.[37] Interestingly enough, both Billie Whitelaw and David Warrilow – two of Beckett's leading actors – have often spoken of themselves as musical instruments set to play out the 'dynamic rhythms of Beckett's word-music'.[38]

Rhythmically patterned, Beckett's later pieces play out a measured and strictly regulated schema even in the face of a clearly failing verbal language. As Ackerley and Gontarski note in their discussion of Beckett's late structuring methods, even with texts of seemingly uncontained polyphony, such as *That Time* (1974), 'manuscripts testify to the care with which the sequence of voices was devised, an order imperceptible to reader or audience but which forms an underlying grid'.[39] Rhythm appears to be the basic structural agent of this grid, functioning, as it were, as linkage and chain. With fragments of language plunging forward, as in the case of *Play* for example, rhythm arrests the gush of words. The tightly orchestrated lighting of this piece, 'opening and shutting'[40] and focused on the three faces, 'imposes its mechanical rhythm on their utterances'[41] and accentuates the periodically repeated blocks of time which alone punctuate a stream of words.

Similarly, syntactically loose sentences abound in Beckett's later works, and yet rhythm seems to make up for the loss in syntactic cohesion, establishing acoustic ties in the texts that result from pattern repetition and weave a 'phonic-instinctual memory' network.[42] In *A Piece of Monologue* (1979), for example,

---

35 John Haynes and James Knowlson, *Images of Beckett* (Cambridge, 2003), p. 109.

36 Gerry McCarthy, 'Emptying the Theater: On Directing the Plays of Samuel Beckett', in Lois Oppenheim (ed.), *Directing Beckett* (Ann Arbor, MI, 1994), pp. 250–67 (p. 258).

37 Knowlson, *Damned to Fame*, p. 447.

38 Whitelaw, *Billie Whitelaw*, p. 78.

39 Ackerley and Gontarski, *The Grove Companion to Samuel Beckett*, p. 356.

40 Beckett, *Play*, p. 157.

41 Bob Mayberry, *Theatre of Discord: Dissonance in Beckett, Albee, and Pinter* (Rutherford, NJ, 1989), p. 32.

42 Julia Kristeva, *Desire in Language: A Semiotic Approach to Literature and Art*, trans. Thomas Gora et al. (New York, 1980), p. 169.

syntactic threads are clearly severed with elided phrases piling up ('Wick turned low. And now. This night. Up at nightfall. Every nightfall. Faint light in room'[43]), but acoustic kinship is established with particular phrasal segments steadily repeated through and across the broken syntax ('he all but said loved ones'[44]). Rhythmic repetition weaves haunting and holding refrains, as Deleuze and Guattari define the term when considering territorialized milieus and forces of chaos: refrains that 'seek, mark, assemble a territory'[45] where the part is related to the whole; tentative skips from chaos, sonic bricks – however permeable – in a verbal edifice of crumbling syntax. The concept of the refrain, as outlined by the two philosophers, takes on particular resonance in Beckett's work where rhythmic motifs and counterpoints ensure a degree of consistency, playing out a palpable form in otherwise disconnected pieces. The previously mentioned refrain 'he all but said loved ones' from *A Piece of Monologue* or the alternation of breaks and voices in *Play* both map a specific pattern along and within the lines of the plays. This pattern is not, however, dependent on linear causalities or narrative logic, but is emergent and intensive, the effect of the dynamic interrelation of different parts. The organization provided by such rhythmic contours is less related to static form and more to a powerful geometry of movement and emergence. The refrain, Deleuze and Guattari remark, is a holding pattern, albeit far removed from 'a formalizing, linear, hierarchized, centralized *arborescent* model'.[46]

Rhythmic Motility

This rhythmic form, which frames, contains and sculpts language in Beckett, is also what eventually removes its symbolic facade and causes it to flow. Rhythmic orchestration allows the playwright to present and at the same time nullify received structures of representation. Julia Kristeva has written extensively on this capacity of the rhythmic to mobilize the structural, semantic and expressive values of the verbal text. Her work holds a significant place in the poststructuralist tradition of the 1970s in that she eschews prioritizing language as semantic register and discourse, directing attention instead to a language-made-body. Kristeva speaks of rhythm as the functioning of bodily drives and 'pulsions' rippling through linguistic structures. This falls under the more general distinction she draws between the semantic and semiotic modalities of the signifying process. For Kristeva, the speaking subject is a dynamic unity of semiotic and symbolic dispositions, where the semiotic is associated with 'a

43 Samuel Beckett, *A Piece of Monologue*, in *Collected Shorter Plays*, p. 265.

44 Ibid.

45 Gilles Deleuze and Félix Guattari, *A Thousand Plateaus: Capitalism and Schizophrenia* (London, 2004), p. 360.

46 Ibid., p. 361.

preverbal functional state'[47] – the realm of the body, the drives, the unconscious – one that precedes the positing of a subject of enunciation and meaning which the symbolic represents (as the realm of language, judgement, the law of the Father).[48] Prior to the symbolic, the semiotic is still present after the onset of the symbolic, the two remaining in a 'necessary dialectic ... which is constitutive of the subject'.[49] Rhythm, according to Kristeva, is an activator of this semiotic modality, reintroducing the body into language, creating more 'throbbing than meaning ... [its] stream go[ing] to our breasts, genitals and iridescent skin'.[50]

In literature, Kristeva sees this rhythmic motility of the semiotic breaking free ('literature as a rhythm made intelligible by syntax'[51]). Citing examples in *Desire in Language* from Philippe Sollers's *H* (among many others) and in words that could apply to Beckett's own idiom,[52] she highlights this potential of rhythmicity for a heteroglossia – 'a *heterogeneousness* to meaning and signification' as she describes it – which genetically dates back to the 'first echolalias of infants'[53] and which is reactivated in language as prosodic rhythm, bringing uttering into speaking and energy vibration into linguistic information. Kristeva dwells on this capacity of the rhythmic to introduce 'wandering or fuzziness into language',[54] through 'an organizing function that could go so far as to violate certain grammatical rules of ... language and often neglect the importance of an ideatory message'.[55] Such is the case with Beckett's rhythmic writing where animated or halting patterns delay the necessary finitude of the sentence by releasing punctuation marks, which imagine the possibility of completion, beyond the limits of the already structured sentence (through a hurried staccato) or by resisting finitude altogether (through a repetitive legato). Take for example the following lines from *Rockaby* (1980) where the protagonist beats time in a rocking chair to the pattern of a halting, obsessively repetitive speech, one that gives rise to a rhythmic schema of hesitation and retarded movement:

> so in the end
> close of a long day

47 Julia Kristeva, *Revolution in Poetic Language*, trans. Margaret Waller (New York, 1984), p. 27.

48 Ibid., pp. 43–5.

49 Ibid., p. 24.

50 Kristeva, *Desire in Language*, p. 163.

51 Kristeva, *Revolution in Poetic Language*, p. 30.

52 Beckett's work itself has often furnished Kristeva's writings with examples. Her short essay 'The Father, Love, and Banishment' (originally published in 1976; reprinted in *Desire in Language*) is entirely devoted to Beckett's work (*Not I* and *First Love*), while references to Beckett frame, elucidate and further her thought in many of her writings.

53 Kristeva, *Desire in Language*, p. 133.

54 Ibid., p. 136.

55 Ibid., p. 134.

in the end went and sat
went back in and sat
at her window
let up the blind and sat
quiet at her window
only window
facing other windows
other only windows[56]

The movement of language here hardly obeys linear narrative development, but sustains, instead, a circular, insistently repetitive rhythm simulating, as it were, the non-progressive, repetitive motion of the rocking chair. In characteristic Beckett fashion, language in *Rockaby* folds back upon itself in a thwarted but always renewed attempt to move forward: 'in the end went and sat/went back in and sat/at her window/let up the blind and sat'. Narrative progression is nullified in constant reversal and revision, just as the rocker's forward inclination is less propulsive motion than the balancing counterpart of the backward pull. The chair's distinctive 'movement-in-place' duplicates itself in language retardation – in the swaying, self-cancelling motion of words. If we look at the piece as a whole, we discover a limited lexicon, one that is endlessly repeated, reshuffled and recombined in ever-aborted attempts at concatenation and release, just as the moving chair is essentially static and only maintains the illusion of motion in its repeated back and forth sway along the arc of its nonetheless static runners. Beating to a rhythm of fits and starts, language swells and leans in damaged cadences, never reaching the 'integrated (w)hole, it strives so hard to be'.[57] What resounds is an unrelenting rhythm, holding back, refusing to let go, resisting the sentence as an arbitrary 'knot of incidental bits'.[58] Evidently, the effort is to hold the essential 'go on' of syntax and let it linger and swell as Krapp does with his favourite utterance, 'Spooool'.[59]

Rhythmic Uttering

The halting or animated rhythmic patterns woven into Beckett's late works do not only pelt words with disruptive cadences but also pulverize their sequences. As Kristeva claims, a 'measured language [is] carried away into rhythm'[60] and

---

56 Samuel Beckett, *Rockaby*, in *Collected Shorter Plays*, p. 277.

57 Enoch Brater, *The Drama in the Text: Beckett's Late Fiction* (New York, 1994), p. 170.

58 Stéphane Mallarmé, 'Mystery in Literature', in Hazard Adams (ed.), *Critical Theory Since Plato* (New York, 1971), p. 694.

59 Beckett, *Krapp's Last Tape*, in *Collected Shorter Plays*, p. 56.

60 Kristeva, *Desire in Literature*, p. 179.

made to bow before its affective realm, before the 'instinctual breakthrough'[61] it effects. I am using 'affective' here as a qualifying term for the overpowering reality realized through rhythm, bearing in mind much recent work on the notion of affect[62] and, more specifically, Brian Massumi's mapping of the term in sharp distinction to emotion. If emotion is understood as qualified intensity framed into socio-linguistic function and meaning, as Massumi argues in his *Parables for the Virtual* – a seminal work on the significance of movement, affect and sensation – affect, on the other hand, is visceral intensity, volatile, infectious and emergent.[63] In Beckett, rhythmic orchestration filters off emotion as socially conditioned expressivity, channelled though language and thus arrested in punctuation, organized in syntactic relational patterns and voiced through intonation markers and prosodic features. What is re-inscribed through consistent metrics is a pre-, extra- or para-linguistic tension, 'more throbbing than meaning',[64] organic pulsation, the violence of material language, 'nothing but emotion' in the Unnamable's words, 'bing, bang, that's blows, ugh, pooh, what else, oooh, aaah, that's love'.[65] Through stuttering, repetitive rhythms or animated staccatos, the characters' voices reach towards us in all their quick starts, fits, curves, rings and bends, offering themselves as modulating tension rather than as 'meaningful' discourse alone. Rhythmic orchestration allows a constant merging of speaking with uttering, of dramatic information with pure energy force. This is the case, for example, with the relentless rhythmic idiom in *Play*: unfolding as 'a little rush then another',[66] it strains and ignores our intellectual response. The moment we pause to 'appreciate' or make sense of what we hear, we are lost. Without refuting semantics altogether, the piece offers, nonetheless, an intensive experience that sweeps the reader/listener off her feet in its immediacy. It urges us to shift from a logic of intellectual exposure to one of visceral encounter. The 'fundamental sounds' played out in Beckett's

---

61 Ibid., p. 167.

62 Discussions of affectivity and emotion have recently taken on new relevance in light of the so-called 'affective turn' that has marked the humanities and social studies. Theorists such as Brian Massumi, Patricia Clough, Gregory J. Seigworth and Melissa Gregg have contributed to this shift of emphasis towards the dynamics of affective expression. Even though there has been no definitive mapping of the term 'affect' and approaches to its economy have varied considerably, it suffices to say that affect as energy, force or incipiency activates a vocabulary of wave dynamics, relationality, motion and potential. Spinoza, Bergson, Deleuze and Guattari are undoubtedly the philosophical precursors of many of these ideas.

63 Brian Massumi, *Parables for the Virtual: Movement, Affect, Sensation* (Durham, NC, 2002), pp. 26–8.

64 Kristeva, *Desire in Literature*, p. 163.

65 Samuel Beckett, *The Unnamable*, in *Three Novels: Molloy, Malone Dies, The Unnamable* (New York, 1991), p. 401.

66 Beckett, *Play*, p. 151.

writing elicit fundamental reactions before shaping into a coherent whole to address our intellect.

This intensive capacity of rhythmically heightened expressivity also casts received notions of expression in a new light. For example, it confounds two basic premises upon which our predominantly Western understanding of expression and the expressing subject has been built: interiority (expression is thought of as the externalization of meaning passed on from sender to receiver) and agency (the wilful act of the singularly bound subject). Instead, in the works I have so far discussed (amongst others by Beckett) the rhythmic dynamism of the expressive body renders it a transmitter and receiver of energy force, extending its regions 'beyond its organic envelope' in a predicament of distributed agency.[67] This contests the received image of the body as a bound organism or as a repository and originator of meaning. Rhythmic uttering implies relatedness, an all-pervasive sharing rather than separation on which the representational logic of language is built. This is what Anna Gibbs in her work on 'synchrony models' described as a 'trajectory in which both [object and subject] are swept up',[68] drawing attention instead to 'the immediacy of what passes between bodies'.[69] Characters in Beckett are as much speakers of 'some truth'[70] as they are vibrating sound boxes or mouthpieces consumed in the violent tension of uttering. The image has been drawn by Beckett, in words uttered by the Unnamable, referring to straining membranes and resonant subjects: 'perhaps that's what I feel, myself vibrating. I'm the tympanum, on the one hand the mind, on the other the world, I don't belong to either.'[71]

Beckett's *Not I*: Hold and Release

It is perhaps *Not I* (1972) which best exemplifies this rhythmic language of affective force and articulated form that we find in Beckett's late plays. The interplay of sucking in (containment) and spilling out (flow) which *Not I* already suggests through the visually prevalent Mouth cavity that pours out the ceaseless torrent of words is also played out in the rhythmic movement of words themselves. In this relentless short play (it lasts hardly 10 minutes in performance), Beckett traces the frantic surge of a voice that he had already explored previously in *The Unnamable*: 'It issues from me, it fills me, it clamours against my walls, it is not

[67] Erin Manning, *Relationscapes: Movement, Art, Philosophy* (Cambridge, 2009), p. 24.

[68] Anna Gibbs, 'After Affect: Sympathy, Synchrony, and Mimetic Communication', in Melissa Gregg and Gregory J. Seigworth (eds), *The Affect Theory Reader* (Durham, NC, 2010), pp. 186–205 (p. 194).

[69] Ibid., p. 193.

[70] Beckett, *Play*, p. 157.

[71] Beckett, *The Unnamable*, p. 376.

mine, I can't stop it, I can't prevent it, from tearing me, racking me, assailing me'.[72] Semantic walls come crumbling down in *Not I* and the dreaded overflow is now staged in this later work, rendered through the rapid, abrupt and disjointed staccato of Beckett's lines:

> found herself in the dark...and if not exactly...insentient...insentient...for she could still hear the buzzing...so-called...in the ears...and a ray of light came and went...came and went...such as the moon might cast...drifting...in and out of cloud...but so dulled... feeling...feeling so dulled...she did not know...what position she was in...imagine!.. what position she was in!..whether standing...or sitting...but the brain–...what?.. kneeling?..yes...[73]

Short terse phrases ('so dulled') escaping the fetters of syntactic organization and with no terminal full-stop or restraining comma to arrest their motion; participles awaiting release ('feeling...feeling so dulled'); dashes halting any potential thread and thus breaking all attempts at concatenation ('but the brain–'); pressing exclamation marks ('imagine!'), questions seeking to maintain a rising intonation ('what?..kneeling?') and to prevent the sentence from drawing to a close – all of these give rise to a frenetic rhythm. The disconnected form of the staccato allows little space for pauses or links between phrases and words; it is threateningly additive rather than reassuringly divisive, while the breakneck speed that Beckett desired for the delivery of the piece necessarily frustrates all of our attempts at coherence and intelligibility, accentuating instead the sense of a threateningly accumulative energy pressing towards total discharge. Rhythm here arrives as the inscription of a gush. It becomes this gush itself, 'this stream...steady stream'[74] along which words freely float, the 'buzzing' in the ears which mocks and defies intelligibility. Interestingly enough, the main device for this rhythmic flowing is the ellipsis which is generally 'the traditional signal for the slowing down of all verbal motion'.[75] Yet, even this yields in 'the dynamic rhythms of Beckett's word music'[76] and becomes, as Brater notes, a 'hurried ellipsis mark[ing] … [its] own Olympic race with time'.[77] A form of caesura in Beckett's hands, ellipsis in *Not I* is less a definitive break than a tenuous bridge along which the frenetic rhythm of the text is carried forth, while breathlessness is inscribed to counter the symbolic appropriation of breath as the limit of a thetic sentence. Words in the piece may momentarily hold back in a slight stutter ('so dulled...feeling...feeling so dulled') or may conjure 'safe', mechanical rhythms ('a ray of light came and went...came and went...'/'in and out of cloud...'), but ultimately these yield to the

72 Ibid., p. 301.

73 Samuel Beckett, *Not I*, in *Collected Shorter Plays*, p. 217.

74 Ibid., p. 219.

75 Brater, *The Drama in the Text*, p. 168.

76 Whitelaw, *Billie Whitelaw*, p. 78.

77 Brater, *The Drama in the Text*, p. 170.

on-moving stream, and simply drip off in a run-on parataxis (that does not turn easily into a 'meaningful' syntaxis or into a narrative string) until the entire text is liquefied ('all that moisture'[78]) and words themselves become confused with tears: 'suddenly saw it wet...the palm...tears presumably...just the tears...sat and watched them dry'.[79] One is reminded of Beckett's *Texts for Nothing*: 'I confuse them, words and tears, my words are my tears, my eyes my mouth.'[80] Even at the end of the piece, this wordshed witnesses no resting period but only a new recharge ('pick it up–')[81] with one more dash mocking all possibilities for a proper cadence.

And yet *Not I* is, at the same time, a piece of rhythmic constraint, featuring numerous halts and breaks that cut across the animated staccato. Beckett's interest in the holding edges of this run-on piece is clearly revealed in his notes for the 1973 Anthony Page production, where he jotted down meticulously all the pauses and hesitations in the text, all the bar rests of his whirling word-music.[82] These may not be initially apparent, as the text is written as a stream of continuous prose lacking the broken line format of poetry that Beckett adopted in *Rockaby*, for example, but they can be easily revealed through a vocalic scanning of the piece. When read aloud, words echo themselves in binding refrains. They stagger across gaps and hesitations, or swell in deliberate prolongations as in the following:

> what position she was in!..whether standing...or sitting...but the brain–
> ...what?..kneeling?..yes...whether standing...or sitting...or kneeling...but the brain–
> ...what?..lying?..yes...whether standing...or sitting...or kneeling...or lying...but the brain still...[83]

As more participles gather (standing, sitting, kneeling, lying) and as the whether–or pattern is opened up to accommodate still more options, the phrase 'but the brain' is not concatenated; there is obviously an effort to contain the rushing stream, holding it fast in the enclosure of repetition ('whether standing...or sitting...'), controlling its surge in ever-attempted reformulations, arresting its frenzy through halting blocks and syncopations ('but the brain–...what?..'). In a piece which refuses symbolic conventions of control but where the need to accommodate the mess still holds, halting rhythmic patterns (woven by pauses, reformulations, prolongations, hesitations) become forms of arrest and chain in place of the missing normative syntax and standard punctuation. They re-enact more primitive conventions of

78 Beckett, *Not I*, p. 218.

79 Ibid., pp. 220–21.

80 Samuel Beckett, *Texts for Nothing*, in *The Complete Short Prose, 1929–1989*, ed. Stanley E. Gontarski (New York, 1995), p. 131.

81 Beckett, *Not I*, p. 223.

82 A facsimile of Beckett's production notes for *Not I* at the Royal Court Theatre in London, in 1973, is included in *The Theatrical Notebooks of Samuel Beckett*, vol. 4: *The Shorter Plays*, ed. Stanley E. Gontarski (New York, 1999), p. 461.

83 Beckett, *Not I*, p. 217.

release and control, offering, as it were, a pressure-reducing valve, which can be opened at intervals as if along a pipe to let off steam ('what position she was in!.. whether standing...or sitting') and then closed off again ('but the brain–...what?.. kneeling?..yes...') to avoid immediate and total discharge.

Rhythm also achieves binding and integration through its repetitive patterns in the piece. Through the multiple verbal reiterations ('what?..who?..no!..she!..'/'... what?..the buzzing?..yes ...') or the repeated intercepts of shrieking laughter and silence, an almost steady rhythmic pattern is inevitably born, a soothing schema of expectation and fulfilment that fosters anticipation and which, as Steven Connor describes 'pucker[s] up the agony of unrelieved elapse into something calculable and roughly predictable',[84] allowing a momentary pleasure of mastering the flow. Words gather in these rhythmic refrains that weave sonorous threads along the broken text and form a momentary constraint, a hold upon the babbling mouth, a cut to heal the gush. In Beckett's piece then, the function of rhythm remains clearly ambivalent, as it features both as a freely flowing energy manifest through the brief sharp bursts of its staccato, but also as an associative chain woven through halts and refrains. Through this chained, articulated flow, Beckett is able to weave a 'meaningful' babbling.

Articulated Arrhythmia

Chained flow: we are back again at the seeming contradiction spelled out at the beginning of this chapter as inherent in the very notion of rhythm, that is, the dialectics between motion and chain, stream and bank, containment and flow. Moving beyond the formalist label often assigned to Beckett's writing in existing literature, I have attempted here to read his rhythmic idiom as a double-edged register of simultaneous orchestration and dissolution. Rhythmic structure in Beckett keeps out 'the mess', as he famously put it in his interview with Tom Driver, but always simultaneously re-inscribes what it seeks to exorcise; 'it admits the chaos and does not try to say that the chaos is really something else'.[85] A double agent, rhythm both binds and unhinges: it contains emotion only to have it more forcefully released, it orchestrates language while pulverizing its sequences, it gives shape to bodies and sends them moving along its waves. A master of speeds, intensities and rhythms, Beckett lets us immerse in his tightly patterned, almost order-obsessed rhythmic grids. And we do. Finding ourselves, in Beckett's own words, 'at bounds of boundless void'.[86]

---

84 Steven Connor, 'Slow Going', paper presented at 'Critical Beckett' conference, School of French Studies, University of Birmingham, 26 Sept. 1998, available at < http://www.stevenconnor.com/slow.htm>.

85 Gordon S. Armstrong, *Samuel Beckett, W.B. Yeats, and Jack Yeats: Images and Words* (Lewisburg, PA, 1990), p. 56.

86 Samuel Beckett, *Worstward Ho* (London, 1999), pp. 46–7.

Chapter 8
Describing Arabesques: Beckett and Dance

Thomas Mansell

'Dance first. Think later. It's the natural order.' is a maxim frequently attributed (somewhat surprisingly) to Samuel Beckett.[1] No doubt it gains traction precisely *because* it sits at odds with the somewhat austere, cerebral Beckett of popular imagination: if *even he* advocates physical abandon over intellect, then surely it can do no harm! As a young man, Beckett himself 'described arabesques of an original pattern'[2] one Bastille Day, much as James Joyce was wont to break 'into spontaneous "spider dances" in the street'.[3] However, the meaning of dance both for and in Beckett, particularly as it relates to his own specific 'musicality', is as complex as the authenticity of the 'quotation' itself.[4]

As we shall see, debates concerning the relationship between music and dance were particularly animated during Beckett's formative years and important for his own artistic development. In his early fiction, they emerge as reflections on the relationship between the mind and the body and, specifically, on attempts to control one with the other, revealing a certain unease which no amount of irony can fully mask. Later, Beckett's own plays would set out certain (and uncertain) movements, and 'choreography' and 'ballet' would become useful metaphors for describing Beckett's work as a whole. However, both the movements and the metaphor are, I shall argue, curiously one-dimensional – as if the only way Beckett (and Beckettians) could reconcile dance with music or body with mind was to pursue precisely this sort of parallelism, with music/mind the leading partner in their respective pairs. Elsewhere, though, Beckett's works seem to guard against the need to 'describe arabesques' with complete command, with the inability of thought or language to do so being accepted as inevitable and even welcome.

---

1 Quoted on various websites, including *goodreads*: <http://www.goodreads.com/quotes/show/123103>; *Reflections of a Rising Humanist*: <http://squarelogic.wordpress.com/2012/05/31/dance-first-think-later-its-the-natural-order-samuel-beckett/>; see also Kathryn Petras and Ross Petras, *Dance First, Think Later: 618 Rules to Live By* (New York, 2011).

2 Samuel Beckett to Thomas McGreevy, Thursday [?17 July 1930], in *The Letters of Samuel Beckett*, vol. 1: *1929–1940*, ed. Martha Dow Fehsenfeld and Lois More Overbeck (Cambridge, 2009), p. 25.

3 Carol Loeb Shloss, *Lucia Joyce: To Dance in the Wake* (New York, 2003), p. 76.

4 Beckett does not state this precisely as quoted, though its origins lie in an exchange in *Waiting for Godot* (see p. 149 below).

Music and Dance: Symphonic Ballets

In a letter of July 1934 to Morris Sinclair, Beckett casts 'music' and 'ballet' not so much as complementary art forms but as mutually exclusive opposites.

> Do not believe that ballet is music. It is precisely because music has a subordinate part in it that ballet annoys me. For serious music cannot be of use. To represent a piece of music in a particular way, by means of dancing, gestures, settings, costumes, etc., is to degrade it by reducing its value to mere anecdote. There are people who cannot achieve satisfaction unless they can see. As for me, to my misfortune no doubt, I cannot go off unless my eyes are closed.[5]

One feels a little sorry for Beckett's then-teenage cousin, who seems to have responded too enthusiastically to an earlier letter in which Beckett spoke of having seen 'a few ballets, among which [Manuel] de Falla's *Tricorne*, with Picasso décor & costumes. You would have loved it.'[6] The fact that 'ballet' is not 'music' need not imply a value-judgement, although for Beckett it evidently does. Nor does Beckett's earlier praise for Joyce's *Work in Progress* – 'when the sense is dancing, the words dance'[7] – present a counterargument, since Beckett also admired how 'when the sense is sleep, the words go to sleep'.[8] Nevertheless, for words to 'dance' (or to 'sleep') does impute to prose more physicality, more vitality than it is generally permitted (Beckett also admired the way Joyce's words 'elbow their way onto the page'[9]), taking mimesis to new levels of embodied identity.

The debate about the relative merits of dance and music was prevalent at the time. In *Terpsichore* (1928), the surrealist Philippe Soupault (with whom Beckett had dealings over the French translation of the 'Anna Livia Plurabelle' section of Joyce's *Work in Progress*[10]) railed against what he saw as the disastrous influence of the *Ballets Russes*.[11] Instead of 'enslaving' dance to music, Soupault argued, we should recognize that 'the essence of one is utterly different to the essence of the other'.[12] However, in 1933 Léonid Massine (principal choreographer of the *Ballets*

---

5 Samuel Beckett to Morris Sinclair (trans. George Craig), n.d. [after 13 July; before 2 Aug. 1934], in *Letters of Samuel Beckett*, vol. 1, p. 215.

6 Beckett to Sinclair, 13 July 1934, in *Letters of Samuel Beckett*, vol. 1, p. 216 n. 2.

7 Samuel Beckett, 'Dante...Bruno.Vico..Joyce', in *Disjecta: Miscellaneous Writings and a Dramatic Fragment*, ed. Ruby Cohn (London, 1983), pp. 19–33: p. 27.

8 For a more specific consideration of literature, dance and *Finnegans Wake*, see Robert McAlmon, 'Mr Joyce Directs an Irish Word Ballet', in Samuel Beckett et al., *Our Exagmination round his Factification for Incamination of Work in Progress, with Letters of Protest*, 2nd edn (London, 1961), pp. 105–16 (esp. pp. 105–6).

9 Beckett, 'Dante...Bruno.Vico..Joyce', p. 28.

10 See *Letters of Samuel Beckett*, vol. 1, pp. 21, 22 n. 2, 24, 28 n. 2, 33, 40–41.

11 Philippe Soupault, *Les Neuf Muses: Terpsichore* (Paris, 1928), p. 20.

12 Ibid., pp. 23–4.

Russes from 1915 to 1921) staged the first of his 'symphonic ballets', the very notion seeming to threaten the ideal of autonomous absolute music so central to Beckett's embryonic aesthetics. London's leading music critic of the time, Ernest Newman, took something of a Beckettian attitude, at least initially. At the premiere of *Les Présages* (on Beckett's birthday, as it happened), Newman was heard to say 'I shall close my eyes and listen to the music' (Tchaikovsky's Fifth Symphony);[13] however, as Irina Baronova comments, 'he must have peeped with at least one eye and liked what he saw as in his review the next day he had the grace to admit that Massine was a genius of the same calibre as the great composer'.[14] Beckett reacted with incredulity to Newman's conversion, which he followed in the pages of *The Sunday Times*:

> Newman has been very plausible on the symphonic ballet. Is he a bad logician on purpose, because he knows how much more persuasive sophistry is? And how appallingly English the sense of humour. Surely a Wagnerite must admire Choreartium [Massine's second 'symphonic ballet, premiered in October 1933] for all the wrong reasons. And to extend a protest against symphony for balletic purposes to a protest against lyric for Lieder purposes surely is nonsense.[15]

Newman had argued that Massine's supposedly controversial fusion of dance and symphonic music was no worse than, say, Schubert's setting to music of poems by Wilhelm Müller in *Winterreise*, a point which Beckett dismissed without offering supporting reasons.

Choreartium was even more provocative than *Les Présages*, according to a logic outlined by another prominent music critic – and friend of McGreevy[16] – Constant Lambert:

> [Tchaikovsky and Stravinsky] would indeed have failed as ballet composers were their work to be satisfying in the concert-hall. But a Beethoven symphony, like a speech in Hamlet or an ode by Keats, satisfies us completely in its present form. Any action which might accompany it would either be an irritating distraction or a superfluous echo.[17]

At least Tchaikovsky had also written ballet scores: *Choreartium* was set to the Fourth Symphony by Brahms (who inherited Beethoven's mantle as the leading

---

13 Irina Baronova, '*Choreartium*: An Insight', *Brolga: An Australian Journal about Dance* 26 (June 2007): 27.

14 Ibid.

15 Beckett to McGreevy, 26 July 1936, *Letters of Samuel Beckett*, vol. 1, p. 362.

16 See *Letters of Samuel Beckett*, vol. 1, p. 314 n. 2.

17 Constant Lambert, 'Music and Action', in Roger Copeland and Marshall Cohen (eds), *What is Dance? Readings in Theory and Criticism* (Oxford, 1983), pp. 203–10 (p. 207).

composer of absolute music (such as sonatas and symphonies), as opposed to the more programmatic, multimedial 'New German Music' inspired by Liszt and Wagner).[18] After his *Symphonie fantastique* (1936), set to Berlioz's eponymous score, Massine committed what for Lambert, as for Beckett, must have been the ultimate effrontery, by creating a piece (which premiered in May 1938) using Beethoven's Seventh Symphony – the 'dearest of the nine'[19] for Beckett, the one appealed to in his 'German letter' of 9 July 1937 to Axel Kaun,[20] and twice thought of by Belacqua in *Dream of Fair to Middling Women*[21] (or in 'What a Misfortune'[22]). When Beckett found out, he was witheringly sarcastic:

> Massine & Co. are here at the new Trocadero. I did not know he had done the 7th Symphony. Cocteau is reported to be making a ballet of [Racine's] Britannicus. With Harpo Marx as Junie I suppose.[23]

In other letters, Beckett disapproved of his elder brother's predilection for dancing ('Frank goes every evening to a dance, + we seem to have nothing to talk about'; 'Frank is well, but overdancing'[24]), whereas he instead preferred to attend concerts and to play the piano, including duets with McGreevy's landlady, Hester Dowden:[25]

> I do not see much of Hester, but it always goes very well when I go round, and we play the Pavane with special reference to the obeisances in the dance.[26]

The 'Pavane' is Maurice Ravel's *Pavane pour une infante défunte*, which Beckett had earlier used as incidental music in 'The Kid', a skit co-written with Georges

---

18 Also see Francis Sparshott, *A Measured Pace: Toward a Philosophical Understanding of the Arts of Dance* (Toronto, 1995), pp. 496–97 n. 13.

19 Beckett to McGreevy, 19 Oct. 1958, quoted in James Knowlson, *Damned to Fame: The Life of Samuel Beckett* (London, 1996), p. 453 (p. 791 n. 40).

20 See *Letters of Samuel Beckett*, vol. 1, pp. 512–16 (p. 514) (Eng. trans. pp. 516–20 (pp. 518–19)).

21 See Samuel Beckett, *Dream of Fair to Middling Women* [1932], ed. Eoin O'Brien and Edith Fournier (London, 1996), pp. 106, 229.

22 See Samuel Beckett, 'What a Misfortune', in *More Pricks Than Kicks* [1934] (London, 1993), pp. 125–60: pp. 149–50 and 160.

23 Beckett to McGreevy, 6 June 1939, *Letters of Samuel Beckett*, vol. 1, p. 660.

24 Beckett to McGreevy, 27 Dec. 1934; 1 Jan. 1935 (Trinity College, Dublin, MS 10402 (passages not included in *Letters of Samuel Beckett*, vol. 1 (see pp. 235 and 239–42)).

25 See Knowlson, *Damned to Fame*, p. 191.

26 Beckett to McGreevy, 19 Mar. 1935, *Letters of Samuel Beckett*, vol. 1, pp. 260, 263 n. 9.

Pelorson at Trinity College, Dublin, in 1931.[27] Beckett's remark proves Theodor Adorno's point, that 'what are taken to be the purest forms (e.g., traditional musical forms) can be traced back even in the smallest idiomatic detail to content such as dance'[28]– a truth which renders highly problematic Beckett's wish to demarcate discrete realms for 'music' and for 'dance'. A diary entry from Beckett's stay in Hamburg the following year furnishes further evidence, with Beckett singularly unimpressed by the attempts of another pianist to 'describe arabesques':

> Arrive Durrieu about 4. First. Look at some Radziwill Radierungen. Usual crew of Saxons begins to trickle in. Butt a Nürnbergerin to play piano, & a Bulgarian. She plays Debussy *Arabesques*, Brahms' *Walzer*, bien worse than I, & Liszt Consolation. Bloody awful.[29]

Dream, *Murphy* and the MMM

Some of these issues surface in Beckett's first novel, *Dream of Fair to Middling Women* (1932, pub. 1992). On the book's second page, we learn that the anti-hero, Belacqua, is in love with the Smeraldina-Rima because

> she mentioned that she cared for nothing in heaven above or the earth beneath or the waters under the earth so much as the music of Bach and that she was taking herself off almost at once and for good and all to Vienna to study the pianoforte. The result of this was that the curds [of her bosom] put forth suckers of Sargasso, and enmeshed him.[30]

The Smeraldina is in fact off to study 'music and eurhythmics in the very vanguardful SchuleDunkelbrau'[31] – a somewhat less abstract and more varied curriculum than she had given Belacqua to understand.

---

27 'We had a nice Cartesian Infanta in the Kid, inarticulate & stupefied, crossing the stage to Ravel's Pavane' (Beckett to McGreevy, 24 Feb. 1931, *Letters of Samuel Beckett*, vol. 1, p. 68).

28 Theodor W. Adorno, *Aesthetic Theory*, trans. Robert Hullot-Kentor, ed. Gretel Adorno, Rolf Tiedemann and Robert Hullot-Kentor (London, 2004), p. 6; see also Andrew Bowie, *Music, Philosophy, and Modernity* (Cambridge, 2007), p. 160 n. 7. The same point was also made by Havelock Ellis (see *The Dance of Life* (London, 1923), pp. 57–8).

29 Samuel Beckett, *German Diaries*, 10 Nov. 1936 (see Roswitha Quadflieg (ed.), *Alles kommt auf so viel an: Das Hamburg Kapitel aus den 'German Diaries'. 2. Oktober–4. Dezember 1936* (Hamburg, 2003), p. 35; see also Knowlson, *Damned to Fame*, p. 236. The German artist Franz Radziwill (1895–1983) was an ambivalent figure at that turbulent time.

30 Beckett, *Dream of Fair to Middling Women*, p. 3.

31 Ibid., p. 13.

> The Dunkelbrau gals were very Evite and nudist and shocked even the Mödelbergers when they went in their Harlequin pantalettes, or just culotte and sweater and uncontrollable cloak, to the local Kino. All very callisthenic and cerebro-hygenic and promotive of great strength and beauty. In the summer they lay on the roof and bronzed their bottoms and impudenda. And all day it was dancing and singing and music and douches and frictions and bending and stretching and classes – Harmonie, Anatomie, Psychologie, Improvisation, with a powerful ictus on the last syllable in each case.[32]

Beckett seems to have in his sights Emile Jacques-Dalcroze's Schule Hellerau-Laxenburg, where his cousin Peggy Sinclair had studied.[33] Lucia Joyce (thought to be the model for the Syra-Cusa) was also a student of Dalcroze.[34] It was indeed near Vienna (lying nine miles to the south), and the Smeraldina did have piano lessons as part of her training,[35] but in most respects this was hardly the devout, intellectual fare that Belacqua might have imagined when she first spoke of her plans and invoked the great name of Bach.

The music/dance relationship is part of a larger anxiety in the novel about the body, very neatly expounded in that initial scene, where Belacqua finds himself particularly affected by 'the béret that she had snatched off to wave when the ship began to draw clear':

> The sun had bleached it from green to a very poignant reseda and it had always, from the very first moment he clapped eyes on it, affected him as being a most shabby, hopeless and moving article. It might have been a tuft of grass growing the way she ripped it off her little head and began to wave it with an idiotic clockwork movement of her arm, up and down, not to flutter it like a handkerchief, but grasping it in the middle to raise it and lower it with a stiff arm as though she were doing an exercise with a dumb-bell.[36]

The Smeraldina's gestures are deemed neither graceful nor spontaneous but mechanical and muscular (though there is also a hint that her naivety is more natural (grass-like) than socially or culturally conditioned (like the handkerchief)). However, Belacqua himself is caught in the same situation, as this is all part of his own quite self-conscious attempt at a display of feeling as he 'works himself up to the little gush of tears that would exonerate him', his mind a 'piston', his

---

32 Ibid., pp. 13–14.

33 See Knowlson, *Damned to Fame*, p. 83; Martin Puchner, *Stage Fright: Modernism, Anti-Theatricality, and Drama* (Baltimore, MD, 2002), p. 170.

34 See Shloss, *Lucia Joyce*, pp. 85, 121–2.

35 She 'never looked like being able to play the piano, but she had a curious talent for improvisation' (Beckett, *Dream of Fair to Middling Women*, p. 14).

36 Ibid., p. 4.

emotion a matter of 'technique'.[37] Very soon, however, Belacqua discovers that this 'fetish [...] refused to work':[38] 'he switched on as usual, after the throttling and expunction, and nothing happened. The cylinders of his mind abode serene'.[39] While he seemed to sneer at the double sense in which the Smeraldina's beret was a 'moving article', this simple simultaneity of sentiment and movement is denied to Belacqua.

Similar themes are played out in *Murphy* (1936, pub. 1938), particularly in Neary's theories – tantalizingly appealing to the eponymous anti-hero – of what he variously terms 'the Apmonia', 'the Isomony' or 'the Attunement'.[40] The ambiguities surrounding Murphy's death – whether it is a deliberate suicide or an unfortunate accident, and what it means to take either possibility as the apotheosis of Murphy's belief-system – share a great deal with *Dream of Fair to Middling Women*. As Beckett worked through these issues in his fiction of the 1930s, his intention, at least in part, seems to have been to ironize that aspect of himself which struggled with the mind/body conundrum and to suggest that any attempts to engender emotional states through premeditated movements are doomed to fail.

However, in *Murphy* any implied polarity between the abstraction of music and the physicality of dance is subverted by a conceit whereby 'music' also functions as a euphemism for sexual relations:

> Celia said that if he did not find work at once she would have to go back to hers. Murphy knew what that meant. No more music.
>
> This phrase is chosen with care, lest the filthy censors should lack an occasion to commit their filthy synecdoche.[41]

What Catherine Laws has termed 'the double image of music'[42] creates something of a crux in Chapter 11.

> Late that afternoon, after many fruitless hours in the chair, it would be just about the time Celia was telling her story, MMM [of the Magdalen Mental Mercyseat

---

37 Ibid.

38 Ibid., p. 5.

39 Ibid.

40 See Samuel Beckett, *Murphy* (London, 1993), p. 6. Murphy's heart is described as being 'like Petrushka in his box'; Beckett's letter to Thomas McGreevy, 22 Sept. 1935, contains a review of Woizikovsky dancing the role (measured against none other than Léonid Massine) (*Letters of Samuel Beckett*, vol. 1, pp. 277–8).

41 Beckett, *Murphy*, p. 47.

42 See Catherine Laws, 'The Double Image of Music in Beckett's Early Fiction', in Marius Buning, Matthijs Engelberts and Onno Kosters (eds), *Beckett and Religion: Beckett/Aesthetics/Politics, Samuel Beckett Today/Aujourd'hui* 9 (Amsterdam and Atlanta, GA, 2000), pp. 295–308 (p. 297).

> (where Murphy worked)] stood suddenly for music, MUSIC, MUSIC, in brilliant, brevier and canon, or some such typographical scream, if the gentle compositor would be so friendly. Murphy interpreted this in his favour, for he had seldom been in such need of encouragement.[43]

The question is whether the 'music, MUSIC, MUSIC' is Neary's, Celia's or some ambivalent combination of the two. In one sense this moment is quite abstract and formal, and almost autistic in its private interpretation of the alliterative acronym. The notion of music as asylum is itself double-edged, and for Beckett MMM might also have signified Robert Burton's description of music in *The Anatomy of Melancholy* as '*mentis medicina maestae* [a roaring-meg against melancholy]'.[44] On the other hand, the appeal to formal autonomy is made with a kind of expressive excess;[45] and there are, perhaps, even more personal associations involved here. The 'typographical scream' alludes to Lucia Joyce's talent for illumination, 'as exemplified in her initial letters to Joyce's *Pomes Penyeach* and to the A.B.C. poem of Chaucer';[46] and MMM might equally refer to the '"Margaret Morris Movement" (M.M.M.)',[47] of which Lucia was a member.[48]

The latter possibility would represent a particularly acute conjunction of the music–dance or mind–body duality: Margaret Morris mentioned Lucia in her memoir (partly because of her famous father, though also for her own qualities as a dancer)[49] and was Lucia's teacher when Beckett saw her dance at the Bal Bullier on 28 May 1929.[50] According to Carol Loeb Shloss, 'Samuel Beckett remembered the excellence of this particular performance and kept his photograph of Lucia in costume for the rest of his life'.[51] Morris's *The Notation of Movement* had

---

43 Beckett, *Murphy*, p. 132.

44 Robert Burton, *The Anatomy of Melancholy*, ed. Holbrook Jackson (New York, 2001), p. 115 (quoting Lemnius, *Instit. cap.* 44); see also Samuel Beckett, *Dream Notebook*, ed. John Pilling (Reading, 1999), p. 114; Beckett, *Dream of Fair to Middling Women*, pp. 38, 85.

45 'Where Apollo fails, Marsyas leaps in, grinning' (Daniel Albright, *Beckett and Aesthetics* (Cambridge, 2003), p. 145).

46 Frank Budgen, *James Joyce and the Making of 'Ulysses'* (London, 1934), p. 195.

47 Margaret Morris, *My Life in Movement* (Garelochhead, Argyll and Bute, 2003), p. ix.

48 A fine selection of photographs from *Margaret Morris Dancing: A Book of Pictures* by Fred Daniels is available at <http://www.a-to-m.com/leftarm/margaret-morris-dancing-photographs-by-fred-daniels/>.

49 See Morris, *My Life in Movement*, p. 65. Incidentally, Morris also remarked that 'I loved Beethoven's Seventh Symphony, and when someone told me it had been called the "Dancing Symphony" I said I would make this name come true' (ibid., p. 31).

50 See Knowlson, *Damned to Fame*, p. 103.

51 Shloss, *Lucia Joyce*, pp. 176, 490 n. 43. The music on that occasion was the *Marche Militaire* by Schubert (see ibid., p. 164), a piece and a form determined by movement that was nevertheless not intended to inspire or to accompany any.

encouraged some to hope that dance could soon be the equal of absolute music, by providing the *sine qua non* for the creation of 'permanent', 'detailed and elaborate' works.[52] Decades later, however, Morris herself acknowledged its limitations, commenting that 'it seems to me obvious that any notation of movement can in reality only notate *positions* and indicate *transitions*'.[53] It is reasonable to speculate that Beckett would have known about the Margaret Morris Movement and that it might have been an important touchstone for him not just in the debate about the relative place of dance and music in the hierarchy of the arts, but also, later, for his own acute concern with issues of notation and authority, text and performance.[54]

'Dance' and the 'Balletic'

Having quoted Beckett's letter to Morris Sinclair, James Knowlson remarked that,

> in spite of this difficulty, it was at this period of [Beckett's] life that the groundwork for his later interest in choreographing movements on stage was laid. When he came to direct his own plays in the 1960s and 1970s, he brought to his task the intense concentration and meticulous precision of the choreographer.[55]

Beyond Lucky's dance in *En attendant Godot* (on which more later), several Beckett works could indeed be described as dances: *Acte sans paroles* (1955) was 'directed *and danced by* Deryk Mandel (Man), for whom it was written'[56] and has been called 'a ballet without music';[57] '*Quad* was composed for the Stuttgart Preparatory Ballet School and performed there in June 1981',[58] and 'no questions arise if we consider

---

52 See H. Levy, 'Introduction', to Margaret Morris, *The Notation of Movement* (London, 1928), pp. 3–5 (pp. 3–4).

53 Morris, *My Life in Movement*, p. 151.

54 Much later, in 1961, Beckett would take up these issues with Igor Stravinsky (the composer of *Petrushka*, among much else) (see Deirdre Bair, *Samuel Beckett: A Biography* [1978] (London, 1990), p. 581; Knowlson, *Damned to Fame*, p. 500).

55 Knowlson, *Damned to Fame*, p. 194.

56 Maurice Harmon (ed.), *No Author Better Served: The Correspondence of Samuel Beckett and Alan Schneider* (Cambridge, MA, 1998), p. 13 n. 2 (my italics).

57 Manako Ôno, 'Actes sans paroles, paroles sans scène', in Manako Okamuro et al. (eds), *Borderless Beckett, Samuel Beckett Today/Aujourd'hui* 19 (Amsterdam and New York, 2008), pp. 403–12 (p. 403) (my translation).

58 Sidney Homan, *Beckett's Theaters: Interpretations for Performance* (London, 1984), p. 246 n. 4. Homan adds, however, that 'the players are, properly, mimes, not dancers' (ibid.). Similarly, in *Quad,* 'by having the figures accumulate from 1 to 2 to 3 to 4 in disciplined, choreographed routines, Beckett sets up expectations for a ritualistic dance. But soon after all four players are present, they begin – incrementally – to disperse, no communal dance having occurred' (Susan D. Brienza, 'Perilous Journeys on Beckett's

Quadrat as a ballet'.[59] A work such as *Footfalls* (1975) is a borderline case: Billie Whitelaw has written that the movements Beckett induced her to make in rehearsals 'started to feel like dance'.[60] The 'mimed fugue'[61] of *What Where* (1983), with its diagrammatic movements, also blurs the boundary between drama and dance. But 'dance' also occurs as a metaphor in discussions of Beckett's non-theatrical works, including *Murphy*, and it is noteworthy that, when it does, it has the curious effect of rendering the subject not more corporeal but more abstract.

Hugh Kenner says that Murphy and Endon's final chess-game[62] 'enacts, as in a ballet, Murphy's fascination with the rituals of the "higher schizoids", and his imperfect grasp of their satisfactions';[63] while John Robert Keller calls it 'a complex dance of isolation and attempts at engagement',[64] which 'in a sense … is a precursor for the dance between Sam and Watt, which also develops an ambiguity of isolation within contact, and the late piece *Quad*'.[65] Of *Human Wishes* (1940), Beckett's unfinished play about Dr Johnson's circle, Ruby Cohn suggests that 'Beckett could not resolve the conflict between the psychological drama he had painstakingly prepared himself to write and the verbal ballet he actually began to write'.[66] Stan Gontarski speaks of the 'paranoid ballet' of the protagonist in *Eh Joe* (1965) 'shuff[ling] about his room […] to shut out prying eyes';[67] Georg Hensel describes the joining and unjoining of hands in *Come and Go* (1965) as 'a little ballet of human relations';[68] and Sidney Homan similarly emphasizes the 'complex, highly stylized "ballet of hands" (as someone called it) between B and L'[69] in *Nacht und Träume* (1982). Discussing Beckett's late prose work *Company* (1979), H. Porter Abbott describes

Stages: Travelling Through Words', in Katherine H. Burkman (ed.), *Myth and Ritual in the Plays of Samuel Beckett* (London, 1987), pp. 28–49 (p. 47)).

59 Hans H. Hiebel, 'Quadrat 1 + 2 as a Television Play', in Marius Buning and Lois Oppenheim (eds), *Beckett in the 1990s*, *Samuel Beckett Today/Aujourd'hui* 2 (Amsterdam and Atlanta, GA, 1993), pp. 335–43 (p. 341).

60 Billie Whitelaw, *Billie Whitelaw … Who He?* (London, 1995), p. 144.

61 Albright, *Beckett and Aesthetics*, p. 7.

62 Beckett, *Murphy*, pp. 136–8.

63 Hugh Kenner, *A Reader's Guide to Samuel Beckett* (Syracuse, NY, 1996), p. 68.

64 John Robert Keller, *Samuel Beckett and the Primacy of Love* (Manchester and New York, 2002), p. 81.

65 Ibid., p. 89 n. 20.

66 Ruby Cohn, *A Beckett Canon* (Ann Arbor, MI, 2001), p. 106.

67 Stanley E. Gontarski, 'The Business of Being Beckett: Beckett's Reception in the U.S.A.', in Mark Nixon and Matthew Feldman (eds), *The International Reception of Samuel Beckett* (London and New York, 2009), pp. 9–23 (p. 21).

68 See Julian Garforth, '"Beckett, unser Hausheiliger?" Changing Critical Reactions to Beckett's Directorial Work in Berlin', in Buning, Engelberts and Kosters (eds), *Beckett and Religion*, pp. 309–29 (p. 322).

69 Sidney Homan, *Filming Beckett's Television Plays: A Director's Experience* (London, 1992), p. 111.

how its meditation on a watch is 'defamiliarized to the monotonous circular ballet of the second hand and its shadow'.[70] Whereas earlier we saw the bodily realities of dance contrasted with the implied purity of absolute music, here dance (especially as exemplified by ballet) is invoked to capture a scene of troubled and troubling communication, somehow emphasizing the lack of real connection and contact. Just as when Wittgenstein writes 'piano playing, a dance of human fingers', the effect is not (as one might think) to bring a somewhat intellectual activity within the ambit of the corporeal, but instead to add yet another layer of abstraction, to divorce the mind from the movement of muscles in order to contemplate it as a purely formal play.[71]

This is not simply a slippage between literal reference to embodied movement and the use of 'dance' as a metaphor, but the fact that all the Beckettian 'dances' (both actual and metaphorical) are inhibited or troubling in some way and that the range of the dance metaphor as applied to Beckett has narrowed to mean something formal or abstract. To some extent, this emphasis is inspired by Beckett's 1975 revival of *Waiting for Godot* at the Schiller Theater, Berlin, as documented by Walter Asmus.

> [Saturday 28 December 1974]
>
> With each sentence Beckett makes a step toward the imaginary partner. Always a step, then the sentence. Beckett calls this a step-by-step approach, a physical theme, which comes up five, six, or seven times and has got to be done very accurately. This is the balletic side of the story. Lucky falls twice, and this mustn't be done realistically, but very cleanly.
>
> Beckett: 'It is a game, everything is a game. When all four of them are lying on the ground, that cannot be handled naturalistically. That has got to be done artificially, balletically. Otherwise, everything becomes only an imitation, an imitation of reality.'[72]

Somehow, through précis and repetition,[73] the notion of the 'balletic' in Beckett Studies has subtly changed, from 'artificial', 'not realistic' or 'not naturalistic' to an almost exclusive emphasis on the 'accuracy' part of the metaphor.

---

70 H. Porter Abbott, *Beckett Writing Beckett: The Author in the Autograph* (London and Ithaca, NY, 1996), p. 19; see Samuel Beckett, *Company*, in *Nohow On: Company, Ill Seen Ill Said, Worstward Ho* (London, 1989), pp. 5–52: pp. 47–9.

71 Ludwig Wittgenstein, *Culture and Value: A Selection from the Posthumous Remains*, ed. Georg Henrik von Wright and Heikki Nyman, trans. Peter Winch, 2nd edn (Oxford, 1998), p. 42.

72 Walter D. Asmus, 'Beckett Directs "Godot"', trans. Ria Julian, in Harold Bloom (ed.), *Samuel Beckett's 'Waiting for Godot'* (Broomall, PA, 2008), pp. 15–24 (p. 22) (originally published in *Theatre Quarterly* 5/19 (1975): 19–26).

73 See, for example, Lawrence Graver, *Samuel Beckett, 'Waiting for Godot'*, 2nd edn (Cambridge, 2004), p. 85; David Bradby, *Beckett: Waiting for Godot* (Cambridge, 2001), p. 116.

> [Lois Oppenheim:] *Why do you use the word 'choreography' in connection with Beckett's plays?*
>
> [Walter Asmus:] Because Beckett himself, when directing *Godot* in Berlin, used the word 'balletic' in the context of the actors' movements. But I think the words 'balletic' and 'choreography' shouldn't be overvalued. It was not that Beckett wanted them to *move* like ballet dancers. It was simply to express the exactitude, and that there was a design in the blocking that had a meaning.[74]

Since this meaning is never spelt out, one is left simply with the 'exactitude' – somehow all the more exacting *because* indeterminate or at least verbally inexpressible. Perhaps we are instead in danger of *undervaluing* the 'ballet'/'choreography' metaphor in seeing it as a straightforward synonym for 'exactitude', to the neglect of all the other facets – beauty, grace, expression, vivacity, to name but a few – that it embraces.

'Any discussion of this kind of stage movement,' advises Jonathan Kalb, 'ought eventually to focus on *Endgame* (1956), which Beckett has said he prefers to *Godot* because of the greater exactitude with which its physical activity is planned'.[75]

> In Beckett's Schiller Theatre production of *Endgame* [1967], Clov's footsteps back and forth from the kitchen to Hamm's chair were of a consistent number and pattern and were always rhythmically timed: 'It's almost like a dance', says Beckett, 'equal number of steps, rhythm kept equal.'[76]

The simile works, so far as it goes: it is like a (certain kind of) dance, in that the movements and timing are prearranged – but there is nothing that says even choreographed pieces should be 'consistent' or 'equal'. The exaggeration was perhaps admitted by Beckett by saying that it was 'almost' like a dance; but Beckett's explicators instead take things even further.

> He normally had a well-thought-out intellectual rationale behind everything that he did, and, in this case, this may have been provided by his readings in the 1930s in the history of Greek philosophy, which would have supplied him with an additional motivation for his emphasis on repetition and pattern. At rehearsals in Berlin, after organising Clov's steps from his kitchen to Hamm's armchair, Beckett referred to the repeated numbers as being 'Pythagorean'. Clearly what he had in mind was Pythagoras' theory in which the universe consisted of a harmonious disposition of numbers, based on the perfect number 10. Again,

---

74 Quoted in John Fletcher, *About Beckett: The Playwright and the Work* (London, 2003), p. 147.

75 Jonathan Kalb, *Beckett in Performance* (Cambridge, 1989), p. 39, n. 94.

76 James Knowlson, 'Beckett as Director', in John Haynes and James Knowlson, *Images of Beckett* (Cambridge, 2003), p. 133.

> using such repeated patterns as a unifying feature, Beckett organised Clov's short steps when he is 'having an idea' into a series of 6 + 4 + 6 + 4.[77]

There is an irony in the way that, just as Beckett felt the need to provide gestural accompaniment to Clov's 'having an idea', Beckett's interpreters feel compelled to offer ideas to accompany this organization of movement. The processes of interpretation and explication – a mixture of observation, erudition and supposition – are marshalled because for some unspoken reason it is necessary or desirable not only to 'describe arabesques' but to *pre*scribe them in minute detail, both before and after the event. But *why* did Beckett usually have 'a well-thought-out intellectual rationale behind everything that he did', if indeed he did, or why do *we* need him to have needed one?

Let Him Dance

To explore these questions, we need to focus not (as Kalb suggests) on *Endgame* but on *Waiting for Godot*, the source of the maxim quoted at the beginning of this chapter:

> POZZO: Well, would you like him to think something for us?
> ESTRAGON: I'd rather he'd dance, it'd be more fun?
> POZZO: Not necessarily.
> ESTRAGON: Wouldn't it, Didi, be more fun?
> VLADIMIR: I'd like well to hear him think.
> ESTRAGON: Perhaps he could dance first and think afterwards, if it isn't too much to ask him.
> VLADIMIR: [*To* POZZO.] Would that be possible?
> POZZO: By all means, nothing simpler. It's the natural order. [*He laughs briefly.*]
> VLADIMIR: Then let him dance.
> [*Silence.*]
> POZZO: Do you hear, hog?[78]

Even allowing for the common practice of attributing to a writer words that he or she has put into the mouth of a fictional character, the transformation of this ironic and disturbing scene into the straightforwardly univocal motto 'Dance first. Think later. It's the natural order.' is something of a travesty. There is nothing permissive or expressive about Lucky's dance, the scene instead being one of exploitation

---

[77] Ibid., p. 133, n. 95.

[78] Samuel Beckett, *Waiting for Godot*, in *The Complete Dramatic Works* (London, 1986), pp. 11–88: p. 39.

and abuse.[79] Pozzo's brief laugh at his notion of 'natural order' hints at a possible oxymoron, but perhaps the desire to give (or receive) orders does indeed come naturally to man.

> VLADIMIR: Tell me to dance.
> ESTRAGON: I'm going.
> VLADIMIR: Dance, hog! [*He writhes.*][80]

Thus, in Act II, Vladimir orders Estragon to give him an order, and, when Estragon refuses, Vladimir resorts to ordering (and obeying) himself. Vladimir's 'let him dance' is no signal to let Lucky off the leash, either metaphorically or literally, having more the sense of 'make him dance'.

Ironically, as others have noted, hardly anyone thinks about Lucky's dance itself.

> In her discussion, [Toby] Zinman (1995) points out its isolation: there are minimal stage directions,[81] it was rarely discussed by Beckett or by actors who performed it, and it is rarely mentioned by critics. I agree, of course, with her assertion that the dance is a 'work of art and as such it is a non-verbal, miniature version of the play itself' (Zinman, 1995: 311.[82] In a sense, the primal importance of the dance has been re-enacted in its non-discussion.[83]

Those discussions that do exist are concerned principally with interpretations of Vladimir and Estragon's attempts to guess what the dance is called ('The Scapegoat's Agony', 'The Hard Stool') and of Pozzo's revelation of the answer ('The Net').[84] Their attempts to understand the non-verbal by means of the verbal are to some extent inevitably futile – and yet we too have no choice but to participate. Zinman cites the English proverb 'to dance in a net' and its origin ('Think not you are undetected. You dance in a nett, and you think no body sees

---

79 The brutality comes over more even forcefully in the English translation, there being, for example, no equivalent for 'hog' in the French original (see Samuel Beckett, *En attendant Godot* (Paris, 1952), p. 55).

80 Beckett, *Waiting for Godot*, p. 82.

81 '[LUCKY *dances. He stops.*] ESTRAGON: Is that all?' (ibid., p. 39).

82 Zinman, 'Lucky's Dance in Waiting for Godot'.

83 Keller, *Samuel Beckett and the Primacy of Love*, p. 169 n. 16 (quoting T.S. Zinman, 'Lucky's Dance in Waiting for Godot', *Modern Drama*, 38/3 (1995): 30–23). Keller suggests that 'it mirrors a core sense of non-recognition, of rupture in the primal dance of life between mother and infant' (ibid.) – but it is the non-discussion itself rather than its potential causes that is of interest to me.

84 See Beckett, *Waiting for Godot*, p. 39; Zinman, 'Lucky's Dance in Waiting for Godot', pp. 309–13; Keller, *Samuel Beckett and the Primacy of Love*, pp. 153, 169–70 n. 16.

you').[85] However, a more specifically Beckettian source might be Kleist's essay on the marionette theatre, in which 'an invisible and incomprehensible force, like a net of iron, seemed to constrain the free play of [the] gestures' of a once-graceful adolescent boy upon becoming self-conscious of that grace.[86] Similarly, one might argue, Beckett's own authorial and directorial movements lost something of their original spontaneity as he was reluctantly compelled to determine in what their quality consisted, in order, hopefully, to reproduce them anew.[87] 'When [Belacqua] tried to mechanise what was a dispensation he was guilty of an abominable confusion'[88] – yet this seems to be not only what Beckett found himself doing later in his career but also what earns our greatest admiration.

For a different perspective on this confusion, I want to consider two contrasting examples of dance-as-communication in Beckett: an apparently successful instance, which is perhaps not so, and a seemingly failed instance, which is perhaps more so. The first comes from *Happy Days* (1961), a work which, despite featuring a middle-aged woman buried up to her waist in earth in Act I and up to her neck in Act II (in a sense *pro*scribing arabesques), was turned into a ballet (*L'Heure esquise* (1908)) by Maurice Béjart.[89] In fact, dance does feature in the '*musical-box tune*' hummed and then sung softly by Winnie at the close of the play:

Though I say not
What I may not
Let you hear,
Yet the swaying
Dance is saying
Love me dear!
Every touch of fingers
Tells me what I know,

85 See Zinman, 'Lucky's Dance in Waiting for Godot'; Keller, *Samuel Beckett and the Primacy of Love*, pp. 169–70 n. 16.

86 Heinrich von Kleist, *On a Theatre of Marionettes*, trans. Gerti Wilford (London, 1989), p. 8. The boy's unsuccessful attempts to repeat a certain particularly winning lifting of his foot also prefigure Pozzo's own almost paralysing pomposity (see ibid., pp. 7–8; cf.: 'The second is never so sweet …' – Pozzo (Beckett, *Waiting for Godot*, p. 29)).

87 Notice, however, that the two suggested sources do not fit squarely together: one assumes that the proverbial 'net', like Kleist's, is (consciousness of) the gaze of the other, whereas in the proverb the net is that of *non*-awareness of the gaze. In any case, Lucky does not dance 'in a nett': his dance *is* 'The Net'.

88 Beckett, *Dream of Fair to Middling Women*, p. 123.

89 See William Hutchings, '"In the Old Style," Yet Anew: *Happy Days* in the "After Beckett"', in Stanley E. Gontarski (ed.), *A Companion to Samuel Beckett* (Oxford, 2010), pp. 308–25 (p. 318). It is, perhaps, the very way that movement is suppressed or denied which attracts a dancer's attention, as well as the ritualized and regulated form of all Winnie's gestures, both physical and verbal.

Says for you,
It's true, it's true,
You love me so![90]

Despite the cruel irony of Winnie's situation and the forced character of her attempts at cheerfulness, her rendition of this tune does at least offer a moment of respite or release, of apparent (and un-awful) consolation. However, what 'the dance is saying' is not beyond doubt – or, if it is, then it is of doubtful value for that very reason. The waltz from Franz Léhar's *The Merry Widow* (1905) is so apt that it is surprising to learn that until quite late in the day Beckett was considering using 'When Irish Eyes Are Smiling' instead, even asking Alan Schneider which he preferred.[91] Their musical characteristics are similar: both share a lilting triple metre (although *The Merry Widow* is somewhat more wistful) and evoke a sentimental nostalgia – but what makes *The Merry Widow* the perfect choice are the *words*.[92]

Ostensibly the dance (music/touch) says, unambiguously and superlatively, what words cannot, yet ironically we can only learn that it does so by means of words, and we only have the singer's word for it. So complete is the communication that one wonders whether it is not in fact redundant: not only does the singer – in this case, Winnie – already know what she is told, but what she is told is the product of her own imagination. The supposed meeting of minds is potentially no more than an illusion, an echo. The pauses and phrasing conditioned by the music (and line-breaks/enjambments) also enable an alternative reading of the first three lines, as a 'Hiberno-English imperative' (where 'let' can also be used with the second-person pronoun and not just (as in Standard English) with the first- and third-person ('let's go'; 'let him have it')).[93] So, in addition to their primary sense of 'although I do not say that which I am not allowed to say in your hearing', the lines could be rendered 'although I do not say that which I am not allowed to, *hear it*, nevertheless, as if I do!' Again, the effect is to produce an equivalence – unnerving to those who are invested in the business of interpretation – between the communion of two souls and a delusory monologue.

A contrasting example comes from *Molloy* (1947, pub. 1951), in the long and justly famous passage where Moran thinks (as he often does) of his bees.

---

90 Samuel Beckett, *Happy Days: A Play in Two Acts*, in *The Complete Dramatic Works*, pp. 137–68: p. 168.

91 See Samuel Beckett to Alan Schneider, 20 May 1961, in Harmon (ed.), *No Author Better Served*, pp. 82, n. 3.

92 In the English adaptation of 1907 by Adrian Ross (Arthur Reed Ropes (1859–1933)).

93 See T.P. Dolan, *A Dictionary of Hiberno-English: The Irish Use of English*, rev. edn (Dublin, 2004), 'Introduction to the First Edition', pp. xxi–xxix (p. xxvi).

> And I thought above all of their dance, for my bees danced, oh not as men dance, to amuse themselves, but in a different way. I alone of all mankind knew this, to the best of my belief.[94]

It is the definition of dance as 'any patterned, rhythmic movement in space and time' that 'enables biologists like Karl von Frisch (in *The Dancing Bees* (1927, trans. 1954)) to describe the movement patterns of non-human creatures, like bees, as dances'.[95] Whereas Winnie's song gave us music with the element of dance deliberately minimized, here is dance without music. Moran is as smitten (by his bees) as Winnie is (by her beloved), if not more so – but he at least hedges his grand claims with multiple caveats. He sets about making sense of the bees' dance, concluding that it is

> a system of signals by means of which the incoming bees, satisfied or dissatisfied with their plunder, informed the outgoing bees in what direction to go, and in what not to go. But the outgoing bees danced too. It was no doubt their way of saying, I understand, or, Don't worry about me. But away from the hive, and busily at work, the bees did not dance. Here their watchword seemed to be, Every man for himself, assuming bees to be capable of such notions.

The assumption is a significant one, which threatens to undermine Moran's entire interpretative exercise. Nevertheless, he continues to elaborate it, in a quasi-scientific way, rhetorically recounting how he has 'classified' and 'measured' a great number of complicated figures, with their 'probable' meanings, taking account of ever more 'determinants': the 'figures', the 'hum', the 'height' and 'doubtless other[s] of which [he] had not the slightest idea' (the admission of ignorance being itself a central pillar of the rational process). In describing his attempts to describe their dance, Moran creates another kind of dance: that of persuasion, although the notional 'public' is acknowledged only to be denied.

Ultimately, Moran's apparent motivation is undone by his own 'raptur[ous]' words: 'Here is something I can study all my life, and never understand':

> And all during this long journey home, when I racked my mind for a little joy in store, the thought of my bees and their dance was the nearest thing to comfort. For I was still eager for my little joy, from time to time! And I admitted with

---

94 Samuel Beckett, *Molloy* [1955], trans. Samuel Beckett and Patrick Bowles, in *Trilogy: Molloy, Malone Dies, The Unnamable* (London, 1994), pp. 5–176 (pp. 169–70); cf. Samuel Beckett, *Molloy* [1947, pub. 1951] (Paris, 2002), pp. 228–30.

95 Roger Copeland and Marshall Cohen, 'What Is Dance?', in (eds), *What Is Dance? Readings in Theory and Criticism* (Oxford, 1983), pp. 1–9 (p. 1). Since von Frisch's study was entitled simply *Aus dem Leben der Bienen*, we should perhaps also credit its English translator, Dora Ilse (Karl von Frisch, *The Dancing Bees: An Account of the Life and Senses of the Honey Bee*, trans. Dora Ilse (London, 1954)).

> good grace the possibility that this dance was after all no better than the dances of the people of the West, frivolous and meaningless. But for me, sitting near my sun-drenched hives, it would always be a noble thing to contemplate, too noble ever to be sullied by the cogitations of a man like me, exiled in his manhood.

As so often with Beckett's narrators, definitive meaning proves elusive in the continual and delicate play of ironic humour: as Moran himself might have put it, 'the purpose of the hum is not to emphasize the dance, but on the contrary to vary it'. The ways in which the passage argues against itself are somehow both obvious and subtle. Moran disparages Western dancing because it is 'meaningless', but admires the dance of the bees precisely because it cannot be tainted by human attempts to understand, to attribute, ascribe or create meaning; and yet this very thought, one feels, can only occur to the seemingly lamentable creature called man.

As the young Beckett recognized (in praise of Joyce), it is the 'endless substantial variations' which 'structural convenience[s]' allow, rather than how little room they leave for manoeuvre, which is to be most valued, the 'interior intertwining of [...] themes into a decoration of arabesques – decoration and more than decoration'.[96] In the 'Publisher's Note' to *Dream of Fair to Middling Women*, John Calder recalls how, although Beckett could see nothing but flaws in the 1978 Odéon revival of *Waiting for Godot*, they 'eventually repaired [...] to a *boîte* a block or two away where, late in the evening, Beckett actually accepted an invitation to get up and dance'.[97] Calder's 'actually', like the popularity of my initial quotation, relies on the incongruity not of a disappointed septuagenarian's dancing, but of Beckett's dancing *per se*. Yet like Lucky, 'He danced. He thought';[98] and thought, and danced. There is little point in being permissively prescriptive about their order, natural or otherwise: in Beckett, while there might be no dance without thought, there is rarely a thought that does not dance – or writhe.

---

96 Beckett, 'Dante...Bruno.Vico..Joyce', p. 22.

97 John Calder, 'Publisher's Note', to *Dream of Fair to Middling Women* (New York, 1992), pp. v–x (p. vi); the equivalent note to the Calder edition is briefer and omits this detail.

98 Vladimir, in Beckett, *Waiting for Godot*, p. 83.

Chapter 9
Not I for Solo Piano: Beckett's Text as Music

Paul Rhys

Origins

As a teenager, late one night I watched a television broadcast of Beckett's *Not I* quite by chance and was both terrified and mesmerized. The words came too fast to understand what was being said, but the image of Billy Whitelaw's mouth surrounded by darkness and the urgent intensity of communication were captivating. Later I found a slim volume on my father's bookshelves containing Beckett's *First Love*, *Not I* and *Imagination Dead Imagine*. It had been a Christmas gift from the composer, Roger Marsh, to my father, and, leaving to study at Oxford, I took the book with me. During my second year at university I read *Not I*, recalled the earlier TV viewing and, for the first time, properly understood the play. I was overwhelmed by the originality of the work and its psychological insights and fascinated by its structure, with its intriguing mixture of patterning and repetition. I understood a self-reflexive or self-referential quality in the writing which seemed to bring about an enhanced awareness of the present moment-in-time during the act of reading the text. Abbott's analysis certainly echoes this second of my encounters with the work:

> In summary, what I am proposing is a fundamental categorical shift in our reading of Beckett, one that moves him out of fiction altogether and relocates him in that rarely occupied subset of autography. … These texts are as distant from fiction as they are from conventional autobiography. … Beckett's subset is writing governed not by narrative form or any species of tropological wholeness but by that unformed intensity of being in the present which at every point in the text seeks to approach itself.[1]

I continued to read Beckett's work whilst studying for a PhD in composition and computer music at Keele (UK) and Northwestern Universities (US). During this period I became acquainted with Luciano Berio's large-scale *Sinfonia*, which sets spoken fragments of Beckett's novel *The Unnamable*

[1] H. Porter Abbot, *Beckett Writing Beckett: The Author in the Autograph* (Ithaca, NY, 1996), pp. 17–18.

alongside other texts in a dense polyphony of voices and instruments. I studied the settings of Mallarmé in Boulez's orchestral song-cycle *Pli Selon Pli* with a view to understanding how the poetry could exert such a force on the music, even when the soprano fell silent for long stretches of time. In the US, I first encountered the music of Morton Feldman through the duo for piano and cello *Patterns in a Chromatic Field* and then the ensemble work, *For Samuel Beckett*. I learned of Feldman's use of a Beckett text for his opera, *Neither*, but only heard this work much later. I became acquainted with the condensed expressivity of György Kurtág's music, although it was nearly a decade later that I heard his moving setting of Beckett's late text, *What is the Word*. In 1995, ten years after reading *Not I* and with my PhD nearly complete, I came across a newspaper advertisement published by the Annenberg-Beckett Foundation, inviting applications from creative artists and scholars to respond to Beckett's work in any shape or form. I proposed to write a piano solo that would be a direct transcription of Beckett's *Not I*, attempting to copy its structure in musical form. It was around this time that I first met the pianist Ian Pace, when he played a very simple synthesizer part in a performance of my ensemble work *Chicago Fall*. I soon became aware of the full extent of his abilities when I attended a solo recital by Pace including a performance of Brian Ferneyhough's *Lemma-Icon-Epigram*. This was a work that I had studied whilst in the US, and I was aware of the considerable technical demands it placed upon the performer, not least the realization of polyphonic textures in which each line is characterized independently by its own rhythmic complexities. Pace performed this challenging work with a precision and commitment that were exhilarating, quite the equal of any recording that I had listened to previously. I resolved to write my piano solo for Pace and was delighted when he agreed.

Analysis of Beckett's Text

My admiration for Beckett's writing and my fascination with the structure of the monologue in *Not I* left me with a determination to understand that structure and to embody it in the music that I would compose. So I set about analysing the text in two complementary ways: first a search for repeating text fragments, then a semantic analysis which sought to reveal narrative continuity and interruption. The printed text of *Not I* consists of a succession of short phrases separated from one another by three dots or ellipses. Other than this, there is almost no other punctuation and a bare minimum of directions for performance. When one reads the play or witnesses a performance one becomes instantly aware of a web of competing trains of thought that constantly interrupt one another, or occasionally develop unimpeded before being cut short in turn (see Figure 9.1). My first step towards understanding the structure of the text was to use a word-processor to search for repeating text fragments or groups of fragments. This approach was a natural extension of habits I had acquired as a computer programmer. I was unaware of the work by literary scholars, such as Rabinovitz,[2] who have used a computer concordance to analyse individual works of Beckett and to investigate their relationship with other works in his oeuvre.

This first analysis made it clear which text fragments repeat ('imagine!..' occurs nine times in the course of the play, and the refrain 'what?..who?..no!.. she!..' five times) and established which fragments do not. It revealed chains of fragments that develop or vary on recurrence ('all that early April morning light.../for on that April morning.../that April morning.../morning sun.../April.../ April morning.../April morning...'). It also became clear that the opening of the printed text ('out...into this world...this world...tiny little thing...') is recapitulated twice towards the end of the work. Beckett clearly wishes the audience of *Not I* to receive the impression that they are witnessing part of a continuous unending torrent of words, reinforced by his directions for the performer to ad-lib extra material before the start and after the end of the written text. But anyone who reads the complete monologue encounters sufficient repetition of its varied themes to have a good idea of how it might continue. It is as if Beckett has given us sufficient enough a fragment of a complex weave to be able to extrapolate its pattern. For all the open-endedness of this text, the author has carefully ensured that the audience receive an experience which may equally be understood as complete.

My second analysis of Mouth's monologue also took its approach from computer programming. In the C programming language and many others like it,[3] indentation of text, associated with the opening or closing curly brace – { or } – is used to delineate the control flow of a programme and to clarify its structure to the human reader. Instructions indented to the right are ignored during the execution of a programme if a conditional statement that precedes them is not fulfilled, or they may be repeated in a loop until a conditional statement is fulfilled. To gain an overview of its structure, a programmer reads only that text situated on the left margin of a programme and ignores the rest. Having been immersed in computer programming to achieve musical results, it seemed logical for me to use this indented text style to interpret and to clarify the complex web of ideas contained in Mouth's monologue. Figure 9.1 demonstrates a section of Beckett's text interpreted in this fashion (although it omits the curly braces that a programmer would use):

---

2 Rubin Rabinovitz, *Innovation in Samuel Beckett's Fiction* (Urbana and Chicago, 1992).

3 Brian W. Kernighan and Dennis M. Ritchie, *The C Programming Language*, 2nd edn (London, 1988).

whole body like gone...
just the mouth...

like maddened...
and can't stop...
no stopping it...

something she–...
something she had to–...

what?..
who?..
no!..
she!.. [*Pause and movement 3.*]

something she had to–...

what?..
the buzzing?..
yes...

all the time the buzzing...

dull roar...in the skull...

and the beam...

ferreting around...
painless...so far...
ha!..so far...

then thinking...

oh long after...
sudden flash...

perhaps something she had to...
had to...tell...

could that be it?..

something she had to...tell...

tiny little thing...
before its time...
godforsaken hole...

Figure 9.1 Interpretation of a section of Beckett's text for *Not I*

This use of indentation helped to identify continuous trains of thought that are interrupted and then resumed. But it also led to a hierarchical organization of Beckett's text, with the primary narrative thread on the left of the page and threads that are progressively less important situated to the right, much in the same way that a Schenkerian analysis of music separates the primary line, or *urlinie*, from what it considers to be secondary detail. When reading the text of

Not I for the first time, one receives the impression of a web of multiple trains of thought, all of equal importance. But a careful reading of the text reveals that there is a hierarchy, including asides which interrupt and sometimes comment on the preceding material. Thus in Figure 9.1 the text 'ferreting around...painless... so far...' comments on the fragment preceding it 'and the beam...' which clearly interrupts the thread of greatest persistence, uniting fragments 'something she had to–.../then thinking.../perhaps something she had to...had to...tell'. On the evidence of the text in my example, the fragment 'ferreting around...' is clearly of less structural importance than 'something she had to...tell...'. This identification of continuity and interruption and clarification of the semantic content and structure of Mouth's monologue, would prove to be critical when it came to the task of representing that text as music.

Beckett's Text as Music

An understanding of the text fragment as the fundamental building block of *Not I* led me to conceive of a musical work built as a mosaic of small musical fragments. Whenever a fragment of speech repeats in Beckett's text, a corresponding musical fragment would repeat in the piano solo. If a fragment of speech is developed or varied as it recurs in the course of the play, so too the musical fragment is developed or varied on its recurrence. The duration of each musical fragment is matched to the duration of its corresponding speech fragment, but, rather than working as a film composer, noting elapsed chronometric time from a video of Billie Whitelaw's performance, I chose the expedient of counting syllables in each text fragment and allocating each syllable the musical duration of one demisemiquaver at a tempo of quaver = 54. This approach was far from exact, but it was practical. It led to a total duration for the musical work slightly in excess of the 12 minutes of Billie Whitelaw's television performance. The counting of syllables was a rule that I carried out with some flexibility since the context and flow of musical ideas often demanded it.

At key moments in the musical work, when there is a particular urgency in Mouth's delivery or an unusual poignancy, Beckett's speech rhythms serve as the source of the music's rhythm (Examples 9.1, 9.2). A whole generation of composers, myself included, had gradually become familiar with the complex rhythmic style of Brian Ferneyhough, and it proved well suited to the task of capturing Mouth's speech rhythms. In this style a slow external pulse is subdivided into several parts, which may then be regrouped. Each of the resulting durations is then subjected to the same process of subdivision and regrouping. The procedure may be carried out repeatedly, provided that the resulting rhythm can be understood and performed by a musician. With the addition of ties to join durational units together and create syncopation, a great richness of rhythmic characterization becomes possible. The rhythmic diversity that in earlier styles might have occupied a whole bar of music now becomes embedded in a single quaver or crotchet pulse.

Example 9.1 Paul Rhys, *Not I*, bars 335–6

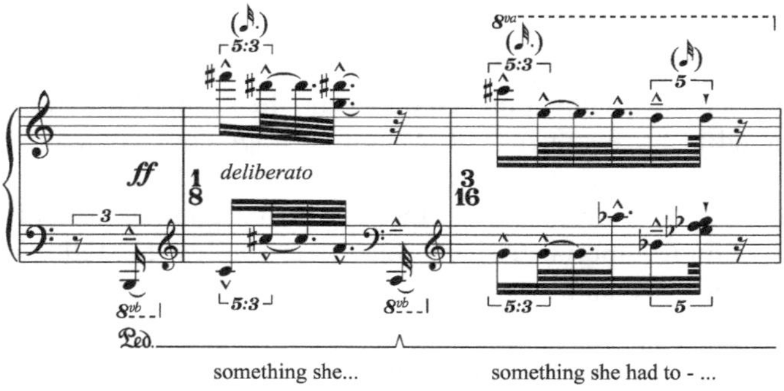

Example 9.2 Paul Rhys, *Not I*, bar 303

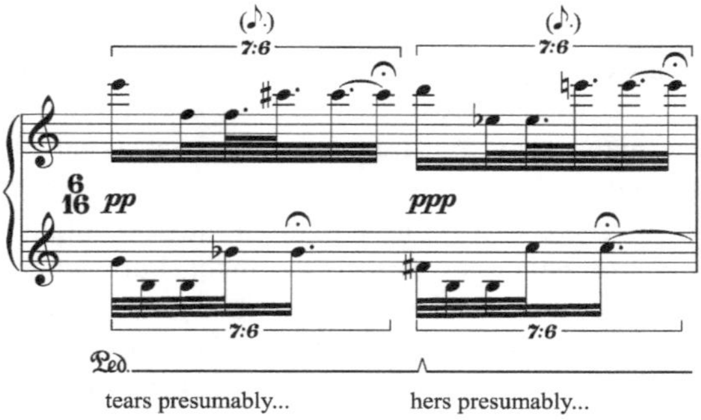

Example 9.3 Paul Rhys, *Not I*, bar 367

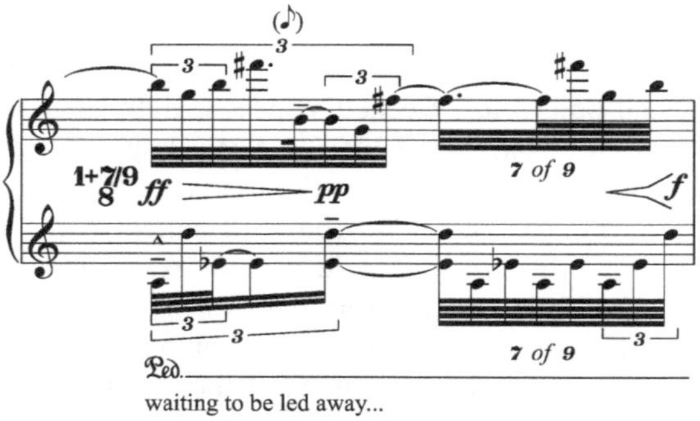

Example 9.4 Paul Rhys, *Not I*, bar 31

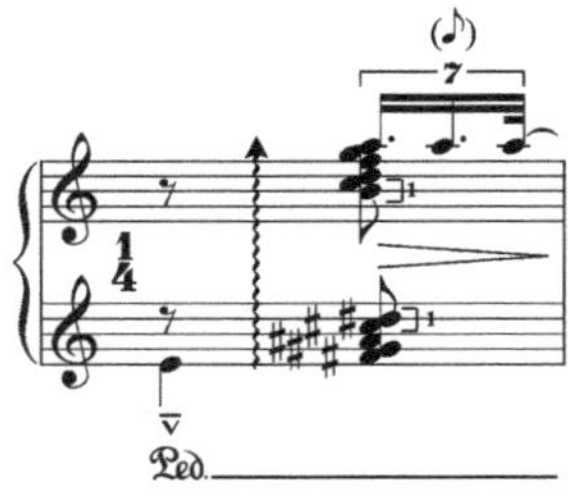
all that early April morning light...

The first half of Example 9.3 demonstrates this style at its simplest: the right hand of the piano part divides the quaver pulse into three; first and last thirds are divided again into three, whilst the middle third is divided into four and regrouped as three-plus-one. I was fortunate that Ian Pace could realize these rhythms with relative ease. It was the flexibility of this rhythmic style, its capacity for capturing the most subtle of rhythmic nuances and metrical displacements, that made it such a valuable tool for representing Beckett's speech rhythms. Occasionally, as in Example 9.2, right and left hands of the piano present slightly different versions of the same speech rhythm; more commonly the hands are synchronized in emphatic statement of the same speech rhythm.

For the greater part, it is the division and syncopation of an external pulse that generates rhythmic variety in the piano music of *Not I*. But occasionally the momentum of this internal division acquires such force that the external pulse is briefly forgotten, and time signatures such as (1+7/9)/8 are a natural consequence (Example 9.3). Such complex time signatures were simplified in my later musical works (*Five Preludes*,[4] *Dialogues*[5]) by a revaluation of the pulse so that the crotchet becomes the unit of duration, and is represented as 1/1 instead of 1/4. This is one example of how the experience of working on *Not I* led me to subsequent musical discoveries.

Whilst Beckett's speech rhythms sometimes serve as the basis for musical rhythm, at other times it is the visual or sonic images of Beckett's writing that serve as inspiration for a musical fragment. As already mentioned, Mouth makes repeated references to 'April morning light' prior to her immersion in darkness, and the resonances of a closely spaced twelve-note chord, spread between the hands

[4] The *Five Preludes* for piano were commissioned jointly by Reading University and Southern Arts and given their first performance by Ian Pace in the Great Hall at Reading University in November 1999.

[5] *The Dialogue* for clarinet and birdsong has been recorded by Andrew Sparling on the Lorelt CD label (Andrew Sparling, *A Place in The Sky* © 2012 Lontano Records Ltd. LNT 135). The 'Dialogue' for alto recorder and birdsong was first performed by Rachel Barnes on 19 November 2010 at the Mumford Theatre, Cambridge.

of the pianist, seemed to achieve this bright, luminous sonority (Example 9.4). Likewise, the buzzing that Mouth repeatedly says she can hear, whether in the ears or in the skull, is represented as a double trill (Example 9.5).

Example 9.5 Paul Rhys, *Not I*, bars 108–9

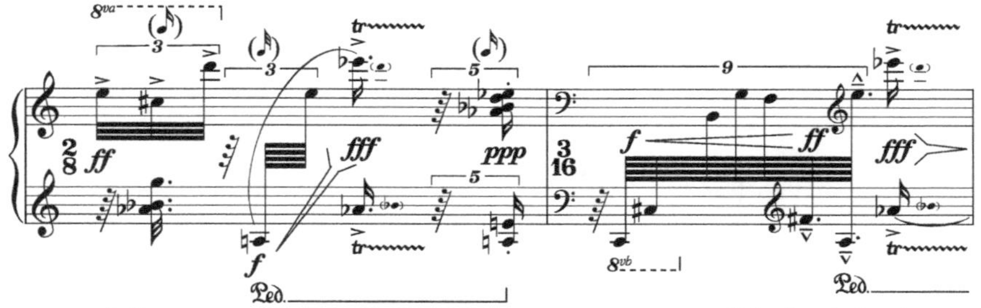

The narrative continuity that lies hidden within the text of Beckett's *Not I* is understood, I suggest, on a subconscious level when we witness a performance of the work. My semantic analysis (above) aimed to bring these continuities to the fore, sometimes uniting fragments of text separated by large intervening spans of time. It was through the use of harmony and voice-leading[6] that I was able to express these continuities and interruptions in the musical version of *Not I*.

Building on the experience of my previous musical works (*Chicago Fall*, *String Quartet No. 1*) the harmony in *Not I* is drawn from a carefully selected twelve-note all-interval series[7] (Example 9.6). Twelve trichords (three-note chords) are excised from the series (Example 9.7) and are used in prime and inversion to construct symmetrical twelve-note chords. Sequential harmonic progressions are then created between pairs of these twelve-note chords, in which each of the voices moves the total distance of a minor third. Example 9.8 shows the progressions between one such pair: in spanning a minor third, all twelve voices move either by semitones and fifths (Examples 9.8a and 9.8b) or by minor thirds (Example 9.8c). It is the last of these progressions that serves as the musical material for the most important refrain of the work, 'what?..who?..no!..she!..' (Example 9.9).

6 'Voice-leading' refers to the motion of each of the lines of music (or voices) in a composition, typically constrained by harmonic considerations. A 'voice' is often understood to be sounding in the mind of the listener, contributing to their understanding of the harmony, even when it has ceased to sound physically (as in Bach's solo cello suites, for example).

7 An all-interval series contains each of the possible intervals (1, 2, 3, 4, 5, 6, 7, 8, 9, 10 and 11 semitones) between adjacent notes, as well as each of the twelve pitch-classes. The convention is to reckon all intervals as if they were ascending; hence the descending fifth in Example 9.6 is labelled +5 or a rising fourth.

Example 9.6 The all-interval series

Example 9.7 Twelve trichords drawn from the series

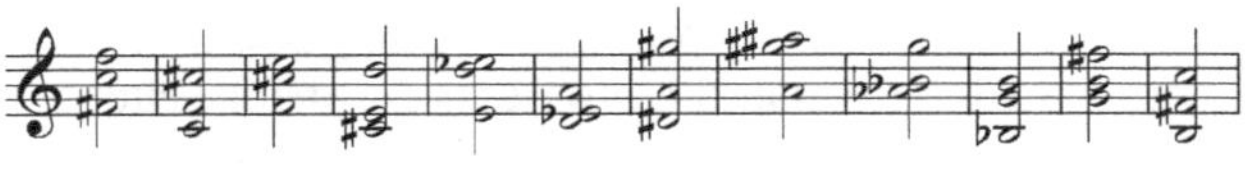

Example 9.8a, b, c Progressions of twelve-note chords

Example 9.9 Paul Rhys, *Not I*, bars 337–40

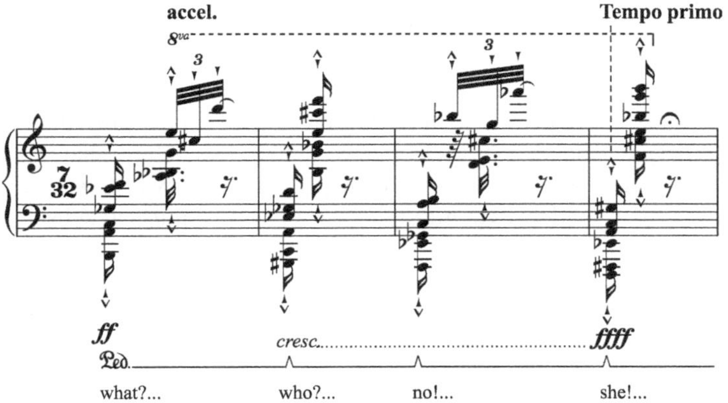

The family of trichords drawn from the all-interval series (Examples 9.6 and 9.7) serve to establish a referential tonality[8] in the piano solo. The harmonic

[8] Whereas the major or minor triad is the chord to which a piece of tonal music repeatedly returns, a wide variety of other chords or pitch-collections fulfil a comparable role in some twentieth-century repertoire. The pitch collection used in this way is described

progressions of Example 9.8 and others like them, lead away from and back to this referential, tonic level. Since these progressions are sequential, the ear is able to project their movement forwards in time. By making use of progressions such as these, it thus became possible to convey the narrative continuity in Beckett's text through continuity of harmonic motion and through the fulfilment, or postponement, of predictable voice-leading.

The schemes in Examples 9.8a and 9.8b span a minor third in four sequential steps and result in rather small-scale harmonic motion. But by moving in the opposite direction around the chromatic circle they occupy ten steps. These progressions of ten chords last longer than the progressions of four chords and, by using them, much longer-term harmonic motion is achievable. Thus the first ten lines of text on the left margin of Figure 9.1 (from 'whole body gone...' up to the start of the recapitulation 'tiny little thing...') are expressed musically as a sequential harmonic progression in ten steps, with the bass of the piano rising chromatically from A to F♯, leading the music back to the tonic level as it reaches the recapitulation. It is through the careful use of register that the intervening music – representing those text fragments to the right of Figure 9.1 – is heard as subsidiary in importance to this principal thread.

An altogether different quality of harmony based on rather more consonant six-note chords (Example 9.10) is reserved for those sections of the monologue that are clearly memory flashbacks. This contrasts with the more dissonant twelve-note harmony that forms the substance of much of the work, as in Example 9.8. Beckett depicts Mouth's mind in a state of frenzy, hurling out one idea after another and retrieving fragments of memories, whether real or appropriated, from every stage of her conscious existence. Indeed the tension and ambiguity in this dialogic story-telling of the self can be understood as part of the reason for Mouth's refusal to acknowledge the account as fully her own, as constituting 'I'. Yet when Beckett writes 'suddenly saw it wet...the palm...tears presumably...hers presumably...no one else for miles...no sound...'[9] it is clear he would have us believe that this is an authentic memory. In sections such as these the gentler harmony of Example 9.10, which also calls for a gentler rhythmic style, is used for the musical substance of the work.

In my piano solo, great care was taken to represent the structure and dramatic contour of Beckett's *Not I*. Yet I always intended for the musical work to have an independent existence in its own right: familiarity with Beckett's play is not considered a necessary condition for appreciation of the music. Nonetheless, the piano score does carry Beckett's text alongside the musical notation, in the hope of inspiring the pianist and guiding his or her interpretation. Indeed the pianist

---

as a 'referential sonority' or a 'referential tonic' and the work that uses it is said to have a 'referential tonality'. For example the pitch collection C–C♯–E–F♯, known as the 'all-interval tetrachord', serves as the referential sonority in a number of the works of Elliott Carter (1908–2012).

[9] Beckett, *Not I*, in *The Complete Dramatic Works* (London, 1986), pp. 380–81.

Example 9.10 Harmony for memory flashbacks

who performs the work takes on a role rather like that of Mouth, possessed with an urgent desire to communicate, yet ultimately frustrated in his or her attempt to do so. The piano solo follows the same emotional contour as the stage work, with its moments of humour, its poignant but fragmented and tenuously caught flashbacks, its build of intensity towards each recapitulation and its robust refrain ('what?..who?..no!..she!..'). Transitions to and from the memory flashbacks are more emotionally charged, I suggest, in the music than in the stage version on account of the change from one harmonic area to another (Examples 9.8 and 9.10). Analogy may be drawn to the memory recall (*Comme un tendre et triste regret*) in the key of G♭ in Debussy's piano prelude *Des pas sur la neige*, a work which is otherwise situated in an icy D-minor and surely makes a nodding reference to Schubert's famous *Winterreise*.

Beckett's stage directions request that the performer should ad-lib material prior to the start of his printed text as the curtain rises and that she should ad-lib once again after the curtain is down and house-lights rise. What we witness, therefore, is a fragment of a much larger unfolding and Mouth's torment may be without end. The entire work should be considered a fragment, in just the same way that it is built of fragments of text. Yet I was never tempted to ask the pianist to improvise material at start and end of the musical work or to ask for a curtain to drop in order to conceal the pianist whilst he or she plays ever more quietly, thus replicating Beckett's fade-in and fade-out on an ongoing torrent of words. In contrast to the written/performed text, the open-endedness of the musical work is achieved by an abrupt start without preparation, and by an abrupt end in which none of the harmonic or thematic processes set in motion find any resolution. As one reviewer described it, this produced 'a curious halt *in media res*'.[10]

Performance and Reception

The completed score of *Not I* was delivered to Ian Pace on 21 November 1995. On that occasion I met with the American composer and cellist Frank Cox who showed me a collection of his scores, many of which demonstrated the same freedom

[10] Charles Krance, 'Review of Inaugural Concert, International Beckett Colloquium of Strasbourg, 31 Mar. 1996' (typewritten translation by colloquium organizer Marek Kedzierski).

of time signatures that I had just begun to explore in my music. A private play-through of the work took place roughly a week later at the home of Ian Pace. The public premiere followed on 9 December in the Great Hall at Reading University. At the time of writing, Pace has delivered a total of nine performances of the work: throughout the UK, in Chicago, and in Strasbourg where the performance was supported by funds from the British Council. Although Pace is the only person yet to have performed the work in public, pianist Nicolas Hodges wrote a clear-sighted appreciation of the work in a letter dated 1 November 1996:

> I was particularly struck by the way you achieved such a differentiated object despite tying yourself so closely to the Beckett. Your solution to that ever-more-frequent association seems to me a strong one in that it avoids charges of vagueness, a fault which one could never attribute to Beckett himself. So much Beckett related music seems to hang on just a few quotes to set the scene: such music is more associated with Beckett's *mood* than his thought … it would be interesting to present it without mentioning Beckett. I'm sure it would have a life of its own, but perhaps one's perception of it would change.

My original intention had always been that the work should 'have a life of its own'. Indeed the work is conceived as a tribute to Beckett, and I suggest that the tribute is made all the more powerfully by an independent work which stands on its own merits and for which I can claim full responsibility. I have toyed with the idea of presenting the piano solo as a multimedia work, performed live on stage at the same time that a video of Billie Whitelaw's performance is projected onto the underside of the raised piano-lid. There is no doubt that the timing of music and video would drift apart, although I believe that correspondences between the two media would still be recognizable. Yet such a presentation would compromise the standing of my work as a separate entity: in all likelihood such multimedia experiments will await a future project.

Mary Bryden has written about the work and referred to other composers, including Morton Feldman, Heinz Holliger and Richard Barrett, who have written music inspired by Beckett.[11] In direct contrast to my own approach, Bryden quotes Richard Barrett on the composition of his 1988 string quartet *I Open and Close* as stating that there was 'no question of a direct "translation" of formal or expressive attributes from Beckett's words into the music that I was writing, even if that were possible'. Indeed Barrett is one composer who uses quotes from Beckett's work to 'set the scene' as Hodges describes it. His 1986 solo for amplified cello *Ne songe plus à fuir* is prefaced by a short quote from *Molloy* and ends with a longer quote from *As the Story Was Told*.

[11] Mary Bryden, 'Reflections on Beckett and Music, with a Case Study', in Lois Oppenheim (ed.), *Samuel Beckett and the Arts: Music, Visual Arts, and Non-Print Media* (New York, 1999), pp. 83–102.

Bryden quotes Ian Pace on the importance of a sense of 'space' in any artwork: 'a sense that the medium is being used to create some sort of dialogue with that which exists outside of itself'. On the relationship between Beckett's text and my music Pace said:

> Beckett's text is breathless, an agglomeration of phrases. Paul's *Not I*, on the other hand, is relentless. It's a continuous stream which is made up of many different sections which join on to the end of each other. ... Before I received it, I expected Paul's piece to bear some resemblance to the Beckett-related works by Holliger. That was the aesthetic world I imagined. However, I was wrong. Paul's piece is quite unlike any other Beckett-inspired work that I've heard.[12]

Retrospect

There is no doubt that Beckett's *Not I* proposes an extreme theatre event. The audience experience a reduction of the visual field to a spotlit mouth in a pitch-black theatre. They witness a speed of vocal delivery that defies intelligibility and a sustained emotional tension that finds no release. Production of the work pushed Billie Whitelaw to extremes of physical endurance. Her memorization of a text containing such an admixture of exact and inexact repetitions and her high-speed delivery were no less a feat. In like fashion, the piano solo based on *Not I* is intentionally an extreme musical work, and a point from which I have retracted to explore other avenues and directions. The technical demands involved in learning and performing the piano solo are considerable, due largely to the rhythmic complexities involved, and the music sustains the same emotional tension and speed of delivery as does the play. It is gentler harmony, such as that demonstrated in Example 9.10, which has come to form the substance of my later works including *Piano Concerto No. 1*.[13] A simpler rhythmic style, sometimes enlivened by time signatures that represent the crotchet as 1/1, has come to dominate my more recent music. But the experience of working with Beckett's text was formative, bringing a narrative flow into my music that had previously been lacking from earlier, more contrapuntal works which seemed to present more architectural forms.

Beckett's work has exerted its influence on many composers, and I was aware of only a small proportion of the music inspired by his example when I embarked upon the composition of *Not I* for solo piano in 1995. Of particular relevance to this discussion are two other musical responses to the same text. A commission from IRCAM in 1979 prompted the renowned conductor, oboist and composer, Heinz Holliger, to compose a 35-minute monodrama for soprano

---

12 Ibid., p. 93.

13 *Piano Concerto No. 1* was first performed on 8 December 2012 in London conducted by Paul Rhys with Ian Pace playing the piano solo.

and magnetic tape, also called *Not I*, which premiered on 15 July 1980 at the Avignon Festival with soprano Phyllis Bryn-Julson. Holliger sets the complete text of Beckett's monologue in a spacious time-frame, almost three times as long as Billie Whitelaw's television performance. His vocal line is sometimes drawn towards recitative, occasionally to real speech, but more often the angularity of Holliger's vocal melody demands a rhythm that is far removed from natural speech. Occasionally Holliger employs expressive melismata, for example when setting the word 'merciful' in the context of Mouth's words 'brought up as she had been to believe...with the other waifs...in a merciful...[*Brief laugh.*]...God... [*Good laugh.*]' The soprano is accompanied by a tape part comprising recorded segments of her vocal line, thereby creating canonic arrangements of the material. As the piece proceeds, the recorded material is subject to increased electronic processing, suggesting ever-increasing psychological disorientation. Holliger himself describes the piece as being composed 'from the basis of a human being who can no longer manage to be an individual: that led me to write a polyphony for as many as sixteen voices'.[14]

More recently the British composer Mark-Anthony Turnage responded to a BBC commission with a work for amplified solo flute and orchestra entitled *Five Views of a Mouth.* The concerto premiered on 18 April 2009 in Glasgow, conducted by Ilan Volkov with Dietmar Wiesner on flute. On this occasion the actress Fiona Shaw delivered a performance of *Not I* as a prelude to the musical work, her pacing of the text much slower than Billie Whitelaw's yet arguably well-suited to the resonant acoustic of a large concert-hall. The five movements of Turnage's work are allocated titles taken from progressively further into Beckett's text, suggesting that there is an underlying programme (1. Out...into this world, 2. Found herself in the dark..., 3. Realised...words were coming, 4. Something she had to..., 5. Out before its time...'[15]). The solo flute, which sometimes plays unpitched breathing sounds into a microphone, seems cast in the role of Beckett's Mouth.

The inherent musicality of Beckett's writing is undoubtedly one of the reasons why it proves to be so alluring to composers, capable of exerting an influence on those as stylistically opposed as Philip Glass and Richard Barrett. Beckett himself spoke of hearing his works in his head prior to committing them to paper and claimed this in particular for *Not I.* It is equally well known that he consciously adopted musical models for some of his works. As Melanie Daiken observes 'much of Beckett's work is music itself: *Waiting for Godot* is operatic repartee; *Lessness* creates development through miniscule block forms like Messiaen's *Neumes rhythmiques*; *Not I* is an elaborated rondeau'.[16] Yet I must admit to a certain sense

---

14 Philippe Albera, 'Beckett and Holliger', in Mary Bryden (ed.), *Samuel Beckett and Music* (Oxford, 1998), pp. 87–97 (p. 94).

15 Mark Anthony Turnage, *Five Views of a Mouth* (London, 2007).

16 Melanie Daiken, 'Working with Beckett Texts', in Bryden (ed.), *Samuel Beckett and Music*, pp. 249–56 (p. 250).

of defeat when pondering in retrospect this circularity of influence: I had sought a literary model as the basis for a musical composition, but that literary work might well have been based on a musical model. John McGrath is perhaps slightly more balanced in his assessment of this issue and makes it clear how Beckett's creative practice remains distinct from musical composition when he observes that 'the crucial element that Beckett borrows from music is the possibility of semantic fluidity; the creation of a language that is both "intelligible" and "inexplicable" at the same time'.[17]

The work of Beckett has not directly served as the basis for any of my other musical compositions since *Not I*. From around 1998 it has been the writings of Baha'u'llah (1817–92), founder of the Baha'i faith, which have gently recast my aesthetic orientation and directed my musical sensibility. *The Fruits of One Tree*[18] uses quartertones to evoke melodic styles of the Middle East alongside music that is more clearly Western in origin. In allusion to Baha'u'llah's symbolism which in turn alludes to Attar's *Conference of the Birds*, my two *Dialogues* of 2001 and 2010 combine the slowed-down recording of birdsong with a solo wind instrument. If I were to return now to Beckett's work, it would undoubtedly be to some of the later, slower-paced writings with their ever more tenuous connection to the physical world.

---

17 John McGrath, 'Musical Repetition in Samuel Beckett's Ill Seen Ill Said', in Mario Dunkel, Emily Petermann and Burkhard Sauerwald (eds), *Time and Space in Words and Music: Proceedings of the First Conference of the Word and Music Association* (Frankfurt, 2012), pp. 31–41 (p. 36).

18 *The Fruits of One Tree* for flute, viola, horn and harp was commissioned by the Arpège Ensemble with funds from Reading University, the Holst Foundation and the Britten-Pears Foundation. The work was first performed on 1 March 2002 in the Great Hall, Reading University.

Chapter 10
The Next Ten Minutes: Morton Feldman and Samuel Beckett[1]

Matthew Goulish

§ In shadow
§ *p.p.p.*
§ Broken comb

§ Grace note
§ *For Samuel Beckett*
§ The stumbling of the sea

§ Green raincoat
§ Anxiety
§ *Vox ignota*

> It is possible that one should speak here about love, in other words about reality, or the probability of answering the sourceless echo.
>
> Arkadii Dragomoshchenko, *Description*

§ In Shadow

Morton Feldman, a composer and professor of music at the State University of New York at Buffalo, had poor eyesight. He wore thick horn-rimmed glasses. He composed leaning over his desk, face close to paper, inking each note chronologically through the score without correction: 'no going back'.[2] In the spring of 1976 he began preliminary work on an operatic composition with words by Samuel Beckett, a commission from Rome's Teatro dell'Opera. He completed three works in July that he considered preparations. These he titled *Orchestra*, *Elemental Procedures* and *Routine Investigations*. *Orchestra* received its premier in Glasgow on 18 September. Feldman attended the concert then travelled to Berlin.[3] At midday on 20 September, he arrived at the Schiller Theater, where rehearsals were underway for *That Time* and *Footfalls*.

---

1 With thanks to Judith Leemann for additional Feldman research.

2 Morton Feldman, *Morton Feldman Says: Selected Interviews and Lectures 1964–1987*, ed. Chris Villars (London, 2006), p. 237.

3 Sebastian Claren, 'A Feldman Chronology', trans. Christine Shuttleworth, in Feldman, *Morton Feldman Says*, p. 270.

> I was led from daylight into a dark theatre, on stage, where I was presented to an invisible Beckett. He shook hands with my thumb and I fell softly down a huge black curtain to the ground.[4]

Feldman invited Beckett to lunch; Beckett accepted, but only drank a beer. He had no acquaintance with Feldman's music, and voiced scepticism about the project.

> He was very embarrassed – he said to me, after a while: 'Mr. Feldman, I don't like opera.' I said to him, 'I don't blame you!' Then he said to me 'I don't like my words being set to music,' and I said, 'I'm in complete agreement. In fact it's very seldom that I've used words. I've written a lot of pieces with voice, and they're wordless.' Then he looked at me again and said, 'But what do you want?' And I said 'I have no idea!'[5]

Feldman produced a score he had written on lines from the script for *Film*. Beckett studied this. Feldman recounted the conversation in an interview eleven years later.

> He asked me, you know, if he did write something for me, what would he write? Just like I ask people that are close to me. Just what is it exactly and what do you think it actually conveys? You see. People think that you have this subject and then you superimpose the whole compositional or the structural process, which might be true for someone that's doing a cartoon strip. But for most artists the structural concerns are uppermost and out of it comes the content which you yourself to some degree are ambiguous about. And in this conversation with Beckett he was a little bit ambiguous about exactly what his subject was. I had to tell him [*laughs*] … at the same time in Berlin, a very close friend of mine was having breast surgery, and she was in a very bad situation. And I said to Beckett, 'Well, of course, compared to Sarah, you're comic relief.' And by 'comic relief' I really mean that there's no … . It's beyond existentialism, you see, because existentialism is always looking for a way out. If they feel that God is dead, then long live humanity. Kind of Camus and Sartre. I mean, there's always a substitute to save you in existentialism. And I feel that Beckett is not involved with that, because there's nothing saving him. … You're not going to arrive at any understanding at all; you're just left there holding this – the hot potato which is life. … I never liked anyone else's approach to Beckett. I felt it was a little too easy; a little too … . Again, they're treating him as if he's an existential hero, rather than a tragic hero. And he's a word man, a fantastic word man. And I always felt that I was a note man. And I think that's what brought me to him.[6]

---

4 James Knowlson, *Damned to Fame: The Life of Samuel Beckett* (New York, 1996), p. 556.

5 Ibid., pp. 556–7.

6 Feldman, *Morton Feldman Says*, p. 232.

In the course of the Berlin conversation, Beckett confessed that a single theme dominated his work. 'May I write it down?' Feldman asked, but Beckett wrote it himself on Feldman's music paper.

> To and fro in shadow, from outer shadow to inner shadow. To and fro, between unattainable self and unattainable non-self.

'It would need a bit of work, wouldn't it?' said Beckett.

At the end of the month, back in Buffalo, Feldman received a card with a note.

> Dear Morton Feldman.
> Verso the piece I promised. It was good meeting you.
> Best. Samuel Beckett.[7]

The handwritten text on the back of the card began as follows.

> Neither
> to and fro in shadow from inner to outer shadow
> –
> from impenetrable self to impenetrable unself
> by way of neither[8]

§ *p.p.p.*

> We cannot understand the manner (call it the method) before we understand its work.
>
> Stanley Cavell, *The Claim of Reason*

Not long after *Neither*, Feldman experienced an extended period of doubt, a crisis he called it, about the work that music does. Is it an art form or simply entertainment? What experience, as an event, can it best accomplish? Perhaps the dramatic breakthroughs he saw unfolding on the canvases of his painter friends, to whom he dedicated compositions (Franz Kline, Philip Guston) precipitated this moment as one he did not want music to miss, this revolutionary breach into which Beckett had also stepped.

> Both Beckett and [art critic Harold] Rosenberg recognized that considering painting to be an act, indeed an action of a performance, also transformed language and the possibilities of writing in general. Beckett grasped earlier

[7] Knowlson, *Damned to Fame*, p. 557.

[8] Morton Feldman, *Neither* [opera, words by Samuel Beckett], hat[now]ART 102 (Basel, 1997).

> than most that while art commentary before the war had tended to tell a story about a line, where it went and what it did once it arrived, the art of the postwar abstractionists made the critic's usual performance impossible. As soon as the painter rejected the idea of the static object to be copied, the critic lost the illusion that criticism was a matter of describing the painting as itself a static object. Beckett's exuberance about the destruction of this illusion stemmed from his recognition that the new painters were assailing the same kinds of conventions he wanted to abandon in writing. Beckett caught the excitement and energy that spring from giving up one hopeless thing, if only for the brief second before the new thing emerges as hopeless in its own way.[9]

Beckett's plays ventured into translational territories, across media, from the visual to the linguistic in an 'effort to find a language for drama that resonated with painting's expressive power'.[10] Feldman for his part, and in his bafflement, found himself abandoning notions of fixed duration, of audience and of the consequences of critical reception. His next series of compositions culminated in *String Quartet (II)* (1983), a work of intricate structure that takes nearly 5 hours to perform (4.52.35, as performed by the Ives Ensemble).[11] His insistent notation for the dynamic of triple pianissimo fixed the music at audibility's brink. The guarantee of sustained strain to hear the strings whisper, to differentiate tone from room noise; the extreme demands on attention as when in twilight one works to recognize the barely perceived: can this tenuous edge be the quartet's labour and reason? In what human circle can such sceptical music meaningfully sound? It is a simpleminded and obvious observation that Beckett laboured under an analogous relationship with not only theatre but also narration and even language. Tentative grip on belief, unsteadiness of the stream of mind, relentless reduction of means and materials (music to notes, text to words) testify to the narrows of the ventures, the zero-degree practice. The pianist John Tilbury said: 'In rehearsal Feldman would help his performers by describing the sounds as *sourceless*. He wanted them to take on that precious quality of transience, of *uncatchability*.'[12] In 1987 Beckett suggested Feldman as the composer for a reworked version of his radio play *Words and Music*, now commissioned by the New York station Voices International.[13] Feldman enthusiastically accepted, but worried that the project would redirect him to faster rhythms and louder volumes.

---

9 Peggy Phelan, 'Lessons in Blindness from Samuel Beckett', *Publication of the Modern Language Association* 119/5 (Oct. 2004): 1279–88 (pp. 1284–5).

10 Ibid., p. 1281.

11 Morton Feldman and the Ives Ensemble, *String Quartet (II)*, hat[now]ART, CD 4-144 (Basel, 2001).

12 John Tilbury, 'On Playing Feldman', available at <http://www.cnvill.net/mftilb.htm>.

13 Beckett withdrew an unsatisfactory version of *Words and Music* from public circulation in 1966 (Feldman, *Morton Feldman Says*, p. 229; Claren, 'A Feldman Chronology', p. 274).

With its theatricalization of the music as it engages in a dialogue-like exchange with two voices, a contested primary material between servant and master, *Words and Music* did necessitate a departure, but Feldman surprised himself by welcoming the changes. He oversaw the production in March and April in New York. Immediately thereafter, he composed *For Samuel Beckett* for chamber orchestra. It premiered on 12 June in Amsterdam. What precisely might that word of dedication connote? It would be his last dedication. Within days he was diagnosed with pancreatic cancer. He died on 3 September 1987 at the age of 61.

§ Broken comb

In a 2012 interview for the *Paris Review*, the poet Susan Howe rehearsed, with characteristic elegance, the weave of mourning and complexity.

> William James says that in times of trauma and crisis a door is opened to a place where facts and apparitions mix. I wrote *Frolic Architecture* shortly after my husband Peter Hare's sudden death from a pulmonary embolism in 2008. I was constructing what I thought was a collaged text, often while listening to Morton Feldman's music and John Adams's *Shaker Loops*. As I moved between computer screen, printer, and copier, scissoring and reattaching words and scraps of letters, I thought, I've never gone as far or felt as free.[14]

This license for creation, like mobility – far, free – she finds in Feldman's orbit. How does his music grant permission? It simply persists. It spools out, unconcerned, occupying microscopically shifting states of mental and emotional exactitude and necessity. Fact or apparition: in Howe's composite poetry, scraps and remnants speak from and for the dead. The poet finds and frames, to sensitize us to their transmissions. Feldman said in a lecture in Toronto:

> And what's fantastic about music, I find, is that there's something so impregnable, something – I wouldn't say it's mysterious – A remark of Whitehead's clarified something for me last week. I don't know what the hell he was referring to – But he said that the reason that something couldn't be defined is because it was too general. I like that. But not that it was so complicated or so esoteric; it was just like – too general to get a handle on. And that's the way I feel about music. Just too generalized. Everything is too generalized. Everything to me is like a found object. A major third is a found object, what the hell, you have no right to write a major third – with or without a context. It's like picking up a broken comb from the floor. Everything. This was when I woke up, that was part of a hallucination, if music could be an art form. Everything sounded like a

[14] Maureen N. McLane, 'The Art of Poetry No. 97: Susan Howe', *Paris Review* 203 (Winter 2012): 144–69 (p. 158).

> found object. Everything didn't seem to be personal. Everything had a fantastic reminiscence about it. Even my own music. And I wrote a piece that I like very much, called *Triadic Memories*, in which I went ahead and treated everything, even my own invention, my own creation, as a series of found objects, no longer even feeling in a sense that I had the capability of making any kind of poetry out of it.[15]

§

> Our deaths are quite near
> also loose-fitting
> Paul Hoover, *Desolation: Souvenir*

§

§ Grace note

> Madame Maurina Press became Morton Feldman's piano teacher when he was twelve. She came out of the Russian tradition, supposedly having taught the Czar's children. She had been close to Scriabin and this is what she gave the young Morton to play, along with Busoni transcriptions of Bach. Feldman felt that, because she wasn't a disciplinarian, she imparted 'a vibrant musicality' as opposed to any kind of 'musicianship.' Perhaps the Feldman sense of registration, pitch and timbre derive from her tutelage. 'The way she would put her finger down, in a Russian way of just the finger. The liveliness of just the finger. And produce "B-flat," and you wanted to faint.'[16]

In 1970 Feldman composed an elegy for his former teacher, titled *Madame Press Died Last Week at Ninety*.

> That title was given to me by my mother. I came back from Europe and called up my mother, and the first thing she said to me was 'Madame Press died last week at ninety.'[17]

John Adams conducted the piece in 1991, on a programme built around a particular unsentimental strain in elegiac American music, the origin of

---

15 Morton Feldman, *Toronto Lecture: April 17th 1982, Mercer Union Gallery, Toronto, Canada*, transcribed by Linda Catlin Smith, available at <http://www.cnvill.net/mfmercer.htm>.

16 Ingram Marshall, 'Notes on the Program', in *American Elegies*, John Adams Conducts the Orchestra of St. Luke's, Elektra Nonesuch, CD 79249-2 (New York:, 1991).

17 Feldman, *Morton Feldman Says*, p. 47.

which Adams traced to Charles Ives. The programme included Adams's own composition *Eros Piano*, about which he wrote:

> *Eros Piano* began as an elegy on the death of Morton Feldman. I was mindful of how John Cage had first described Feldman's music as 'erotic' but then later decided that it was heroic. I have always felt that both of Cage's descriptions were correct. As examples of extended musical architecture, of a radically new attitude toward the flow of time, Feldman's works – especially the late ones – are certainly heroic in what they attempt. But on the microscopic level, his music was always sensuous, erotic, obsessed with gradations of touch and the subtlest shifts of color.
>
> Another feature of Feldman's music ... I call the 'fetish,' the obsessively reiterated motive or gesture ... creating musical structures by lingering over and over on a single small detail. 'Madame Press' is a case in point.[18]

Madame Press Died Last Week at Ninety repeats a two-note motif. The first note, extremely brief, a kind of grace note, drops into the lower, longer second note, sustained and dying away – quick attack, slow decay – 'A coo-coo clock goes off and never stops.'[19] *The HarperCollins Dictionary of Music* has this to say about the grace note:

> An ornament played very quickly just before a main note; it is performed just before the beat and gives a sharp accent to the main note. The grace note is usually printed in small type. Its time value is not counted in the rhythm of the measure, being borrowed from the duration of a note either immediately before or immediately after it.[20]

The grace note of *Madame Press* is an *appoggiatura*, a *leaning* or *resting* note, of the short type found in Baroque musical ornamentation.[21] It strikes a brief harmonic dissonance, the tension of which the main note instantly resolves. For other composers an ornament in excess, the grace note for Feldman becomes the fundament, the drawing near of the horizon. In another touch shared with Beckett, he lowers the threshold of what constitutes an event, theatrical or sonic. In the 50-minute opera *Neither*, the solo soprano voice commences at roughly 4 minutes, singing the first phrases on an insistent single note assigned to each individual syllable.

> to and fro in shadow from inner to outer shadow
>
> –

18 Marshall, 'Notes on the Program'.

19 Ibid.

20 Christine Ammer (ed.), *The HarperCollins Dictionary of Music* (New York, 1995), p. 169.

21 Ibid., p. 12.

from impenetrable self to impenetrable unself by way of neither

–

as between two lit refuges whose[22]

At about the 6-minute point, the introduction of a double grace note steps up to the same repeating note, as if unfolding it into an equally insistent triadic formulation, as the words continue, now with each receiving the triad treatment, a major structural shift within the confines of *Neither.*

doors once
neared gently close, once turned away from
gently part again[23]

§ *For Samuel Beckett*

Rome's Teatro dell'Opera presented the first performance of *Neither* on 8 June 1977, conducted by Marcello Panni with a set by Michelangelo Pistoletto. The Italian audiences, finding opera devoid of conventional dramatization unendurable, greeted the performance with tumultuous protests.[24] Nearly ten years later, on 30 May 1986, the New York Philharmonic Orchestra, with Gunther Schuler conducting, performed *Coptic Light*, Feldman's last orchestral work. A remark by the *New York Times* reviewer that he was 'the most boring composer in musical history' left Feldman devastated.[25] The following year, the presentation of *For Samuel Beckett* in Amsterdam marked the final dedication piece. Feldman had composed seven other such dedications through the years: *For Bunita Marcus*, *For Christian Wolff*, *For Frank O'Hara*, *For Franz Kline*, *For John Cage*, *For Philip Guston* and *For Stefan Wolpe*. The list reads like a circle of artist colleagues, protective perhaps in mutual recognition, as claims to and reminders of community, the conviction (Feldman's) that 'the wish and search for community are the wish and search for reason'.[26] What precisely might that word of dedication – *For* – connote? What of Beckett, if anything, prompted or can be located in *For Samuel Beckett*? Or does the dedication suggest only the coincidental happy timing of friendship? Feldman composed the piece for an ensemble of 15 instruments, with 7 of those doubled: flute, oboe, clarinet, bassoon, horn, trumpet and trombone. The single tuba, harp, piano, vibraphone, violin, viola, cello and double bass complete the band of 22.[27]

---

22 Feldman, *Neither*.

23 Ibid.

24 Claren, 'A Feldman Chronology', p. 271.

25 Ibid., p. 274.

26 Cavell, *The Claim of Reason*, p. 20.

27 Morton Feldman, *For Samuel Beckett*, Classic Production Osnabrück, CD 999 647-2 (Georgsmarienhütte, Germany, 1999).

The music begins as if already in progress, its start like an interruption. It proceeds as pure extended exposition, no development, no resolution, always restarting. If the instruments ever cohere into sections, such coherence is fleeting, as high horn repetitions insist on a note against the ground of an ever-shifting texture, instruments trading roles in constant circulation. There is something in this single note insistence, the 'fetish' that John Adams pinpointed, of 'cries that have not been smothered by the construction of concepts',[28] cries against the passage of time, ineffable gestures in the wordless world this music maps, 'at the same time a protest against the irreversible and (thanks to reminiscence) a victory exacted from the irreversible, a means of resuscitating the same in the form of the other'.[29]

§ The stumbling of the sea

Comparisons of Feldman's rhythm to ocean waves or to breathing[30] miss the dynamic subtlety of the laws that govern both the music and such natural phenomena that it echoes, a dynamic subtlety that is the rhythm's reason. As the poet Paul Hoover put it, 'except for the stumbling of the sea, nature has no rhythm. The measure of the ... image is that of traffic between two yellow lights.'[31] Across the span of a periodic lull, a phrase elongates or foreshortens, yet the listener recognizes a repetition. In the landscape of equivalent if not equal parts, the breath, if it is breathing one thinks of, is irregular, as singular as an organism but communal, like a dissonant flocking in odd pulsations. The body subjects memory, as it does all embodied acts, to the variations of the organic, part habit and part perpetual readjustment. Beckett wrote of something similar in his essay on Proust.

> The laws of memory are subject to the more general laws of habit. Habit is a compromise effected between the individual and his environment, or between the individual and his own organic eccentricities, the guarantee of a dull inviolability, the lightning-conductor of his existence. Habit is the ballast that chains the dog to his vomit. Breathing is habit. Life is habit. Or rather life is a succession of habits, since the individual is a succession of individuals.[32]

For Samuel Beckett sits alongside Beckett's bleakness, an accompaniment like the pulsing vein in the dog's neck, below the chain, beside the vomit – its exuberance,

---

28 Isabelle Stengers, *Thinking With Whitehead*, trans. Michael Chase (Cambridge, MA, and London, 2011), p. 42.

29 Vladimir Jankélévitch, *Music and the Ineffable*, trans. Carolyn Abbate (Princeton, NJ, and Oxford, 2003), p. 97.

30 Peter Niklas Wilson, 'Capturing the Moment: Morton Feldman's *For Samuel Beckett*', liner notes to Morton Feldman, *For Samuel Beckett*.

31 Paul Hoover, *Sonnet 56* (Los Angeles, 2009), p. 64.

32 Samuel Beckett, *Proust* (New York, 1957), p. 8.

its love, however unlikely, is insistent: 'the excitement and energy that spring from giving up one hopeless thing, if only for the brief second before the new thing emerges as hopeless in its own way'.[33] Each dedication in its obstinate tenderness acknowledges the inspiration drawn from the admired work of a friend, as listener assumes identity of source. Like Wallace Stevens's *Snow Man*,

> One must have the mind of winter
> To regard the frost and the boughs.
> For the listener, who listens in the snow,
> And, nothing himself, beholds
> Nothing that is not there and the nothing that is.[34]

§

> All song is bent
> by a silent measure
>
> Jay Wright, *Music's Mask and Measure*

§

§ Green raincoat

For the 1976 concert in Glasgow, immediately before his meeting with Beckett in Berlin, Feldman wrote the following programme note.

> One of the compositional quirks I'm most lucky about is the almost total state of amnesia immediately after completing a composition. … I write that I'm fortunate about this (the Talmud refers to an Angel of Forgetfulness); what I mean to say is that this broken memory makes possible the never ending stopping of my pen. It is that which you repeat not from memory but from the lack of it which is the 'substance' that interests me most.[35]

Regarding the repeated two-note theme of *Madame Press*, the questions remain: why those two notes? Why not two other notes? Why not three notes or four? The theme recalls the teacher, or the memory of the teacher evokes the theme. The teacher's name, spoken by the composer's mother, invokes the memory of the teacher's finger touching a key, to which the composer now adds an adult

---

33 Phelan, 'Lessons in Blindness from Samuel Beckett', p. 1285.

34 Wallace Stevens, *Selected Poems*, ed. John N. Serio (New York, 2009), p. 7.

35 Morton Feldman, *Musica Nova: Third Festival of Contemporary Music in Glasgow* (programme booklet, 1976), cited in Morton Feldman, *Morton Feldman*, Col Legno, CD 20070 (Frankfurt, 2001).

grace note to supplement the child's B♭. The smallest of fragments retains the whole, found, like a broken comb, in a birdcall from Mozart's *Magic Flute*. To use Whitehead's formulation, repetition gives way to immediacy.

> But 'process' is the rush of feelings whereby second-handedness attains subjective immediacy; in this way, subjective form overwhelms repetition, and transforms it into immediately felt satisfaction; objectivity is absorbed into subjectivity.[36]

What thought does this two-note aggregate arouse? After his break with fixed duration, Feldman spoke, in a 1984 interview, of his attempts to perform for any listener the same disorienting breaking of memory from which he claimed he congenitally suffered.

> What I'm interested in is not so much memory now, but what happens in a long piece that becomes memorable. And I'm always asking myself, you know, just because you want to say I want to have a madeleine, to taste it again, or I want to go out and smell a flower to … . Just because you set it up, you see, doesn't mean in a sense that it's going to become memorable. And I keep on bringing back things, almost as if I'm asking myself, is this the line that's memorable? And you don't know what is memorable, what's not memorable. I was very touched years ago when I saw *Krapp's Last Tape*. The thing is just going along, just rolling along, and then he talks about seeing a girl on the other side of a station, a provincial station. And he kept silent. He brings it back, the girl in the green raincoat. And I forgot it. That's all it was, it was the girl in the green raincoat. That has influenced me very much in my work.[37]

It is not difficult to imagine Feldman's interest in the loops and replays of language, the recapitulations of a life, facilitated for the aging Krapp by his tape recorder. Each replay supplants the original, less a repetition than that first time to the nth degree. In the lyrical *Rothko Chapel* of 1971, Feldman treated the composition's temporality as a loose musical/autobiographical chronology, tracking through his life's stages.

> The piece begins in a synogoguey type of way; a little rhetorical and declamatory. And as I get older the piece gets a little abstract, just like my own career. … Then there is the tune in the middle of the piece, a dialogue between a soprano and tympani and viola, which was a little Stravinsky on purpose: I wrote that tune the day Stravinsky died [6 April 1971] … and the piece ends with the memory of a piece that I wrote when I was 14.[38]

---

[36] Alfred North Whitehead, *Process and Reality* (New York, 1978), p. 155.

[37] *Morton Feldman in conversation with John Mackenzie, November 1984*, available at <http://www.cnvill.net/mfmackenzie.pdf>.

[38] Feldman, *Morton Feldman Says*, p. 66.

The impulse of the musical self-quotation, this youthful viola tune that he elsewhere referred to as a 'photograph',[39] gives way in the late works to the revelation of the perfect fragment. Written or found, appropriated or invented, the question dissolves if the fragment remains. The disorientations of inexact repetition that play out in real time are not simply the product of slippage between one iteration and the next. The disorientation is one of the permeability of the self, of the individual as a succession of individuals, hearing and rehearing anew a sourceless echo, repeated not from memory but from its lack, until unexpectedly the broken memory disgorges a fantastic reminiscence. 'What remains of all that misery?' Krapp asks into his tape recorder. 'A girl in a shabby green coat, on a railway-station platform? No?'[40]

§ Anxiety

If *Waiting for Godot* contemplated what cyclical time makes visible or the world that waiting brings into view,[41] *Krapp's Last Tape* ruminates on those sounds that become audible in unmeasured time's circumambulations: those sonic events, those voices, one recognizes as one's own. For his latest (last) tape, recorded after playing again one particularly heartfelt confession, Krapp dictates:

> Just been listening to that stupid bastard I took myself for thirty years ago, hard to believe I was ever as bad as that. Thank God that's all done with anyway.[42]

Each replay marks an increased distance from the moment of recording. The effect confers on each self-fragment the appearance of artefact. Such artefactualization dismantles and reforms the self, in all its flimsy ephemerality and stubborn depth, against a background of darkness and silence. 'Be again, be again', the old man muses into his microphone and 'What's a year now?' before his recursive speech gives way to distracted song.

> KRAPP:
> [*sings*]
> Now the day is over,
> Night is drawing nigh-igh,
> Shadows – [*coughing, then almost inaudible*] – of the evening
> Steal across the sky.[43]

---

[39] Ibid., p. 93.

[40] Samuel Beckett, *Krapp's Last Tape*, in *The Collected Shorter Plays of Samuel Beckett* (New York, 1984), p. 58

[41] See Phelan, 'Lessons in Blindness from Samuel Beckett'.

[42] Beckett, *Krapp's Last Tape*, p. 62.

[43] Ibid.

In his lecture notes for a brief consideration of anxiety, Roland Barthes, citing Freud ('There is something about anxiety that protects its subject against fright'), wrote: 'often, I've been told, birdsong, a song of suffering and of anger'.[44] Those feelings that cannot be spoken must be sung to keep back the frightful engulfing silence. In one still moment, the stage directions describe Krapp's lips moving without sound as he listens as his younger self listens and speaks at once: 'Past midnight. Never knew such silence. The earth might be uninhabited.' The line comes very near the end. The end of what? The tape, his life, the play, the world. 'One comes out of a Theatre to find oneself in another Theatre.'[45] In his 1965 lecture *The Anxiety of Art*, Feldman wrote:

> Where in life we do everything we can to avoid anxiety, in art we must pursue it. This is difficult. Everything in our life and culture, regardless of our background, is dragging us away. Still, there is this sense of something imminent. What is imminent, we find, is neither the past nor the future, but simply – the next ten minutes. The next ten minutes. … We can go no further than that, and we need go no further. If art has a heaven, perhaps this is it.[46]

The idea anticipates the strange temporalities of his last compositions, the intricate minutiae of each momentary tonality spooling out in boundless durational extrusion. He might have exchanged 'imminent' (impending) for 'immanent' (inherent), the word so favoured of philosophy. He might have said that in addition to the present being all there is, inhering in the present is the fact of perishing. Each moment dies away, as we will die away, as others have died away before us. In waiting a world comes into view, but one must wait, or participate in the apparatus that makes the viewing possible, in order for the worldhood of such a world to announce itself.[47] So it is with close listening, the mode of attention that constitutes art's utopian afterlife. Attending to each note – quick attack, slow decay – becomes an act of mourning.

§ *Vox ignota*

Feldman's *String Quartet (II)* makes its impossible demands of attention on the listener. Its relentlessness echoes the unbroken prose of *The Unnameable*,

---

44 Roland Barthes, *The Neutral*, trans. Rosalind E. Krauss and Denis Hollier (New York, 2005), pp. 208, 259 n.; see Sigmund Freud, *Beyond the Pleasure Principle*, trans. James Strachey (New York: Bantam, 1959), p. 30.

45 Hélène Cixous, *Zero's Neighbor Sam Beckett*, trans. Laurent Milesi (Cambridge, 2010), p. 64.

46 Morton Feldman, *Give My Regards to Eighth Street: Collected Writings of Morton Feldman*, ed. B.H. Friedman (Cambridge, 2000), p. 32.

47 Kathleen Stewart, *Ordinary Affects* (Durham, NC, and London, 2007), p. 109.

the third in Beckett's trilogy of novels. Beckett's words and Feldman's notes both seem to begin *in medias res*, as if any reader or listener's arrival interrupts the infinite flow. The experience that these works frame and structure, although exhausted, or, as Gilles Deleuze famously said, following the exhaustion of the possible in all its permutations,[48] paradoxically proceeds with its own exuberance, persisting well past any recognized meagre human limits. 'Keep going, going on, call that going, call that on. ... Perhaps that is how it began.'[49] But what am I writing? This is not solely an exercise in determining commonalities between these two artists. In one moment from his *Philosophical Investigations*, Ludwig Wittgenstein asked:

> Well, how do I know [how to continue]? ... If that means 'Have I reasons?' the answer is: my reasons will soon give out. And then I shall act, without reason.[50]

Wittgenstein's 'giving out' may be another name for exhausting the quotidian possible, the simple permutation of all combinatorial patterns of notes, of stones in one's pockets, of memories or inventions, of reason and the reasonable. (All sources recede into darkness.) The crossroads have been reached and passed. The imaginary future when reason has given out might as well be now. Let's say that it is. How do we behave then? What words do we speak? What music do we make?

> This is thy hour O Soul, thy free flight into the wordless,
> Away from books, away from art, the day erased, the lesson done.[51]

> I mourn'd, and yet shall mourn with ever-returning spring.[52]

In the time when time is no more, freed from duration, in death's wake and the state of perpetual loss, after we have lived to witness our own funerals, when we have never gone so far, nor felt so free, to what voice do we attend? Vladimir Jankélévitch, philosopher of music, put it this way.

> It is silence that allows us to hear *another voice*, a voice speaking *another language*, a voice that comes *from elsewhere*. This unknown tongue spoken by an unknown voice, this *vox ignota*, hides behind silence just as silence lurks behind the superficial noise of daily existence.[53]

---

48 Gilles Deleuze, *Essays Critical and Clinical*, trans. Daniel W. Smith and Michael A. Greco (Minneapolis, 1997), pp. 152–74.

49 Samuel Beckett, *The Unnameable* (London, 1994), p. 293.

50 Wittgenstein quoted in Cavell, *The Claim of Reason*, p. 19.

51 Walt Whitman, 'A Clear Midnight'.

52 Walt Whitman, 'When Lilacs Last in the Dooryard Bloom'd'.

53 Jankélévitch, *Music and the Ineffable*, p. 151.

Perhaps the whisper of Feldman's music was never more than this: a sonic analogy for his permanent condition of a limited visual field, translating his need to look closely, that is, with one's eyes close to the object of study, into an imperative for others to listen closely, I mean nearly, to the source: to draw closer. He and Beckett shared the same silence. Maybe that accounted for their peculiar bond, despite the celebrated contrasts of their personalities. Unlike the benign void of his compatriot John Cage, from which sonic events would reliably, miraculously issue like mushrooms from imperceptible spores, Feldman's silence promised no such turning back from absence to presence. Silence operates as his music's threat, not absence at all, but abyss, the only reliable presence, not zero but nothing. It pressurizes his sounds with imminent oblivion. Beckett's words and Feldman's notes must refuse to acquiesce and insist on, even struggle for, audibility, their survival. The limited means by which they do so, their astringent vocabularies, testify to their irreducibility: notes and words like kernels left from the harrow. Out of the silence after the end of time they whisper one last unlikely song, traces of a voice, unknown, familiar.

§§§

Chapter 11
Beckett's Apertures and Overtures

Mary Bryden

Many people are familiar with that great hymn to the ego, the popular song 'My Way'. In lyrics of what John Sutherland has termed 'ineffable banality',[1] the song's narrator is at the end of his life, facing 'the final curtain' of his own mortality. Looking back, his life appears to be full of setbacks. There were times, he recalls, when he 'bit off more than I could chew … ate it up … spit it out … faced it all … and did it my way'. Although innumerable artistes have performed and recorded the song, the Canadian song-writer Paul Anka wrote the English lyrics with Frank Sinatra in mind. The song became irrevocably associated with him, partly because Sinatra had by then (1968) actually lived the kind of life described in the song. Nevertheless, the song had originally sprung from a French collaboration between the flamboyant singer Claude François (who recorded it in 1967), Jacques Revaux and Gilles Thibault, under the title 'Comme d'habitude'. In fact, the French predecessor is a much more gentle and wistful song, in which the motif 'comme d'habitude [as usual]' punctuates a reconstruction of a typical day in the life of a couple in which one partner offers habitual tenderness while the other offers habitual indifference. Thus, whereas the English song is an inflated retrospective, looking back over an entire life, the French original is written entirely in the present and future tenses, tremblingly anticipating the small instances of rejection which lie ahead at different points of the day.

Much less well-known than Sinatra's 'My Way' is Samuel Beckett's 'my way'. I refer here to the short poem, 'my way is in the sand flowing', written in the late 1940s.[2] The poem is also anticipating an end – a cessation to all the 'harrying' and 'fleeing' – but its context could hardly be more different. While Sinatra's song looks back across all the blows and brawling and proclaims that 'each careful step along the byway' had been 'planned' and 'charted', Beckett's poem traces a meandering, uncertain trail, where footsteps are hidden in sand and water. Within these moist environments – sea, rain and mist – the human organism becomes subject to a similar dissolubility. Living takes place in the interstices between brief

---

1 John Sutherland, 'Frank Sinatra's My Way: The Song that Refuses to Die', *The Guardian* (15 Oct. 2012).

2 Samuel Beckett, 'my way is in the sand flowing', in *Collected Poems: 1930–1978* (London, 1984), pp. 58–9. In this edition, as in their first publication, the French original and its translation are set out on facing pages.

openings and closings, 'between the shingle and the dune'. Meanwhile, the shifting sand, evoking hourglasses, also marks out the unremitting passage of time.

Written not long before *En attendant Godot*, this poem may readily be aligned with the womb/tomb tropes to be found in that play, as also in many other areas of Beckett's output. However, rather than manifesting a conventional disquiet in the face of the transience of time and the ephemerality of the world, the voicer of this poem derives a paradoxical sense of fulfilment from being cast adrift between the first tread and the last. The second stanza replaces 'my way' with 'my peace': 'my peace is there in the receding mist'. Thus, the poem proclaims first an attachment to the cessation of the shuttling between apertures – 'these long shifting thresholds' – and then an accommodation to the image of that aperture being not only closed, but being welcome to be closed: 'live the space of a door/that opens and shuts'. The French original is even more hospitable towards the notion of closure. Its direct address to the passing instant – 'cher instant je te vois [dear moment I see you]' – is a lyrical apostrophe to a moment in the future achieved by living through moments as yet still murkily impending. Nevertheless, as will be examined later, the poem manages to keep both modes in play. While it caresses the idea of a definitive full stop, such closure is held at bay by the persistence of movement.

Beckett's attunement to musicality and sound is particularly apparent in the French original of this poem, and especially in its masterly first line, with its rhythmic succession of sibilants: 'je suis ce cours de sable qui glisse'.[3] Reminiscent of Krapp's savouring and elongating of the word 'spooool',[4] the poem is strung between an extraordinarily rich series of vowel sounds built upon 'ou' and 'u', including 'suis', 'cours', 'dune','pluie', 'fuit', 'poursuit', 'jour', 'brume', 'recule', 'fouler', 'mouvants', 's'ouvre'. These sounds encourage lingering, suggesting that the ideas they denote are allies rather than aliens. They are, nonetheless, intersected by harsher elements: the plosive 'p' of the hammering rain, in 'la pluie d'été pleut sur ma vie [the summer rain rains on my life]', and the alveolar consonants of 'd'été', which can be spat out. There is, in addition, a cutting, painful edge supplied by the repeated 'ee' sound, which Ruby Cohn has termed 'the repetitive long "i" keening vowel, eliciting sadness'.[5]

The English translation of the poem has a much more spiky and uncertain character than the French original. Instead of two five-line stanzas, it offers a five-line stanza followed by a four-line second stanza, containing an emphatically lengthy and somewhat awkward 13-syllable second line. In contrast to the pulsing 'longs seuils mouvants' of the French, this line ends with 'these long shifting

---

3 The dual meaning of 'je suis' ('I am' and 'I follow') cannot be captured by the English translation, though it could be argued that 'my way' encapsulates notions both of being (the ability to utter a possessive pronoun being reliant upon a being capable of possessing) and of movement (wayfaring).

4 Samuel Beckett, *Krapp's Last Tape*, in *Collected Shorter Plays of Samuel Beckett* (London, 1984), p. 56.

5 Ruby Cohn, *A Beckett Canon* (Ann Arbor, MI, 2001), p. 158.

thresholds'. However, the English translation accentuates a tendency already there in the French. Although the poem appears to culminate with the image of a closing door, it is the notion of shifting and transiting which preoccupies the attention throughout and which gains ascendancy over the notion of finitude. Notably, the 'harrying fleeing' of the voicer's life is said to occur not 'from its beginning', but, in a more cyclical way, '*to* its beginning to its end' (my italics). Moreover, in the French original, the door does not simply close ('ferme'), but 'se referme', the verb's prefix 're' acknowledging the movement's infinite availability for repetition.

Hence, the prominent line-end placement of the word 'thresholds' in the English version is significant. A threshold is neither inside nor outside and can offer no more than a temporary home. Moreover, since the thresholds themselves are 'long', 'shifting' and multiple, there is a sense in which the whole poem becomes a kind of threshold art. In this respect, it could be said to resemble music, which offers identifiable steps and progressions towards other such steps, but never on a durable or fixed basis. As Alfred Döblin wrote of music in 1910: 'Le son est achevé, rond, lisse, on peut le retenir; il retentit, passe et a bientôt disparu sans laisser trace; il est saturé, masse sans vie, il n'indique ni passé ni avenir, n'a ni parents ni enfants. [The sound is completed; rounded and smooth, it can be held on to; it rings out, passes, and has soon disappeared without trace; it is saturated, a lifeless mass, it indicates neither past nor future, and has neither parents nor children.]'[6] Each sonic step, he goes on to observe, is devoid of inbuilt value; it can accrue significance only by means of the passage from one to another: 'La cohérence des sons réside entièrement dans le mouvement de l'un vers l'autre; le son particulier n'a de sens que comme porteur et transmetteur d'un mouvement. [The coherence of sounds resides entirely in the movement from one towards the other; the particular sound has meaning only as conveyor and transmitter of a movement.]'[7]

Beckett's poem thus offers a paradox which is also offered by music: it breaks the silence by its articulation, by its apparent selection of one 'way' rather than another, and yet its transient dynamic also dissolves the basis upon which 'my way' could achieve any kind of settled context or identity. Some exploration of this may be seen in the composer Rhian Samuel's 2006 setting of 'my way is in the sand flowing' for baritone and piano.[8] In the piece, which begins with the elastic direction, *Con moto, ma molto rubato*, Samuel succeeds in highlighting key words by either tipping down or rising into them by means of an abrupt and extended pitch interval. In the first stanza, the words 'sand', 'shingle', 'dune', 'rain', 'me' and 'life' are all picked out in this way. Then, after a crescendo and an acceleration in tempo, the words 'harrying' and 'fleeing', rapidly repeated, are

---

6 Alfred Döblin, *Sur la musique*, trans. Sabine Cornille (Paris, 2002), p. 55.

7 Ibid., p. 60.

8 Rhian Samuel, *The Flowing Sand* (London, 2006). The piece was commissioned by the School of European Studies, Cardiff University, with funds from the Arts Council of Wales.

shot out like bullets, hustled along by coursing piano triplets. In the second stanza, the voice reaches higher than ever before for the words 'long shifting', then to fall away steeply once again for the sustained word, 'thresholds'. However, as the voice approaches the final image of the door, the prevalent pattern is disrupted. A pause ensues after 'opens', giving way to a three-bar piano passage filled with variations in structure, time signature and volume. It is as if a multitude of human transactions have been condensed into a brief but intense episodic unit. Finally, after a tumult of rising demisemiquavers on the piano, the voice resumes with the connective 'and', creating expectations of another downward (and this time definitive) leap towards closure. Yet, this time, the voice unexpectedly slides not downwards but upwards, from D to E, ending with a curtailed and staccato note on the word 'shuts'. By allowing the poem's last word to bounce into the air in this way, Samuel perfectly respects the manner in which Beckett's poem refuses to impose any simple linear development between opening and closing, beginning and ending.

In this context, it may be observed that Beckett's door in 'my way is in the sand flowing' is not a revolving one, which simultaneously admits and ejects. It is a door which is capable of providing a blockage to a wayfarer. In many of Beckett's late works, sparse and austere chambers with closed doors provide a space of enclosure, willed or otherwise. The Austrian composer Heinz Holliger once said:

> As a musician, I'm also attracted by the musicality of Beckett's texts, even if this musicality seems to exclude any added music. Sometimes, it all seems to take place in an empty room, from the acoustic point of view. No sound can penetrate it; it's a completely closed universe, where you can't hear any echo, not even your own voice.[9]

Yet, can this perception hold good for long? Even while apparently sealed within a space, the figures in Beckett's plays are repeatedly attuning themselves to an offstage space or focusing on an aperture (doors or windows) through which sounds could conceivably penetrate. In the television play *Eh Joe*, while never leaving his room, Joe parts or opens every movable partition (door, window, curtain, cupboard) in an intensity of looking and a 'mounting tension of *listening*'[10] for the woman's voice which addresses him. The woman's voice in the stage play *Rockaby* is heard telling of lingering 'quiet at her window facing other windows',[11] straining for sight of another, while Reader in the stage play *Ohio Impromptu* speaks of the intensity of waiting for intimations of sound or light from beyond. The declared absence of these elements – 'Through the single window dawn shed

9 Philippe Albèra, 'Beckett and Holliger', trans Mary Bryden, in Mary Bryden (ed.), *Samuel Beckett and Music* (Oxford, 1998), pp. 87–97 (p. 94).

10 Samuel Beckett, *Eh Joe*, in *Collected Shorter Plays*, p. 202.

11 Samuel Beckett, *Rockaby*, in *Collected Shorter Plays*, p. 277.

no light. From the street no sound of reawakening'[12] – serves only to draw attention to their hypothetical presence.

There is, however, a profound ambiguity attaching to these apertures, as with the door and opaque window in the television play *Ghost Trio* (1977), which are both '*imperceptibly ajar*' and yet have '*No knob*'[13] with which to manipulate them. *Ghost Trio* takes place in a rectangular room, though with access to other zones: a corridor beyond the door, a window, and a mirror (replicator of space). Within this permeable space, a male figure appears to be waiting for a woman known to him.[14] The triadic structure of the play is made up of the 'Pre-action', in which a female voice describes the elements of the chamber; the 'Action', in which, the female voice having announced that 'He will now think he hears her', the male figure tenses and moves about the room before settling back on a stool; and finally the 'Re-action', in which the expectant male figure is visited by a small boy who shakes his head, presumably indicating that the woman will not appear. During the play, surges of music are heard at prescribed points, the extracts being taken from the largo of Beethoven's Fifth Piano Trio, op. 70, no. 1, commonly known as the 'Ghost Trio'. The use of Beethoven's 'Ghost Trio' was not, according to Beckett, at the origin of his composition. What he was wrestling with was the need to render apparent a sudden mental turmoil, as he told Ruby Cohn: 'I wanted a calm scene which revealed an inner storm as the camera approached'.[15] The problem is a challenging one: how may an 'inner storm' be made perceptible on stage in a still, seated figure? Beckett's solution, he said, was to set up a relationship between the figure and the geometrical zones surrounding him: 'the figure resisted me, so I resorted to rectangles'.[16] These rectangles are multiple – the door, the window, the pallet, the mirror, the cassette player, the room itself – but two of them, the door and the window, are especially significant because they are apertures to without.

The fact that the door and window are agents of negotiation with external spaces emerges only gradually in the course of the play. In the second part of the play, the male figure first '*listens with right ear against door*' and then '*pushes door open half-way clockwise, looks out*'.[17] Afterwards, he moves to the window and '*pushes window open half-way clockwise, looks out*',[18] while in the third part he opens the window again, admitting '*faint sound of rain*'.[19] However, the first non-verbal sound, the '*Faint music*', is heard in relation to the door. Insofar as the door constitutes an opening, we might draw attention here to the derivation of the

[12] Samuel Beckett, *Ohio Impromptu*, in *Collected Shorter Plays*, p. 287.

[13] Samuel Beckett, *Ghost Trio*, in *Collected Shorter Plays*, p. 248.

[14] At draft stage, the play appeared under the title 'Tryst' (see the notebook: University of Reading, MS 1519/1).

[15] Cohn, *A Beckett Canon*, p. 339.

[16] Ibid, p. 339.

[17] Beckett, *Ghost Trio*, p. 250.

[18] Ibid.

[19] Ibid., p. 252.

musical term 'overture' from the late Latin *apertura* (opening). On its passage into English it relates also to the French noun *ouverture*, which, as well as denoting an opening, can mean an open*ness*, a making-available of oneself for the reception of some external event or atmosphere.

Ghost Trio brings together all these associations. In the first place, Beethoven's piece, with its tremolo, pulsing qualities and startling dynamic contrasts, already contains haunting resonances which led to its nickname the 'Ghost Trio'. As Lawrence Kramer remarks, 'this slow movement is so very extraordinary, so deliberately out of the ordinary that it seems to be challenging the very conception of ordinary life'. Strindberg's play *The Ghost Sonata* also nods towards Beethoven, and Kramer observes of Strindberg that: 'clearly the sound of Beethoven's slow movement was echoing, ghostlike, in his ears, and it is still possible, another century later, to hear it on the same spectral terms'.[20] Beckett was aware that Beethoven had included, on the same compositional sheet, not only sketches for the slow movement, but also for a planned opera based upon Shakespeare's *Macbeth*, which would feature a chorus for the trio of witches. Beckett acknowledges this additional supernatural association by writing in the margin 'Macbeth theme' at specific points of his typescript.[21] As James Knowlson remarks, '"The Ghost" retained for Beckett something of *Macbeth*'s doom-laden atmosphere and involvement in the spirit world'.[22] Indeed, in relation to the failed encounter which lies achingly at the heart of *Ghost Trio*, Graley Herren observes that: 'the choice of "The Ghost" as theme is also significant because it implies from the start that F's [the male figure's] anticipated tryst will not take place, at least not in the material world, because his lost love has joined the spirit world of the dead'.[23]

The 'Ghost Trio' first occurs in the play in relation to an aperture (the door) and is moreover reliant upon an act of intense openness on the part of the listener. It attaches to, is even generated by, the encounter with the door. As the play progresses, the male figure is repeatedly drawn to the door as a site of expectation, only to return to hunch over the cassette player. Meanwhile, short extracts of the 'Ghost Trio' are heard, though the fact that they are non-consecutive[24] implies that they are playing in a wider field of affect and memory than that which would be produced by purely mechanical means. In noting the relationship between the

---

20 Lawrence Kramer, 'Saving the Ordinary: Beethoven's *Ghost Trio* and the Wheel of History', *Beethoven Forum* 12/1 (Spring 2005): 50–81 (p. 52).

21 For more detail on the stages of the draft work, see Mary Bryden, Julian Garforth and Peter Mills (eds), *Beckett at Reading: Catalogue of the Beckett Manuscript Collection at the University of Reading* (Reading, 1998), pp. 44–6.

22 James Knowlson, *Damned to Fame: The Life of Samuel Beckett* (London, 1996), p. 622.

23 Graley Herren, *Samuel Beckett's Plays on Film and Television* (New York and Basingstoke, 2007), p. 77.

24 The relevant bars are stipulated by Beckett in a note at the end (*Ghost Trio*, p. 254).

trudging of the male figure between door and cassette player on the one hand, and the progression through different parts of the music on the other, the words of David Lidov are apt: 'Motion is one of the essential illusions of music, like the closely related one of reappearance. (We do not say that a theme "recurs" but that it "returns" – as if it had been staying somewhere else in the meantime).'[25] Insofar as the playing of the music seems to be closely connected to a desired or anticipated event over which the listener has no control (the arrival of 'her'), it indeed seems to go through cycles of fading and then resurfacing. In the light of the ghostly resonances associated with the Beethoven piece, its reappearances might be likened to the French 'revenant' which, as well as being the present participle 'returning' or 'coming back', is also a noun meaning 'ghost'.

There is undoubtedly a restrained and remote quality to *Ghost Trio*, especially since its central male figure is mediated to the audience by a separate, female voice, as outlined earlier. The voice describes itself as 'a faint voice', the light is 'faintly luminous',[26] the music is '*faint*', and when the small boy appears at the end, after '*Faint sound of steps*' and '*Faint sound of knock*', he simply '*shakes head faintly*' before receding into the dark.[27] However, this faintness is not to be mistaken for numbness or insentience. On the contrary, though he is prone to uncertainty and irresolution, the male figure is caught up in an act of engrossed listening, which the strains from the 'Ghost Trio' seem to accentuate. The music, then, participates in a wider phenomenon of acute attentiveness, where the ear is attuned for the slightest variation in the ambient soundscape. Picking up on Curtis Roads's work on transient auditory phenomena,[28] David Toop writes of those microsounds which are

> audible but in their brevity as micro-events, their infinitely subtle fluctuations, or their placing at the threshold of audible frequencies, they lie outside the conventional notion of pitch, tone and timbre. They are difference; the differentiation of one voice from another, or the activation of one instrument from another.[29]

The male figure in *Ghost Trio* is, as his '*tense pose*' indicates,[30] indeed listening for difference and seemingly using music as some kind of vehicle for that differentiation. Yet, as the music surges and then ebbs, he seems to be straining to hear something which is barely distinguishable from silence – a silence with

---

25 David Lidov, *Is Language a Music? Writings on Musical Form and Signification* (Bloomington, IN, 2005), p. 146.

26 Beckett, *Ghost Trio*, p. 248.

27 Ibid., p. 253.

28 Curtis Roads, *Microsound* (Cambridge, MA, 2004).

29 David Toop, *Sinister Resonance: The Mediumship of the Listener* (New York and London, 2010), p. 60.

30 Beckett, *Ghost Trio*, p. 250.

impetus, similar to that described by David Toop: 'Silence can occupy space with the stealth of fine white sand in subtle movement, an unoccupied chair in an empty room, an abandoned car, sifted flour falling on a chopping board, the cooling of boiled water.'[31] In the silence, the male figure can 'sound out' his environs, moving to listen intently at the opening: 'The phrase [sounding out] gives a sense of outer movement counterbalanced by cautious ingress, which is to listen and investigate *with openness*'.[32] 'Ouverture', in other words, is here seen in association with aperture.

The version of 'Ghost Trio' Beckett owned was the performance by Daniel Barenboim (piano),[33] with Barenboim's then wife Jacqueline du Pré (cello) and Pinchas Zukerman (violin), recorded in 1970,[34] which was used for the BBC2 recording of the play in 1976 (broadcast in 1977). By the time Beckett wrote *Ghost Trio* in 1976, du Pré had already been stricken with the illness from which she would eventually die in 1987 when only in her early forties. The collaboration of the three musicians produced a performance of riveting intensity, uncanny in its evocation of a spirit world, and, over 40 years later, a cult item on YouTube. One of the salient characteristics of the performance is a refusal to domesticate the piece or to make bearable its unbearable qualities. For Barenboim, to play Beethoven does require an act of courage. As he told Edward Said: 'The element of courage is the most important. … [I]f you have a *crescendo* in Beethoven that goes to the end, and then there is a *subito piano* that creates the illusion of a precipice, you have to do that. You have to go to the precipice, to the end, and then not fall.'[35]

That sense of risk, of sound always being preyed upon by silence, is palpable in Barenboim's performance of the 'Ghost Trio'. It is also apparent in much of his own commentary on sound:

> Sound … is not an object, such as a chair, which you can leave in an empty room and return later to find it still there, just as you left it. Sound does not remain in this world; it evaporates into silence. Sound is not independent – it does not exist by itself, but has a permanent, constant and unavoidable relationship to silence.[36]

---

31 Toop, *Sinister Resonance*, p. 63.

32 Ibid., p. 63 (my italics).

33 See James Knowlson: 'When I asked [Beckett] directly what he meant by this note ['Macbeth' written on the first typescript], he explained that the record sleeve of his own recording (the version made by Daniel Barenboim) linked this Piano Trio with Beethoven's music for an opera based on *Macbeth*' (*Damned to Fame*, p. 621).

34 A film of Barenboim, du Pré and Zukerman performing the 'Ghost Trio', directed by Christopher Nupen, was re-released on DVD in 2004 (Opus Arte/Allegro Films).

35 Daniel Barenboim and Edward W. Said, *Parallels and Paradoxes: Explorations in Music and Society* (London, 2004), p. 62.

36 Daniel Barenboim, *Everything is Connected: The Power of Music*, ed. Elena Cheah (London, 2008), p. 7.

Unless sound is prolonged by the infusion of additional energy or by intervening techniques (the sustaining pedal on the piano, the use of legato, the reversing of bow direction for the violin, and so on), it will be swallowed up by silence: 'After the sound is produced, it immediately begins to decay. ... Sustaining the sound is in any case an act of defiance against the pull of silence, which attempts to limit the length of the sound.'[37] However, if sound always either 'interrupts the silence or evolves out of it' and then gives way to silence in 'one last moment of expressivity', there is nevertheless an unparalleled peace to be found in playing it, insofar as 'one can control, through sound, the relationship between life and death'.[38]

The idea of moving from silence to silence, and, by extension, from cradle to grave, has an obvious Beckettian resonance. Beyond this, however, what, in the light of Barenboim's observations, is the status of the recorded music in *Ghost Trio*? On one level, Beethoven's 'Ghost Trio' may be thought of as a constant, or at least recurrent, companion to the stage transactions. It makes itself heard in insistent fragments, and the conclusion of the piece (from bar 82 to the end) coincides with the conclusion of the play, succeeded by a final silence and fade.[39] On the other hand, the extracts specified by Beckett are not consecutive. They fold back on themselves and then roll forward again. Thus, one cannot think of the piece as a kind of continuo, accompanying the action in a constant and subliminal way, despite being inaudible in parts. On the contrary, the music is very carefully apportioned, as is its volume, which ranges variably between 'faint', 'progressively fainter', 'audible', 'slightly louder', 'louder' and 'growing'. Though avoiding properly musical terms for the music, Beckett, in acknowledgement of the full sonic repertoire he has put together, reserves these directions for the sounds made by the apertures, for example '*Crescendo creak of door opening*' and '*Decrescendo creak of window slowly closing*'.

The fact that the male figure appears to be transfixed both by the music and by the need to check for any sign of the woman's approach suggests a link between the music and the woman. Does the music generate the possibility of the woman's appearance? Or does the music provide an alternative resource, one which somehow absorbs the space left empty by the woman? It might be imagined that the male figure is able to engineer the interventions and impact of the music. He does, after all, sit in intimate proximity to the cassette player, in a manner reminiscent of Krapp with his tape recorder. Yet the music appears to play unreliably; moreover, at the close of the second part of the play, it is the female voice commanding 'Stop'

37 Ibid., p. 8.

38 Ibid., pp. 8–10.

39 For a close analysis of Beckett's progressive intensification of the musical engagement in *Ghost Trio*, across different stages in the work's genesis, see Franz Michael Maier, '*Geistertrio*: Beethoven's Music in Samuel Beckett's *Ghost Trio*', in Angela Moorjani and Carola Veit (eds), *Samuel Beckett: Endlessness in the Year 2000*, *Samuel Beckett Today/Aujourd'hui* 11 (Amsterdam and New York, 2001), pp. 267–78.

which halts the music.[40] Despite this, her succeeding interjection 'Repeat' in fact results not in a repeat but in a looping-back of the music to a much earlier point.

Even the assumption that the musical extracts heard by the audience are matched in their volume and duration by what is heard by the protagonist cannot exceed the status of an assumption. What does seem clear is that the music in *Ghost Trio*, though tightly rationed by Beckett and repeatedly curtailed on stage, is a site of radical possibility and unpredictability, operating in fields which only partially conjoin the ambit of the male figure. As Franz Michael Maier has argued:

> The music ... is much more energetic and lively than the protagonist who is introduced by the voice simply as the 'sole sign of life'. Silently cowering, he appears as a mere sign, whereas the music becomes audible in its own right. Following its own independent rules, it cannot be limited to a simple link in the sequencing of actions.[41]

Moreover, though visual information is available in *Ghost Trio*, clues have to be actively sought among 'shades of grey',[42] layers of dust, and silent gestures (the head-shaking of the small boy). Sound, on the other hand, as Barenboim points out, 'penetrates the human body and is therefore more directly connected to it'.[43] Notably, just three years before he began to write *Ghost Trio*, Beckett told Charles Juliet that 'l'ouïe prend de plus en plus d'importance par rapport à l'oeil [the sense of hearing is increasingly becoming more important than that of sight]'.[44]

The visit by the small boy in *Ghost Trio* does not bring resolution, but only an apparent deferral. Though he stands '*before open door*',[45] the oilskin-clad boy does not enter the room, and the male figure himself remains on the threshold. With the wordless encounter at an end, a divarication is implemented as the boy recedes along the corridor and the protagonist slowly closes the door and reinserts himself into the room and the music. Yet if the boy's visit does not bring fulfilment, neither does the music act as an agent of resolution, even though its playing seems to be imperative to the protagonist. Insofar as the absent woman is able to summon expectation, one may presume her anterior existence. As such, the music appears to participate on some level with an act of memory. As Barenboim observes, 'the importance of the ear cannot be overestimated. ... It forces us to remember with thought. Recollection, after all, is memory with thought; a young man remembers, an old man recollects'.[46]

---

40 Beckett, *Ghost Trio*, p. 251.

41 Franz Michael Maier, '*Geistertrio*: Beethoven's Music in Samuel Beckett's *Ghost Trio* (Part 2)', *Samuel Beckett Today/Aujourd'hui*, 12 (2002) pp. 313–20: p. 316.

42 Beckett, *Ghost Trio*, p. 248.

43 Barenboim, *Everything is Connected*, p. 25.

44 Charles Juliet, *Rencontre avec Samuel Beckett* (Paris, 1986), p. 31.

45 Beckett, *Ghost Trio*, p. 253.

46 Barenboim, *Everything is Connected*, pp. 25–6.

Beyond this, may anything secure or worthwhile be said about the function of music in *Ghost Trio*? First, that perhaps music is an ally in the *avoidance* of resolution, which may constitute an unwanted form of closure. This observation would not apply to all acts of music. It would need to be the kind of music which itself has apertures, which is 'leaky' and permeable. The apertures of *Ghost Trio* – the door and window – might usefully be aligned with the wider context of what Lawrence Kramer has termed 'hermeneutic windows', which provide

> sites of engagement through which the interpreter and the interpreted animate one another. What we see or hear at such windows can, of course, always be recuperated for the symbolic order. But by resisting or deferring that recuperation, … we can understand more than the symbolic order allows.[47]

The symbolic order of language indeed seems unequal to the task of analysing this enigmatic collaboration between Beckett and Beethoven. This hope seems in any case to be a forlorn one in many musico-literary contexts, since, as Kramer asserts, 'the very premise of musical narratology is the recognition that music cannot tell stories'.[48] Yet music can intersect with internal narratives and 'embody a certain relationship to the signifying process'.[49] This relationship may usefully be aligned with Julia Kristeva's concept of the semiotic. This precedes the imaginary and the symbolic, which both rely upon a separation of subject and object. The semiotic drive, on the other hand, 'is impulsive, rhythmic, dynamic, plural, untotalized, supercharged. In these respects it is very like music when music excites us most'.[50]

Ghost Trio is built upon a very specific piece of music. It is specific to the audience, but it is also (seemingly) specific to the protagonist. For him, it may be presumed to embody the 'pulsion' of the semiotic. As Kramer observes:

> Only the music that listeners identify closely with their own lives, music they find meaningful, can do this. The semiotic is articulated as an immediacy only through an already-significant symbolic that endows the immediacy of the semiotic with an already-reflective meaning.[51]

The audience witnesses this apparently semiotic connection between protagonist, music and absent woman. At first they do this vicariously and remotely, but, as the aural and spatial negotiations across opening and closing portals unfold over time, their involvement is more intimately recruited.

---

[47] Lawrence Kramer, *Classical Music and Postmodern Knowledge* (Berkeley and Los Angeles, 1995), p. 21.

[48] Ibid., p. 110.

[49] Ibid., p. 20.

[50] Ibid., p. 19.

[51] Ibid,. p. 20.

The two works which have formed the principal focus of this chapter – 'my way is in the sand flowing' and *Ghost Trio* – are separated by almost 30 years and represent two very different genres: poetry and television drama. Yet both focus on human wayfarers driven by an inner compulsion to move between points which are only temporarily fixed, whether they be 'the shingle and the dune' of the poem, or the pallet and stool of the play. On one level, these wayfarers are beset by environmental adversity. The voicer of the poem reports that 'the summer rain rains on my life', just as the male figure in *Ghost Trio* peers from the open window at '[r]ain falling in dim light'.[52] Nevertheless, both works attach significance to apertures as sites of dynamic interchange. In 'my way is in the sand flowing', the door is not the 'final curtain' of Sinatra's 'My Way'. Rather, 'the space of a door that opens and shuts' is one which is predicated upon the subjunctive mood – 'when I may cease' – and such cessation is constantly deferred by the 'long shifting thresholds'. In *Ghost Trio*, the door and the window offer some form of transit or communion, and the ending of the play does not suggest that the male figure's threshold encounter with the small boy, his 'hood glistening with rain', is a final one.[53] Moreover, this impression is facilitated by the interventions of the music, which does not provide a finale or coda, but, rather, persistently threads through the affective transactions taking place on stage. In this sense, music in both cases unsettles finitude and renders it inconclusive. In 'my way is in the sand flowing', the poem's aural and rhythmical qualities seem to outweigh the conceptual status of closure, as Ruby Cohn describes: 'The flow of sound enhances that feeling of entropic infinitude'.[54] In *Ghost Trio*, the 'flow of sound' survives its moments of faintness and intermittence. Daniel Barenboim points out that, while total silence can ensue within a piece of music, 'it is temporary death, followed by the ability to revive, to begin life anew. … In the world of sound, even death is not necessarily final.'[55] In these as in many of his other compositions, Beckett demonstrates that 'my way' traverses spaces in which apertures are never irrevocably sealed, and sound is never definitively abated. Like the 'sand flowing' in the hourglass, the investment of energy may appear infinitesimal, but it is always sufficient to generate a reprise.

---

52 Beckett, *Ghost Trio*, p. 253.

53 Ibid.

54 Cohn, *A Beckett Canon*, p. 158.

55 Barenboim, *Everything is Connected*, pp. 10–11.

Chapter 12

Ohio Impromptu: Reading Blanchot, Hearing Beckett

Sara Jane Bailes

(one)

> Friendship is not a gift, or a promise; it is not a form of generosity. Rather, this incommensurable relation of one to the other is the outside drawing near to its separateness and inaccessibility. Desire, pure impure desire, is the call to bridge the distance, to die in common through separation.
>
> Maurice Blanchot, *The Writing of the Disaster*

On the cover of Samuel Beckett's short play, *Ohio Impromptu*, written in English in 1980, is a black and white photograph, a still from the play's original production at Ohio State University, Columbus, in 1981.[1] The image still captivates me, even as I recall it, as it did from the moment I first set eyes on it in the 1989 Grove Press paperback edition where the play is published along with two of Beckett's other 'shorts', *Catastrophe* (1982) and *What Where* (1983), the latter the final playtext Beckett wrote. It is both an arresting image and an image of arrest: it captures the imagination for the way in which its subjects seem detained by something they are nevertheless willing to endure, compliant in their resistance. As with many of Beckett's figures, particularly in the later works, they appear stone-like, fixed, unmovable, unmoving. My recollection of the image is this: two old men, who appear almost identical, are seated at a large, white table. Each wears a black coat. Both have improbably long white hair. Their posture is almost identical: they appear to be one and the same figure; they mirror one another though they are not the same. These two figures possess

[1] *Ohio Impromptu* was written for Stan Gontarski, who wrote to Beckett in February 1980, asking him to write a play for his symposium and festival due to take place in Ohio as part of celebrations that would mark Beckett's 75th birthday. Beckett responded a month later saying he would do his best and by May of that year was at work on a text. By mid-December he had finished the short play, and, according to Pierre Astier, in his account of its genesis, a typescript of *Ohio Impromptu* arrived in the mail. The play premiered on 9 May 1981. See Pierre Astier 'Beckett's "Ohio Impromptu": A View from the Isle of Swans', in Stanley E. Gontarski (ed.), *On Beckett: Essays and Criticism* (New York, 1986), pp. 394–404 (pp. 395–6).

a quality of reclusiveness, cloistered, as if over time and for many years they have drawn back from the everyday world, receding into a state of diminished existence. One sits at the end of the white table, the other at its side to the right of the first. Their heads are bowed, each propped up by the right hand, the same but different. The position of the hand is remarkable in that one's attention is drawn to it: it appears to prop up the head and shade the brow and eyes, hiding each figure's face by casting a downwards shadow that conceals the eyes. The image suggests a profound weariness and a desire to retreat from perception – from perceiving as from being perceived, and to withdraw from the light. They do not look; they listen. The left hand of each figure lies at rest on the table. Yet despite its depiction of a weariness one might associate with prolonged attention to a situation, the image also depicts a mood that is imminent and expectant: the figures are engaged in an activity that is unfinished and it is unclear when it began or how it will end. In front of the man seated at the top end of the table an unusually large book lies open on what appears to be its final pages which are lined with faint print. The figure who sits before the book looks as if he is beginning to read, or perhaps he is approaching an end. Perhaps the other listens. They are united in a state of apprehension. The presence of the book distinguishes them: it sets them apart and brings them together. It provides the bridging of a distance between them. In the foreground of the image a large black, wide-brimmed hat sits on the table.

(two)

++ They take seats, separated by a table, turned not toward one another, but opening, around the table that separates them, an interval large enough that another person might consider himself their true interlocutor, the one for whom they would speak if they addressed themselves to him: 'Forgive me for having asked you to come to see me. I had something to say to you, but at present I feel so weary that I'm afraid I am unable to express myself.' – 'You are feeling very weary?' – 'Yes, weary.' – 'And this came upon you suddenly?' – 'To tell the truth, no, and if I even took the liberty of calling you, it was because of this weariness, because it seemed to me that it would facilitate the conversation. I was even entirely sure of this, and still now I am almost sure of it. Only I had not realized that what weariness makes possible, weariness makes difficult.'[2]

Many years later, as I began to read the above text which follows the preliminary 'Note' in Maurice Blanchot's *The Infinite Conversation*, a familiar narrative unfolded of two weary men, separate yet bound together by the limits and necessity of a conversation they seem compelled to continue. A strange feeling, in

[2] This and all following references to Blanchot's text are from the following edition: *The Infinite Conversation* (Minneapolis: University of Minnesota Press, 1993), p. xiv.

reading Blanchot, of having been here before: the image of two men, aged, weary, conscious of their weariness yet brought to consciousness by virtue of its existence, came back to me. Sat at a table, each propping up his forehead with hand, with long white hair falling upon shoulders, the two figures, Reader (R) and Listener (L), from Beckett's dramaticule, *Ohio Impromptu,* now seemed to illustrate Blanchot's articulation of two weary figures encountering one another. In the act of reading – itself a form of visual 'listening' or ingesting conducted through the ocular exchange between eye and text – my encounter with Blanchot's text returned me to this earlier Beckettian double-act. Reading *The Infinite Conversation*, which Blanchot wrote in 1969 in French, I experienced a prolonged, ekphrastic moment, albeit inverted, where the image as described above seemed to precede the subject of the text, hovering in my mind's eye as I now read it. Blanchot's text 'appeared' by way of the recollected image. Weeks later, I was many pages into Blanchot's discussion of the ontology of writing as the outside of discourse, where literature is understood as that which exists beyond everyday language inventing a reality of its own, a discussion he unravels in prose which transports comprehension to the edges of abstraction. Unable to forget the Beckettian image, I gave in to my own curiosity and retrieved a copy of *Ohio Impromptu* in order to revisit it by seeing it again and in order to reread the playtext and listen to its reverberation, recovering from it what it wished to tell. In that moment, it was as if I had never ceased reading the play. Here, now, I was simply resuming a conversation.

When Deleuze speaks of the 'visions' and 'auditions' of language in 'Literature and Life', referring to them as the 'veritable Ideas that the writer sees and hears in the interstices of language, in its intervals', one is reminded instantly of the musicality of language and image as abstract materials that 'become' or come to life through resonance and reverberations that are peculiar to literature. Literature proposes an act of composition in which one is never singular. It is conversant, a mode of transmission that carries us beyond language itself, much as music, when performed, is able to transport the listener far beyond the organization of notes upon a page. There is a sense, too, that such visions and auditions take place not only within the works of one writer but across different texts and literatures, as if one writer calls to another, either blindly or with conscious intent.[3] This, then, might be one way to begin thinking about the function of the reader: as a mediator or conductor, as one who steps in like an operator to connect a call. In the company of Blanchot and Beckett, visions and auditions correspond through word, idea and image both through the acts as well as in the depiction of the acts of reading and listening as corresponding states of attentive apprehension. That is, the processes of reading and listening are doubled: performed (by the actual reader/spectator) and performative (performed within the text the reader reads or sees performed). The event of reading becomes central to both writers, this event the very focus of the drama of these two texts.

[3] Gilles Deleuze, *Essays: Critical and Clinical*, trans. Daniel W. Smith and Michael A. Greco (Minneapolis, 1997), p. 5.

(three)

What does it mean to say that one *reads*? That is, when reading a text, what is it we are actually doing or, as Blanchot phrases the demand, 'what happens to the one who is reading?'[4] This gestures towards a number of considerations that motivate the concerns of this chapter: to think about the way that the implicit dialogic structure of reading and listening as dramatized in *Ohio Impromptu* resembles a musical 'call' and 'response' that opens up the text to meanings which occur beyond the spoken dialogue between R and L. *Ohio Impromptu* is scored in such a way that its movement – its motivation – seems to issue from beyond the text that appears central to the drama, that is, the book that is being read aloud by R to L. How does this brief playtext establish a series of open circuits that reveal not only the story to be told, but also the impulse that moves Reader to read and Listener to hear and then to interrupt (in order to hear better) and then to once again continue? In the stark predicament Beckett creates for the play, he calls our attention not to the story itself – a sort of red herring – but to what *occurs*, that is, what presents itself between Reader and Listener. Yet without the reading of this surrogate text (the story written in the book which R continues to read to L) this *other* text, an invisible score that exists prior to the reading of the book, would not become apparent. It becomes evident through the interruptions with which Beckett punctuates the text which are indexed by Listener's knocks upon the table. Interruption operates as rhythmic response, as both a halting mechanism and a permissive beat: L knocks, R pauses, then repeats a sentence, L knocks again, R pauses or continues. Interruption arrives as a form of interlocution and as the intervention of an 'other' through a signal (Listener's 'knock') that Reader should cease reading in order that the act of listening may be repeated. The tenuous transportations of language underscore our separateness from each other in the moment in which they become necessary, an idea central to Blanchot's thinking about the possibilities of literature. This same notion is palpably and physically rendered through Beckett's plays. Yet it is these same transportations that also remind us of the human desire to memorialize and to remain. Writer and translator Alberto Manguel describes literature as 'civic action', for it is preservative, it is 'memory'. In that sense reading can be understood as our attempts to 'reclaim[ing] the right to this human immortality'.[5] Reading and listening instigate an act of sharing, yet what of the status of those (silent) images that are released by words and which are attendant upon language as ghostlike reverberations around them, articulating literature in that particularly intimate and haunted space that opens up between writer and reader yet which remains private? In the very act of reading there is much at stake that moves beyond the temporally situated act itself which is activated or

---

4 Blanchot, *The Infinite Conversation*, p. 321.

5 Alberto Manguel, 'Power to the Reader', available at <www.alberto.manguel.com/>.

paused by the opening and the closing of the book. Words are a distraction away from the subject that wishes to be discussed, yet that same interference can lead towards the profounder meanings of a text and its production.

In *The Infinite Conversation* Blanchot keeps calling the reader to attention *as reader*, stalling and reminding one, in the offer of the book, of the task taken on to which one might now be committed: the attempt to understand what it is *to read*. Not that Blanchot makes light of this endeavour. He states: 'The book is a night that would become a day: a dark star, unilluminable and calmly giving light. Reading transforms into light that which is not of the order of illumination.'[6] A darkened tread, then, into the spill of light from a dark star. By considering Blanchot and Beckett's texts together, I am interested in the way that reading – its fictional representation and the experience of the act itself – can be perceived as an attempt to create continuity at the same time as it performs a kind of interruption that takes place between image or the act of image-making and text; an interruption from Beckett, for example, while I began to read Blanchot, which marked my reading and which, at times, seemed paradoxically to articulate itself as an interruption from Blanchot reminding me that Beckett *had never ceased being read*. Many the year since I had immersed myself fully in the works of Beckett and here now this strange recall. Call waiting. Beckett on hold. The presence of Beckett's writing as part of my reading recurs again through the act of writing, here and now. And so on. An infinite conversation or one that is at least without end, even if such conversations are punctuated by suspension or pause. So again I pose the question: What happens to the one who is reading? What does reading ask of us? How might reading and listening constitute an act that approximates the communicative modes of music with its ability to deliver resonant but abstract meaning?

(four)

> No answer – no matter how persuasive – will ever have enough strength to resist indefinitely the question that sooner or later will summon it.
>
> Edmond Jabès, *Cut of Time*

The 'beginning' of Blanchot's *The Infinite Conversation* poses a riddle simply in the way that it commences for it does not announce itself as thus but retracts from a clear point of departure. The book begins with a 'Note' (by Blanchot) followed by what appears to be an eleven-page exchange printed in italics written in the third person singular. This narrative reports on the events of an encounter between two weary figures, one summoned by the other, who are engaged in a conversation that began 'long ago'.[7] Yet it remains unclear where the book

6 Blanchot, *The Infinite Conversation*, p. 318.

7 Ibid., p. xiii.

itself begins and what the function of the figures (they are not quite 'characters') in this oblique, unannounced drama might be. (The situation parallels that of *Ohio Impromptu*). That question riddles its way through into the body of the text, beyond the foreword, the translator's acknowledgments and into Section 1 of the book, 'Plural Speech: The Speech of Writing', through Blanchot's intricate passages that quietly evacuate language, reducing it of its excess and crowded implications and connotations. Meaning constantly evades but returns to the reader as she moves forwards, almost as if it were ancillary, situated at the back of the words, carried by them but not of them. Reading *The Infinite Conversation* one begins to understand that certain conditions make possible the experience of understanding. The reader becomes aware of the impulse or movement towards communication (of speech, language, idiom or of the will itself) that seems compressed by Blanchot's writing. An interrogative impetus is always already present in a text, it is insistent and it returns through the reader's sustained encounter with the text: when does *The Infinite Conversation* begin? The question is, surely, always already there. (Then why ask it?)

Let me state certain conditions that seem obvious. The reader becomes aware of the presence of the question (when did this text begin?) *as an answer* upon opening a book: the book is a response. It is already a response. Opening the book-as-object one embarks upon a search – the *quest* of question – for the book as a book. The book must *become* a book beyond its material presence as an object in order to *be* a book. To know the book begins by locating its beginning and then having the sense of following it through to an end. It is to have understood its passage and content, its 'order that submits to *unity*' as Blanchot describes in the 'Note '. Imagining that we are reading a book we settle and regard it with the eye of a reader, from the position of one who reads books and feels one knows what it is to read a book. This position is predicated on the assumption that we already understand how to read, not just that we are able to read. One assumes that there is something *to* read, something to be understood. Furthermore, we are aware that this *something* involves not only the words themselves, but the countless acts of memory provoked by reading that each individual brings to a text. This engagement approximates the act of listening to music, where the music itself may not denote anything literal at all, but the listener assumes that there is something to be understood and discovers this by engaging though listening. Yet the possibility of meanings remain dependent upon the web of extra-textual associations, memories and expectations that accompany each act of listening. Reading is a performative, receptive act but it is also constitutive, as is listening: both activities occur through (silent) doing. *The Infinite Conversation* challenges the very assumptions and conditions of reading. Turning its pages we may no longer read as we have read. We will be called upon to surrender the need to decipher language in a way that makes us feel in possession of the existence of meaning, to slacken our hold, therefore, as we proceed. Blanchot proposes a different set of relations, a structure of collaboration that beckons the reader into a kind of reciprocity that begins (and proceeds) without knowing and which is founded upon the ability to become present: 'Reading is ignorant. It begins with what it reads and in this way discovers the force of a beginning. It is receiving and hearing, not the power to decipher and analyze, to go beyond by developing or to go back before by laying bare; it does not comprehend (strictly speaking), it attends.'[8] Less an act of domination, it is a sustained and repeatable gesture of surrender through a specific kind of attendance.

Opening a book, one actualizes reading. The turn of each page repeats the act of summoning. We look for signs – headings, subheadings, footnotes, indicators. One reads a book as if it were a map to a country one already holds within. We wonder where and how it will begin, this infinite conversation – has it already begun? – this open journey, how it will launch itself, become familiar, and bring familiarity to what it describes. This is the immensity of the 'when' of the question, a spatial and temporal enquiry. Where will the encounter take place? How will Blanchot bring us in? When will the book have begun? When I read Blanchot, where has Beckett ended and Blanchot begun *to be read*? Reading Blanchot, I hear Beckett. In 'III: The Absence of the Book (the Neutral, the Fragmentary)', Blanchot's final series of episodes in *The Infinite Conversation*, he turns to criticism and the writing of Sade and Beckett in a brief essay titled 'Words Must Travel Far'.[9] Here he proposes that certain books that are written are unreadable or at least not written to be read. Blanchot suggests, for example, that while Sade may have wished to be read, his books did not. Works such as these, 'come closer … to the movement of writing and to the movement of reading'. The approach one must adopt to reading such texts is more akin to the auditory: 'The term hearing would befit this act of approach better than reading. Behind the words that are read, as before the words written, there is a voice already inscribed, not heard, not speaking; and the author, close to this voice, is on an equal footing with the reader – each nearly merged with the other, seeking to recognize it.'[10] For Blanchot, all writing is auditory, an act of listening. To a certain extent, a fact made evident by certain texts, writer and reader share in the same circumstance: to seek to recognize.

(five)

Ohio Impromptu begins with the following stage direction: '*L=Listener. R=Reader. As alike in appearance as possible.*'[11] Reader and Listener are synchronous, 'as alike … as possible', duplicates, nearly identical though ambiguous in their similarity and ultimately separate. This separation necessitates an attempt to commune through the

8 Ibid., p. 320.

9 Ibid., pp. 326–31.

10 Ibid., pp. 328–9.

11 Samuel Beckett, *Ohio Impromptu*, in *The Complete Dramatic Works* (London, 1990), p. 445.

act of reading and listening to a text, and for each to bear witness to the other. As L listens to what the story tells, a tale of loss and mourning, R appears to become engaged by *how* the story is able to 'tell' and how one might prevent its ending (by knocking, by signalling for repetition). He seems to listen not only to the words of the text but to the absences it marks, for example, and the absence (of the reality of the events it remembers) its telling also communicates. The reader of the play (or spectator of its performance) cannot be sure of the identity of the subject of the story being told; whether it is autobiographical or not; whether these two are one and the same or not; or whether the protagonist (referred to as 'he') represents L, while the visitor in the story, who comes to L and reads, is R. The way in which the words read aloud by R and listened to by L can be understood is complicated by the formal composition of the play. It remains deliberately ambiguous whether the tale recounts details from L's or R's life or whether we should understand them as one. In addition, the conditions that make possible a 'real' exchange (of spontaneous dialogue, for example) are denied the protagonists: everything is instead mediated by the presence of the book which sits between the two characters. Yet it is also the book's presence that enables both *the* story and *their* story (in the here-and-now temporality of the play, reading and listening) to go on. The story within the book – possibly fictional, possibly a memoir and intended to allow for both to be assumed – acts as transmitter between the two and, within the structure of the play, as a script within a script. It establishes the text's metatheatricality while underscoring the tension between absence and presence (of identity) that haunts the play. The terms used to describe the characters – Listener (who we presume listens) and Reader (who we presume reads) – and the promise of something to be told suggested by their reciprocal pairing limits the possibilities. Of what can the characters speak? What manner of meaning will their exchange convey? Will they, rather, bear witness to the emptiness of language, as many Beckett characters do, nevertheless presiding over that void, or will they instead replace impromptu speech with the recitation of an already written text that has (possibly) already been heard? If there is something to read, a tale to tell, who has authored the text? In other words, what is being listened to? Or, what is being listened *for*?

As a reader or spectator of this play, one arrives upon a set of circumstances that are already established but which nevertheless seem to be stalling or caught up in the attempt to delay any kind of conclusion, a characteristic common in Beckett's works. The circumstance, or 'scene', as described earlier from the image on the cover of the playtext, conveys a specific mood that is weighed down by a sense of attenuated deferral. The figures appear hesitant but resigned. In the staging of the play, the two characters are already present, sat within a pool of light before the artificial lights beyond the interior world of the piece fade up, signalling the beginning of the play where the scene is already underway. L and R are seated at a 'plain white deal table'.[12] R begins by turning a page. Pause. He commences:

---

12 'Deal' refers to the material the table is made of, a soft wood that can be easily sawn, usually either fir or pine.

R: (*Reading*): Little is left to tell. In a last –
[*L knocks with left hand on table*.]
Little is left to tell.
[*Pause. Knock.*][13]

So it begins, and systematically falters in its beginning, a beginning (as all beginnings in Beckett) that describes the beginning of an end. But perhaps this already assumes too much.

Can we surmise from this that *Ohio Impromptu* is a play that *begins*? Or is it, rather, that Beckett searches for a way to avoid beginning, just as the play describes the avoidance of an ending? They are there; the book is open; a process continues. The musical rhythm soon established back and forth, between Reader and Listener, of reading aloud punctuated by a knock, pause, repeat, pause, knock, read, listen, proceed and so on, describes not so much even a process of continuation but rather a process of endless interruption as a means of development. As R reads from the book, L interrupts by knocking on the table with his left hand. R responds by stopping and repeating the words 'Little is left to tell', a motif that persists throughout, pausing again (in doubt?) before the moment that has provoked L to knock. Each knock calls a change that is registered by the way in which R reads, pausing (withholding) or else repeating lines from the open book. But the question the play poses is more complex than the pattern or musical scoring articulated by what the spectator sees and hears. The series set up by the movement of the text is, in a sense, conducted by L; that is, it both commences and is interrupted by L, repeats and is again interrupted by L paused by R (pre-empting a knock?), then continues and is interrupted yet again by L's knock and so on. It establishes a series of echoes and repetitions, recurring like motifs throughout the text, that condition the meaning of the play, so that the work itself is underwritten by what Harry White describes with insightful precision as 'a musical conception of meaning'.[14] The status of language itself is, as White notes in his discussion of the significance of musical serialism in Beckett's later plays, 'downgraded from that of sole intelligencer to compositional technique'.[15] Instead, it is the impetus of the work as well as its interruptedness that drives the meaning of the text rather than the scant details we are given of character, location (we learn, for example, that the Isle of Swans can be seen from the window of the single room where the protagonist of the narrative now lives) and events within the story. Questions turn and are rephrased in the mind of the spectator: one wonders not exactly who is reading but rather who is being read and what reading is for; what does it *do* here between and for these two figures? Not who listens, but what is being listened for. Reading

13 Beckett, *Ohio Impromptu*, p. 445.

14 Harry White, '"Something is Taking its Course": Dramatic Exactitude and the Paradigm of Serialism in Samuel Beckett', in Mary Bryden (ed.), *Samuel Beckett and Music* (Oxford, 1998), pp. 159–71 (p. 165).

15 Ibid.

and listening are the subject of the play. Each interruption registers a switch in direction, alters the tempo, and delivers a new movement or development within the overall composition. As Reader, R possesses a dual function: he both listens to the book *and* reads it. Reading – a reading that allows or attends – is an act of interpretative understanding.[16] The terms 'Reader' and 'Listener' are less stable than we might assume, and Beckett's play attempts to dramatize that dissolve. L both hears and dictates the reading. He reads R's attempts to read just as R listens for how L is reading him.

L's series of knocks belong to a system that forms part of an unspoken speech act to be negotiated by and between R and L, as well as by the spectator as another who listens. The interruption of the knock causes R to momentarily cease speaking and his response is to repeat a sentence or phrase. At other times the knock signals for R to continue, to move on from a pause as L follows the narrative. The knock (and the repetition it calls for) signals an arrest. Its necessary presence is what constitutes conversation in this situation and enables the spectator (from beyond the performance or the reading of the text) to perceive this exchange between L and R *as dialogue*, albeit a dialogue in which only R speaks and L is silent. Yet it appears to be the reverse – R is caught in recitation while L is the one who speaks or who at least determines the movement and direction of the text. But what of the interruption that interrupts L, the rupture in what *he* hears that causes him to knock in the first instance? How does this 'other' function in the text as a part of (its) language and compositional structure? In other words, how might we account for, or read, the interruption that causes L to knock? Blanchot considers interruption not only as a call but as a response to 'the strangeness, to the infinity between us'. This asks us to think of interruption as more than simply a break in or from language, but rather as something altogether more profound: 'let us understand that the arrest here is not necessarily or simply marked by silence, by a blank or a gap (this would be too crude), but by a change in the form or the structure of language'.[17] The interruptions and pauses that structure the exchange between R and L are not merely indicative of intervals or breaks. They announce the division that separates these two, a limit that marks the impossibility of their sameness.

When L interrupts R's reading it allows L to linger longer over the previously spoken line, as if he now listens for something other than the words themselves so as to hear in them more than can be spoken: to hear, in other words, what is now absent but which prompted the words to be written. Blanchot refers to the origin and otherness present in literature as *reverberation*, a condition or movement distinct from resonance, which 'does no more than bring us back sentimentally to our own experience'. Continuing, he articulates the effect of reverberation on the

---

[16] Paul de Man, *Blindness and Insight: Essays in the Rhetoric of Contemporary Criticism* (Minneapolis, 1983). p. 65. In 'Impersonality in the Criticism of Maurice Blanchot', de Man discussed Blanchot's notion of reading, referring to Heidegger's formulation of the reader as listener in a footnote.

[17] Blanchot, *The Infinite Conversation*, p. 77.

reader/listener thus: 'This reverberation is not, then, the image that resounds (in me, the reader, and on the basis of my self), it is rather the very space of the image, the animation proper to it, the point of its springing forth where, speaking within, it already speaks entirely on the outside.'[18] Let us now return to Beckett's text, to a later moment in *Ohio Impromptu* where the knock and consequent repetition of passages of text occur and layer this reading through the light of the distinction Blanchot makes between resonance and reverberation. The play is reaching its end. R continues after a pause:

> Finally he said, I have had word from–and here he named the dear name–that I shall not come again. I saw the dear face and heard the unspoken words, No need to go to him again, even were it in your power.
> [*Pause.*]
> So the sad–
> [*Knock.*]
> Saw the dear face and heard the unspoken words, No need to go to him again, even were it in your power.
> [*Pause. Knock.*]
> So the sad tale a last time told they sat on as though turned to stone.[19]

Within the play (as in its duration as a performance) R and L are now more advanced in the diminishing progression of the book being read. Several things come to one's attention considering the tension and movement of *Ohio Impromptu* in relation to Blanchot's discussion. First, in repeating the line, 'Saw the dear face and heard the unspoken words', R omits the pronoun 'I' removing the signifying presence of self-identification from the narrative voice. The knock itself performs a number of things, producing a shorthand to language, a rhythmic code that carries an excess of significance beyond its sound. It signals that L hears something (or someone) else in the words R reads. It announces (firmly, abruptly) the need to hear the words again (or else to continue on from a pause), to turn back in order to rehear their meaning or to hear what they do not say (twice in the text this refrain comes after the phrase 'heard the unspoken words') but also for the reverberation around these words which is, in any case, alluded to by the significance of 'heard the unspoken words'. But also, there is the knock itself – a blunt, hollow sound, a gesture more usually associated with the request to enter through a doorway or threshold – which substitutes speech and interrupts language, indicating the need for repetition or a second hearing. L prolongs the experience of the text in this way, extending its temporal limits. Above all, the repetitive knocking in *Ohio Impromptu* alerts us to the possibility of meaning or intention outside of speech to which L listens again

18 Ibid., p. 321.

19 Beckett, *Ohio Impromptu*, p. 447.

in order to hear more clearly. Beckett's play, anything but an impromptu, brings us closer to this other voice, the shudder of the other ushered forth through language, and Blanchot's writing is equally concerned with bringing our attention to the potentiality of this movement within literature. The exchange between R and L – interrupted and interrupter – is presented as a series of repetitive sequences that deliberate but progress, acknowledging the inevitability of absence and silence that occupy speech. This sense of 'movement' comes about through a series of precisely choreographed stanzas, so that, to return to Harry White's proposition concerning the explicit serialism of Beckett's late plays, 'dramatic advancement' is achieved 'by means of an unfolding structure'.[20] Blanchot reminds us that 'silence is still only a deferred speech, or else it bears the signification of a difference obstinately maintained'.[21] Through its composition, where *hearing* the words spoken brings more resonance to the text than the significance of the words themselves, *Ohio Impromptu* advances often by turning back on itself and through the partial repetition of motifs. It seems to articulate silence as part of speech rather than its deferral, a dimension of speech that is usually smothered by language in its never-ending tide of meaningless surrogacies and approximations. Here, instead, silence is articulated through the replay and recitation of language activated by its being read. It advances incrementally as a half-spoken, half-muted dialogue. As the play opens (it has already begun), we are already nearing an end and 'little is left to tell'. When it begins, the telling (by R) is interrupted (by L), establishing a method whereby speaking is composed as a musical recitation. R and L, each attentive to the other's silences, listen out for one another's interruptions which reveal that which drives them to speak but which itself will remain forever concealed. It is the presence of a voice that cannot be spoken that they have come together to articulate. This voice remains within speech yet beyond the reach of language.

In Beckett's novels and texts for theatre, as in Blanchot's extensive, ruminative consideration of the 'work' of literature, the voice within speech is distinguished as separate from but always in relation to language. Referring to Beckett's novel, *The Unnamable*, Simon Critchley describes this narrative voice that speaks to us as one that is driven or *being* driven, 'drawn on by a speaking that does not begin and does not finish, that cannot speak and cannot but speak'.[22] Or, as Blanchot writes with reference to the same text, 'when the talking stops, there is still talking; when the language pauses, it perseveres; there is no silence, for within that voice the silence eternally speaks.'[23] We find a similar predicament in the disarticulatory

[20] White, '"Something is Taking its Course"', p. 168.

[21] Blanchot, *The Infinite Conversation*, p. 76.

[22] Simon Critchley, 'Who Speaks in the Work of Samuel Beckett?', in Thomas Pepper (ed.), *The Place of Maurice Blanchot*, Yale French Studies 93 (Connecticut, 1998), pp. 114–30 (p. 126).

[23] Maurice Blanchot, 'Where Now? Who Now?', in Gontarski (ed.), *On Beckett*, pp. 141–9 (p. 141). Blanchot discusses the question of 'who is doing the talking' in Beckett's novels.

flow of the protagonist, Mouth, in *Not I*, and in the endlessly repeating serialism of the suffering souls, M, W1 and W2 trapped in urns in *Play*, where in both of these examples the 'being driven' is dramatized by the sequencing, precise repetitions and refrains as well as by the stage image itself. Mouth and heads are isolated. Speech overtakes the possibility of physical being or presence; it advances before it and remains after it. Character is all but gone, 'I' itself is being extinguished if not already extinct. In Blanchot's essay, which focuses on Beckett's trilogy, he refers to the 'terrible discovery' that fuels this drive in Beckett's work, a drive which brings us closer to the origin of speech and speaking and is reflective of the labour to which literature in its different forms commits itself, that is, to articulate the voice of the silence that eternally speaks. We might therefore think of *Ohio Impromptu* as an attempt to articulate the inevitable silence that exists not for each of us as individuals but rather as that enveloping, collaborative duet of silence made still more prominent by the presence of two, a silence that is, paradoxically, only ever made known through speech. R and L, however, begin to evidence silence as a mode of sharing and cooperation. Is this an attempt to articulate its presence and absence in language, therefore, in order to suggest that in silence there is no such difference? R and L have relinquished (or simply exhausted) the attempt at *real* speech or the attempt at unscripted, impromptu dialogue as offering the possibility of meaningful exchange. Instead they listen to the telling of a tale that might bring them together: 'With never a word exchanged they grew to be as one.'[24] They read and listen together to the arrival, the sound and the cadences of words, words as the symptom of an impulse and as recitation, without conversing, until the book itself delivers them to an unreachable place, 'Of mindlessness. Whither no light can reach. No sound. So sat on as though turned to stone. The sad tale a last time told'.[25] In the final line of the playtext, R recites that 'Nothing is left to tell' and in this moment, as he closes the book, an event already foreshadowed by the reading of the sad tale, there is an uncanny awareness of a beginning as of an ending, of an unending return, and of the vast expanse of the nothing beyond the book that remains to be told. It is the only moment in which the two figures look at each other, a self seeing itself, perceiving itself and being perceived, and hold one another's gaze, 'unblinking. Expressionless. Ten seconds. Fade out.'[26]

(six)

In his essay, *The Exhausted*, Deleuze ascribes a coded system to Beckett's oeuvre which he divides into three types of language – *language I, II and III*. For Deleuze, this charts the ways in which language and words themselves are gradually exhausted of possibility in Beckett's work from the novels through

24 Beckett, *Ohio Impromptu*, p. 447.

25 Ibid., p. 448.

26 Ibid.

the theatre works to the lesser known works for television. Applying Deleuze's theory to Beckett's work in general, and here specifically to *Ohio Impromptu*, it is important to remember the critical and tenacious status Deleuze confers upon exhaustion as a trope, equally upon the exhausted person as one who is both 'sufficiently disinterested' and 'sufficiently scrupulous', a paradox that reminds us of the ghostly appearance of Blanchot's two figures at the beginning of *The Infinite Conversation* for whom '*what weariness makes possible, weariness makes difficult*'. Deleuze states: 'But only an exhausted person can exhaust the possible, because he has renounced all need, preference, goal, or signification.'[27] *Language III*, described as 'the language of images and spaces', suggests a way we might think about the function and materiality of language in *Ohio Impromptu*. Beckett's incorporation of a prewritten text as speech read from a book, rhetorically mimics the fictional, therefore, while at the same time retaining the resemblance of the (auto-)biographical. Combined with the pauses, silence and repetitions that L's 'knock' gives rise to, this sufficiently distances language from its obligation to represent everyday spontaneous dialogue within the drama, as if this were already a thing of the past, and instead discovers other routes through signification.

In the notion of a language of images, Deleuze distinguishes his appropriation of the term 'image' from memory image, describing image as 'process'. For Deleuze, image is emptied of either the personal or the rational. In the image, language is separated from the transmission of voices and the more tactile, familiar association of objects. Instead, it relates to 'immanent limits that are ceaselessly displaced – hiatuses, holes, or tears that we would never notice, or attribute to mere tiredness, if they did not suddenly widen in such a way as to receive something from the outside or from elsewhere'.[28] His description of what such ruptures potentially reveal is as relevant to Beckett's text as to Blanchot's earlier work *The Space of Literature* and, later, *The Infinite Conversation*. In Blanchot's writing, the sense that something is received from the outside pervades cumulatively through his steady, attentive deployment of language, a use of language that aims to liberate itself from the burden of representation and which will eventually reassess the presumption of the narrative 'I' in literature, much as Beckett's plays and novels became increasingly dedicated to such a task. These efforts seem to compress language, as Blanchot persuades it back from false surfaces and limits, in the same way that Beckett also strives to advance language into other submissions and behaviours. Language floats, hovers, waits. It echoes. It reverberates. It *sounds*. Gradually we become aware that its function is no longer, therefore, only to *tell*. In Beckett's writing, this is (also) the work language is made to do, a kind of labour that is closer allied to the potential abstraction of visual engagement or to that auditory 'language' that is peculiar and particular to musical notation. Language proposes a rhetorical performance of an outside articulated by characters as they persist, wearily, in the rehearsal of conversation under exhausted and exhaustive

27 Deleuze, *Essays*, p. 154.

28 Ibid., pp. 158–9.

circumstances. It is night – the stars shine darkly. The book is to be read. Both Beckett and Blanchot move the reader to consider not only the outside of language but to attend to it in the very act of reading (that is, encountering), to 'transform into light that which is not of the order of illumination'.[29] *Ohio Impromptu* stages this as a performative duet that operates through a series of interrupted attempts made by L and R to tell and hear told the nothing that is left to tell, as music that is yet to be written but which has already been heard.

[29] Blanchot, *The Infinite Conversation*, p. 318.

Chapter 13
FOURSOME[1 2 3 4]

Christof Migone

[1] Prelude. In 2003 I was working with choreographer Lynda Gaudreau to devise a workshop for P.A.R.T.S. in Brussels. Briefly stated, we established a series of visual and textual sources that the students would then be asked to translate into movement. For one of those triggers I placed myself in front of a camera, close-up on my face, and proceeded to describe the movement of a performance of Beckett's *Quad I* was watching on a monitor (not visible to the camera) – this was the 1982 version, *Quadrat 1 + 2* for German television. My description was matter-of-fact, a Dan Graham-like deadpan (featured in Episode 4 below). I was simply trying to keep pace with the movement of the four players as they move around and through a square.

[2] In 2007 I was invited by Kelli Dipple of the Intermedia Art division (now defunct) at the Tate Modern to produce a work as part of the event, 'The Long Weekend 2007'. The piece would be on-line and on-air on Resonance FM. I was keen to develop further the translation of Beckett's wordless piece into sound through various descriptive strategies, so I produced *Foursome*, a radio work in four episodes featuring four Montreal-based choreographers (Dana Gingras, k.g. Guttman, Tammy Forsythe and Marie-Claude Poulin) translating Beckett's piece for a radio audience. In a sense, the choreographers replaced the four percussive instruments of the original: drum, gong, triangle, woodblock. Where in the original each instrument followed one player, here the following was more generalized and exhaustive – and thereby bound to fail. They performed various attempts: describing in words as they watch the piece and then from memory, moving in space and on the page, circling around a microphone and then the microphone circling around them. The empty centre which is avoided at all costs in *Quad* is here embodied by a piece which surrounds another without ever taking complete hold of it.

[3] Each episode traces an always meandering and provisional trajectory. *Foursome* is a *dis*-orienting, *dis*-ordered and *dis*-articulated narrative where failure in interpretation is foregrounded. A quadraphonic quadrangle where voices, paces and noises are intertwined to concoct a radio portrait of a most un-radiogenic work. *Quad* might be wordless but it is not soundless. The percussion which accompanies the original however was not used in *Foursome*. The reasons are in part practical: when the choreographers' voices were recorded at the same time as they watched *Quadrat 1 + 2* on a video monitor it was important to capture only their voices and also to have them untethered by headphones. The other consideration was the conceptual strategy to focus on the translation by the choreographers of the gestural into the aural. While *Foursome* uses *Quad* merely as a departure point, it could perhaps function as an alternate soundtrack for *Quad*, albeit one that injects out-of-synch aural subtitles or proposes a distracting and unnerving commentary.

[4] The transcription is accurate insofar as it attempts to represent the multivocal radio work. It works under a predilection for the prefix *dis-* mentioned in the preceding note. The tempo of the various sections of each of the episodes, as well as the various layered and interrupted voices, are conveyed in text in a manner that accentuates the repetitive patterns of Beckett's original. As for meaning, the ekphrastic method is featured here to convey what I would call a naked opacity – not to give words to a wordless play, but to rhythm the pieces (both *Foursome* and *Quad*) on the page through wordless words, words that abide by the always sidestepped centre. Here the challenge is to produce a somatic presence in the midst of the semiotic. The original audio works can be heard on <christofmigone.com>.

EPISODE 1

TAMMY FORSYTHE: Play, pause. Press play. Ok, there alright. *Quadrat I + II*, von Samuel Beckett. OK, sorry, movement four, never mind. OK, around the edges, squared. 1 comes in, 2 comes in, 3 comes in, 4 comes in. Then they disappear in the dark. Let's see. Pivot 1.

MARIE-CLAUDE POULIN: They walk, quite fast, like someone is behind them or more led by a thought, a single thought, which is carrying them from one place to the other.

DANA GINGRAS: A square, one figure, diagonal line, a circle, black centre spot moving around the centre avoiding the centre up to the outside.

K.G. GUTTMAN: An empty space. *Quad 1*. I think it is wood. By Samuel Beckett. There is only light on the square. And a figure appears. Figure 2. Starts walking in a steady rhythm. Light only lit. Figure 2, two figures. Around the border and square. So, defining the space through him walking or walking. I think the focus is ... .

MCP: They walk, quite fast, like someone is behind them or more led by a thought, a single thought, which is carrying them from one place to the other. Insects or I don't know like destiny is decided already. They cross each sometimes, coincidence. The circle in the centre. Changing direction. Head down. The thought is leaving nothing behind. No past. Feet, quick feet, and joined hands, head down. Heavy heavy back. Curved upper back. Invisible walls. Corners. Only the corners blocked by the walls. The mental, mental is very present. The dress is floating on the floor. Shadows. Together, but very alone. More alone than together. Parallel. Avoiding, only avoiding. Going only forward. Nothing backwards. Infinite. There's like a dance sometimes, like a dance, a conscious dance. Shadows. Four people, four shadows. The white centre. Dirty, dirty floor. A space which is square, which is not too big. Like suspended in the dark. Like if the dark was infinite, so a square which is defined by its colour. And, it's maybe grainy, maybe a bit yellow, brown. There's light on it. And it's finishing where the darkness starts. I think there's four people, maybe three. but I think four. And they are occupying the space, they advance. I don't know if they walk, but they are not static. They move very slowly and their path is also defining the limits of their space. They are quite regular in their speed. And they make me feel the presence of time or the unfolding of time. A bit like sand which is falling into an hourglass. I think they have a costume. I think each of them is dressed in a monochrome costume. I'm not sure. I feel the four corners of that space. They stop, maybe. And they start again. I can watch forever. I feel that this space is suspended in a bigger space, but also suspended in time. I don't know from where the light is coming. I don't know who are these people. And they go forward. I don't think they go backward. I think they can only go forward. They have something on their head, each covering their hair. We don't see the hair. We see ... . I don't remember if we see the faces. It's like I remember the face but without nose, mouth and eyes. I think one is blue and maybe the other is red, and the other yellow. But I'm not sure, maybe they are also only dressed the same colour like the floor. I don't remember exactly. I think they are more walking than anything else. I think they look ... . they stop their eyes somewhere like a punctuation in their trajectory. I don't know if they go lower, if they sit or they walk down. I don't think, I think they just walk. They are walking around or they are walking along the borders. And maybe they overpass sometimes each other. Maybe they walk together sometimes. I don't know if they look back. Maybe the space is bigger, because they need space, they are four people. But at the same time the space appears small to me. Because the outside space is very present. I don't know if they are moving maybe their hands, their fingers, small gestures, like their eyes which stop. And it's like they are sliding very slowly on the surface of the floor, like they would be transported without effort.

TF: Blue screen. Press play, pause. Circle.

KJG: A figure appears, walking in a steady rhythm.

TF: OK, never mind.

KJG: Around the corner. Defining the space through.

TF: OK, never mind. Around the edges, square.

DG: Diagonal, straight, circle. Second figure.

TF: Ok. One two three. Pivot. Their arms are folded.

KJG: I would say there is a kind of steadiness to it.

DG: Bigger moves, two figures moving around the centre point.

TF: There doesn't seem to be any set pattern. One two three stop.

KJG: Focuses down. Figure 2. Figure 2, two figures.

TF: A square.

DG. Shadows. Figures.

KJG: Pivot.

DG: There's something in the centre. Avoiding.

KJG: One orange figure.

One two three four five. One two three four. One two three. One two three four five pivot. There is no eye contact between. There's no visible stuff along. Keeping track. Figures.

Pivot. Immediacy. Approach. There's all this darkness around the square. Avoiding. Pattern. Bodies leaning forward. Coming from. In a consistent pattern. There's a grid. Shadow. Fluidity. Avoiding. Pivot. Four figures. Looking down. Lonely. Pivot. Wait a minute. Made for television. One figure. Back to the exterior, go the edges of the quadrant. One two three four. Two figures. Go through the edges. Pivot. Counter-clock. Steady, firm, circling halfway. A map.

Go forward. Two figures, three figures. Corners. Torture. Around the outside. Pivot. Wait. Top of it. Centre. One two three four. One two three four five. An incompletion. Pivot. Twice. Ok. Wait. Move. Ok. Steady. They are going, they're going. Steady. Semi-circle. Sharp corners. Figures one two three and four. No circling. Small, together. Pivot. They seem to be falling forward. They are moving slower.

Together. Pivot. Coming together. Impossible to describe. I don't know how big the square was. Pivot. Corners, face down. Towards the centre. Pivot.

Pivot. Pivot. One two three four five six. Corner. Exterior. Where they come from. Four figures behind. Pivot one two three four five six. Wait.3.528

Falling forward. In front of the body, lilting, lurching. A body walks. Makes a triangle, pivots. Avoids white figure. Avoids yellow figure. Sometimes it's more acute, more sharp. Kind of cultish figure. Looks cultish. Quite bright. Avoiding the centre. Always avoiding. Lugubrious. Bowing.

Silent steps.

EPISODE 2

An empty space, *Quad*
1, I think it's wood, by Samuel Beckett, there's only light on the square and a figure appears, Figure
2, starts walking in a steady rhythm light only lit, figure
2, two figures, around the border, on square, so, pivot, defining the space through, approach, him walking or her walking, there's no pausing, I think the focus is down, black perimeter, or I imagine the focus to be down, pivot, I would say, pivot, there's kind of a steadiness to it, and the second figure, black rim, catches on to the steadiness, there's, entering the system, one orange figure, focus is down,
1
2
3
4
5, spine is curved,
1

2
3
4
5
1
2
3
4
5, staring at feet, avoid the circle, the two figures don't look at each other I would imagine, there are three figures, around the centre, they are quite equidistant apart, shuffle around, they are only on the edges, they are magical feet, three figures, and the third figure, crossing, would enter into that kind of, crossing three figures crossing, the entrances are not noticeable, this is all going way too quickly, shadow on the figures, getting ahead of myself, yellow figure, focus is down, leaning forward, there's no eye contact between the figures, figures in a triangle, only looking down at the feet, pivot, there's no taking, around the outside, there's no, pivot, planning, OK, turning quickly, fourth box, four figures, absorption with the space, case down, getting mixed up which, pivot, who is which, pivot, which is which, looking down, who is who, there's an approach, kind of a lozenge, and a retreat, shoulders hunched, many times, shadow, so much so that approach looks like, crossing, the retreat, and the retreat looks like the approach, avoiding each other, again looking down, tips, I wonder if any, pivot, turn, at any time any of the figures look up, towards the tips, I think that is not allowed, constant, in the system, away from the centre, towards the tips, burning, everyone is wearing shoes, loud shoes, four figures, each at a corner, maybe that's why everyone's looking down, slowly, and the fourth figure emerges, avoiding the centre, there's kind of a fluidity, one approaches, to their movements, one retreats, one exits two are left, and it's quite,
1
2
3
4
5
6, amazing that they are all looking down, around the perimeter walking, retreating, blue figure leaves, facing each other and then, counterclockwise, pulling at the last minute, shuffle yes shuffle, looking down, maybe they can see each other's heels, one figure, steady, around the perimeter, shuffle, always around the perimeter, pivot, two figures facing each other, triangle after, near the centre, insistence, around, around outline, I don't know on what, no circling, straight lines, kind of insistence, to the work, turning the corner shuffle, yellow figure, pivot, maybe insisting on, cross the centre turn, approaching, yellow figure has disappeared, corner are big, white figure has disappeared, they make the perimeter, crossing, they fix the perimeter, blue, go forward, as a shadow turns, red has a shadow, upper left hand page, pivot, turn, four steps, it's not broken, they're going they're going, it's incredibly, pace is steady, steady, faces down, and loud, there's no light on the perimeter, yes I would say the piece is really loud, last box, one figure, retreating, no it's quite quiet, blue figure, there's a kind of silent inner, turn, approach and retreat, and going

away, back up, avoid the centre, approach and retreat, walks turn coming together now, coming together, figures
1
2
3 and
4,
1
2
3
4
5
6, all have sharp corners, perimeter, corner
1
2
3
4
5
6, then crossing the square, corner, I imagine they cross the space completely but sometimes they have to stop, towards each other, and, two figures, turn only 90 degrees so they don't, turn it around, backs into each other, quite complete, so it is always, towards the centre, an incompletion, medium fast yes, across the space, no gaze, steady, bottom right, towards incompletion, steady incomplete, quite quick, sharp corners, gaze down, figures
1
2
3 and
4,
1 silent,
2 silent,
3, blue figure,
4 turning clockwise,
5 steps,
6 maybe, very steady, there's no increase, there's no crescendo, figures are direct, there's an accumulation of figures
1
2
3 and
4, across the space, they don't walk backward, pivot, blue figure and strangely, corner, I would say, approach the centre, towards the corner, avoid the centre, it's not about the centre, the perimeter, it's about the lines, the white figure, no it's about the feet,
1
2, they look down,
4 figures behind, they turn corners, exited, the feet keep walking, red figure following blue figure,

1
2
3 towards the centre, pivot, in hard shoes, I'm not doing this in the right order, I can't imagine the ending, walking, pause, I have no idea what the fuck the ending is, turn, the tempo is medium, tempo, there's an acceleration, is medium, and the figures meet, no circling, and cross, approaching centre, but generally tempo is medium, makes the triangle, I am imagining the, just triangles, sometimes, and squares, pattern that each figure makes, yellow figure, sometimes, red figure, it is a 90-degree corner, avoids blue figure, there are no faces, avoids white figure, shoulders and feet mostly, avoids yellow figure, more acute, corner not the centre, figures are tall just shoulders and slim, he distinguishes the centre from the corner, more sharp, sluggish, but there's a steady rhythm, ahead of retreating blue figure, in each step, corner, tracing the square not the centre, so corner, no matter what, white figure is, sometimes the body shifts more acutely, yellow figure behind red figure, sound is loud but steady, because the weight, red figures behind blue, is heard, going forward, turning, through each step, four bodies, there's not an attack necessarily, centre's lit, against the floor with the foot but there's a, quite bright, kind of solid landing, avoiding the centre, it's about contact, three figures, full foot contact, sluggish, I would say that the gaze looking down, approaching the centre, creates a curve in the spine, but hesitant.

A square
one figure diagonal line
a circle black centre spot moving around the centre
avoiding the centre up to the outside
moving around the outside straight line
diagonal into the centre around
moving to the opposite corner diagonal straight circle
second figure enters I can't remember if the colour is blue, red, yellow or white
a hooded figure
lit so that there's a shadow in front of the figure as the figure moves
two figures moving around the centre point
moving around each other moving around the outside
triangles a square circles
numbers four three two
a third figure enters
moving in the same pattern
frantic stepping
moving around
moving around a centre point
there's something in the centre
they avoid something
avoiding
not sure what the intention is
pivoting

pivoting around
pivoting around the centre
avoiding the centre
there's a fourth figure
a fourth figure enters
again I can't remember the colour if it's blue yellow red white
huddled hurried
they're moving around each other
keeping
keeping track
keeping track
it continues
we've lost a figure
we have three figures in the space
there's an urgency
very very clear parameters
a border an outline
I started to think about the space outside of the square
there's all this darkness around the square
triangle within a square
the veiled hooded figures huddled marching moving
there are shadows
shadows outside of the box
where did the figures come from?
is there a backstage?
where did they come from?
they come they enter they leave
I want to know what's outside of the box
they move in a consistent pattern
tense tension an elastic pulling equidistant
space in between figures
the negative space the shapes colours
obsessive
what's in the centre?
we've lost a figure
three figures two figures one figure
it starts again
one two three four around the centre
out to the edge around
what is it about the centre?
what is it about the centre that is so compelling?
steady steady firm
a map there's some kind of map
an inner logic

so the figures continue doing this pattern
it continues.

And it’s like they are sliding very slowly on the surface of the floor like they would be transported from... without that they have to make an effort.

PlaypausepressplayokalrightquadratoneplustwonevermindaroundtheedgessquareonecomesintwocomesinthreecomesinfourcomesindisappearallinteractingleftandthentheydisappearbottomrightokpivotarmsarefoldedbottomrightpivotcolorscolorspivotallgoingokoppositepatterncounterclockwisepivottwofigurespivotonetwothreefoursixoksixonetwothreefourfivesixpivotonetwothreefourfivesixintothefirstbodyonetwothreefourcameinokohdirectionalpivotpivotokbodycameinfirstbodypivotonsixquieterslowslowernowordsnomovementreallyotherthanfigureswalkinglessspeednowordsdirectionmovingspecificveryspecificnothingstaticcalmernowtwofigurespivotcultishIdon’tknowanythingaboutitwhentheyleavethesquaresluggishimmediacyandurgencyfiguresfiguresnevermindcreepyorangefigureIdon’tknowanythingaboutitveiledfiguredeathcreepyendlessfewerstepsthantheotherfiguresoksobodiesleaningforwardshuffleshuffleshufflelugubriousslowlyshuffleshuffleshuffletheflooorwasasquaremadefortelevisionabcsooppressiveanothershufflemathematicalshuffleshuffleshuffleowbackIcan’tI’matalossforwordsactuallytothecirclewalkingclockwisepivotexteriorhopelesssoifthecamerawasshootingstopgoaroundpivotpointfigureokonetwothreestoponetwobackturnmiddleavoidthemiddlecentreturnturnturnturnpivotsomekindofmathematicaltwofiguresokstoptowardswowbottomlefthandcorneravoidavoidit’snotonefigurequickspacefastspacepivotturnavoidavoidjusttwostepstoprightbooksstepstorturepivotavoidpivotonetowardsanotherpivotoksoavoidavoidyouwanttwofiguresonetwothreefourfivesixturnturnexteriorpivotcounterclockwiseturnturnthreefourfivesixokwaitwaitdoesn’treallymattersixcirclearoundthecentrewaitturnturnonewhat’sgoingonokokexteriorallgotwofiguresfiguretogoonethreefiguresremainfourthfigurepivotonetwothreefourfivesixexpandtheatricalplatformmiddlerepetitivethesamemediumwalkstowardsthecentrepivotpivotavoidavoidfirstfigureshuffleshuffleshuffleonefigureclockwisefollowingwaitreturnavoidthecentrebodyfollowsthefirstbodyfollowsthethirdbodyavoidavoidwalkaroundflowsthefirstbodytwofiguresgoesaroundturningsecondbodycircleenterwalkingaroundtowardsoneanothertowardsthecentreavoidthecentrethreebodies.

EPISODE 3

step step step step
ouououououououououououououou ouououououououououououououou
centre
ouououououououououououououou ouououououououououououououou
turn step step step step figures one step step step step avoid centre step step step step
ouououououououououououououou
centre step step step step pivot three figures step step step step
around the border
focus is down
spine is curved
staring at feet

there's no eye contact between the figures
only looking down at the feet
they stop they stop they step they stop
maybe
and they and they and they start again
maybe maybe
and they start again
again looking down
and they start again
ouououououou ouououououou ouououououou
there's kind of a fluidity to their movements
insistence
maybe insisting on approaching and retreating

they fix the perimeter
it's incredibly steady and loud
I would say the piece is very loud
approach and retreat
turn back up
approach and retreat
turn go forward

there's no crescendo
so it's constant
and strangely, I would say, it's not about the centre
it's about the lines

they turn corners
the feet keep walking
they look down

I can't imagine the ending
I'm not sure what the ending is

when the figures meet and cross
the tempo is medium
there's an acceleration
sometimes the body shifts more acutely
but there is a steady rhythm
in each step
no matter what

step step step step corner step step step centre around the centre avoid centre
step step step step

enter fourth figure
step step step step
corner
step step step step
through centre
step step step step
step step step step
step step step step
go around and pivot
step step step step
corner
step step step step
fourth figure exits
step step step step
centre
step step step step
oooooooooooooooooooooooooooooooooooooooooooooo
corner
oooooooooooooooooooooooooooooooooooooooooooooo
oooooooooooooooooooooooooooooooooooooooooooooo
oooooooooooooooooooooooooooooooooooooooooooooo
oooooooooooooooooooooooooooooooooooooooooooooo
step step step corner corner
around the perimeter
black exterior
lit centre
step step step
approach look down
step step step step
start retreat
corner step
oooooooooooooooooooooooooooooooooooooooooooooo
oooooooooooooooooooooooooooooooooooooooooooooo

I see a square a space which is square which is not too big like suspended in the dark like if the dark was infinite so a square which is defined by its colour and its maybe grainy maybe a bit yellow brown there's light on it and its finishing where the darkness starts I think there's four people maybe three but I think four and they are occupying the space they advance I don't know if they walk but they are not static they move very slowly and their path is also defining the limits of their space they are quite regular in their speed and they make me feel the presence of time or the unfolding of time a bit like sand which is falling into an hourglass I think they have a costume I think each of them is dressed in a monochrome costume I am not sure I feel the four corners of that space they stop maybe and they start again I can watch forever I feel that this space is suspended in a bigger space but also suspended in time I don't know from where the light is coming I don't know who are these people I think there are women and also men and they go forward I don't think they go backwards I think they can only go forward and sometimes take pauses they have something on their head which covers their hair we don't see their hair I don't remember if we see their faces it's like I remember the face but without nose, mouth and eyes.

oooooooooooooooooooooooooooooooooooooooo
oooooooooooooooooooooooooooooooooooooooo

ouououououououououououou ouououououououououououou
step step step step step step step step step
avoid centre go around
step step step step step step step step step
go go go go go
ouououououououououououou ouououououououououououou
around the centre
ouououououououououououou ouououououououououououou

takoute thnothingree tammmusty blugeometrye bluel agonem screeseen atpress aplay pause losstake threok etammy press play othek alrighmiddlet ththeyink ofok thofe sebendingcret movinga okancient moving ok avoidinavoiding thgoe dotg thfaste dopacet aroquickund the edccornerges squaleftre evtopery theslowerre doearoundsn't onnevere disappdisappearsear piseem tospeeding bevot firust ime Ibig oksaw thispivogoingt okavoid movcounterclock wisemshuffle ethrid ment tfigurehe whopivotle time piany sensevot therememberir aronems atwore fthreeolded sfourhuffle shnouffle buwordsmping intfigureo shuavoidffle opivotn twshuffleo threbacke stopivotp ssenseet pfour figuresattern fiset uavoidp guabout thisre goinpieceg couno armsnter clono visiblekwise yspecifica avonever anyiding thstatice circhowle thpivotrid figusppedre pivoincreasest pivooranget pessenceivot onofe twavoido thrimmediacyee oranandge figuurgencyre pivopivott shuffloke bacsok avoibodiesd tlefto thleaninge lshuffleeft pivforwardot pivowordst arepetitivevoid threpetitivee circlexite nomovement woouchrds nook moveupment reallmovingy othexiter thcounteran sofigureme kindof benenterst forwarquited nseemso awhatrms sptheecific pivheckoting wisith thgoinge leonft fotogetherot pivturnot pivopivott hunnowchback speswitcheded intheycreases whavehen thimpossibleey leatove thfiguree squaoutre figurunderstandes leatelevisionding bupivott I doneon't ktwonow anythreething abfourout it ofivek ssixo bopivotdies leavoidaning foroneward thtwoere's threea gfourrid whfiveat wsixas tmorehe direslowerction I'mcalmer not sureally surfigurese shuffle shuffle shuffle third figure enterminds coseeming towknowards onanythinge anotheshuffler shushuffleffle shurepetitiveffle pivolt turdon turnotn turknown thethirdy mfigureust hentersave coturnunted thcountedeir stepstepss thedescribere mwhatust hcornersave mbeen sopivotme kindof mastopthematical nnoo wowordsrds nevero wogords circaroundle atraversevoid thtorturee midgeometrydle thigones inothings tortouture geomeoftry goquickne ostepk soslower yotwou wstespant nowalkthing otout othef nothcentreing thelre's adon't loknowng boavoiddy gcounterown oclockk thiwises bmeansody thfigureis laentersst bosemidy iscircle slofullwer thaavoidn antheybody eoklse turln pivcanot avbeoid thcomfotablee centwither Isilence dblueon't kdoesnow hnotow bireallyg thmattere squaimpossiblere watos oppodescribesite pivavoidots turpivotn tuonern turtwon pivthreeot counfourterclowckwise figtopure enteleftrs figurcornere eavoidnters avoavoidids semiquietercircle aroundslower tsluggishhe coneenter fuextendll circlpivote arounoned ththee cewholenter whtimeat thbendinge heoverck is gseemoing oton obek II cacann byae comfothirdrtable witfigureh silpivotence osenseut aonegain ctwoounterclokwise pivothreet onfoure fourtshuffleh fiavoidgure bnolue ewordsnter bnolue nomovementw thehey siswitch diregonection thpivote doespeeds iincreasest resenseally maoftter imposurgencysible tlongero debutscribe sbodiestays thleaninge saforwardme mrepetitiveedium fashufflest fashufflest imshufflepossible tthirdo undfigureerstand impentersossible toturn figturnure otheyut mustI whaveonder hcuntedow ltheiroud itsteps waones itwon tthreehe stfourudio pivtheyot pivneverot pivgoot pivaroundot oneverne twogeometry thrgoneee fookur gosoes tyouo thwante ennothingter shoutuffle shuofffle shufnothingfle shgouffle ptoivot gtoo ttheo thbottome top lerightft figuhandre bottomovem rigfigureht tuentersrn avoiavoidsd avanyoid pivofullt oncirclee twoko thcanree fobeur fivcomfotablee siwithx twsilenceo figublueres qnotuieter sjustlow moimpossiblere slowtoer slodescribewer caimpossiblelmer fotour figurunderstandes enpivotter ppivotivot oonene twtwoo

EPISODE 4

eeeeeeeeeeeeeeeeeeeeee
ouououououououououououou
eeeeeeeeeeeeeeeeeeeeee
ouououououououououououou
eeeeeeeeeeeeeeeeeeeeee
ouououououououououououou
eeeeeeeeeeeeeeeeeeeeee
ouououououououououououou
eeeeeeeeeeeeeeeeeeeeee
ouououououououououououou
eeeeeeeeeeeeeeeeeeeeee
ouououououououououououou
aaaaaaaaaaaaaaaaaaaaaa
eeeeeeeeeeeeeeeeeeeeee
ouououououououououououou
aaaaaaaaaaaaaaaaaaaaaa
eeeeeeeeeeeeeeeeeeeeee
ouououououououououououou
aaaaaaaaaaaaaaaaaaaaaa

A square in the centre of the image – a white hooded figure moves around the square – now there's a second person dressed the same but in blue – they move along the lit square in the centre of the image – they move along the sides of the square – then towards the centre – they avoid each other – then go back to the corners – then along the edges then back to the centre – avoid each other at the centre – now there's a third one that comes in red one – so there's red blue and white – along the edges – towards the centre – avoid each other – back into the corner all in unison – now there's a fourth one that just came in at the top right – so a yellow a blue a red and a white – along the edges – they all walk towards the centre – avoid each other – turn around – back to the edges – centre – corners – walk along the edges of the square – towards the centre of the square – avoid each other to the corners – walk along the edges centre – now the white one left – so there's just three the yellow red and blue ones – they go towards the centre – avoid each other – go to the corners – walk along the edges – then into the centre – walk towards the corner – then along the edges – the blue one just left at the bottom left of the screen – so there's just the yellow and red left – they walk along the edges – walk towards the centre – avoid each other – go towards the corner – walk along the edges – walk towards the centre – avoid each other – go towards the corner – walk along the edges – walk towards the centre – walk towards the corner – the red one has left – so it's just the yellow one by itself – walks towards the centre – avoids the centre – walks to the corner – walks along the edges – walks towards the centre – corner – edges – centre – walks to the corner – walks along the edges – back to the other corner – the white has just come in – it's the white and yellow now – they walk towards the edges – from one corner to the other – back towards the centre – avoid each other and the centre – into the corner – walk along the edges – now walk towards the centre – they walk towards the corner – walk along the edges to the other corner – now walk down to the centre – avoid each other – go back to the corner – the red one just came in at the bottom right of the screen – they walk towards to the centre – walk into the corner – walk along the edges – back into the centre – back into the corner – walk along the edges – towards the centre – into the corner – walk along the edges – they all walk around at the same speed – you hear the shuffling of the feet – the fourth one just came in at the bottom left of the screen – so there's four of them now – blue red yellow and white – walk towards the centre – they go to the corners – walk along the edges to the other corner – back to the centre – avoid each other – they go into the corners – walk along the edges – back into the corner – they go towards the centre – walk along the edges – back into the corner – the yellow has left – the three of them now walk along the edges – go towards the centre – and walk along the edges – from the corner going into the centre – avoid each other – go back into the corner – the move back into the centre – into the corner – the white one just left from the top left of the screen – it's just red and blue left – walk along the edges – into the centre – avoid each other and the centre – and go to the corner – walk along the edges – back towards the centre – and to the corner – and the edges – back towards the centre – avoid each other – into the corners – the red one just left at the bottom right of the screen – so it's just blue left – walk along the edges – to the corner – go into the centre – avoid the centre itself – go to the other corner – walk along the edges – back towards the centre – walk towards the corner – along the edges now – back towards the centre – avoid the centre – yellow one just came back from the top right of the screen – yellow and blue walk towards the edges – now towards the centre – avoid each other – back into the corner – walk along the edges – back into the centre – they go back towards the corner – walk along the edges – back into the centre – avoid each other – go back to the corner – the white one just came in at the top left of the screen – go into the corner – walk along the edges – walk towards the centre – avoid each other and the centre – go into the corners – walk along the edges – back into the centre – avoid each other – go into the corners – walk along the edges – back into the centre – back into the corner – the bottom right of the screen the red one just came in – there's four of them blue red yellow and white – walk along the edges – into the centre – back into the corner – walk along the edges – back towards the centre – into the corners – walk along the edges – back into the centre – out to the corners – the blue one left from the bottom left of the screen – three of them left – walk along the edges – towards the centre – out into the corners – walk along the edges – into the centre – out towards the corners – walk along the edges – into the centre – out to the corners – the yellow one left from the top right of the screen – two of them left red and white – walk along the edges – into the corner – walk along the edges – towards the centre – out into the corners – walk along the edges – into the centre – out towards the corners – top left of the screen the white one left – so it's the just the red left now – walk along the edges – in towards the centre – out to the corner – walk along the edges – in towards the centre – out to the corner – walk along the edges – in towards the centre – out towards the corner – the blue one just came in from the bottom left of the screen – so there's two of them now – red and blue – towards the centre – out into the corner – walk along the edges – in towards the centre – avoid the centre – out into the corner – walk along the edges – in towards the centre – out into the corners – the top right yellow just came in – there are three of them red yellow and blue – walk along the edges – in towards the centre – out into the corners – walk along the edges – in towards the centre out towards the corners – walk along the edges – in towards the centre – out towards the corner – top left of the screen the white came in – so there are four of them white yellow red and blue – walk along the edges – in towards the centre.

Okpress playa squareand rollinggoing outsidethe perimeter, quadratone andtwo bysamuel beckettsecond. Figureenters pressplay goingaround theoutside ofthe perimeterstep inby samuelbeckett. Intothe centreavoiding centretwo figureshunched overgoing aroundthe outsideof theperimeter, intothe centrestepping ared figureenters thesquare. Threefigures secondfigure intothe centreavoiding thecentre, aroundavoiding thecentre, almostcoming togetherbut notquite. Hunchedover threefigures steppingavoiding thecentre – allone twothree onetwo threeone twothree fouralmost comingtogether butnot quitehunched. Overone, twothree, onetwo, threeone, twothree, onetwo, threefour alongthe outsidesavoid thecentre. Onetwo, threealmost, comingtogether butnot quitehunched overinto. Thecentre: onetwo, threeone, twothree, onetwo, threeone, twothree, andfour.

Sharp turnsaroundthe corners, neverlookingat each otherthered figure. Hasenteredrepeating a patternagainpattern going nowherethatstays that maintainsitselfhurried figures – cloakedfiguressharp figure contactneverlooking to eachotherhooded. Figure andoutagain hurried, figurestheblue figure hasjustentered the spacesteppingcoming together; movingapartand out againconstantmovement pattern thatgoesnowhere. Stepping awayonetwo, one, twoboundaryone, two magnetsarecoming together. Threefiguresin the spacenothinghas changed. Patterncontinuesone two threesteppingaround, hurried. Figurescloackedfigures no eyecontactwe: have fourfiguresin the squareboundarycoming together, andsteppingaway and outagainwe are backtofour. Figures nothinghaschanged (boxed inconstantstepping), one twoonetwo. One twoperimeterboundary. One twothreecoming together inpatterncontinues. Three figuresworkingopposite sides ofthespaces, following shadowssteppingemptiness of thecentreof, the squarefigureone. Two: threefollowingthe (nothing haschangedcontinues) we haveawhite and redfigureleft moving. Soundbalancingthe space, everythingmovestowards the centrepointof the space.

Around.
Around.
In never.
Space.
Towards the centre.
Around.
Out.
In.
Around.
Out.
In.
Never reaching the centre point.
Falling forward.
Lilting lurching.
Black on the screen.
Slow steady steps.
Moving much slower.
Wait.
Two figures.
Lilting lurching.
Slow heavy steps.
Same pattern as before.
Two white figures.
Following each other.
Hunched over walking.
Space between the two.
Slower rate.
Hunched over.
Fourth figure.
Pattern same as before.
Rotation.
Third figure has entered.

Three figure left in the space.
Rotation diagonal.
Time continues as before.
Repetition.
Metronome pulse.
Two figures.
Pattern continues as before.
A metronome.
A pulse.
And now the screen is black.
I lost track of the figures.
The screen is black.
Lost track of the figures.

Chapter 14

Music in Beckett's *Nacht und Träume*: Vocality and Imagination[1]

Catherine Laws

Introduction: Beckett, Schubert and Romanticism

Beckett's love of music is frequently commented upon, and Schubert is the composer to whom he refers most frequently in his works. Specific compositions by Schubert are invoked alongside those of Beethoven, particularly in some of the early novels and short stories, and throughout his life Beckett held a particular love for Schubert's lieder, sometimes singing them himself at the piano.[2] However, it is only in the radio play *All That Fall* (1956) and the television play *Nacht und Träume* (1982) that we hear actual extracts of Schubert's music. In *All That Fall* we twice hear music from 'Death and the Maiden', early and late in the play, while *Nacht und Träume* is named after a Schubert lied, and the only sounds in the play are a few bars from the end of the song.

A number of writers have considered the significance of Schubert to Beckett, observing a certain commonality of thematic concerns: lone figures journeying through barren landscapes, ambiguous encounters along the way, the persistent desire for the comfort of company in the face of ultimate isolation, and the hovering presence of death. However, this commentary is mostly characterized in very broad terms, musically speaking, and is often heavily influenced by Beckett's comment to his cousin John: 'I think the opening of Schubert's *String Quartet in A minor* is more nearly pure spirit than any other music.'[3] (The exception here is Franz Michael Maier, whose analyses are more detailed but take a different tack to my own.[4])

---

[1] For a full discussion of the role of music in Beckett's work, see Catherine Laws, *'Headaches Among the Overtones': Music in Beckett/Beckett in Music* (Amsterdam and New York, 2013).

[2] Chris J. Ackerley and Stanley E. Gontarski, *The Grove Companion to Samuel Beckett* (New York, 2004), p. 515.

[3] Mary Bryden, 'Beckett and the Sound of Silence', in (ed.), *Samuel Beckett and Music* (Oxford, 1998), pp. 21–46 (p. 42).

[4] In particular, see Franz Michael Maier, 'Two Versions of *Nacht und Träume*: What Franz Schubert Tells Us about a Favourite Song of Beckett', in Dirk van Hulle and Mark Nixon (eds), 'All Sturm and no Drang', *Samuel Beckett Today/Aujourd'hui* 18 (Amsterdam

Paul Lawley comments on the recurrence in both Beckett and Schubert of the idea that 'the comfort of company is itself the occasion for suffering'.[5] Both repeatedly evoke situations in which the companionship provided by another is complicated by ambiguity with regard to his or her status or intentions. As Lawley says, Beckett clearly took comfort in Schubert's music, but he still referred to his repeated listenings to *Winterreise* as 'shivering through the grim journey again'.[6] There is certainly no simple solace to be found for Beckett in Schubert, just as, following Mary Bryden, music in general in Beckett is 'never a rapturous or transformatory force'.[7] I argue that this is certainly the case in *Nacht und Träume*.

More broadly, as has recently been much discussed, Beckett's relationship to Romanticism is complex and contradictory. He is distrustful of heroic transcendence and, as Mark Nixon has noted, dismissive of the sentimentalism of much Romantic writing, taking delight in mockery and misquotation.[8] However, Beckett's reading of Romantic literature was wide. As Nixon and Dirk van Hulle point out, 'no matter how tongue-in-cheek Beckett's references to Romanticism are, they keep recurring with a remarkable persistence throughout his work'.[9] In particular, as Nixon and Matthew Feldman have shown, in the 1930s his focus on German literature and philosophy was extensive and his note-taking substantial.[10] Nixon identifies Beckett's particular association of German literature, music and philosophy with qualities of seriousness, tragedy and a specific relationship to ideas of love and sex. The use of Beethoven in his first novel, *Dream of Fair to Middling Women* (and then again, much later, in *Ghost Trio*) is part of this, and the influence of German Romantic music, most especially that of Beethoven and Schubert, emerges in a number of works but is itself complex and differentiated: the music of these composers is employed for very different purposes.

Of course, despite both being generally subsumed under the category of early musical Romanticism, Beethoven and Schubert hold very different positions in

---

and New York, 2007), pp. 91–100; Franz Michael Maier, 'The Idea of Melodic Connection in Samuel Beckett', *Journal of the American Musicological Society* 61/2 (2008): 373–410.

5 Paul Lawley, '"The Grim Journey": Beckett Listens to Schubert', in Angela Moorjani and Carola Veit (eds), *Samuel Beckett: Endlessness in the Year 2000, Samuel Beckett Today/Aujourd'hui* 11 (Amsterdam and New York, 2001), pp. 255–67 (p. 258).

6 James Knowlson, *Damned to Fame: The Life of Samuel Beckett* (London, 1996), p. 682; see also p. 685.

7 Bryden, 'Beckett and the Sound of Silence', p. 42.

8 Mark Nixon, 'Beckett and Romanticism in the 1930s', in Van Hulle and Nixon (eds), *All Sturm and no Drang*, pp. 61–76 (p. 64).

9 Dirk van Hulle and Mark Nixon, 'Introduction', in (eds), *All Sturm and no Drang*, pp. 9–11 (p. 9).

10 Mark Nixon, '"Scraps of German": Samuel Beckett reading German Literature', in Matthijs Engelberts, Everett Frost and Jane Maxwell (eds), *'Notes diverse holo', Samuel Beckett Today/Aujourd'hui* 16 (Amsterdam and New York, 2006), pp. 259–82; Matthew Feldman, *Beckett's Books: A Cultural History of the Interwar Notes* (London, 2006).

the Western musical canon. In terms of historical musicology, Beethoven is the archetypal humanist pioneer, pushing classical ideas to their limits, if not beyond, and extending the scope of music's ambition to seriousness and grandness of scale. In contrast, and despite his own symphonic achievements, Schubert's music is characterized – sometimes overtly negatively, especially historically – as intimate in its concerns and detailed in its mapping of emotional territory. Concomitantly, and following the influence of an essay by Schumann, Schubert's music has often been characterized as feminine in quality, contrasted with the 'virile power' of Beethoven.[11]

Given his background and musical experience, Beckett is likely to have been at least vaguely aware of these general characterizations: his use of music supports this. With Schubert, as with the paintings of Caspar David Friedrich, Beckett finds a close affinity with the decidedly unheroic strain of German Romanticism, which focuses on the melancholic figure isolated in an indifferent world.[12] There is, then, a strong link between Beckett's sense of the gap between the self and the world and his attraction to particular strains of Romantic art, music and literature. If Beethoven's music seems to offer the young Beckett confirmation of the limits of rational thought and the irreconcilability of subject and object, Schubert's seems to reinforce the paradox that results: absolute isolation coupled with the impossibility of finally relinquishing traces of the idea that encounters with others, real or imagined, might produce temporary distraction and even comfort.

My own interest lies in what the music *does* in the works, exploring the relationship between Beckett's use of music and other characteristics of his work. In both *All That Fall* and *Nacht und Träume*, the writer's understanding – and use – of the specific qualities of Schubert's music is apparent. As with his use of Beethoven in *Ghost Trio*, Beckett here seems interested in what we *do* with music, how active listening involves an imaginative engagement with the expressive content of (especially Romantic) music. This engagement can be perceived as productive, constituting a working through or imaginative enactment of selfhood in the world.

In *All That Fall* the precise features of the soundscape were of great concern to Beckett.[13] However, it is the framing of Maddy's journey with extracts from Schubert's 'Death and the Maiden' – the lied or quartet movement[14] – emanating

---

11 Susan McClary, *Feminine Endings: Music, Gender, and Sexuality* (Minnesota and Oxford, 1991), p. 18.

12 For full discussions of Beckett's complicated relationship to Romanticism, see Van Hulle and Nixon (eds), *'All Sturm and no Drang'*.

13 Clas Zilliacus, *Beckett and Broadcasting* (Åbo, 1976), p. 69.

14 Beckett specifies Schubert's 'Death and the Maiden', but there is some uncertainty as to which work he was referring to: the lied to a text by Matthias Claudius, composed by Schubert in 1817 (D.531) or the *String Quartet in D Minor* (D.810) from 1824, which uses the theme from the lied as the basis for the second-movement variations. Critics do not agree on this. The original BBC production by Donald McWhinnie used extracts from

from the 'ruinous old house' of a 'very old woman' that supports the themes of the play: birth, youth and fertility versus barrenness, sterility, physical decline and death. As in *Ghost Trio*, the music operates not entirely realistically: it is apparently located in the house, yet continues to grow louder or softer even when Maddy stops moving. It is as if the degree of attention to the music brings it into focus, rather than the acoustical fact of its relative proximity. The music again projects absence – death during childhood and the 'poor woman' – but also invokes the productive powers of the imagination, in this case through Maddy's conjuring of her own ambiguous other(s): the suffering woman and the looming figure of Death. This creates a lyrical and affective counterpart to what cannot quite be said.

Music provides a similar counterpart in *Nacht und Träume*, but here there are no words; the music operates in relation to the visual composition and its specific televisual qualities. Examining this helps to elucidate what Schubert means in Beckett's work, in this instance what his music signifies in *Nacht und Träume*. This is a slightly different question to the one that is more often touched upon: what Schubert means to or for Beckett. While one might argue that Beckett's personal affinity with Schubert's music is responsible for the passing references in his work, it is hard to believe that this in itself would warrant inclusion of the music as part of the dramatic fabric, especially with a writer as fastidious as Beckett. This is not to deny that there are connections between Beckett's love of the music and the ways in which he uses it. But the more complex question is quite how the music contributes to the overall effect of the television play. There are two sides to this: the detail of Beckett's musical choices – exactly what he takes from Schubert and why – and the impact of his particular use of the voice.

'To close the eyes and see that hand': The Context of *Nacht und Träume*

Nacht und Träume was written in 1982 for Süddeutscher Rundfunk at the request of its then director, Reinhart Müller-Freienfels. Beckett directed the production, which was viewed in 1983 by an audience of two million.[15] At around 10 minutes it is one of Beckett's shortest plays, and one of very few with no spoken text (alongside *Quad* and *Breath*). The only sound is the humming and then singing of a few bars from the close of the Schubert lied from which the play takes its title.

The scene is almost static, formally composed and dimly lit by 'evening light'. In the foreground of a room, to the left, light fades up just sufficiently for us to see the upper body, right profile, of a man (A) seated with his head bowed and hands resting on a table in front of him. The last seven bars of the vocal part of Schubert's

the string quartet. In researching his American production for Voices International, Everett Frost found no comments on the choice of music in the BBC Written Archive. Frost used the lied (Everett Frost, e-mail, 7 Mar. 2007).

15 Knowlson, *Damned to Fame*, p. 683. A DVD of the production is now available from Suhrkamp Verlag (Frankfurt, 2008).

'Nacht und Träume' (D827) are heard, hummed quietly by a male voice. The light fades, leaving only a little light on A. The very last three bars of the Schubert are then heard again, this time sung with words, and after this the light fades on A as he bows his head to rest on his hands.

Just enough light remains to confirm the man's continued presence while his dream commences: light fades up on an identical figure, B, seated as A but suspended in the top right of the picture and seen in left profile. Aside from the profiling, at this point the only difference between the images is that B is lit by 'kinder light' than A. Out of the dark above and beyond B, a hand appears and rests gently on his head. It moves away, disappearing from view, and then its pair appears and holds a cup to B's lips. This hand withdraws, reappears with a cloth and gently wipes B's brow, then moves away and disappears. B raises his head and gazes upwards, as if at the face of the invisible figure with the hands. He then raises his right hand towards the figure, with the palm upwards, and one of the ministering hands reappears and rests on B's. B gazes at the joined hands, and then raises his left hand and rests it on the joined pair. The hands are lowered to the table, B lowers his head to rest on them, and the other hand of the ministering pair reappears and rests on B's head. The light then fades out on this image and the evening light and light on A fade up. From this point onwards, we are presented with a complete reprise of these events, including the humming and singing. The only difference is the focus and the speed: everything takes place in slightly slower motion, and this time the camera zooms in to observe the action around B in close-up. At the end of the action the camera pulls out again, slowly, to the original position, the dream fades out, and then the light on A fades, leaving a dark screen.

The origins of the play lie in Beckett's abandoned *Mime du rêveur* from 1954, a mime play which repeatedly stages a dream though with far more peripheral and semi-comic action than *Nacht und Träume*.[16] However, Ruby Cohn and Mark Nixon both point out the additional relationship to an unpublished poem in Beckett's 1977 'Sottisier Notebook': 'one dead of night/in the dead still/he looked up/from his book/from that dark/to pore on other dark'.[17] As he peers into the dark, the man seems to project himself, or another version of himself, into that space and sees by 'taper faint' that his book is 'faintly closed' by 'a hand not his/a hand on his'.[18] As Nixon says, in this poem, as in *A Piece of Monologue*

[16] Ruby Cohn, *A Beckett Canon* (Ann Arbor, MI, 2005), pp. 210–12.

[17] Mark Nixon comments on the prevalence of 'dead of night' situations in Beckett's late work, noting the recurrence of the phrase in *...but the clouds...* and *A Piece of Monologue*. However, in the context of plays that incorporate Schubert's music, this reference calls up Beckett's 1956 letter to Nancy Cunard in which he describes coming up with the idea of *All That Fall* 'in the dead of t'other night' (Mark Nixon, '"Unutterably Faint": Beckett's Late English Poetry', *Fulcrum* 6 (2007): 507–21 (p. 511); George Craig et al., *The Letters of Samuel Beckett*, vol. 2: *1941–1956* (Cambridge, 2011), p. 631.

[18] Quoted in Nixon, '"Unutterably Faint' ", p. 511; also noted in Cohn, *A Beckett Canon*, p. 374.

(begun around this time), *Stirrings Still* and some of the fragments of late poems in English, the phrases seem to suggest 'existence brought to a kind of threshold by projecting death into the darkness as well as releasing dream and alternate existential states':[19] this remains central to *Nacht und Träume*. James Knowlson points out the additional relationship to a line in *Company*, written just a couple of years earlier: 'What a help that would be in the dark! To close the eyes and see that hand!'[20]

For some, the scenes of comfort in this play are too maudlin.[21] However, most critics seem to agree with Knowlson that the abstract formal symmetry, the schematic working through of the actions, and the full-scale repetition all operate so as to undercut the sentimentality.[22] As Ulrika Maude points out, the self-consciously virtual quality of the scene, with its apparently free-floating images, softly lit and carefully framed and re-framed, has a similar effect.[23] David Pattie makes the same point, adding that, as the dream emerges, 'the image takes on a kind of precariousness, an increased fragility, because it seems to have no secure relation to the rest of the screen'.[24] Moreover, as Jonathan Kalb says, the specificity of the actions, simple but attended to with intense focus, renders the experience at once familiar and strange.[25]

There are similarities here with techniques used in Beckett's other television plays. The scrutinizing of a simply and formally constructed scene, viewed first from far off and then close up, is a feature of *Ghost Trio* in particular. Enoch Brater argues that the paring down of the elements in Beckett's television plays – the reduction of language, minimizing of spatial contextualization and use of geometric forms – produces pieces which are in part about the mediating power of the art form itself and its effect on perception.[26] Certainly, Beckett exploits the properties of filming to self-conscious effect, but as Jonathan Bignell points out, this kind of metacommentary has more in common with avant-garde film and video art than the broadcast drama of the time.[27] Moreover, some of the techniques

---

19 Nixon, '"Unutterably Faint"', p. 511.

20 Knowlson, *Damned to Fame*, p. 682.

21 Martin Esslin, for instance, finds the play 'too sentimental' ('Towards the Zero of Language', in James Acheson and Kateryna Arthur (eds), *Beckett's Later Fiction and Drama* (Basingstoke, 1987), pp. 35–49 (p. 46)).

22 Knowlson, *Damned to Fame*, p. 683; Jonathan Kalb, *Beckett in Performance* (Cambridge, 1989), p. 97.

23 Ulrika Maude, *Beckett, Technology and the Body* (Cambridge, 2009), pp. 128–9.

24 David Pattie, 'Coming out of the Dark: Beckett's TV Plays', *Journal of Beckett Studies* NS 18/1–2 (2009): 123–35 (p. 133).

25 Kalb, *Beckett in Performance*, p. 97.

26 Enoch Brater, 'Towards a Poetics of Television Technology: Beckett's *Nacht und Träume* and *Quad*', *Modern Drama* 28 (1985): 48–54 (p. 51).

27 Jonathan Bignell, 'Beckett in Television Studies', *Journal of Beckett Studies* NS 10/1–2 (2001): 105–18 (p. 106). Bignell explores Beckett's television work (primarily the

are already to be found in the stage plays, although the television context makes the effects a little simpler to achieve technically. The placing of images in separate pools of light was explored in earlier stage plays such as *Not I*, *Play* and *That Time* (as well as appearing again around the same time as *Nacht und Träume* in the initial, stage version of *What Where* (1983), and slightly later in the SDR television production, *Was Wo*, filmed in 1985.[28] Similarly, the complete repetition of events had been examined earlier in *Play* and in the SDR production that had preceded *Nacht und Träume*, *Quadrat I and II* (originally entitled *Quad*).

The formalized qualities of *Nacht und Träume* contrast with the lyricism of the Schubert melody. At the same time, the apparently stark and simple imagery produces an array of symbolic and cultural associations. The offering of the drink and wiping of the brow inevitably suggest the Eucharist, and this is emphasized by the chalice-like shape of the cup used in Beckett's production. James Knowlson notes that the chalice, cloth and comforting hand are images often found in religious painting and points out the relationship to the painterly tradition in which 'a vision often appears in the top corner of the canvas, normally the Virgin Mary, Christ ascended in his glory, or a ministering angel'.[29] Herren goes further, arguing that the play explicitly invokes Christ's prayer in the Garden of Gethsemane on the night before his crucifixion, as related in the Gospels of Mark, Matthew and Luke and subsequently depicted in a whole range of Italian and Dutch Old Masters. Herren cites the examples of Bellini, Mantegna, El Greco, Correggio and Gossaert, pointing out the frequent inclusion of the cup, cloth or ministering hands, the tradition of depicting Christ with hands and gaze raised upwards towards an angel and the spotlighting techniques (the latter used more broadly in these schools of painting so loved by Beckett and reproduced in much of his work for theatre and television).[30] Herren also traces the conceptual importance of Dante to the genesis of the play, drawing a specific link to Dante's depiction of worshippers gazing upwards to the Virgin Mary in *Paradiso*.[31] Additionally, Beckett apparently told the cameraman, Jim Lewis, that the cloth was an allusion to the veil that Veronica

---

pieces produced by the BBC) in the context of television drama of the 1960s and 1970s.

[28] Nevertheless, it is important to note the different impact of the televisual context for the viewer, compared to live performance in a theatre. David Pattie explores this in some depth ('Coming out of the Dark').

[29] Knowlson, *Damned to Fame*, p. 682.

[30] Graley Herren, '*Nacht und Träume* as Beckett's Agony in the Garden', *Journal of Beckett Studies* NS 11/1 (2002): 54–70. Chris Ackerley has also produced a set of annotations to Beckett's TV plays, tracing Beckett's numerous textual and visual references and highlighting relationships across the oeuvre. Chris Ackerley, '"Ever Know What Happened?": Shades and Echoes in Samuel Beckett's Television Plays', *Journal of Beckett Studies* NS 18/1–2 (2009): pp.136–164.

[31] Graley Herren, *Samuel Beckett's Plays on Film and Television* (New York, 2007), pp. 151–8.

used to wipe Jesus' brow on the way to Calvary which was then believed to retain the imprint of Christ's face.[32]

Beckett's works are infused with religious references, primarily Christian – this was his educational and cultural inheritance, after all – but the images of *Nacht und Träume* are the most explicit. However, as Herren acknowledges, the play is not 'about' these things in any simplistic way.[33] Beckett distils the essentials from these sources, distancing the symbols from their explicit Christian context. The concentration on the figure of the dreamer and the dreamt self and, I will argue, the use of the music are such that it is the act of longing, of imagining and re-imagining the comfort of the hands, that becomes the prime focus, rather than the substance or context of the act: the what, the who or the why. Moreover, as Herren says, the effect is to emphasize the confluence of the experiences of the artistic subject and the viewer: as Beckett noted in his German diary, 'the art (picture) that is a prayer, releases prayer in the onlooker'.[34] Just as the subject strains towards the heavens for comfort, solace, absolution, we gaze at the screen, hoping for – what? Illumination? Catharsis? Some form of transcendence? And, of course, Beckett re-enacts a game all too familiar from other works:

> *Nacht und Träume* replicates the conditions of its own creation. Just as A envisions a replica of himself (B) receiving the succor he longs for, so, too, does Beckett conjure up a character (A) capable of such a vision. In other words Beckett dreams up a dreamer dreaming his dream.[35]

We are reminded of lines from *Company* (written a couple of years earlier, in 1979), where Beckett invokes the 'Devised deviser devising it all for company'.[36] This mirroring, then, is another productive strategy that adds layers of complexity to the apparently simple and abstract play, complicating its sentimental surface.

The laying on of hands has a clear religious symbolism, especially in the traditions of religious art that Beckett draws upon (and Knowlson comments on Beckett's general fascination with images of hands in paintings, noting that a reproduction of Dürer's etching of praying hands hung on the wall of his room at Cooldrinagh[37]). However, aside from the religious connotations this signals a more general desire for the company of or union with another that is so prominent in Beckett's work, the late work especially. As Herren points out, actual touch is relatively unusual in Beckett's plays,[38] but even here, yet again,

---

32 Knowlson, *Damned to Fame*, p. 682.

33 Herren, '*Nacht und Träume* as Beckett's Agony in the Garden', p. 56.

34 Ibid., p. 55.

35 Graley Herren, 'Splitting Images: Samuel Beckett's *Nacht und Träume*', *Modern Drama* 43/2 (Summer 2000): 182–91 (p. 186).

36 Samuel Beckett, *Company* (New York, 1980), p. 46.

37 Knowlson, *Damned to Fame*, p. 682.

38 Herren, 'Splitting Images', p. 187.

the physicality of this moment is undercut by the disembodiment of the hands. We are denied the subjective context of fully drawn 'characters' – or even full bodies – touching one another. Instead, as Catherine Russell says, *Nacht und Träume* offers 'an enactment of a relationship *qua* relationship',[39] distilled to a phantasmal minimum, without individuation. The hands are possibly female, as would be expected from the implied association with the Virgin Mary or Veronica, though this is uncertain. The published script does not specify, and, in letters to Müller-Freienfels prior to the production, Beckett initially stated a preference for creating an androgynous impression, but then decided upon female though with the caveat that there should still be some ambiguity ('I think no choice but female for the helping hands. Large but female. As more conceivably male than male conceivably female'[40]). Surprisingly, then, it turns out that the cast list given at the end of his SDR production is all male. Yet the effect is pretty much as described by Beckett: to me, the hands and wrists appear more female in shape – relatively narrow – but in the close–up the fingers are surprisingly long. The dim lighting helps to preserve the uncertainty. So whereas in *Ghost Trio* the awaited other is definitely female, here it is only probably so. But even this is enough to evoke Beckett's many other depictions of figures anticipating or re-imaging the presence of a woman; these include *Krapp's Last Tape*, *Ghost Trio*, *Footfalls*, *...but the clouds...* and *Rockaby*. Moreover, in this respect the choice of Schubert's music with its gendered associations or, at the very least, its comparable interest in evoking the female presence, seems particularly appropriate.

Beckett's reference to the veil wiping the brow reminds us that true images of Christ's face subsequently become known as Veronicas – *vera icons* or true images. Here, though, there is no such thing as an unquestionably 'true', unambiguous image, either on the cloth or more generally. The formal structuring of space and time, along with the 'foregrounded virtuality' of the images discussed by Maude[41] ensure a sense of suspended reality. The release from suffering is projected as an imaginative possibility, but into a liminal space mediated and circumscribed by technology. Anna McMullan discusses the tension in Beckett's late work between the controlling force of technology, over both the body and the powers of perception, and its production of virtual bodies as a 'strategy of survival and creativity … as a kind of prosthetic imagination'.[42] This is apparent in *Ghost Trio* but is also certainly the case in *Nacht und Träume* where the locus of power and authority, in the form of the production of images – and, I will argue, the music – is equally complex and ambiguous, but the repeated conjuring of the dream of

---

39 Catherine Russell, 'The Figure in the Monitor: Beckett, Lacan, and Video', *Cinema Journal* 28/4 (Summer 1989): 20–37 (p. 32).

40 Knowlson, *Damned to Fame,* p. 683.

41 Maude, *Beckett, Technology and the Body*, p. 130.

42 Anna McMullan, 'Virtual Subjects: Performance, Technology and the Body in Beckett's Late Theatre', *Journal of Beckett Studies* NS 10/1–2 (2000– 2001): 165–72 (p. 168).

solace offers a trace of creative resistance to its own impossibility. Both plays use music to summon the virtual company of an absent other, though this is nothing so substantial as an assertion of transcendence, redemption or the suspension of suffering. Rather, it suggests the endlessly re-played echo of the refusal to abandon that possibility.

'Come again ...': Beckett and Schubert's Lied

Beckett's use of Schubert, then, has an important role to play in all this, perhaps in seeming to trigger the dream but more particularly in the state of suspension, or in-betweenness, that is produced through the tension between the self-conscious constructedness of the images, the complexities of their origin and the ambiguities of authority. The coupling or doubling of figures is a much remarked upon feature of Beckett's work, but the specific mirroring of visually identical figures is perhaps most reminiscent of *Ohio Impromptu*, written two years earlier. In *Nacht und Träume*, as with many of Beckett's other pairings, the status of the relationship seems clear at first, with the sequential precedence of A suggesting priority over the 'copy' B. However, as Graley Herren points out, this is undermined by the fact that our understanding of A, such as it is, becomes dependent upon B:[43] what we see happen to one figure informs what we know of the other, but all of this remains uncertain, unsettled, ill–defined. Many of Beckett's earlier plays cast couples in the form of a speaker–listener duo – obvious examples are Winnie and Willie in *Happy Days*, the present and past selves in *Krapp*, or the speaker and auditor in *Not I* – but here we experience a slightly different version: two identical, silent listeners. This produces a variation on what Pierre Chabert refers to as Beckett's representations of 'the tension present in the act of listening'.[44] In *Nacht und Träume* the music is hummed and sung softly, drawing us into the world of the play, but it is nevertheless quite clearly heard, and in general the idea of intense listening to small sounds is something that becomes more prevalent in Beckett's later work. Beckett commented more than once that, as he grew older, the sense of hearing was becoming more important.[45] In *Sounds* (1973), for example, a contrast is set up between straining to hear even the tiniest sounds of a still night ('never quite for nothing even stillest night') and the possibility that complete stillness might allow the listener to 'let himself be dreamt away to where none at any time ... where no such thing no more than ghosts make nothing to listen for no such

[43] Herren, 'Splitting Images'; id., '*Nacht und Träume* as Beckett's Agony in the Garden', pp. 54–70.

[44] Bernard Beckerman, 'Beckett and the Act of Listening', in Enoch Brater (ed.), *Beckett at 80/Beckett in Context* (New York, 1986), pp. 149–167 (p. 150).

[45] Charles Juliet, *Conversations with Samuel Beckett and Bram van Velde*, trans. Janey Tucker (Leiden, 1995), pp. 147, 152.

thing as a sound'.[46] The combination of dreaming and listening prefigures that in *Nacht und Träume.*

Critics comment on the affective power of the lied and its role in creating the 'strange, haunting beauty' of the work[47] (though those for whom the play is too sentimental often attribute this to the music, too[48]). James Knowlson suggests that the play 'evokes perhaps more clearly than any other of Beckett's plays that "purity of spirit" that had long been important in his life as well as his work'.[49] In echoing Beckett's own words about the 'pure spirit' quality of Schubert's music (quoted earlier), Knowlson seems to imply that the two bodies of work are united in intention and affective power. C.J. Ackerley is more explicit, attributing the characteristics of this work to Beckett's adoption of Schubert: *Nacht und Träume* has a 'strange romantic beauty – a quality to which B responded in Schubert's lyricism and made very much his own'.[50] Ackerley goes as far as to suggest that Beckett's late prose and drama are 'like' lieder in their 'intricate fusion of words and music'.[51] However, Beckett never really does 'fuse' words and music, and certainly not in *Nacht und Träume*: the two are rarely heard together. More often, music contributes to the discourse, sung or listened to in the gaps between the words (as in *Ghost Trio*, for example, or *Words and Music*, *Cascando* and most of the time in *All That Fall*), and if they do come together it is only when both are taken from another source, as is the case here: the fusion is Schubert's.

Instead, I would suggest that Beckett draws on the Romantic sensibility of the music, threading it into the fabric of the work, using its expressive power but also showing us how it is used. He reflects back the ways in which we use music for sentimental succour, to call up and recall the affective qualities of particular ideas or memories. In this respect the play is both sentimental and not: the sentiment is simultaneously directly invoked and offered up as an object for reflection.

The question, then, concerns the specifics of quite how the music is used to contribute to this. The song was composed probably in 1822 or 1823, but only published in 1825.[52] The text, slightly modified from that published by Heinrich

---

46 Samuel Beckett, *Sounds*, in *The Complete Short Prose 1929–1989* (New York, 1995), pp. 267–8.

47 Ackerley and Gontarski, *The Grove Companion to Samuel Beckett*, p. 398.

48 Daniel Albright, for example, gives *Nacht und Träume* as the prime example of what he sees as Beckett's occasional tendency to sentimentalize music (*Beckett and Aesthetics* (Cambridge, 2003), p. 148).

49 Knowlson, *Damned to Fame*, p. 683.

50 Chris Ackerley, 'Inorganic Form: Samuel Beckett's Nature', *Journal of the Australasian Universities Modern Language Association* 103–4 (2005): 79–102 (p. 101).

51 Ibid., p. 100.

52 Carl Schachter, 'Text and Motive in Four Schubert Songs', in David Beach (ed.), *Aspects of Schenkerian Theory* (New Haven and London, 1983): 61–76 (p. 71).

Josef von Collin,[53] appeals for suspension of being in the atemporality of sweet dreams: 'Kehre wieder, heil'ge Nacht/Holde Träume, kehret wieder' [Come again, hallowed night/Sweet dreams, come again]'.[54] The song evokes this moment of liminality in the refuge of dreams, between ordinary consciousness and its absence, between day and night (it is 'evening light' that comes and goes in the play) and perhaps between life and death. While Beckett's love of Schubert was ongoing throughout his life, it is perhaps worth noting that this play emerges after what Mark Nixon describes as the renewed importance of German poetry to Beckett in the late 1970s.[55]

It is Schubert's lied, each time, that precedes the fading of the light on A and the commencement of the dream. Moreover, the implication of the only words we hear, from the last three bars of the song ('Holde Träume, kehret wieder') is that the music prompts the dream, and that its first appearance to us is in fact a repetition of many prior conjurings. Thus the particular use of the music subtly underlines the residual creativity of the imagination. But whose imagination is this? Importantly, the source of the voice is somewhat uncertain, a point that seems to elude most commentators.[56] On the one hand, seeing a lone male figure and hearing a male voice implies the association of the two, and the fact that the music is hummed confirms that it is not background music played from a recording. Similarly, the sequencing, with the music appearing to prompt the dream, might suggest that the music is produced by the dreamer. On the other hand, Beckett specifies only that a male voice hums and sings but not whether this is the voice of the seated figure. As Erik Tonning says, the voice is 'unplaceable' in this sense.[57] Importantly, to my mind, in Beckett's production the visual image does not operate quite as a representation of the sound: the voice is relatively soft, but nevertheless quite clearly projected, with a good tone and a little vibrato – it sounds trained or at the very least considerably practised. It is hard to imagine this sound produced by

---

53 Carl Schachter suggests that Schubert perhaps held a manuscript copy of the text, and that changes were made to the published version (ibid.).

54 James Knowlson gives the translation as 'Return, sweet night!/Return, O you sweet dreams' (*Damned to Fame*, p. 682); Noel Witts offers 'Come back, hallowed night/ Gracious dreams, come back again' ('Beckett and Schubert', *Performance Research* 12/1 (Mar. 2007): 138–144 (p. 140); Ackerley and Gontarski have another variant: 'Sweet dreams, come back' (*The Grove Companion to Samuel Beckett*, p. 398).

55 Nixon, '"Unutterably Faint"' p. 509. James Knowlson notes that Beckett's working title for the play was originally 'Nachtstück', and Graley Herren speculates that Beckett may, therefore, have originally planned to use the Schubert lied of that name. As Herren says, there are similarities between the two lieder but the lyrics of 'Nachtstück' are explicitly concerned with death and finitude, compared to the more ambiguous dreamscape of Collin's 'Nacht und Träume' (Knowlson, *Damned to Fame*, p. 681; Herren, *Samuel Beckett's Plays on Film and Television*, p. 146).

56 Graley Herren acknowledges this point, as does Erik Tonning (Herren, 'Splitting Images', p. 183; Erik Tonning, *Samuel Beckett's Abstract Drama* (Oxford, 2007), p. 249).

57 Tonning, *Samuel Beckett's Abstract Drama*, p. 249.

an entirely still body, such as on the screen. In this sense the diegetic status of the voice is uncertain. It seems curiously disembodied, but nor is it fully disconnected from the viewed figure. It is not produced in such a way as to imply external objectivity: not a narrator, overseer of the action (such as the female voice in *Ghost Trio*) or another kind of authority figure. The association with the images is too weak to assume a simple equation of voice and image, but too strong for us to suppose a 'stand–in' for the author. The music does not seem to be produced by the dreamer or the dreamed self, but nor does it seem to be part of the dream: it hovers, with uncertain agency and origins.

Tonning makes a similar point, arguing that Beckett demonstrates a kind of 'double vision' through the enfolded layering of objective process and subjective engagement. The cycle of dreaming, light, images and music seems to offer a meditative, 'desire-driven' mode of participation in an impersonal, endless pattern, but the residues of subjectivity remain in the enactment from one representation to the next. As Tonning says, 'a need to engender consolation is poignantly evoked, but the need is simultaneously shown as the very means by which the serial pattern unfolds and reproduces itself'.[58] As with the complexities of the image production, then, the music creates an ambiguity with regard to subjective and authorial intentionality. This, to my mind, is what finally undercuts the possibility of unalloyed sentimentality: the expressive content of the music is present but free-floating, operating as if personalized and from within the fabric of the play but untethered to a specific body or consciousness.

Importantly, the extract from the song is heard without piano accompaniment. Unlike the use of the cassette in *Ghost Trio* or the record in *All That Fall*, this is not a recording of a professional performer imported into the play. The fact that the music is produced within the play has a rather different effect, as with Maddy's humming of the 'Death and the Maiden' theme. Heard through the voice of someone within the play, the music operates more intimately, as part of a personal expressive vocabulary. Instead of forming part of the scene or the environment of the play, hummed or sung music is adopted, becomes part of what that individual is or has to say within the play. This effect is one that Beckett uses elsewhere when characters hum or sing – Winnie, for example, or Krapp – but in *Nacht und Träume* the voice is decoupled from the figure. Similarly, the absence of the harmonic context usually provided by the piano uproots the melody. Noel Witts comments on the ways in which the piano accompaniment often acts a kind of landscape for the lone singer/traveller in Schubert's lieder.[59] But here the wanderer has no landscape to traverse. The vocal line, like the partial, floating images, lacks context: the figure lacks ground. Catherine Russell describes the play as producing a 'refuge of subjectivity … the subject here is suspended in time, in space and in discourse'.[60] The use of the music is central to this.

58 Ibid., p. 250.

59 Witts, 'Beckett and Schubert', p. 142.

60 Russell, 'The Figure in the Monitor', p. 31.

The impact of this absence of piano accompaniment needs further consideration. Graley Herren is the only commentator to pay real attention to this matter. He argues that while 'the piercing beauty of Schubert's score works in part to mitigate Collin's lyrical distress',[61] Beckett's splitting of vocal line from accompaniment and his use of only the last few bars pushes in the opposite direction, denying us what Herren perceives as the consolatory effect of the full musical context:[62] 'Beckett's adaptive strategies all work to exacerbate the very threat that Schubert had sought to ameliorate'.[63] I agree that Beckett's compositional choices serve to underscore the uncertainty and ambiguity but for rather different reasons.

However beautiful Schubert's song is, it is hard to agree that the divorcing of vocal line from harmony in itself concentrates the anguish. Heard alone, the vocal phrases incorporated by Beckett have a melancholic lyricism and simplicity. Melodically, the song is remarkably solid. From the opening phrase (sung to 'Heil'ge Nacht') onwards, the vocal line stays very much within the same, relatively narrow range, many of the phrases simply finding different ways to wander around the same territory of a fourth, between the D♯ of the first note and the A♯ that follows (see Music Example 14.1). The third and fourth lines of the first verse are sung to exactly the same melody as those of the second (the lines we hear in Beckett's play). And in both verses the final melodic line starts lower, initially rising through a B-major chord but then essentially restating the same melody as the third line, but in a steadier, more drawn out rhythm. The only real deviation from any of this material takes place at the opening of the second verse ('Die belauschen sie mit Lust'), where the music makes an unusual harmonic shift, apparent in both vocal line and accompaniment. However, we do not hear this passage in Beckett's play. As Charles Rosen notes, one of the ways in which Schubert's music differs from Beethoven's is the preference for melodic sequences that do not lend themselves easily to motivic development (and Rosen chooses 'Nacht und Träume' to exemplify his point[64]). Melodically, then, one might argue that Beckett actually chooses the most stable musical material for use within the play.

Moreover, heard out of the context of the Schubert song, the melody used by Beckett implies simpler harmonies than those provided by Schubert, if still somewhat ambiguous.[65] On hearing tonal melodies, listeners tend to 'fill in' implied harmonies, at the very least experiencing a sense of harmonic direction

---

[61] Herren, *Samuel Beckett's Plays on Film and Television*, p. 147.

[62] Ibid., p. 148.

[63] Ibid., p. 147.

[64] Charles Rosen, 'Schubert's Inflections of Classical Form', in Christopher H. Gibbs (ed.), *The Cambridge Companion to Schubert* (Cambridge and New York), pp. 72–98 (p. 95).

[65] Franz Michael Maier describes the content of the melody in similar terms, though with a somewhat different contextual emphasis ('The Idea of Melodic Connection in Samuel Beckett', pp. 399–400).

Example 14.1 Schubert, 'Nacht und Träume', melody

or 'pull' towards implied cadence points. This experience is not dependent upon a technical understanding of harmony or the ability to articulate it in musical terms, it derives from our ongoing, everyday experience of hearing music of the Western tonal tradition, in classical, jazz, folk and pop musics. In this instance, I argue, the ways in which a listener is likely to 'fill in' or imagine the harmonic context of the melody are somewhat different to what Schubert actually does, and the impact of Beckett's decision to omit the accompaniment is significant in this respect.

With melody only, the imagined harmony implied by the initial, hummed, phrases (from bar 21) is likely to be very simple: a straightforward perfect cadence in C♯-minor, stated twice. The rising and falling phrase of the last three bars (to 'holde Träume, kehret wieder') are clearly in B-major, and retrospectively (or on the repetition of events) this might then colour the way one hears the preceding phrases. It is possible, for example, to start to hear the preceding phrases in B, with C♯-minor harmonies under the descending phrase and F♯ under the final note of each of these initial phrases. But these minor variations on quite how one 'fills in' the implied harmonies are insignificant here, nor is it important whether or not the listener is aware of the musical detail: what matters is that one is unlikely to imagine the harmony that is, in fact, provided by Schubert, since his choices are not obvious or easily predictable. While the implied harmonies are reassuringly simple, the reality of Schubert's accompaniment is quite different. In the full context, with piano accompaniment, the harmonic effect of those first phrases is more unexpected and unsettled, due to Schubert's use of a chromatic rising passage in the tenor part of the piano left hand, F♯–F𝄪–G♯ (see Music Example 14.2). In particular, the chord under the first hummed notes incorporates the F×: we start on a chromatic passing chord, with bass notes that are the leading note and tonic of B-major but harmony that instead operates some distance from this main key, as a cadence from $D\sharp^{7}$ to G♯-minor: the submediant of B-major. This resolves in a relatively straightforward manner, through a circle of fifths (D♯–G♯-minor–C♯–F♯–B) to take us back into the solidly B-major rising and falling line with which the vocal melody ends. The musical analysis helps to explain the different impacts of the unaccompanied vocal line used by Beckett compared to the same section in the accompanied song. Put simply: while Beckett starts his melody from what is, in the full context, a moment of uncertain, transitory harmony, the decision to omit the piano accompaniment leave us blissfully unaware of this.

Example 14.2 Schubert, 'Nacht und Träume', bars 21–7 (excerpt used by Beckett without accompaniment)

Beyond this, considering Schubert's harmonic choices more carefully reveals the ways in which Beckett's ambiguous doubling of dreamer and dreamt self is reflected in his decision to use only the end of the lied and to omit the accompaniment. The particular harmonic inflection described above, involving the F× in Schubert's harmonization of the closing lines, is not new in the lied: it is hinted at in the piano prelude and used in the equivalent section of the first verse. Additionally, at this later stage in the song the F× is significant in its enharmonic echoing of the striking harmonic contrast employed by Schubert in bars 15–19, for the opening of the second verse (see Music Example 14.3). At this point, the harmony shifts unexpectedly to G-major, a surprising modulation in B-major (even if prefigured by the F♯–F×–G♯ progression in the piano bass line in the first verse, bars 7–8). This progression is disconcerting – again, any listener familiar with Western tonal harmony will recognize this on some level – and yet it takes us into the reassuring harmonic world of the major chord. The experience is ambiguous in quality for the listener. Carl Schachter argues that this harmonic change might be seen as a musical mapping of the dreamworld evoked by the words. As he says, the short section around G-major operates simultaneously on two levels: it 'crystallizes around a most transitory musical event',[66] creating an unsettling, floating harmonic moment, and yet 'while we are immersed in it, it assumes the guise of the most solid of harmonic entities': a major triad.[67] For Schachter, this dual use of the F𝄪/G, as the bass passing note (as F𝄪) and the root of a major triad (G), combines 'in a single sonority two different and contrasting orders of reality' and so 'gives this song a great central image; the song embodies a musical symbol of dreams'.[68]

Example 14.3 Schubert, 'Nacht und Träume', bars 15–19

Of course, Beckett omits this section. In this sense, in musical terms he decouples the dreamer and the dreamt, splitting one from the other. This mirrors the visual undermining of the priority of A over B, the 'between' state of the imagery and the resulting uncertainties over the status and origin of the play's material. Similarly, in the lieder, the F𝄪 heard under the 'kehre' in bar 21 – the point at which the humming in Beckett's play begins – is significant, subtly recalling the more substantial evocation of the dream state in bars 15–19. But again, in Beckett's version we do not even hear this echo: the melodic line carries no indication of the harmonic complexities underneath, but is left to float freely, without grounding. If the melody projects a solidity or serenity, Schubert uses the unsettling harmonic recontextualizations to undermine this, whereas Beckett provides a comparable effect through the specific use of the voice within the context of the film.

Overall, in terms of the melodic content, the decision to leave out the accompaniment, and the omission of the middle part of the song, Beckett's choices

66 Schachter, 'Text and Motive in Four Schubert Songs', p. 73.

67 Ibid., p. 74.

68 Ibid., p. 73.

simplify the musical impact, if anything minimizing the more disturbing elements. This contrasts with Herren's argument that the lied is incorporated precisely so as to undermine its redemptive spirit.[69] Nevertheless, I agree with Herren that Beckett's strategies undermine the possibility of simple solace from music and that the ultimate effect is one of instability and uncertainty. But the sentiment and the possibility of solace are real and present. It is not Beckett's musical selections from the Schubert that undermine these (unlike in the re-compositional strategies apparent in *Ghost Trio*[70]) but the particular deployment of that material. Perhaps this is what Deleuze means when he writes: 'The monodic, melodic voice leaps outside the harmonic support, here reduced to a minimum, in order to undertake an exploration of the pure intensities that are experienced in the ways the sound fades. A vector of abolition straddled by music.'[71] To my mind the simple beauty and repetitive quality of the lines Beckett chooses to include produce a meditative quality that matches that of the visual images and their pacing. Moreover, I would argue that this decision emphasizes the more sentimental and romantic side of the music, compared to the unsettling harmonic changes of the Schubert song, but that Beckett needs to invoke this effect and then undermines it in other ways. It is the free-floating decontextualization of the voice, the use of humming and the relationship between these aspects of the music and the approach to scene-making that are significant in this respect.

'A voice comes to one in the dark. Imagine'

Beyond the musical detail, Beckett's decision to use an untrained male voice of uncertain origin and to incorporate humming as well as singing, lends a particular quality to the music in *Nacht und Träume*. What takes place when I sing to myself or hum a tune composed or sung by another? On one level, the individual is always drawing up something that has soaked into his or her memory, often without conscious intent. Either the repeated hearing of a tune or something in the tune has resonated with me, embedding it in my head and making it part of me. It then sometimes emerges without conscious intent: I 'find myself' humming or singing the tune for no apparent reason. And in then singing it for myself, I embed it further, re-voicing it in my own vocal timbre, re-composing the melody into the fabric of my self. In this respect, Beckett's decision to use an unaccompanied voice of uncertain origin, rather than a recording of the song, is a manifestation of his production of memory and subjectivity as material for re-creation: the song

69 Herren, *Samuel Beckett's Plays on Film and Television*, p. 148.

70 I discuss this in Catherine Laws, 'Beethoven's Haunting of Beckett's *Ghost Trio*', in Linda Ben-Zvi (ed.), *Drawing on Beckett: Portraits, Performances, and Cultural Contexts* (Tel Aviv, 2003), pp. 197–214.

71 Gilles Deleuze, *Essays Critical and Clinical*, trans. Daniel W. Smith and Michael A. Greco (London and New York, 1998), p. 172.

emerges from someone's voice, someone's memory and is reproduced as undiluted presence, a pure manifestation of selfhood. As Steven Connor writes, 'giving voice is the process which simultaneously produces articulate sound, and produces myself, as a self-producing being'.[72] The embodied moment of recalling the song through vocal production itself brings memory into being, in that moment, without apparent cause and effect yet with some connection to the context or situation. This forms a musical counterpart to what David Pattie characterizes as broadly typical of Beckett's television plays from *Ghost Trio* onwards:

> The world presented in these plays has no depth; there is no strong sense of another space beyond the lit area, no clear idea of a world beyond the image, no sense of a past beyond the consciously willed creation of a past – in fact, no suggestion beyond simple assertion that past and future are anything other than empty.[73]

At the same time, this vocality is not, can never be, a manifestation of undivided selfhood. Firstly, it is provoked by another; the song comes from someone else (Schubert, in this instance, but also from the performers who manifest the song in sound – those who have been heard singing the song, primarily Dietrich Fischer-Dieskau for Beckett). In this sense, embedded in one's own vocalizing is that of at least one other. Secondly, in singing aloud to 'myself', the sound goes out into the world and I hear it as external to me. As Connor says, 'if I hear my thoughts as a voice, then I divide myself between the one who speaks, from the inside out, and the one who hears the one who speaks, from the outside in'.[74] This is as true of any vocalized sound, not only speech. Finally, from another's perspective, listening in to someone singing is, outside of the situation of performance, both peculiarly intimate and strangely distancing. That is, we seem to be granted temporary access to an unselfconscious manifestation of the individual, but the very act carries connotations of eavesdropping, a transgression of boundaries that makes us all too aware of our outsider status, our otherness.

In this way, 'singing to myself' produces a situation which doubles identification and estrangement. Individual subjectivity and memory are deeply entwined within the vocalizing, expressed by the action of humming or singing, but the provocation for the very action of self-expression comes from another, and that action effects an estrangement from the voice, its externalizing. When humming or singing a tune to myself, I produce a version of myself at the same time as listening in to myself as if from outside, and as soon as I listen as if from outside, it is no longer quite myself that I hear. In this sense, I am always a ventriloquist, my own voice carrying the traces of others, received back into myself as somewhat other. Yet that

[72] Steven Connor, *Dumbstruck: A Cultural History of Ventriloquism* (Oxford, 2000), p. 3.

[73] Pattie, 'Coming out of the Dark', p. 134.

[74] Connor, *Dumbstruck*, p. 6.

trace of selfhood and of individual memory is material: I still seem responsible for the vocal action. Beckett rehearses this familiar situation, which evokes selfhood and otherness, but at the same time he retains the ambiguity as to quite who sings. He invokes the patterns by means of which vocal subjectivity and the solace of company are produced, but the uncertain presence leaves the experience without depth or origin. In this he exploits to great effect music's ability to carry subjectivity without specificity of character.

Hearing the melody first without words has a particular impact. Lawrence Kramer asks: 'Isn't it true that most of us can recall … occasions on which song became deeply moving, not as an expressive fusion of text and music, but as a manifestation of the singing voice, just the voice, regardless of what it sang?'[75] On such occasions, he suggests, the text does not matter, but a particular understanding, empathy or affinity is produced, a quality Kramer characterizes as 'songfulness'. By including the humming, Beckett momentarily produces this quality. Briefly, we experience that free-floating sense of expression without semantics, and hearing someone singing to himself resonates with one's own sense of voice, producing a connection beyond the individual. But again, the repetition of the vocalizing within an ongoing cycle and with ambiguous origin undercuts the immersion in this moment of identity.

The particular use of music in the play, then, mirrors the doubling of images and the ambiguities of agency, action and identity. This uncertainty of status is emphasized by the repetitive cycle in which the images and the vocalizing are caught up: the creative agency of the imagination persists in the determination to carry on (re-)producing the dream and the song, but this content can never be clearly tethered to an individual consciousness or body. The cycle seems to take on its own mechanistic objectivity, yet cannot exist without the trace of the subject.

Overall, then, it is hard to agree with Jonathan Kalb that the Schubert in 'Nacht und Träume' lulls the dreamer to sleep,[76] or that, as Sidney Homan suggests, the music offers pure comfort ('If A lacks B's woman, he has the lovely Schubert lied'[77]). As with the use of 'Death and the Maiden' in *All That Fall*, the comfort and identification – company of a kind – is part of what is offered by the use of Schubert's music, but the details of Beckett's choices complicate our reception of the expressive aural surface.

As Mark Nixon says, 'if Beckett's late work tends to move towards an inevitable end, it also frequently projects that point in imagination or dream'.[78] Here, as in *All*

---

75 Lawrence Kramer, 'Beyond Words and Music: An Essay on Songfulness', in Walter Bernhart, Steven Paul Scher and Werner Wolf (eds), *Word and Music Studies: Defining the Field* (Amsterdam and Atlanta, GA, 1999), pp. 303–19 (p. 304).

76 Jonathan Kalb, 'The Mediated Quixote: The Radio and Television Plays, and *Film*', in John Pilling (ed.), *The Cambridge Companion to Beckett* (Cambridge, 1994), pp. 124–44 (p. 141).

77 Sidney Homan, *Filming Beckett's TV Plays* (Lewisburg, PA, 1992), p. 114.

78 Nixon, '"Unutterably Faint"', p. 516.

That Fall, music is used as a means of trying to imagine the unimaginable – the inexpressible is conjured partly by the excision of words. In *All That Fall*, though, the music frames numerous attempts to negotiate and even defuse the coming of death by talking about or otherwise evoking it, both directly and indirectly. In *Nacht und Träume* the emphasis is on the productive imagining and re-imagining of release, transcendence and absolution. This contrast is exemplified by the qualitative difference between Maddy humming the 'Death and the Maiden' theme, with its direct thematic associations and identificatory powers, and the sustained ambiguities of voice and image in *Nacht und Träume*. In both plays, the significance and expressive impact of Beckett's use of music reveals his subtle understanding of the qualities and associations of Schubert's songs.

Select Bibliography

Acheson, James, 'Beckett, Proust, and Schopenhauer', *Contemporary Literature* 19/2 (1978): 165–79.

Ackerley, Chris, 'Inorganic Form: Samuel Beckett's Nature', *Journal of the Australasian Universities Modern Language Association* 103–4 (2005): 79–102.

—— '"Ever Know What Happened?" Shades and Echoes in Samuel Beckett's Television Plays', *Journal of Beckett Studies* NS 18/1–2 (2009): 136–64.

—— and Stanley E. Gontarski (eds), *The Grove Companion to Samuel Beckett: A Reader's Guide to His Works, Life, and Thought* (New York: Grove Press, 2004).

Adorno, Theodor W., *Philosophy of Modern Music*, trans. Anne Mitchell and Wesley Blomster (London: Continuum, 2003).

—— *Aesthetic Theory*, trans. Robert Hullot-Kentor, ed. Gretel Adorno, Rolf Tiedemann and Robert Hullot-Kentor (London: Continuum, 2004).

Albèra, Philippe, 'Beckett and Holliger', in Mary Bryden (ed.), *Samuel Beckett and Music* (Oxford: Oxford University Press, 1998), pp. 87–97.

Albright, Daniel, *Beckett and Aesthetics* (Cambridge: Cambridge University Press, 2003).

Ammer, Christine (ed.), *The HarperCollins Dictionary of Music* (New York: HarperCollins, 1995).

Antoine-Dunne, Jean, 'Beckett and Eisenstein on Light and Contrapuntal Montage', in Angela Moorjani and Carola Veit (eds), *Samuel Beckett: Endlessness in the Year 2000, Samuel Beckett Today/Aujourd'hui* 11 (Amsterdam and New York: Rodopi, 2001), pp. 315–23.

Armstrong, Gordon S., *Samuel Beckett, W.B. Yeats, and Jack Yeats: Images and Words* (Lewisburg, PA: Bucknell University Press, 1990).

Asmus, Walter D., 'Beckett Directs "Godot"', trans. Ria Julian, in Harold Bloom (ed.), *Samuel Beckett's 'Waiting for Godot'* (Broomall, PA: Blooms Literary Criticism, 2008), pp. 15–24; originally in *Theatre Quarterly* 5/19 (1975): 19–26; repr. in Stanley E. Gontarski (ed.), *On Beckett: Essays and Criticism* (New York: Grove Press, 1986): 280–90; and as 'Walter Asmus' Rehearsal Diary', in Dougald McMillan and Martha Fehsenfeld (eds), *Beckett in the Theatre: The Author as Practical Playwright and Director*, vol. 1: *From Waiting for Godot to Krapp's Last Tape* (London: John Calder, 1988), pp. 136–48.

Astier, Pierre, 'Beckett's "Ohio Impromptu": A View from the Isle of Swans', in Stanley E. Gontarski (ed.), *On Beckett: Essays and Criticism* (New York: Grove Press, 1986), pp. 395–6.

Aviram, Amittai F., 'The Meaning of Rhythm', in Massimo Verdicchio and Robert Burch (eds), *Between Philosophy and Poetry: Writing, Rhythm, and History* (New York: Continuum, 2002), pp. 161–70.

Bair, Deirdre, *Samuel Beckett: A Biography* [1978] (London: Vintage Books, 1990).

Barenboim, Daniel, *Everything is Connected: The Power of Music*, ed. Elena Cheah (London: Weidenfeld and Nicolson, 2008).

Barenboim, Daniel, and Edward W. Said, *Parallels and Paradoxes: Explorations in Music and Society* (London: Bloomsbury, 2004).

Baronova, Irina, '*Choreartium*: An Insight', *Brolga: An Australian Journal about Dance* 26 (June 2007): 27.

Barrett, Richard, *Ne songe plus à fuir* (London: United Music Publishers, 1986).

—— *I Open and Close* (London: United Music Publishers, 1988).

Barthes, Roland, *Image Music Text*, trans. Stephen Heath (London: Fontana Press, 1977).

—— *The Neutral*, trans. Rosalind E. Krauss and Denis Hollier (New York: Columbia University Press, 2005).

Basu, Dipak (ed.), *Dictionary of Pure and Applied Physics* (London: CRC Press, 2001).

Beckerman, Bernard, 'Beckett and the Act of Listening', in Enoch Brater (ed.), *Beckett at 80/Beckett in Context* (New York: Oxford University Press, 1986), pp. 149–67.

Beckett, Samuel, *'All That Fall' and Other Plays for Radio and Screen* (London: Faber & Faber, 2009).

—— *'Alles kommt auf so viel an': Das Hamburg Kapitel aus den 'German Diaries'. 2. Oktober–4. Dezember 1936*, ed. Roswitha Quadflieg (Hamburg: Raamin-Presse, 2003).

—— *Collected Poems: 1930–1978* (London: John Calder, 1984).

—— *Collected Shorter Plays of Samuel Beckett* (London: Faber, 1984).

—— *Company* (New York: Grove, 1980).

—— *Company* [1980], in *Nohow On: Company, Ill Seen Ill Said, Worstward Ho* (London: John Calder, 1989), pp. 5–52.

—— *The Complete Dramatic Works* (London: Faber & Faber, 1986).

——*The Complete Short Prose 1929–1989*, ed. Stanley E. Gontarski (New York: Grove, 1995).

—— 'Dante...Bruno.Vico..Joyce', in Samuel Beckett et al., *Our Exagmination round his Factification for Incamination of Work in Progress, with Letters of Protest*, 2nd edn (London: Faber & Faber, 1961), pp. 1–22; repr. in Samuel Beckett, *Disjecta: Miscellaneous Writings and a Dramatic Fragment*, ed. Ruby Cohn (London: Calder, 1983), pp. 19–33.

—— *Dream of Fair to Middling Women* [1932], ed. Eoin O'Brien and Edith Fournier (London: Calder, 1996).

—— *Dream Notebook*, ed. John Pilling (Reading: Beckett International Foundation, 1999).

—— *En attendant Godot* [1949] (Paris: Éditions de Minuit, 1952).
—— lectures on Gide and Racine, Trinity College Dublin, Michaelmas 1931 (notes taken by Rachel Burrows, née Dobbin, TCD Mic 60).
—— *The Letters of Samuel Beckett*, vol. 1: *1929–1940*, ed. Martha Dow Fehsenfeld and Lois More Overbeck (Cambridge: Cambridge University Press, 2009); vol. 2: *1941–1956*, ed. George Craig et al. (Cambridge: Cambridge University Press, 2011).
—— *Molloy* [1947, pub. 1951] (Paris: Éditions de Minuit, 2002); Eng. trans. [1955] in *Trilogy: Molloy, Malone Dies, The Unnamable*, trans. Samuel Beckett and Patrick Bowles (London: John Calder, 1994), pp. 5–176.
—— *Le Monde et le pantalon* (Paris: Éditions de Minuit, 2010).
—— *More Pricks Than Kicks* [1934] (London: John Calder, 1993).
—— *Murphy* [1936, pub. 1938] (London: John Calder, 1993).
—— *Nohow On: Company, Ill Seen Ill Said, Worstward Ho* (London: John Calder, 1989).
—— *Proust* (New York: Grove Press, 1957); repr. in *Proust, Three Dialogues* (London: John Calder, 1965); French trans. Édith Fournier (Paris: Éditions de Minuit, 1990).
—— 'Proust in Pieces', in *Disjecta: Miscellaneous Writings and a Dramatic Fragment*, ed. Ruby Cohn (London: John Calder, 1983), pp. 63–5.
—— *Selected Poems* (London: John Calder, 1999).
—— *The Theatrical Notebooks of Samuel Beckett*, vol. 4: *The Shorter Plays*, ed. Stanley E. Gontarski (New York: Grove Press, 1999).
—— *Three Novels: Molloy, Malone Dies, The Unnamable* (New York: Grove, 1991).
—— *Three Plays: Ohio Impromptu, Catastrophe, What Where* (New York: Grove Press, 1984).
—— *Trilogy: Molloy, Malone Dies, The Unnamable* (London: John Calder, 1994).
—— *Worstward Ho* (London: John Calder, 1983).
—— Letters to Thomas McGreevy, TCD MS 10402.
Benoist-Méchin, *La Musique et l'immortalité dans l'œuvre de Marcel Proust* (Paris: Simon Kra, 1926).
Benson, Stephen, 'Beckett, Feldman, Joe and Bob: Speaking of Music in Words and Music', in Suzanne M. Lodato and David Francis Urrows (eds), *Essays on Music and the Spoken Word and on Surveying the Field* (Amsterdam: Rodopi, 2005), pp. 165–80.
Benveniste, Emile, *Problems in General Linguistics*, trans. Mary Elizabeth Meek (Coral Gables, FL: University of Miami Press, 1971).
Bergson, Henri, *Essai sur les données immédiates de la conscience*, in *Œuvres*, ed. André Robinet (Paris: Presses Universitaires de France, 1959).
—— *La Perception du changement*, in *Œuvres*, ed. André Robinet (Paris: Presses Universitaires de France, 1959).
—— *Le rire: Essai sur la signification du comique*, in *Œuvres*, ed. André Robinet (Paris: Presses Universitaires de France, 1959).

Bignell, Jonathan, 'Beckett in Television Studies', *Journal of Beckett Studies* NS 10/1–2 (2001): 105–18.

Blackman, Maurice, 'The Shaping of a Beckett Text: *Play*', *Journal of Beckett Studies* OS 10 (1985): 87–107.

Blanchot, Maurice, *The Space of Literature*, trans. Ann Smock (Lincoln: University of Nebraska Press, 1982).

—— 'Where Now? Who Now?', in Stanley E. Gontarski (ed.), *On Beckett: Essays and Criticism* (New York: Grove Press, 1986), pp. 141–9.

—— *The Infinite Conversation*, trans. Susan Hanson, Theory and History of Literature 82 (Minneapolis: University of Minnesota Press, 1993).

—— *The Writing of the Disaster*, trans. Ann Smock (Lincoln: University of Nebraska Press, 1995).

Bloch, Ernst, *Essays on the Philosophy of Music*, trans. Peter Palmer (Cambridge: Cambridge University Press, 1985).

Bowie, Andrew, *Music, Philosophy and Modernity* (Cambridge: Cambridge University Press, 2007).

Bradby, David, *Beckett: Waiting for Godot* (Cambridge: Cambridge University Press, 2001).

Branigan, Kevin, *Radio Beckett: Musicality in the Radio Plays of Samuel Beckett* (Bern: Peter Lang, 2008).

Brater, Enoch, 'The *I* in Beckett's *Not I*', *Twentieth Century Literature* 20/3 (1974): 189–200.

—— 'Towards a Poetics of Television Technology: Beckett's *Nacht und Träume* and *Quad*', *Modern Drama* 28 (1985): 48–54.

—— *The Drama in the Text: Beckett's Late Fiction* (New York: Oxford University Press, 1994).

Brentano, Franz, *Untersuchungen zur Sinnespsychologie* (Hamburg: Meiner, 1979).

Brindle, Reginald Smith, *Serial Composition* (Oxford: Oxford University Press, 1966).

Brienza, Susan D., 'Perilous Journeys on Beckett's Stages: Travelling Through Words', in Katherine H. Burkman (ed.), *Myth and Ritual in the Plays of Samuel Beckett* (London: Associated University Presses, 1987), pp. 28–49.

Brun, Bernard, 'Sur le *Proust* de Beckett', in Jean-Michel Rabaté (ed.), *Beckett avant Beckett: Essais sur le jeune Beckett: 1930–1945* (Paris: PENS, 1984).

Bryant-Bertail, Sarah, 'The True-Real Woman: Maddy Rooney as *Picara* in *All That Fall*', available at <http://archive.today/Gnjvi>.

Bryden, Mary, 'Beckett and the Sound of Silence', in (ed.), *Samuel Beckett and Music* (Oxford: Oxford University Press, 1998), pp. 21–46.

—— 'Reflections on Beckett and Music, with a Case Study', in Lois Oppenheim (ed.), *Samuel Beckett and the Arts: Music, Visual Arts, and Non-Print Media* (New York: Garland, 1999).

—— (ed.), *Samuel Beckett and Music* (Oxford: Oxford University Press, 1998).

—— Julian Garforth and Peter Mills (eds), *Beckett at Reading: Catalogue of the Beckett Manuscript Collection at the University of Reading* (Reading: Whiteknights Press and Beckett International Foundation, 1998).

Budgen, Frank, *James Joyce and the Making of 'Ulysses'* (London: Grayson and Grayson, 1934).

Burton, Robert, *The Anatomy of Melancholy*, ed. Holbrook Jackson (New York: New York Review of Books, 2001).

Calder, John, 'Publisher's Note', in Samuel Beckett, *Dream of Fair to Middling Women* (New York: Arcade Publishing/Riverrun Press, 1992), pp. v–x; ed. Eoin O'Brien and Edith Fournier (London: John Calder, 1996), pp. v–ix.

Cavell, Stanley, *The Claim of Reason* (New York: Oxford University Press, 1979).

Cixous, Hélène, *Zero's Neighbor Sam Beckett*, trans. Laurent Milesi (Cambridge and Malden, MA: Polity Press, 2010).

Cohn, Ruby, *A Beckett Canon* (Ann Arbor: University of Michigan Press, 2001).

Connor, Steven, *Dumbstruck: A Cultural History of Ventriloquism* (Oxford: Oxford University Press, 2000).

—— 'I Switch Off: Beckett and the Ordeals of Radio', in Debra Rae Cohen, Michael Coyle and Jane Lewty (eds), *Broadcasting Modernism* (Gainesville: University Press of Florida, 2009), pp. 274–93.

—— 'Slow Going', paper presented at 'Critical Beckett' conference, School of French Studies, University of Birmingham, 26 Sept. 1998, available at <http://www.stevenconnor.com/slow.htm>.

Compagnon, Antoine, *La Troisième République des Lettres* (Paris: Éditions du Seuil, 1989).

Cooke, Deryck, *The Language of Music* (Oxford: Oxford University Press, 1959).

Copeland, Roger, and Marshall Cohen, 'What Is Dance?', in (eds), *What Is Dance? Readings in Theory and Criticism* (Oxford: Oxford University Press, 1983), pp. 1–9.

Critchley, Simon, 'Who Speaks in the Work of Samuel Beckett?', in Thomas Pepper (ed.), *The Place of Maurice Blanchot*, Yale French Studies 93 (New Haven, CT: Yale University Press, 1998), pp. 114–30.

Daiken, Melanie, 'Working with Beckett Texts', in Mary Bryden (ed.), *Samuel Beckett and Music* (Oxford: Oxford University Press, 1998), pp. 249–56.

Dandieu, Arnauld, *Marcel Proust, Sa révélation psychologique* (Paris: Firmint-Didot, 1930).

Davidson, Donald, *Inquiries into Truth and Interpretation* (Oxford: Oxford University Press, 1984).

—— *Subjective, Intersubjective, Objective* (Oxford: Oxford University Press, 2001).

—— *Truth, Language and History* (Oxford: Oxford University Press, 2005).

Debrock, Guy, 'The Word Man and the Note Man: Morton Feldman and Beckett's Virtual Music', in Lois Oppenheim (ed.), *Samuel Beckett and the Arts: Music, Visual Arts and Non-Print Media* (New York: Garland Publishing, 1999), pp. 67–82.

Deleuze, Gilles, *Essays Critical and Clinical*, trans. Daniel W. Smith and Michael A. Greco (Minneapolis: University of Minnesota Press, 1997).

—— *Francis Bacon: The Logic of Sensation*, trans. Daniel W. Smith (Minneapolis: University of Minnesota Press, 2004).

—— and Félix Guattari, *A Thousand Plateaus: Capitalism and Schizophrenia* (London: Continuum, 2004).

De Man, Paul, *Blindness and Insight: Essays in the Rhetoric of Contemporary Criticism*, 2nd rev. edn, Theory and History of Literature 7 (Minneapolis: University of Minnesota Press, 1982).

Döblin, Alfred, *Sur la musique*, trans. Sabine Cornille (Paris: Éditions Payot & Rivages, 2002).

Dolan, T.P., *A Dictionary of Hiberno-English: The Irish Use of English* (Dublin: Gill & Macmillan, 1998; rev. edn 2004).

Dragomoshchenko Arkadii, *Description*, trans. Elena Balashova and Lyn Hejinian (Los Angeles: Sun & Moon Press, 1990).

Ellis, Havelock, *The Dance of Life* (London: Constable & Company, 1923).

Esslin, Martin, *Mediations: Essays on Brecht, Beckett, and the Media* (London: Eyre Methuen, 1980).

—— 'Towards the Zero of Language', in James Acheson and Kateryna Arthur (eds.), *Beckett's Later Fiction and Drama* (Basingstoke: Macmillan, 1987), pp. 35–49.

Fauconnet, André, *L'Esthétique de Schopenhauer* (Paris: Félix Alcan, 1913).

Farber, Stephen, 'A Half-Dozen Ways to Watch the Same Movie', *New York Times: Movies* (13 Nov. 2005), <http://www.nytimes.com/2005/11/13/movies/13farb.html?pagewanted=1>.

Feldman, Matthew. *Beckett's Books: A Cultural History of the Interwar Notes* (London: Continuum, 2006).

Feldman, Morton, *Toronto Lecture: April 17th 1982, Mercer Union Gallery, Toronto, Canada*, transcribed by Linda Catlin Smith, available at <http://www.cnvill.net/mfmercer.htm>.

—— *Give My Regards to Eighth Street: Collected Writings of Morton Feldman*, ed. B.H. Friedman (Cambridge: Exact Change, 2000).

—— *Morton Feldman in Conversation with John Mackenzie, November 1984*, available at <http://www.cnvill.net/mfmackenzie.pdf>.

—— *Morton Feldman Says: Selected Interviews and Lectures 1964–1987*, ed. Chris Villars (London: Hyphen Press, 2006).

Fletcher, John, *About Beckett: The Playwright and the Work* (London: Faber & Faber, 2003).

Foster, David, 'Spatial Aesthetics in the Film Adaptation of Samuel Beckett's *Comédie*', *Screen* 53/2 (2012): 105–17.

—— 'Becoming Present, Becoming Absent: Movement and Visual Form in the Film Adaptation of *Comédie*', *Journal of Beckett Studies* NS 21/1–2 (2012): 157–80.

Fraisse, Luc, 'Le "Proust" de Beckett: Fidélité médiatrice et infidélité créatrice', in Marius Buning, Matthijs Engelberts and Sjef Houppermans (eds), *Samuel Beckett: Crossroads and Borderlines, Samuel Beckett Today/Aujourd'hui* 6 (Amsterdam and Atlanta, GA: Rodopi, 1997), pp. 365–86.

—— *L'Éclectisme philosophique de Marcel Proust* (Paris: Presses Universitaires Paris Sorbonne, 2013).

Freud, Sigmund, *Beyond the Pleasure Principle*, trans. Gregory C. Richter (Peterborough, ON: Broadview Editions, 2011).

Frisch, Karl von, *The Dancing Bees: An Account of the Life and Senses of the Honey Bee*, trans. Dora Ilse (London: Methuen, 1954).

Frisch, Karl von, *Erinnerungen eines Biologen* (Berlin: Springer-Verlag, 1957).

Frost, Everett C., 'Fundamental Sounds: Recording Samuel Beckett's Radio Plays', *Theatre Journal* 43/3 (1991): 361–76.

—— 'A "Fresh Go" for the Skull', in Lois Oppenheim (ed.), *Directing Beckett* (Ann Arbor: University of Michigan Press, 1997), pp. 186–219.

—— 'The Note Man on the Word Man: Morton Feldman on Composing the Music for Samuel Beckett's *Words and Music* in *The Beckett Festival of Radio Plays*', in Mary Bryden (ed.), *Samuel Beckett and Music* (Oxford: Oxford University Press, 1998), pp. 47–55.

—— Preface to Samuel Beckett, *'All That Fall' and Other Plays for Radio and Screen* (London: Faber & Faber, 2009), pp. vii–xxiii.

Garforth, Julian, '"Beckett, unser Hausheiliger?" Changing Critical Reactions to Beckett's Directorial Work in Berlin', in Marius Buning, Matthijs Engelberts and Onno Kosters (eds), *Beckett and Religion: Beckett/Aesthetics/Politics, Samuel Beckett Today/Aujourd'hui* 9 (Amsterdam and Atlanta, GA: Rodopi, 2000), pp. 309–29.

Georgiades, Thrasybulos, *Musik und Rhythmus bei den Griechen: zum Ursprung der abendländischen Musik* (Hamburg: Rowohlt, 1958).

Gibbs, Anna, 'After Affect: Sympathy, Synchrony, and Mimetic Communication', in Melissa Gregg and Gregory J. Seigworth (eds), *The Affect Theory Reader* (Durham, NC: Duke University Press, 2010), pp. 186–205.

Gide, André, *Morceaux choisis*, 20th edn (Paris: Gallimard, 1928).

—— *Paludes, Romans et récits: Œuvres lyriques et dramatiques 1*, ed. Pierre Masson (Paris: Gallimard, 2009).

—— *Les Faux-monnayeurs*, Romans et récits: *Œuvres lyriques et dramatiques* 2, ed. Pierre Masson (Paris: Gallimard, 2009).

—— *Journal des Faux-monnayeurs, Romans et récits: Œuvres lyriques et dramatiques* 2, ed. Pierre Masson (Paris: Gallimard, 2009).

—— *The Counterfeiters*, trans. Dorothy Bussy, Kindle edn (New York: Vintage, 1973).

—— *The Journal of the Counterfeiters*, trans. Justin O'Brien, Kindle edn (New York: Vintage, 1973).

Glasmeier, Michael, and Gaby Hartel, '"Three Grey Disks": Samuel Beckett's Forgotten Film, *Comédie*', in Caroline Bourgeois (ed.), *Comédie* (Paris: Éditions du regard, 2001), pp. 77–85.

Glass, Philip, *Opera on the Beach* (London: Faber & Faber, 1988).

Goldstein, E. Bruce, *Encyclopedia of Perception* (London: Sage, 2010).

Gontarski, Stanley E., *The Intent of Undoing in Samuel Beckett's Dramatic Texts* (Bloomington: Indiana University Press, 1985).

—— 'Staging Himself, or Beckett's Late Style in the Theatre', in Marius Buning, Matthijs Engelberts and Sjef Houppermans (eds), *Samuel Beckett: Crossroads and Borderlines, Samuel Beckett Today/Aujourd'hui* 6 (Amsterdam and Atlanta, GA, Rodopi, 1997), pp. 87–110.

—— 'The Business of Being Beckett: Beckett's Reception in the U.S.A.', in Mark Nixon and Matthew Feldman (eds), *The International Reception of Samuel Beckett* (London and New York: Continuum, 2009), pp. 9–23.

—— 'Revising Himself: Performance as Text in Samuel Beckett's Theatre', *Journal of Modern Literature* 22/1 (1998): 131–45.

Goodridge, Janet, *Rhythm and Timing of Movement in Performance: Drama, Dance and Ceremony* (London: Jessica Kingsley Publishers, 1999).

Graver, Lawrence, *Samuel Beckett, 'Waiting for Godot'*, 2nd edn (Cambridge: Cambridge University Press, 2004).

—— and Raymond Federman (eds), *Samuel Beckett: The Critical Heritage* (London: Routledge, 1979)

Green, Burdette, and David Butler, 'From Acoustics to *Tonpsychologie*', in Thomas Christensen (ed.), *The Cambridge History of Western Music Theory* (Cambridge: Cambridge University Press, 2002), pp. 246–71.

Grotowski, Jerzy, *Towards a Poor Theatre* (New York: Simon & Schuster, 1968).

Guralnick, Elissa S., *Sight Unseen: Beckett, Pinter, Stoppard, and Other Contemporary Dramatists on Radio* (Athens: Ohio University Press, 1996).

Harmon, Maurice (ed.), *No Author Better Served: The Correspondence of Samuel Beckett and Alan Schneider* (Cambridge, MA: Harvard University Press, 1998).

Harper, Margaret, 'Yeats's Wild West: Cuchulain and the Cowboy' (plenary lecture presented at the DUCIS conference 'A New Ireland? Representations of History Past and Present in Literature and Culture', Falun, 3–4 Nov. 2011).

Haynes, John, and James Knowlson, *Images of Beckett* (Cambridge: Cambridge University Press, 2003).

Heffernan, James A.W., *Museum of Words: The Poetics of Ekphrasis from Homer to Ashbery* (Chicago, IL: University of Chicago Press, 1993).

Heidegger, Martin, *Being and Time*, trans. John Macquarrie and Edward Robinson (Bodmin: Blackwell, 2001).

Henry, Anne, 'Proust du côté de Schopenhauer', in (ed.), *Schopenhauer et la création littéraire en Europe* (Paris: Klincksieck, 1989), pp. 149–64.

—— *Marcel Proust: Théories pour une esthétique* (Paris: Klincksieck, 1981).

Herren, Graley, 'Splitting Images: Samuel Beckett's *Nacht und Träume*', *Modern Drama* 43/2 (Summer 2000): 182–91.
—— 'Nacht und Träume as Beckett's Agony in the Garden', *Journal of Beckett Studies* 11/1 (2002): 54–70.
—— *Samuel Beckett's Plays on Film and Television* (Basingstoke: Palgrave, 2007).
—— 'Different Music: Karmitz and Beckett's Film Adaptation of *Comédie*', *Journal of Beckett Studies* 18 (2009): 10–31.
Hiebel, Hans H., 'Quadrat 1 + 2 as a Television Play', in Marius Buning and Lois Oppenheim (eds), *Beckett in the 1990s*, *Samuel Beckett Today/Aujourd'hui* 2 (Amsterdam and Atlanta, GA: Rodopi, 1993), pp. 335–43.
Hollier, Dennis, 'Timeliness and Timelessness', in Thomas Pepper (ed.), *The Place of Maurice Blanchot*, Yale French Studies 93 (New Haven, CT: Yale University Press, 1998).
Holliger, Heinz, *Not I*: *Monodrama for Soprano and Tape* (Mainz: Schott, 1980).
Homan, Sidney, *Beckett's Theaters: Interpretations for Performance* (London: Associated University Presses, 1984).
Homan, Sidney, *Filming Beckett's Television Plays: A Director's Experience* (London: Associated University Presses, 1992).
Hoover, Paul, *Sonnet 56* (Los Angeles: Les Figues Press, 2009).
—— *Desolation: Souvenir* (Richmond, CA: Omnidawn Publishing, 2012).
Hume, David, *A Treatise of Human Nature*, ed. Lewis Amherst Selby-Bigge (Oxford: Clarendon Press, 1888).
Hutchings, William, '"In the Old Style," Yet Anew: Happy Days in the "After Beckett"', in Stanley E. Gontarski (ed.), *A Companion to Samuel Beckett* (Oxford and Chichester: Wiley-Blackwell, 2010), pp. 308–25.
Jabès, Edmond, *From the Book to the Book: An Edmond Jabès Reader*, trans. Rosmarie Waldrop (Hanover, NH: Wesleyan University Press, 1991).
Jaeger, Werner, *Paideia: The Ideals of Greek Culture*, vol. 1: *Archaic Greece: The Mind of Athens*, trans. Gilbert Highet (New York: Oxford University Press, 1986).
Jankélévitch, Vladimir, *Music and the Ineffable*, trans. Carolyn Abbate (Princeton, NJ, and Oxford: Princeton University Press, 2003).
Jesson, James, '"White World. Not a Sound": Beckett's Radioactive Text in *Embers*', *Texas Studies in Literature and Language* 51/1 (2009): 47–65.
Jun, Irena, interview by Antoni Libera, in *Women in Beckett*, ed. Linda Ben-Zvi (Urbana and Chicago, IL: University of Illinois Press, 1990), pp. 47–50.
Juliet, Charles, *Rencontre avec Samuel Beckett* (Paris: Éditions Fata Morgana, 1986).
—— *Conversations with Samuel Beckett and Bram van Velde*, trans. Janey Tucker (Leiden: Academic Press, 1995).
Kalb, Jonathan, *Beckett in Performance* (Cambridge: Cambridge University Press, 1989).

—— 'The Mediated Quixote: The Radio and Television Plays, and *Film*', in John Pilling (ed.), *The Cambridge Companion to Beckett* (Cambridge: Cambridge University Press, 1994), pp. 124–44.

Karmitz, Marin, and Elisabeth Lebovici, 'Entretien', in Caroline Bourgeois (ed.), *Comédie* (Paris: Éditions du regard, 2001), pp. 14–25.

Keller, John Robert, *Samuel Beckett and the Primacy of Love* (Manchester and New York: Manchester University Press, 2002).

Kennedy, Michael, *The Concise Oxford Dictionary of Music*, 4th edn (Oxford: Oxford University Press, 1996).

Kenner, Hugh, *A Reader's Guide to Samuel Beckett* (Syracuse, NY: Syracuse University Press, 1996).

Kernighan, Brian W., and Dennis M. Ritchie, *The C Programming Language*, 2nd edn (London: Prentice-Hall, 1988).

Kivy, Peter, *Authenticities: Philosophical Reflections on Musical Performance* (Ithaca, NY, and London: Cornell University Press, 1995).

Kleist, Heinrich von, *Über das Marionetten Theater und andere Schriften* (Munich: Wilhelm Goldmann, n.d.).

—— *On a Theatre of Marionettes*, trans. Gerti Wilford (London: Acron Press, 1989).

Knowlson, James, *Damned to Fame: The Life of Samuel Beckett* (London: Bloomsbury, 1996).

—— 'Beckett as Director', in John Haynes and James Knowlson, *Images of Beckett* (Cambridge: Cambridge University Press, 2003).

Kramer, Lawrence, *Classical Music and Postmodern Knowledge* (Berkeley and Los Angeles: University of California Press, 1995).

—— 'Beyond Words and Music: An Essay on Songfulness', in Walter Bernhart, Steven Paul Scher and Werner Wolf (eds.), *Word and Music Studies: Defining the Field* (Amsterdam and Atlanta, GA: Rodopi, 1999), pp. 303–19.

—— 'Saving the Ordinary: Beethoven's "Ghost" Trio and the Wheel of History', *Beethoven Forum* 12/1 (Spring 2005): 50–81.

Kristeva, Julia, *Desire in Language: A Semiotic Approach to Literature and Art*, trans. Thomas Gora, Alice Jardine and Leon S. Roudiez (New York: Columbia University Press, 1980).

—— *Revolution in Poetic Language*, trans. Margaret Waller (New York: Columbia University Press, 1984).

Kurth, Ernst, *Grundlagen des linearen Kontrapunkts: Bachs melodische Polyphonie* (Bern: Drechsel, 1917).

Lambert, Constant, 'Music and Action', in Roger Copeland and Marshall Cohen (eds.), *What is Dance? Readings in Theory and Criticism* (Oxford: Oxford University Press, 1983), pp. 203–10.

Lawley, Paul, '*Embers*: An Interpretation', available at <http://www.english.fsu.edu/jobs/num06/jobs06.htm>.

—— '"The Grim Journey': Beckett Listens to Schubert', in Angela Moorjani and Carola Veit (eds), *Samuel Beckett: Endlessness in the Year 2000, Samuel*

Beckett Today/Aujourd'hui 11 (Amsterdam and New York: Rodopi, 2001), pp. 255–67.

Laws, Catherine, 'The Double Image of Music in Beckett's Early Fiction', in Marius Buning, Matthijs Engelberts and Onno Kosters (eds), *Beckett and Religion: Beckett /Aesthetics/Politics, Samuel Beckett Today/Aujourd'hui* 9 (Amsterdam and Atlanta, GA: Rodopi, 2000), pp. 295–308.

—— 'Music in *Words and Music*: Feldman's Response to Beckett's Play', in Angela Moorjani and Carola Veit (eds), *Samuel Beckett: Endlessness in the Year 2000, Samuel Beckett Today/Aujourd'hui* 11 (Amsterdam and New York: Rodopi, 2001), pp. 279–90.

—— 'Beethoven's Haunting of Beckett's *Ghost Trio*', in Linda Ben-Zvi (ed.), *Drawing on Beckett: Portraits, Performances, and Cultural Contexts* (Tel Aviv: Assaph, 2003), pp. 197–214.

—— *Headaches Among the Overtones: Music in Beckett/Beckett in Music* (Amsterdam and New York: Rodopi, 2013).

Leblanc, Cécile, 'Proust et la "bande à Franck": Présence et influence de la musique française de la fin du dix-neuvième siècle', in Nathalie Mauriac Dyer, Kazuyoshi Yoshikawa, and Pierre-Edmond Robert (eds.), *Proust face à l'héritage du XIXe siècle: Tradition et métamorphose* (Paris: Presses Sorbonne nouvelle, 2012), pp. 203–17.

Lefebvre, Henri, *Rhythmanalysis: Space, Time and Everyday Life*, trans. Stuart Elden (New York: Continuum, 2004).

Le Juez, Brigitte, *Beckett before Beckett* (London: Souvenir Press, 2009).

Leriche, Françoise, 'Wagner', in Annick Bouillaguet and Brian G. Rogers (eds), *Dictionnaire Marcel Proust* (Paris: Honoré Champion, 2004), pp. 1073–4.

Levy, Ernst, *A Theory of Harmony* (Albany: State University of New York Press, 1985).

Levy, H., 'Introduction', in Margaret Morris, *The Notation of Movement* (London: Kegan Paul, Trench, Trubner & Co., 1928), pp. 3–5.

Levy, Shimon, *Samuel Beckett's Self-Referential Drama: The Sensitive Chaos* (Brighton: Sussex Academic Press, 2002).

Lidov, David, *Is Language a Music? Writings on Musical Form and Signification* (Bloomington: Indiana University Press, 2005).

Lindley, Elizabeth, and Laura McMahon (eds), *Rhythms: Essays in French Literature, Thought and Culture* (Oxford: Peter Lang, 2008), pp. 11–25.

Lotze, Hermann, *Metaphysik: Drei Bücher der Ontologie, Kosmologie und Psychologie*, ed. Georg Misch (Leipzig: Meiner, 1912).

Macklin, Gerald, 'Writing by Numbers: The Music of Mind in Samuel Beckett's *Pas*', *French Studies Bulletin* 76 (Autumn 2000): 10–13.

Maier, Franz Michael, '*Geistertrio*: Beethoven's Music in Samuel Beckett's *Ghost Trio*', in Angela Moorjani and Carola Veit (eds), *Samuel Beckett: Endlessness in the Year 2000, Samuel Beckett Today/Aujourd'hui* 11 (Amsterdam and New York; Rodopi, 2001), pp. 267–78.

—— '*Geistertrio*: Beethoven's Music in Samuel Beckett's *Ghost Trio* (Part 2)', in Marius Buning, Matthijs Engelberts and Sjef Houppermans (eds), *Pastiches, Parodies and Other Imitations*, *Samuel Beckett Today/Aujourd'hui* 12 (Amsterdam and New York: Rodopi, 2002), pp. 313–20.

—— 'Melodisch, Melodie', in Karlheinz Barck et al. (eds), *Ästhetische Grundbegriffe: Historisches Wörterbuch in sieben Bänden* (Stuttgart: Metzler, 2002), vol. 4, pp. 38–58.

—— 'Two Version of *Nacht und Träume*: What Franz Schubert Tells Us about a Favourite Song of Beckett', in Dirk van Hulle and Mark Nixon (eds), *'All Sturm and no Drang'*, *Samuel Beckett Today/Aujourd'hui* 18 (Amsterdam and New York: Rodopi, 2007), pp. 91–100.

—— 'The Idea of Melodic Connection in Samuel Beckett', *Journal of the American Musicological Society* 61/2 (2008): 373–410.

Mallarmé, Stéphane, 'Mystery in Literature', in Hazard Adams (ed.), *Critical Theory Since Plato* (New York: Harcourt Brace Jovanovich, 1971), pp. 692–4.

Manning, Erin, *Relationscapes: Movement, Art, Philosophy* (Cambridge, MA: MIT Press, 2009).

Mansell, Thomas, 'Different Music: Beckett's Theatrical Conduct', in Marius Buning et al., *Historicising Beckett/Issues of Performance*, *Samuel Beckett Today/Aujourd'hui* 15 (Amsterdam and New York: Rodopi, 2005): 225–39.

Marks, Lawrence, 'Synesthesia and the Arts', in W.R. Crozier and A.J. Chapman (eds), *Cognitive Processes in the Perception of Art* (Amsterdam: Elsevier, 1984), pp. 427–59.

Massumi, Brian, *Parables for the Virtual: Movement, Affect, Sensation* (Durham, NC: Duke University Press, 2002).

Maude, Ulrika, *Beckett, Technology and the Body* (Cambridge: Cambridge University Press, 2009).

Mayberry, Bob, *Theatre of Discord: Dissonance in Beckett, Albee, and Pinter* (Rutherford, NJ: Fairleigh Dickinson University Press, 1989).

McAlmon, Robert, 'Mr Joyce Directs an Irish Word Ballet', in Samuel Beckett et al., *Our Exagmination round his Factification for Incamination of Work in Progress, with Letters of Protest* [1929], 2nd edn (London: Faber & Faber, 1961), pp. 105–16.

McCarthy, Gerry, 'Emptying the Theater: On Directing the Plays of Samuel Beckett', in Lois Oppenheim (ed.), *Directing Beckett* (Ann Arbor: University of Michigan Press, 1994), pp. 250–67.

McClary, Susan, *Feminine Endings: Music, Gender, and Sexuality* (Minneapolis and Oxford: University of Minnesota Press, 1991).

McGrath, John, 'Musical Repetition in Samuel Beckett's *Ill Seen Ill Said*', in Mario Dunkel, Emily Petermann and Burkhard Sauerwald (eds), *Time and Space in Words and Music: Proceedings of the First Conference of the Word and Music Association* (Frankfurt: Peter Lang, 2012), pp. 31–41.

McLane, Maureen N., 'The Art of Poetry No. 97: Susan Howe', *Paris Review* 203 (Winter 2012): 144–69.

McMullan, Anna, 'Virtual Subjects: Performance, Technology and the Body in Beckett's Late Theatre', *Journal of Beckett Studies* NS 10/1–2 (2000–2001): 165–72.
Milly, Jean, *Les Pastiches de Proust* (Paris: Armand Colin, 1970).
Mitchell, W.J.T., *Picture Theory* (Chicago, IL: University of Chicago Press, 1994).
Morris, Margaret, *The Notation of Movement* (London: Kegan Paul, Trench, Trubner & Co., 1928).
—— *My Life in Movement* (Garelochhead, Argyll and Bute: International Association of MMM, 2003).
Nattiez, Jean, *Proust musicien* (Paris: Christian Bourgois, 1984).
Naturel, Mireille, *Proust et Flaubert: Un secret d'écriture*, 2nd edn (Amsterdam and New York: Rodopi, 2007)
Nixon, Mark, '"Scraps of German": Samuel Beckett Reading German Literature', in Matthijs Engelberts, Everett Frost and Jane Maxwell (eds), *'Notes diverse holo', Samuel Beckett Today/Aujourd'hui* 16 (Amsterdam and New York: Rodopi, 2006), pp. 259–82.
—— 'Beckett and Romanticism in the 1930s', in Dirk van Hulle and Mark Nixon (eds), *'All Sturm and no Drang', Samuel Beckett Today/Aujourd'hui* 18 (Amsterdam and New York: Rodopi, 2007), pp. 61–76.
—— '"Unutterably Faint": Beckett's Late English Poetry', *Fulcrum* 6 (2007): 507–21.
—— *Samuel Beckett's German Diaries 1936–1937* (London: Continuum, 2011).
Ojrzyńska, Katarzyna, 'The Journey through the Dying World of Boghill in Samuel Beckett's Radio Play, *All That Fall*', in Magdalena Cieślak and Agnieszka Rasmus (eds), *Images of the City* (Cambridge: Scholars Publishing, 2009), pp. 284–93.
—— 'O muzyce i metamuzyce we wczesnych słuchowiskach Samuela Becketta', *Tekstualia* 20/1 (2010): 89–101.
Ôno, Manako, 'Actes sans paroles, paroles sans scène', in Manako Okamuro et al. (eds), *Borderless Beckett, Samuel Beckett Today/Aujourd'hui* 19 (Amsterdam and New York: Rodopi, 2008), pp. 403–12.
Overbeck, Lois More, 'Audience of Self/Audience of Reader', *Modernism/modernity* 18/4 (2011): 721–37.
Pattie, David, 'Coming out of the Dark: Beckett's TV Plays', *Journal of Beckett Studies* NS 18/1–2 (2009): 123–35.
Pavis, Patrice, *Analyzing Performance: Theater, Dance, and Film*, trans. David Williams (Ann Arbor, MI: University of Michigan Press, 2003), pp. 131–47.
Phelan, Peggy, 'Lessons in Blindness from Samuel Beckett', *Publication of the Modern Language Association* 119/5 (Oct. 2004): 1279–88.
Perloff, Marjorie, 'The Silence that is not Silence: Acoustic Art in Samuel Beckett's *Embers*', in Lois Oppenheim (ed.), *Samuel Beckett and the Visual Arts: Music, Visual Arts, and Non-Print Media* (New York: Garland Publishing, 1998), pp 247–68.

Petras, Kathryn, and Ross Petras, *Dance First, Think Later: 618 Rules to Live By* (New York: Workman, 2011).
Pilling, John, 'Beckett's Proust', in Stanley E. Gontarski (ed.), *The Beckett Studies Reader* (Gainesville: University Press of Florida, 1993).
—— '*Proust* and Schopenhauer: Music and Shadows', in Mary Bryden (ed.), *Samuel Beckett and Music* (Oxford: Oxford University Press, 1998), pp. 173–8.
—— *Beckett before Godot*, 2nd edn (Cambridge: Cambridge University Press, 2004).
Piroué, Georges, *Proust et la musique du devenir* (Paris: Denoël, 1960).
Pollack, Barbara, 'The Effective Conductor: A Matter of Communication and Personality', in Glenn Daniel Wilson (ed.), *Psychology and Performing Arts* (Amsterdam: Swets & Zeitlinger, 1991), pp. 155–64.
Porter Abbott, H., *Beckett Writing Beckett: The Author in the Autograph* (London and Ithaca, NY: Cornell University Press, 1996).
Porter, Jeff, 'Samuel Beckett and the Radiophonic Body: Beckett and the BBC', *Modern Drama* 53/4 (2010): 431–46.
Prieto, Eric, *Listening In: Music, Mind, and the Modernist Narrative* (Lincoln: University of Nebraska Press, 2002).
Proust, Marcel, *À la recherche du temps perdu*, ed. Jean-Yves Tadié et al., 4 vols (Paris: Gallimard, 1987–89); Eng. trans.: *In Search of Lost Time*, trans. C.K. Scott-Montcrieff and Terence Kilmartin; rev. D.J. Enright, 6 vols (London: Vintage 1996); ed. Christopher Prendergast, 7 vols (London: Penguin, 2002).
—— 'À propos du "style" de Flaubert', in *Contre Sainte-Beuve*, ed. Pierre Clarac and Yves Sandre (Paris: Gallimard, 1971), pp. 586–600; Eng trans.: 'On Flaubert's "Style"', in *Against Sainte-Beuve and Other Essays*, trans. John Sturrock (London: Penguin, 1994), pp. 261–74.
—— *Carnets*, ed. Florence Callu and Antoine Compagnon (Paris: Gallimard, 2002).
—— *Contre Sainte-Beuve*, ed. Pierre Clarac and Yves Sandre (Paris: Gallimard, 1971).
—— *Lettres*, ed. Françoise Leriche et al. (Paris: Plon, 2004).
Puchner, Martin, *Stage Fright: Modernism, Anti-Theatricality, and Drama* (Baltimore, MD: Johns Hopkins University Press, 2002).
Rabinovitz, Rubin, *Innovation in Samuel Beckett's Fiction* (Urbana and Chicago, IL: University of Illinois Press, 1992).
Raimond, Michel, *La Crise du roman: Des lendemains du Naturalisme aux années vingt* (Paris: Corti, 1966).
Ricœur, Paul. *The Rule of Metaphor*, trans. Robert Czerny (London: Routledge & Kegan Paul, 1986).
Rivière, Jacques, *Études (1909–1924): L'Œuvre critique de Jacques Rivière à la Nouvelle revue française*, ed. Alain Rivière (Paris: Gallimard, 1999), pp. 586–92.
Roads, Curtis, *Microsound* (Cambridge, MA: MIT Press, 2004).

Rosen, Charles, 'Schubert's Inflections of Classical Form', in Christopher H. Gibbs (ed.), *The Cambridge Companion to Schubert* (Cambridge and New York: Cambridge University Press), pp. 72–98.
Rowell, Lewis, 'The Subconscious Language of Musical Time', *Music Theory Spectrum* 1 (Spring 1979): 96–106.
Ruland, Heiner, *Expanding Tonal Awareness: A Musical Exploration of the Evolution of Consciousness Guided by the Monochord*, trans. John Logan (London: Rudolf Steiner Press, 1992).
Russell, Catherine, 'The Figure in the Monitor: Beckett, Lacan, and Video', *Cinema Journal* 28/4 (Summer 1989): 20–37.
Samuel, Rhian, *The Flowing Sand* (London: Stainer & Bell, 2006).
Schachter, Carl, 'Text and Motive in Four Schubert Songs', in David Beach (ed.), *Aspects of Schenkerian Theory* (New Haven, CT: Yale University Press, 1983): 61–76.
Schmid, Marion, 'The Birth and Development of À la recherche du temps perdu', in Richard Bales (ed.), *The Cambridge Companion to Proust* (Cambridge: Cambridge University Press, 2006), pp. 58–73.
Schneider, Alan, *Entrances: An American Director's Journey* (New York: Viking Press, 1986).
Schoenberg, Arnold, *Theory of Harmony*, trans. Roy Carter (Berkeley: University of California Press, 1992).
Schopenhauer, Arthur, *The World as Will and Representation*, Vol. 1., trans. R.B. Haldane and J. Kemp (London: Kegan Paul, Trench, Trübner & Co., 1909); trans. Judith Norman and Alistair Welchman, ed. Christopher Janaway, Judith Norman and Alistair Welchman (Cambridge: Cambridge University Press, 2010).
Scruton, Roger, *The Aesthetics of Music* (Oxford: Oxford University Press, 1997).
Sembos, Evangelos, *Principles of Music Theory* (Morrisville, NC: Lulu Press, 2006).
Shainberg, Lawrence, 'Exorcizing Beckett', available at <http://www.samuel-beckett.net/ShainExor1.html>.
Shloss, Carol Loeb, *Lucia Joyce: To Dance in the Wake* (New York: Farrar, Straus and Giroux, 2003).
Simms, Bryan, *The Atonal Music of Arnold Schoenberg, 1908–1923* (Oxford: Oxford University Press, 2000).
Soupault, Philippe, *Les Neuf Muses: Terpsichore* (Paris: Émile Hazan, 1928).
Sparshott, Francis, *A Measured Pace: Toward a Philosophical Understanding of the Arts of Dance* (Toronto and London: University of Toronto Press, 1995).
Steinberg, Michael, *The Symphony: A Listener's Guide* (Oxford: Oxford University Press, 1995).
Stengers, Isabelle, *Thinking With Whitehead*, trans. Michael Chase (Cambridge, MA, and London: Harvard University Press, 2011).
Stewart, Kathleen, *Ordinary Affects* (Durham, NC, and London: Duke University Press, 2007).

Stevens, Wallace, *Selected Poems*, ed. John N. Serio (New York: Alfred A. Knopf, 2009).

Strickland, Edward, *Minimalism: Origins* (Bloomington: Indiana University Press).

Surprenant, Céline, '"An Occult Arithmetic": The Proustian Equation according to Beckett's *Proust*', *Journal of Romance Studies* 7/3 (2007): 47–58.

—— 'Couldn't Write', review of Gilles Philippe (ed.), *Flaubert savait-il écrire, Une querelle grammaticale (1919–1921)* (Grenoble, 2004), *Times Literary Supplement* (6 May 2005): 22.

Sutherland, John, 'Frank Sinatra's My Way: The Song that Refuses to Die', *The Guardian* (15 Oct. 2012).

Tilbury, John, *On Playing Feldman*, available at <http://www.cnvill.net/mftexts.htm>.

Tonning, Erik, *Samuel Beckett's Abstract Drama* (Oxford: Peter Lang, 2007).

Toop, David, *Sinister Resonance: The Mediumship of the Listener* (New York and London: Continuum, 2010).

Turnage, Mark Anthony, *Five Views of a Mouth* (London: Boosey & Hawkes, 2007).

Van Hulle, Dirk, and Mark Nixon, 'Introduction', in (eds), *'All Sturm and no Drang', Samuel Beckett Today/Aujourd'hui* 18 (Amsterdam and New York: Rodopi, 2007), pp. 9–11.

White, Harry, 'Something is Taking Its Course: Dramatic Exactitude and the Paradigm of Serialism in Samuel Beckett', in Mary Bryden (ed.), *Samuel Beckett and Music* (Oxford: Oxford University Press, 1998), pp. 159–71.

—— *Music and the Irish Literary Imagination* (Oxford: Oxford University Press, 2008).

Whitehead, Alfred North, *Process and Reality* (New York: Macmillan, 1978).

Whitelaw, Billie, *Billie Whitelaw ... Who He? An Autobiography* (London: Hodder & Stoughton, 1995).

Wittgenstein, Ludwig, *Culture and Value: A Selection from the Posthumous Remains*, ed. Georg Henrik von Wright and Heikki Nyman, trans. Peter Winch, 2nd edn (Oxford: Basil Blackwell, 1998).

Witts, Noel, 'Beckett and Schubert', *Performance Research* 12/1 (Mar. 2007): 137–44.

Wood, Rupert, 'An Endgame of Aesthetics', in John Pilling (ed.), *The Cambridge Companion to Beckett* (Cambridge: Cambridge University Press, 1994), pp. 1–16.

Worth, Katharine, 'Beckett and the Radio Medium', in John Drakakis (ed.), *British Radio Drama* (Cambridge: Cambridge University Press, 1981), pp. 191–217.

—— 'Words for Music Perhaps', in Mary Bryden (ed.), *Samuel Beckett and Music* (Oxford: Oxford University Press, 1998), pp. 9–20.

Wright, Donald, *Du discours médical dans* À la recherche du temps perdu: *Science et souffrance* (Paris: Honoré Champion, 2007).

Wright, Jay, *Music's Mask and Measure* (Chicago, IL: Flood Editions, 2007).

Yeats, William Butler, *Essays and Introductions* (London: Macmillan, 1961), pp. 153–64.

—— *Collected Plays* (London: Macmillan, 1982).

You, Haili, 'Defining Rhythm: Aspects of an Anthropology of Rhythm', *Culture, Medicine and Psychiatry* 18/3 (Sept. 1994): 361–38.

Zilliacus, Clas, *Beckett and Broadcasting: A Study of the Works of Samuel Beckett for and in Radio and Television* (Åbo: Åbo Akademi, 1976).

Zinman, T.S., 'Lucky's Dance in *Waiting for Godot*', *Modern Drama* 38/3 (1995): 308–23.

Zuckerkandl, Victor, *The Sense of Music* (Princeton, NJ: Princeton University Press, 1971).

Zurbrugg, Nicolas, *Beckett and Proust* (Gerrards Cross, Bucks: Colin Smythe, 1987).

Select Discography

American Elegies, John Adams Conducts the Orchestra of St. Luke's, Elektra Nonesuch, CD 79249-2 (New York:, 1991).

Morton Feldman, *For Samuel Beckett*, Classic Production Osnabrück, CD 999 647-2 (Georgsmarienhütte, Germany, 1999).

—— *Morton Feldman*, Col Legno, CD 20070 (Frankfurt, 2001).

—— *Neither* [opera, words by Samuel Beckett], hat[now]ART 102 (Basel, 1997).

—— and the Ives Ensemble, *String Quartet (II)*, hat[now]ART, CD 4-144 (Basel, 2001).

Index

Note: numbers in brackets preceded by *n* are footnote numbers. Bold page numbers indicate figures and musical examples. All works are by Beckett except where indicated otherwise.